THE GERMANS

THE GERMANS

Public Opinion Polls, 1967-1980

Edited by
Elisabeth Noelle-Neumann
Institut für Demoskopie Allensbach

Greenwood Press

Westport, Connecticut • London, England

Library of Congress Cataloging in Publication Data
Main entry under title:

The Germans—public opinion polls, 1967-1980.

Includes index.
1. Public opinion—Germany (West) 2. Germany (West) —Public opinion. 3. Social surveys—Germany (West) 4. Germany (West)—Statistics. I. Noelle-Neumann, Elisabeth, 1916- . II. Institut für Demoskopie.
HN460.P8G47 303.3′8′0943 81-1075
ISBN 0-313-22490-9 (lib. bdg.) AACR2

Library of Congress Catalog Card Number: 81-1075
ISBN: 0-313-22490-9

First published in 1981

Greenwood Press
A division of Congressional Information Service, Inc.
88 Post Road West, Westport, Connecticut 06881

Printed in the United States of America

10 9 8 7 6 5 4 3 2 1

CONTENTS

FOREWORD

The Germans are an interesting people, interesting in the sense of the Chinese curse: "May your children live in interesting times." Outsiders are intensely concerned about the Germans. There is still the question: Can they be trusted not to revert to Nazism or militarism? Is this German democracy real?

There is obviously no definitive way to resolve the anxieties that Germany's past produces in others. There was good reason to be optimistic about Wilhelmine Germany—the most advanced welfare state of its time with the largest Social-Democratic party in the world, which pledged its strength to oppose war. Weimar Germany in the late 1920s appeared to be the very model of a progressive democratic society marked by, among other things, an innovative artistic and academic culture. Yet the promise of both Reichs produced fires that caused the deaths of many millions and came close to destroying Western liberal society.

Is the Federal Republic of Germany another mirage, one which may become the catalytic agent for the final collapse of the West? Should we fear the consequences of the economic miracle that has restored Germany to its position as the strongest power in Western Europe?

Those like myself who have become optimistic about the future of Germany may find evidence for hope in the extensive data gathered over the past three decades by the Institut für Demoskopie on the views of the West German population. The large majority, interviewed by Elisabeth Noelle-Neumann and her colleagues, hold strong democratic views. They reject the recent past of their country. They view the Bonn Republic as the best system Germany has had during this century.

What is more significant than the positive views expressed by the majority is the generational differences. In every case reported, the younger cohorts hold the most democratic opinions, and, over time, the proportions with positive views about the Hitler period have declined sharply. Thus by 1980, the percentage holding that things had gone best for Germany in the 1933-1939 period had fallen to 3 percent, down from 42 in 1950 and 10 in 1963. Belief that the "National Socialist government was an unjust government, a criminal regime" increased from 54 percent in 1964 to 71 percent in 1978. In 1975 those expressing anti-Semitic opinions, saying that they do not want to be with Jews or to have them as friends, numbered 16 percent among the population as a whole, ranging, however, from 9 percent of youth, 16 to 29 years of age, to 32 percent among those over 60. And by contrast, 44 percent of all queried reject National Socialists as possible friends or associates.

By an overwhelming majority, 74 percent, Germans felt in 1975 "that the democracy we have in Germany is the best form of government." Only 9 percent agreed with the alternative statement that "there is another form of government that is better." When questioned over the years about the optimum political party system, the proportion replying "several parties," increased steadily to 68 percent in 1978; another 24 percent preferred a two- or three-party system. Those in favor of only one party fell to 5 percent, down from 24 in 1950 and 11 in 1956.

The Germans seemingly have learned that there is wisdom in dispersing political power. When asked in 1980 to evaluate the worth of having a small third party, the Free Democrats, represented in parliament thereby preventing either major party from gaining a majority and thus "establishing their policies completely," most rejected majority government. Only 23 percent agreed with the statement, "I don't think it necessary to have the FDP. The strongest party should be able to establish its policies completely without having brakes applied by a smaller party."

The acceptance of democratic norms may also be seen in the answers to questions about women's rights. Those agreeing that "in a marriage husband and wife should hold equal rights" rose from 48 percent in 1954 to 75 in 1979. Fully 88 percent of youth, 16-29 years of age, held this view in 1979 compared to 61 percent among those 60 years or older.

The opinion data suggest that the Germans have become less nationalistic than some other Europeans. As of 1979, over two-thirds of the German population not only strongly support the European Community, they would like to see it expand "to become a political community—a united Europe." Over three-fifths favor the European Parliament having power "to determine the policies of member countries, in certain matters." Only 31 percent, however, believe "that we Germans should increase our influence and assume more of the leadership" in the community. Three-fifths feel that the fact that "Foreign workers from these [European Community] countries have the right to live and work here whenever they wish" is good. When asked in 1972 whether they should accept "the present German-Polish border—the Oder-Neisse Line," which incorporates a sizable segment of prewar German territory in Poland, only 18 percent said they "shouldn't accept this," down from 59 percent in 1964.

The West Germans seemingly have become reconciled to the division of their country. In 1976, close to two-thirds said that they do not think "that East and West Germany will ever be reunited again." The proportion who replied that reunification "is the most important question West Germany faces" declined steadily from 45 percent in 1959 to 31 in 1963, 18 in 1967, 1 in 1976 and less than one percent in 1980.

There is, of course, much more in this volume than politics. German values are changing rapidly in ways that may astonish traditionalists. Less than half of those under 30 years of age believe that marriage is a necessary institution. While 44 percent of people over 62 years old say they would not mind people living together without marriage, fully 86 percent of those under 30 hold this view. More surprisingly, 83 percent of the youth cohort would not mind a couple having a child without being married, compared to 34 percent among those 60 and older. The belief that homosexuality is a "vice," the opinion of close to half the adult population in 1963, dropped to less than a quarter by 1976.

Americans, on the whole, will be pleased with the opinions Germans hold about them. As of 1980, majorities say they "like" Americans, that they are "efficient, capable in business," "progressive, stay in step with the times," "mechanically-minded, inventive," people who "put personal freedom first," and that they are "very patriotic, proud of their country." On the other hand, 53 percent are not confident "that the United States is capable of taking a wise leadership role today," compared to 34 percent who have some confidence.

Elisabeth Noelle-Neumann and the Institut für Demoskopie are to be congratulated for their reporting on over three decades of record keeping on German attitudes on a myriad of topics. The Institute ranks in the forefront among polling organizations the world over. As one who has visited its headquarters and has had the pleasure of conversations about survey analysis with Professor Noelle-Neumann over the years, I can testify to the reliability of the findings reported here. The continued willingness to make these data available to the English-language public attests to the concern which Professor Noelle-Neumann and her colleagues have for the international community.

Seymour Martin Lipset
Stanford, California
January, 1981

PREFACE

Fifteen years ago the first volume of the Germans was published. It contained the results of surveys conducted by the Allensbach Institut Für Demoskopie between 1947 and 1966. Now that the second volume is available, I have feelings very similar to those I had when the first appeared. Such a book discloses a lot. It sweeps one's country with a broad searchlight and reveals many unflattering things. It is perhaps somewhat embarrassing to see the taste one's compatriots have in furnishing their houses (p. 12), or to see how blatantly dull human sympathy has become: A growing number of people say that under no circumstances could they find the time to do voluntary work in charitable organizations; yet a growing number of the same people confirm that the work charitable organizations do is indispensable (pp. 147-48). Such a book exposes a people's poor calculating skills and knowledge of history (pp. 73-74). It reveals that fewer and fewer people can recognize a linden tree leaf—and the slight increase in those who know a maple tree does not make up for the increased ignorance (p. 78). In the past the Germans were considered idealists—but how much of that idealism remains? More and more Germans today say that having a good time is the primary goal in their lives (p. 38).

Such a collection of survey results does not necessarily present a favorable picture of one's country, particularly if it really includes everything that might interest an international audience. However, nothing has been retouched for this edition; no survey has been included or excluded because its results were particularly favorable or unfavorable. As a German I feel that the publication of these surveys is advantageous even if reading this volume stimulates negative ideas, as long as those ideas are in line with reality. What is depressing is to face foreign prejudices about one's country that may be true in the individual case but are not true of the general tendency. A case in point is the prevailing idea about the relationship of Germans to the National Socialist Regime. Many foreigners reason that it is not merely an idea that the majority of the Germans were enthusiastic supporters of National Socialism, otherwise, Germans would have offered more resistance. Perhaps only people who live or have lived under a dictatorship, where any deviation from the party line is a threat to life, are able to understand what the Germans of 1977 have in mind when they say, in anonymous public opinion-poll interviews, that offering resistance did not make sense once the National Socialist Regime was firmly entrenched (p. 113). Many foreigners imagine that when Germans talk about National Socialism, they are only trying to justify themselves and to demonstrate their own innocence. However, when asked in 1978, the Germans had quite a different recollection of the years following the collapse of the Reich, the years between 1945 and 1947. Hunger is what people characteristically recall from those years. But a large majority of the population also mentions their happiness that the Hitler era was over and their joy that freedom of opinion and the press had been regained (p. 104).

Actually, after an initial period of exuberant hopes, it is usually a minority that is enthusiatic about any dictatorship, but this minority consists of enough people to stage mass demonstrations and roaring street scenes. At the same time, totalitarian propaganda has sufficient impact on even a critically minded portion of the population so it adopts convictions and forms judgments without realizing that, in doing so, it has accepted large portions of the dictatorial ideology. In the results of the surveys conducted between 1947 and 1980 one can clearly see that the reality of National Socialism was not understood in its entirety immediately after 1945. As late as the mid-1960s, many people had illusions about the era. By 1964, 55 percent of the German populace grasped the idea that the National Socialists had formed a criminal regime (p. 113). In the last survey on this subject, conducted in 1978, 71 percent had come to this understanding.

The reader will notice that results from 1953 and 1979 are compared in many parts of the book. Why exactly these two years? Through good fortune, in 1953 the Allensbach Institute developed a questionnaire for a research project supported by UNESCO. It was designed to investigate the attitudes of the German people in six areas: family and neighborhood, work and leisure, politics and the church. In 1979 the Interversa Corporation in Hamburg, under its President Dr. Horst Stuetzer, made it possible to repeat the entire 1953 survey. Neither the subjects nor the wording of the questions were changed, and only questions about television were added. One of the most striking results of this longitudinal study is the amazing rise in sociability (pp. 56, 57, 85). Many other results appear to be paradoxical, but this is precisely what makes them so well suited to correcting our simplistic ideas about the development of a society. For example, in spite of the decrease in households containing more than a single generation, the study reveals a tendency to embrace more generations in the idea of the family (pp. 22, 23).

This book contains no detail of the methodological principles of Allensbach surveys. These principles have already been described in a book that has been translated into many languages and is expected to be published soon in English by the University of Chicago Press. The Allensbach election forecasts have been used in seven consecutive German Federal elections as proof of the high accuracy of the methods applied by Allensbach.

It would have been ideal if the space available for this foreword had permitted me to discuss the wording of questions in more detail; for instance, it is one of our principles to avoid abstract concepts as often as possible because large parts of the population tend to think visually and emotionally. This explains the great number of dialogues in the questionnaires. We present complicated subjects through the speech of two fictitious persons to bring the subjects to life; or we tell stories, such as the one about the West German vacationing at the Black Sea and meeting an East German (p. 123). Using this method, our question about how Germans from the two separated parts of Germany still feel about each other is easily posed and spontaneously answered.

I want to thank Wolfgang J. Koschnick, head of the English-Language Foreign-Liaison Department at the Allensbach Institute; without his initiative this second volume of the Germans would never have appeared. The main burden in selecting the material from the Allensbach archives and in translating and editing was borne by Dr. Erna Begus, Ms. Maria Marzahl, and Ms. Mary Siwinski. I thank them for their enthusiasm and perseverance.

Elisabeth Noelle-Neumann
Allensbach on Lake Constance
August 1981

EXPLANATORY NOTES

This book comprises the results of surveys of various kinds and sizes. By consulting the illustration on page 6, you can find out about the sample upon which any given table is based.

Tables not marked by any symbol contain the results of surveys conducted among a representative cross-section of the population, each based on interviews with 2,000 persons aged 16 and over in the Federal Republic of Germany and West Berlin. Respondents were selected according to the quota system. Results obtained by this means are presented as in the following table:

Question: *"Generally speaking, are you interested in politics?"*

	January 1980
	%
Yes	48
Not very much	43
Not at all	9
	100

Results which relate to other sectors of the population, or which were obtained by interviewing different samples, are distinguished by a capital letter in the left-hand margin of the table. For instance, tables marked with an "A" contain the results of polls of statistically representative samples of 1,000 persons aged 16 and over in the Federal Republic of Germany and West Berlin. The full list of samples appears at the end of this section.

All tables indicate the month and the year in which the survey was taken, not the date of evaluation.

Percentages

Wherever the percentages add up to more than 100, more than one answer could be given to the question. If only one answer could be given because the possibilities were mutually exclusive, the percentages always add up to 100.

An "x" in a table instead of a number indicates that less than 0.5 percent of the respondents chose this response alternative.

Abbreviations

Some tables give demographic breakdowns, e.g. results by sex, age, occupation, etc. If no demographic groups are given, the results refer to the total population.

EDUCATION. ELEMENTARY denotes education at a ''Hauptschule'' (normally nine years) or at a secondary school up to the tenth grade. The INTERMEDIATE group consists of persons whose schooling was terminated upon receiving the ''Mittlere Reife'' certificate, after completing their tenth year at school. SECONDARY consists of persons who have completed 13 years of secondary education and have passed the final examination (''Abitur''), entitling them to study at a university.

OCCUPATION. These groups include both persons engaged in the respective occupations and the members of their families who do not work. For example, UNSKILLED WORKERS or SKILLED WORKERS comprise not only the workers, but also their families—housewives, for instance.

The term ''Gainfully employed persons'' (''Berufstaetige'' in German) is used to describe the entire labor force except for the unemployed. ''Employed persons'' (''berufstaetige Arbeitnehmer'') comprises the total labor force except for the self-employed and the employers, while ''public servants'' applies to those public employees who enjoy life-time employment (''Beamte'').

REGIONAL DISTRIBUTION. The following subdivisions were made according to the size of the town in which the respondent lived: VILLAGES (less than 2,000 inhabitants), SMALL TOWNS (2,000 to 20,000 inhabitants), MEDIUM-SIZED CITIES (20,000 to 100,000 inhabitants), LARGE CITIES (more than 100,000 inhabitants).

PARTY PREFERENCE. A classification of respondents who expressed a distinct preference for one of the major parties. Other respondents were not included.

Eligible voters are those persons aged 18 and over in the Federal Republic without West Berlin.

Symbols

(O) = OPEN QUESTION. In this case the questionnaire did not contain any pre-choice response alternatives; the actual replies given by respondents were noted down. To evaluate the replies, they had to be ''coded,'' in other words, grouped together in common categories.

(X) = SPLIT-BALLOT TECHNIQUE. Where it was felt that the sequence of response alternatives might influence the result, a procedure known as the "split-ballot technique" was employed. In this case, the alternatives were read out in the reverse order in half of the interviews. The results of these "split" questions have been combined, and an average has been taken which is neutral to the extent that the effect of the sequence has been eliminated.

(L) = LIST, (C) = CARDS. Tables marked by an "L" or a "C" are based on interviews in which a list of response alternatives or a set of cards containing response alternatives were presented to the respondents.

(ill.) = ILLUSTRATION. Here respondents were shown an illustration during the interview in order to make a specific situation easier to understand. For examples, see pages 55 and 297.

List of Samples

without symbol	=	2,000 persons aged 16 and over in the Federal Republic and West Berlin
A	=	1,000 persons aged 16 and over in the Federal Republic and West Berlin
B	=	500 persons aged 16 and over in the Federal Republic and West Berlin
C	=	2,000 persons aged 18 and over in the Federal Republic without West Berlin
D	=	8,500 persons aged 16 and over in the Federal Republic and West Berlin
E	=	2,000 car owners and drivers between 18 and 70 years of age in the Federal Republic and West Berlin
F	=	1,000 persons aged 18 and over in the Federal Republic without West Berlin
G	=	1,000 persons aged 18 and over in the Federal Republic and West Berlin
H	=	260 men aged 16-55 in the Federal Republic and West Berlin
I	=	1,000 persons aged 55 and over in the Federal Republic and West Berlin

Ranges of Error

The survey results compiled in this book are based upon sample surveys, each comprising only a small portion of the universe and chosen according to mathematical-statistical principles (a representative cross-section). Such percentages which are projected onto the whole hold true within clearly defined margins of error. A means of measuring these ranges of error is the σ, or "standard deviation," the values for which can be found on the following page.

The following is an example of the correct use of the table:
If 20 percent of 2,000 respondents give a certain answer, one looks at the point of intersection of the column for $p = 20$ and the line for $n = 2{,}000$, and finds 1.80. This means that the actual percentage of the universe from which the sample was drawn is 20 ± 1.80, that is to say, between 18.2 and 21.8 percent.

RANGES OF ERROR

Values of 2 σ in percentages
Level of significance: 95.45 percent

n = Size of sample
p = Frequency of any one item in the universe in percentages

n	p 50 / 50	40 / 60	30 / 70	25 / 75	20 / 80	15 / 85	10 / 90	8 / 92	5 / 95	2 / 98
100	10.00	9.80	9.20	8.66	8.00	7.14				
150	8.16	8.00	7.52	7.08	6.52	5.82				
200	7.10	6.94	6.52	6.14	5.68	5.06	4.26			
250	6.32	6.20	5.82	5.50	5.06	4.52	3.80	3.42		
300	5.80	5.68	5.30	5.00	4.64	4.14	3.48	3.14		
400	5.00	4.90	4.60	4.32	4.00	3.56	3.00	2.70	2.18	
500	4.48	4.40	4.12	3.88	3.60	3.20	2.68	2.42	1.94	
600	4.10	4.00	3.78	3.56	3.28	2.92	2.46	2.22	1.78	
700	3.78	3.70	3.48	3.28	3.02	2.70	2.26	2.04	1.64	
800	3.54	3.46	3.26	3.06	2.84	2.52	2.12	1.90	1.54	1.00
1,000	3.16	3.10	2.90	2.64	2.52	2.26	1.90	1.70	1.38	0.83
1,200	2.90	2.84	2.66	2.50	2.32	2.06	1.74	1.56	1.26	0.82
1,400	2.70	2.62	2.46	2.32	2.14	1.92	1.62	1.44	1.18	0.76
1,600	2.50	2.44	2.30	2.16	2.00	1.80	1.50	1.36	1.10	0.70
1,800	2.36	2.32	2.18	2.04	1.90	1.68	1.42	1.28	1.02	0.66
2,000	2.24	2.20	2.06	1.94	1.80	1.60	1.34	1.20	0.98	0.62
2,500	2.00	1.96	1.84	1.72	1.60	1.42	1.20	1.08	0.88	0.56
3,000	1.84	1.80	1.68	1.58	1.46	1.30	1.10	1.00	0.80	0.52
4,000	1.58	1.54	1.46	1.38	1.26	1.12	0.94	0.86	0.68	0.44
5,000	1.40	1.38	1.30	1.22	1.12	1.00	0.84	0.76	0.62	0.40
6,000	1.30	1.28	1.20	1.12	1.04	0.92	0.78	0.70	0.56	0.36
7,000	1.20	1.18	1.10	1.04	0.96	0.86	0.72	0.64	0.52	0.34
8,000	1.12	1.10	1.04	0.96	0.90	0.80	0.68	0.60	0.48	0.32

σ = standard deviation; a means of measuring the mean error.

In the case of n and p the binomial distribution is noticeably asymmetrical and therefore clearly differs from the normal distribution. As the positive and negative values of σ are in this case not equal, they are not given.

I. THE PEOPLE

PERSONAL DATA

POPULATION GROWTH IN THE FEDERAL REPUBLIC OF GERMANY

POPULATION SIZE Yearly average of the territory within the federal boundaries of January 1, 1979

	1950	1955	1960	1965	1970	1975	1980
Total population in 100,000's	50,809	52,382	55,433	58,619	60,651	61,829	61,300

AGE AND SEX	1960				1970				1980			
	Men %	Women %		Total %	Men %	Women %		Total %	Men %	Women %		Total %
Under 16	11.7	11.2	=	22.9	12.5	11.9	=	24.4	11.1	10.5	=	21.6
16 - 29	11.0	10.5	=	21.5	9.4	8.9	=	18.3	10.4	9.9	=	20.3
30 - 44	8.4	10.2	=	18.6	11.1	10.4	=	21.5	11.0	10.3	=	21.3
45 - 59	9.2	11.6	=	20.8	6.9	9.5	=	16.4	7.9	9.4	=	17.3
60 and over	6.7	9.5	=	16.2	7.7	11.7	=	19.4	7.3	12.2	=	19.5
Total	47.0	53.0	=	100.0	47.6	52.4	=	100.0	47.7	52.3	=	100.0

MARITAL STATUS	1960			1970			1980		
	Men %	Women %	Total %	Men %	Women %	Total %	Men %	Women %	Total %
Single	45.0	39.2	41.9	44.1	37.1	40.4	43.7	35.5	39.4
Married	51.2	46.3	48.6	52.4	47.2	40.7	51.7	47.2	49.3
Widowed	2.8	12.7	8.0	2.4	13.5	8.2	2.6	14.4	8.8
Divorced	1.0	1.8	1.5	1.1	2.2	1.7	2.0	2.9	2.5
	100.0	100.0	100.0	100.0	100.0	100.0	100.0	100.0	100.0

Source: Statistisches Jahrbuch für die Bundesrepublik Deutschland 1979; 1980: Allensbach projection.

NUMBER OF PERSONS IN PRIVATE HOUSEHOLDS

	1950 %	1960 %	1970 %	1980 %
One person	19.4	20.6	25.1	29.3
Two persons	25.3	26.5	27.1	28.5
Three persons	23.0	22.6	19.6	18.0
Four persons	16.2	16.0	15.3	14.7
Five or more persons	16.1	14.3	12.9	9.5
	100.0	100.0	100.0	100.0
Average number of persons per household	2.99	2.88	2.74	2.50

OCCUPATIONAL DISTRIBUTION

	1950 %	1960 %	1970 %	1980 %
Blue-collar workers	45.9	47.6	45.8	41.5
Farm workers	4.9	1.9	0.9	0.8
White-collar workers	16.0	22.9	31.2	36.1
Public servants	4.0	4.7	5.6	8.7
Self-employeds, professionals	11.1	11.0	9.1	8.0
Farmers	18.1	11.9	7.4	4.9
	100.0	100.0	100.0	100.0

NET MONTHLY INCOME of the chief earner of the household

	1965 %	1970 %	1975 %	1980 %
under 799 DM	65	30	18	6
800 - 999 DM	19	29		
1,000 - 1,249 DM	16	22	20	9
1,250 - 1,499 DM	x	10	23	15
1,500 - 1,999 DM	x	5	20	35
2,000 - 2,499 DM	x	4	10	16
2,500 - 2,999 DM	x	x	5	9
3,000 and over	x	x	4	10
	100	100	100	100

SOURCE: Statistisches Jahrbuch 1955, 1962, 1972, 1979; 1980: Allensbach projection

CONSUMER PRICE INDEX for average consumer group
1970 = 100

1965	1966	1967	1968	1969	1970
87.9	90.9	92.4	94.9	96.7	100

1971	1972	1973	1974	1975	1976	1977	1978	1979	1980
105.3	111.1	118.8	127.1	134.7	140.8	146.3	150.1	156.1	164

NUMBER OF COMMUNITIES BY POPULATION

	1950*		1960		1970		1980	
Community population	Number	%	Number	%	Number	%	Number	%
Under 1,000	16,606	68.7	17,340	70.7	15,198	67.5	3,146	36.9
1,000 - 2,000	4,306	17.8	3,673	15.0	3,506	15.6	1,624	19.1
2,000 - 5,000	2,155	8.9	2,201	9.0	2,211	9.8	1,702	20.0
5,000 - 20,000	865	3.6	1,011	4.2	1,246	5.6	1,557	18.3
20,000 - 100,000	177	0.8	227	0.9	290	1.3	423	4.9
100,000 and over	48	0.2	53	0.2	59	0.2	67	0.8
	24,157	100.0	24,505	100.0	22,510	100.0	8,519	100.0

POPULATION BY COMMUNITY SIZE

Number of community residents	1950* %	1960 %	1970 %	1980 %
Under 1,000	15.7	13.2	10.6	2.4
1,000 - 2,000	11.9	9.1	8.1	3.8
2,000 - 5,000	13.0	12.1	11.2	8.9
5,000 - 20,000	15.3	16.0	18.9	24.7
20,000 - 100,000	13.6	16.0	18.8	25.8
100,000 and over	30.5	33.6	32.4	34.4
	100.0	100.0	100.0	100.0

*Excluding the Saar

SOURCE: Statistisches Jahrbuch fuer die Bundesrepublik Deutschland 1979; 1980: Allensbach projection

The Representative
Cross-Section of the Population

Federal Republic of Germany and West Berlin — Population 16 years of age and over

Sources: Statistisches Jahrbuch für die Bundesrepublik Deutschland 1978, 1979 and projections of the Institut für Demoskopie Allensbach. Figures for education from the Institut für Demoskopie Allensbach.

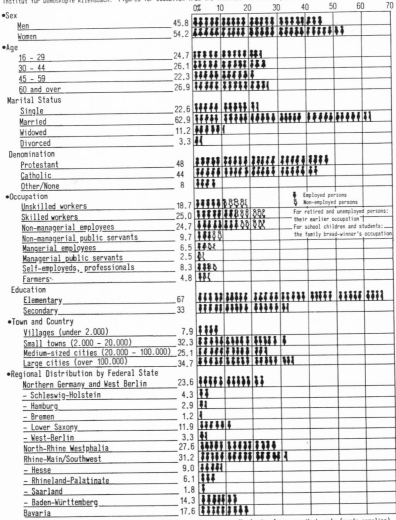

Category	%
•Sex	
Men	45.8
Women	54.2
•Age	
16 - 29	24.7
30 - 44	26.1
45 - 59	22.3
60 and over	26.9
Marital Status	
Single	22.6
Married	62.9
Widowed	11.2
Divorced	3.3
Denomination	
Protestant	48
Catholic	44
Other/None	8
•Occupation	
Unskilled workers	18.7
Skilled workers	25.0
Non-managerial employees	24.7
Non-managerial public servants	9.7
Mangerial employees	6.5
Managerial public servants	2.5
Self-employeds, professionals	8.3
Farmers	4.8
Education	
Elementary	67
Secondary	33
•Town and Country	
Villages (under 2.000)	7.9
Small towns (2.000 - 20.000)	32.3
Medium-sized cities (20.000 - 100.000)	25.1
Large cities (over 100.000)	34.7
•Regional Distribution by Federal State	
Northern Germany and West Berlin	23.6
- Schleswig-Holstein	4.3
- Hamburg	2.9
- Bremen	1.2
- Lower Saxony	11.9
- West-Berlin	3.3
North-Rhine Westphalia	27.6
Rhine-Main/Southwest	31.2
- Hesse	9.0
- Rhineland-Palatinate	6.1
- Saarland	1.8
- Baden-Württemberg	14.3
Bavaria	17.6

Employed persons
Non-employed persons
For retired and unemployed persons: their earlier occupation
For school children and students: the family bread-winner's occupation

•For these categories, interviewers have to conduct their interviews on the basis of a prescribed quota (quota sampling).
Based on 2.000 respondents, each figure represents 40 interviews

RESIDENCE

Question: *"If you could choose freely, where would you prefer to live—in the country, in a small town, in a medium-sized city or in a large city?"*

	1950 June %	1970 March %	1972 Nov. %	1976 June %	1977 May %	1980 Jan. %
In the country	25	27	27	34	37	35
In a small town	20	18	22	21	26	22
In a medium-sized city	24	26	27	24	23	25
In a large city	27	27	21	17	12	14
Undecided	4	2	3	4	2	4
	100	100	100	100	100	100

	January 1980					
	Country %	Small town %	Medium-sized city %	Large city %	Undecided %	
Total population	35	22	25	14	4	= 100
Men	34	24	23	16	3	= 100
Women	35	21	27	13	4	= 100
AGE GROUPS						
16 - 29	32	15	29	18	6	= 100
30 - 44	29	24	29	15	3	= 100
45 - 59	39	21	22	15	3	= 100
60 and over	40	28	21	9	2	= 100
OCCUPATION						
Unskilled workers	38	21	24	14	3	= 100
Skilled workers	35	22	24	15	4	= 100
Non-managerial employees and public servants	32	22	27	15	4	= 100
Managerial employees and public servants	29	26	26	14	5	= 100
Self-employeds, professionals	25	24	34	15	2	= 100
Farmers	71	18	7	2	2	= 100

MOBILITY

Question: *"Could you tell me whether you've always lived here in this town or whether you moved here from somewhere else?"*

C

	Have lived here - always	with interruptions	Moved here	
	%	%	%	
Total population - 1953	40	7	53	= 100
Total population - 1979	42	7	51	= 100
AGE GROUPS				
18 - 29	55	5	40	= 100
30 - 44	39	6	55	= 100
45 - 59	42	8	50	= 100
60 and over	36	8	56	= 100
OCCUPATION				
Unskilled workers	47	5	48	= 100
Skilled workers	45	7	48	= 100
Non-managerial employees and public servants	42	7	51	= 100
Managerial employees and public servants	30	7	63	= 100
Self-employeds, professionals	38	12	50	= 100
Farmers	69	x	31	= 100

C

	Total		Men		Women	
	1953	1979	1953	1979	1953	1979
"Would you like to move away from here?"	%	%	%	%	%	%
No	70	85	71	85	68	85
Yes	24	9	23	7	25	11
Undecided	6	6	6	8	7	4
	100	100	100	100	100	100

	May 1976				
The respondent's residential area is -	Total pop.	Villages	Small towns	Medium cities	Large cities
	%	%	%	%	%
Loosely settled, with small yards or open spaces	62	68	70	66	47
Very densely settled, houses built close to one another	32	20	22	28	51
Sparsely settled, only a couple of houses	6	12	8	6	2
	100	100	100	100	100

TYPE OF HOUSING

C

	Fall 1979 Apartment house %	Single-family dwelling %	Farmhouse %	Villa, country house %		
Total population	60	34	5	1	=	100
OCCUPATION						
Unskilled workers	68	26	6	x	=	100
Skilled workers	61	37	2	x	=	100
Non-managerial employees and public servants	68	30	1	1	=	100
Managerial employees and public servants	52	45	1	2	=	100
Self-employeds, professionals	47	47	2	4	=	100
Farmers	7	19	74	x	=	100

HOME OWNERS

Question: *"Do you or someone in your household own a house or a condominium?"*

D

	Spring 1979 One-family house %	Two-family house %	Multiple family unit %	Condominium %	Vacation house or apartment	None of these		%
Total population	31	10	3	4	1	53	=	102
OCCUPATION								
Unskilled workers	26	9	1	2	x	63	=	101
Skilled workers	30	10	1	3	x	47	=	101
Non-managerial employees and public servants	27	9	2	5	1	58	=	102
Managerial employees and public servants	38	9	4	7	1	43	=	102
Self-employeds, professionals	40	16	9	7	3	32	=	107
Farmers	58	30	4	1	x	11	=	104
TOWN AND COUNTRY								
Villages	49	18	2	2	x	31	=	102
Small towns	43	15	2	4	x	38	=	102
Medium cities	30	10	2	4	x	56	=	102
Large cities	17	5	3	5	1	70	=	101

RENTERS AND LODGERS

Question: *"Do you live in your own house, or do you rent, or do you lodge with someone?"*

C

	Fall 1979				
	Rental/Official Housing*	Own house	Lodger	Own condominium	
	%	%	%	%	
Total population	49	46	1	4	= 100
OCCUPATION					
Unskilled workers	61	36	2	1	= 100
Skilled workers	53	43	2	2	= 100
Non-managerial employees and public servants	55	37	3	5	= 100
Managerial employees and public servants	42	50	2	6	= 100
Self-employeds, professionals	31	64	3	2	= 100
Farmers	6	94	x	x	= 100

*Housing provided by employer

HOME IS BIG ENOUGH

Question: *"Do you feel that you don't have enough rooms, that your home is too small, or is it big enough?"*

C

		Home is -			
		Big enough	Not quite	Much too small	
		%	%	%	
Total population	1953	62	19	19	= 100
	1979	79	16	5	= 100
Total tenants	1979	69	23	8	= 100
OCCUPATION					
Unskilled workers		70	21	9	= 100
Skilled workers		68	26	6	= 100
Non-managerial employees and public servants		68	23	9	= 100
Managerial employees and public servants		72	18	10	= 100
Self-employeds, professionals		74	22	4	= 100
Farmers		80	x	20	= 100

NEIGHBORLINESS

Question: *"Do you have any neighbors or tenants in your building who give you a hard time?"*

C

	Total population		Men		Women	
	1953	1979	1953	1979	1953	1979
	%	%	%	%	%	%
No, none	80	89	82	89	79	88
Yes	16	9	15	9	18	9
No answer	4	2	3	2	3	3
	100	100	100	100	100	100

Question: *"What would you probably miss most if you* had *to move?"* (L)

C

	1953	1979
	%	%
My group of friends	36	62
My present house, apartment	42	57
Relatives who live here	38	45
The landscape	47	43
Neighbors of mine	16	25
Burial place of family members	28	22
This street, this part of town	14	21
Fellow club members	8	14
I wouldn't like to work for another company	13	13
Sports pals	8	11
Our church, our congregation, the parish	17	10
Our get-togethers at the corner pub	4	4
Political party friends	2	1
Wouldn't miss anything	12	2
Other / no response	4	2
	289	332

STYLES OF LIVING

Question: *"There are six living rooms pictured here. Which of these rooms do you like best - I mean to say, which would you choose if you were to live in one of them?"* (In case there are questions: *"Leaving aside the price of the furniture".)* (ill.) See illustration on the next page.

A

	August 1977							
No.	1	2	3	4	5	6	Undecided	
	%	%	%	%	%	%	%	
Total population	11	18	18	18	18	15	2	= 100
Men	11	15	16	18	22	15	3	= 100
Women	11	20	20	17	17	14	1	= 100
AGE GROUPS								
16 -29	14	10	5	12	30	29	x	= 100
30 - 44	14	15	14	14	25	15	3	= 100
45 - 59	9	18	29	19	15	9	1	= 100
60 and over	6	30	28	26	4	4	2	= 100
OCCUPATION								
Unskilled workers	7	17	16	28	15	16	1	= 100
Skilled workers	11	13	19	20	19	17	1	= 100
Non-managerial employees and public servants	14	18	17	12	23	15	1	= 100
Managerial employees and public servants	10	18	21	10	23	16	2	= 100
Self-employeds, professionals	11	26	18	12	23	6	4	= 100
Farmers	7	30	26	19	9	9	x	= 100

A TELEPHONE AT HOME?

D

	1962	1966	1971	1976	1979	1980
	%	%	%	%	%	%
Yes	20	25	41	58	71	78

GARDEN

Question: *"Do you have a garden - an ornamental garden or a vegetable garden?"*

D

	Spring 1979				
		Size of locality			
	Total population	Under 5,000	5,000 - under 20,000	20,000 - under 100,000	100,000 and over
	%	%	%	%	%
Ornamental garden	30	31	36	31	26
Vegetable garden	24	44	33	21	11
No garden	46	25	31	48	63
	100	100	100	100	100

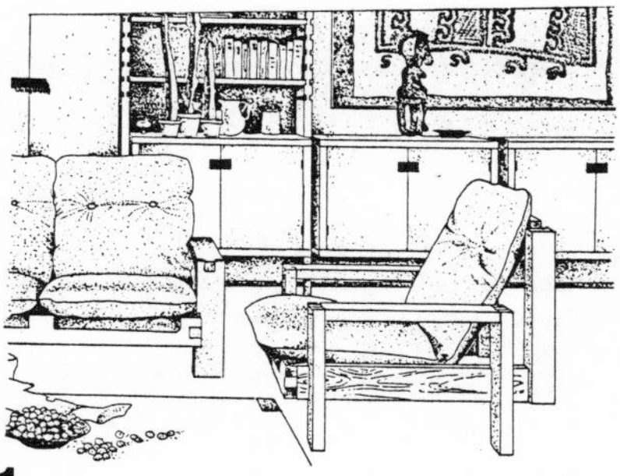

1

2

3

4

5

6

THE IDEAL HOME AND REALITY

Question: *''Everybody has his own idea of the ideal home, apartment, residential area, physical surroundings, etc. What sort of ideas do you have? A list of various things has been drawn up. Could you tell us which of the things on the list correspond to your idea of the ideal home?''* (L)
''And could you describe your present home?''

	June 1976					
	Ideal Total	Reality Total	Villages	Small towns	Medium-sized cities	Large cities
	%	%	%	%	%	%
One-family house	76	41	69	51	42	14
Central heating, hot water, bath	74	66	58	64	69	71
Garden attached to house	71	54	81	65	54	27
Sunny area, lots of green	70	47	65	57	46	28
Peaceful, not much noise	68	52	71	61	50	32
Pleasant neighbors	67	48	55	50	46	44
Convenient transport facilities	53	46	24	36	54	64
Near place of work	42	31	33	32	30	30
Suburb of a town	41	36	10	30	58	47
In the country, in a village	30	36	86	50	13	3
Near business district	22	26	6	17	30	45
Vacation area, health district	21	13	22	22	8	3
Inner court or place nearby where one can meet people and talk	14	8	7	9	6	8
Fashionable residential district	14	3	x	2	8	4
New housing area	13	26	11	29	33	28
Cozy, old-fashioned type of rooms	11	6	8	7	4	6
Locality with places of historical interest	10	7	7	9	7	5
City center, old part of town	8	14	1	8	15	26
Apartment house, multiple-family dwelling	6	43	18	36	48	68
A house which is of historical value	6	1	2	2	x	1
Multi-storied building	2	5	x	3	5	11
Industrial area	1	7	2	3	7	15
	720	616	636	643	633	580

IDEAL BIG CITY

Question: "*What would be ideal conditions for a big city?*" (C)

	1980 February %
Reasonable rents	81
Good subway, streetcar and bus connections	78
Clean air	78
Good job opportunities	75
Little noise from the street in the residential areas	75
Comfortable pedestrian facilities	73
Job security	72
Good chances for earning money	70
Nice residential areas in the surroundings	70
Well-equipped playgrounds	65
Friendly, obliging neighbors	61
Good train connections in all directions	60
Sufficient nursery schools	60
Good, safe bicycle paths	53
Flowing downtown traffic	50
Adequate, easy-to-follow road signs in the city	46
Good freeway connections	45
Sufficient apartments in the inner city	42
Centrally located	38
Home office for important businesses in trade and industry, banks, insurance companies	30
A large airport	25
A sufficient number of taxis	25
A number of good hotels	24
	1,296

CULTURAL INSTITUTIONS AND OTHER ATTRACTIONS

Question: *"When you think of the cultural institutions of an ideal big city - what is the ideal, what must there be in order for you to want to live there?"* (C)

Question: *"Now to restaurants and stores. What should there be in a big city? What would be ideal in your opinion?"* (C)

February 1980

Cultural institutions	%	Restaurants and stores	%
Good schools	74	Well-located supermarkets	75
Possibilities for continuing education	65	Large department stores	73
Interesting old city center, nice old houses	60	Nice, attractive stores downtown	73
Newspapers with good local sections	58	Small bars, pubs	66
Theater, opera, where international stars appear	56	A market with individual stands	64
Universities, institutions of higher learning	48	Good pastry shops, cafés	60
Extensive libraries	48	Inviting sidewalk cafés	56
Various museums	47	Lively pedestrian zones	61
Volkstheater (folk theater)	46	Folk festivals, fairs	55
Concerts with famous musicians	43	Little stores on the corner	52
Convention center for various events	40	Specialty restaurants for gourmets	50
Large selection of movie theaters	40	Modern, elegant restaurants	44
Art exhibitions	38	Inviting snack bars	39
Diverse selection of lectures	34	A flea market where one can buy everything	39
Critically-oriented cabaret	32	Truly good discotheques	31
		Bars, night clubs	31
	729		869

SPORTS AND LEISURE TIME FACILITIES

Question: *"Thinking of sports, hiking and leisure time, which of these things would be especially important to you in an ideal big city?"* (C)

	February 1980				
	Total	Age groups			
	pop.	16-29	30-44	45-59	60 and over
	%	%	%	%	%
Public gardens, parks in the city	87	84	87	89	90
Nice places for outings nearby	82	77	83	84	84
Hiking trails in the area	74	63	76	77	79
Heated swimming pools	69	77	77	71	53
Sports facilities for everyone	66	77	75	63	48
Groups, clubs for various hobbies and pastimes	58	67	64	56	43
A large zoo	52	46	54	52	57
Large-scale sports events	42	47	45	46	31
An indoor ice rink	32	41	35	29	23
An observatory tower with a good view of the city	30	23	28	30	38
None of these	1	1	1	1	3
	593	603	625	598	549

MORE NOISE OR LESS?

Question: *"Much is said about noise, I mean the noise of traffic, industry, the big cities, etc. Do you feel there is more noise now than 10 years ago, or was it just as bad then?"*

	More noise today	Just as bad then	Don't know	
	%	%	%	
Total population - September 1965	90	6	4	= 100
- March 1979	84	11	5	= 100

MOST POPULAR CITIES

Question: *"If we were going to give a prize for the ideal German big city: which of the cities you know would you choose?"* (Only *one* answer!) (O)

February 1980

Munich	Berlin	Hamburg	Duesseldorf	Frankfurt	Cologne	Stuttgart	Hanover	Other/ no city chosen
%	%	%	%	%	%	%	%	%
31	15	11	6	6	5	4	3	19 = 100

Question: "*Could you tell me which of the things on the cards that you have just picked out have been put into effect in (aforementioned city), as you see it? If there is something you are not sure about, say what you suspect is the case.*" (C)

	February 1980			
	Munich	Berlin	Hamburg	Duesseldorf
	%	%	%	%
TRAFFIC CONDITIONS				
Good subway, streetcar and bus connections	71	74	74	57
Lively pedestrian malls	58	45	46	47
Good train connections in all directions	52	38	58	55
Comfortable pedestrian facilities	48	52	45	53
Good freeway connections	43	30	42	53
Adequate, easy-to-follow road signs in the city	31	36	29	30
Centrally located	29	23	27	38
Flowing downtown traffic	23	36	26	30
A large airport	22	29	18	28
A sufficient number of taxis	18	26	22	24
Good, safe bicycle paths	14	18	19	10
	409	407	406	425
EMPLOYMENT				
Good job opportunities	55	57	61	66
Good chances for earning money	53	56	56	59
Job security	39	47	42	47
Home office for important businesses in trade and industry, banks, insurance companies	26	26	27	34
	173	186	186	206
SHOPPING				
Large department stores	67	72	69	71
Nice, appealing stores in the downtown area	67	65	59	67
Easily accessible supermarkets	56	53	61	50
Markets with stands where one can shop	55	42	53	41
Little stores on the corner	27	39	35	28
Flea market where one can buy simply everything	24	33	31	22
	296	304	308	279
RESIDENCE				
Nice residential areas in the surroundings	57	46	52	50
Interesting old city center, nice old houses	45	33	39	59
Clean air	32	35	32	24
Friendly, obliging neighbors	29	36	23	21
Well-equipped playgrounds	29	34	27	20
Sufficient nursery schools	24	33	26	17
Little noise from the street in the residential areas	20	27	24	24
Reasonable rents	16	33	17	17
Sufficient apartments in the inner city	14	23	19	14
	266	280	259	246

continued

continued

	Frankfurt %	Cologne %	Stuttgart %	Hanover %
	February 1980			
TRAFFIC CONDITIONS				
Good subway, streetcar and bus connections	69	63	67	60
Lively pedestrian malls	38	41	47	36
Good train connections in all directions	63	62	60	60
Comfortable pedestrian facilities	42	54	47	55
Good freeway connections	53	41	35	29
Adequate, easy-to-follow road signs in the city	28	38	28	31
Centrally located	42	38	25	29
Flowing downtown traffic	29	28	28	26
A large airport	42	23	18	17
A sufficient number of taxis	24	19	17	29
Good, safe bicycle paths	11	19	9	26
	441	426	381	398
EMPLOYMENT				
Good job opportunities	63	51	64	47
Good chances for earning money	63	51	49	40
Job security	51	40	55	41
Home office for important businesses in trade and industry, banks, insurance companies	40	28	20	26
	217	170	188	154
SHOPPING				
Large department stores	72	69	74	58
Nice, appealing stores in the downtown area	63	66	71	61
Easily accessible supermarkets	65	59	63	59
Markets with stands where one can shop	43	54	41	43
Little stores on the corner	33	35	37	41
Flea market where one can buy simply everything	25	22	12	20
	301	305	298	282
RESIDENCE				
Nice residential areas in the surroundings	49	48	61	55
Interesting old city center, nice old houses	51	57	34	43
Clean air	16	20	30	31
Friendly, obliging neighbors	27	41	36	29
Well-equipped playgrounds	28	27	39	28
Sufficient nursery schools	23	29	30	29
Little noise from the street in the residential areas	17	15	18	24
Reasonable rents	21	17	18	31
Sufficient apartments in the inner city	24	14	16	17
	256	268	282	287

continued

continued	February 1980			
	Munich	Berlin	Hamburg	Duesseldorf
	%	%	%	%
EDUCATION, INFORMATION				
Good schools	57	55	59	47
Possibilities for continuing education (vocational school, evening classes, etc.)	57	57	55	50
Newspapers with good local sections	45	45	44	38
Universities, institutions of higher learning	47	50	46	27
Various museums	49	47	42	24
Large zoo	41	50	46	10
Extensive libraries	43	43	38	23
Convention center for various events	31	41	41	24
Diverse selection of lectures	26	30	29	17
	396	418	400	260
ENTERTAINMENT				
Theater, opera, where international stars appear	53	62	52	45
Folk festivals, fairs	48	35	41	32
Volkstheater ("folk theater"), where plays in dialect are presented	42	28	42	17
Large-scale sports events	41	41	33	39
Art exhibitions	39	40	36	23
Concerts with famous musicians	38	46	39	26
Large selection of movie theaters	35	43	42	40
Truly good discotheques	28	29	26	25
Critically-oriented cabaret	27	35	20	24
	351	359	331	271
GOING OUT				
Small bars, pubs	56	63	52	57
Good pastry shops, cafés	51	60	51	48
Specialty restaurants for gourmets	48	53	44	40
Inviting sidewalk cafés, where one can sit along the street	47	59	31	49
Modern, elegant restaurants	39	46	34	45
Inviting snack bars	30	31	31	31
A sufficient number of good hotels	20	28	22	22
Bars, nightclubs where one isn't overcharged	18	26	18	20
	309	366	283	312
SPORTS - RECREATION				
Public gardens, parks in the city	79	74	71	70
Nice places for outings nearby	73	60	62	66
Heated swimming pools	60	60	64	56
Sports facilities where everyone can go	52	51	48	40
Hiking paths in the surrounding area	51	48	45	38
Associations and clubs for various hobbies and leisure time activities	44	43	42	37
Indoor ice rink	28	30	17	24
Observation tower with a good view of the city	20	30	23	4
	407	396	372	335

continued

	February 1980			
	Frankfurt %	Cologne %	Stuttgart %	Hanover %
EDUCATION, INFORMATION				
Good schools	47	61	63	53
Possibilities for continuing education (vocational school, evening classes, etc.)	56	57	56	57
Newspapers with good local sections	46	38	53	52
Universities, institutions of higher learning	41	47	25	35
Various museums	43	39	33	50
Large zoo	55	45	48	47
Extensive libraries	32	35	32	36
Convention center for various events	37	23	34	26
Diverse selection of lectures	30	19	28	16
	387	364	372	372
ENTERTAINMENT				
Theater, opera, where international stars also appear	55	45	42	38
Folk festivals, fairs	35	38	53	36
Volkstheater (''folk theater''), where plays in dialect are also presented	31	41	34	22
Large-scale sports events	42	34	39	33
Art exhibitions	43	29	31	28
Concerts with famous musicians	41	33	28	29
Large selection of movie theaters	45	30	26	36
Truly good discotheques	30	26	18	21
Critically-oriented cabaret	20	18	12	16
	342	294	283	259
GOING OUT				
Small bars, pubs	56	51	48	52
Good pastry shops, cafés	56	54	61	64
Specialty restaurants for gourmets	49	36	32	48
Inviting sidewalk cafés, where one can sit along the street	44	34	33	29
Modern, elegant restaurants	50	34	42	38
Inviting snack bars	31	32	31	38
A sufficient number of good hotels	29	22	16	16
Bars, nightclubs where one isn't overcharged	21	17	17	16
	336	280	280	301
SPORTS - RECREATION				
Public gardens, parks in the city	66	73	79	81
Nice places for outings nearby	73	78	82	74
Heated swimming pools	59	59	61	57
Sports facilities where everyone can go	46	43	48	45
Hiking paths in the surrounding area	46	49	70	59
Associations and clubs for various hobbies and leisure time activities	48	49	41	43
Indoor ice rink	21	22	13	22
Observation tower with a good view of the city	29	17	35	16
	388	390	429	397

FAMILY LIFE

Question: *"If we're talking about family, whom would you think of? Whom do you include in your family?"*

C

	1953 %	1979 %
Children	70	68
Spouse	70	67
Parents	28	35
Brothers and sisters	19	29
Grandchildren	5	10
Parents-in-law	3	8
Son-in-law, daughter-in-law	4	7
Uncle, aunt, nephew etc., distant relatives	2	7
Grandparents	1	4
Brother-in-law, sister-in-law	2	3
Don't have a family, am alone	3	1
	207	239

Question: *"Would you say that you have a lot of relatives?"*

C

	Have a lot %	Average %	Few %		
Total population - 1953	49	30	21	=	100
1979	44	32	24	=	100

RELATIVES WITHIN REACH

Question: *"Where do most of your relatives live?"*

C

	1953 %	1979 %
Right here in the same town, in the vicinity	48	45
Right here in the same state	25	28
Farther away, in other parts of West Germany, in West Berlin	17	16
East Germany	10	7
Abroad	6	3
All over the place/no response	15	11
	121	110

FAMILY SUPPORT

Question: *"Do you personally contribute to supporting the family or to supporting relatives?"*

C

Support -	Total 1953 %	Total 1979 %	Men 1953 %	Men 1979 %	Women 1953 %	Women 1979 %
family in the same household	49	47	75	68	28	29
family not in the same household	3	1	3	2	2	1
relatives	5	3	6	2	5	3
No	46	51	21	29	68	68
	103	102	105	101	103	101

SMALLER HOUSEHOLDS

Question: *"How many people - counting both children and adults - live in your household, including yourself?"*
"Could you please tell me with the aid of this list, which persons are included in your household?" (L)

C

Number of persons -	1953 %	1979 %
6 or more persons	15	4
5 persons	13	8
4 persons	20	19
3 persons	23	21
2 persons	19	30
1 person	10	18
	100	100
Average number of persons	3.6	2.8

Household consists of -	1953 %	1979 %
My husband/my wife	64	65
Son/daughter	54	43
Father/mother	19	12
Brother/sister	11	7
Grandson/granddaughter	4	2
Son-in-law/daughter-in-law	4	1
Father-in-law/mother-in-law	4	2
Nephew/niece/uncle/aunt	4	x
Brother-in-law/sister-in-law	2	1
Grandparents	1	1
Other relatives	1	1
One person	10	18
	178	153

IDEAL FAMILY SIZE

Question: "*What do you think is the ideal family size - father, mother and how many children?*" (O)

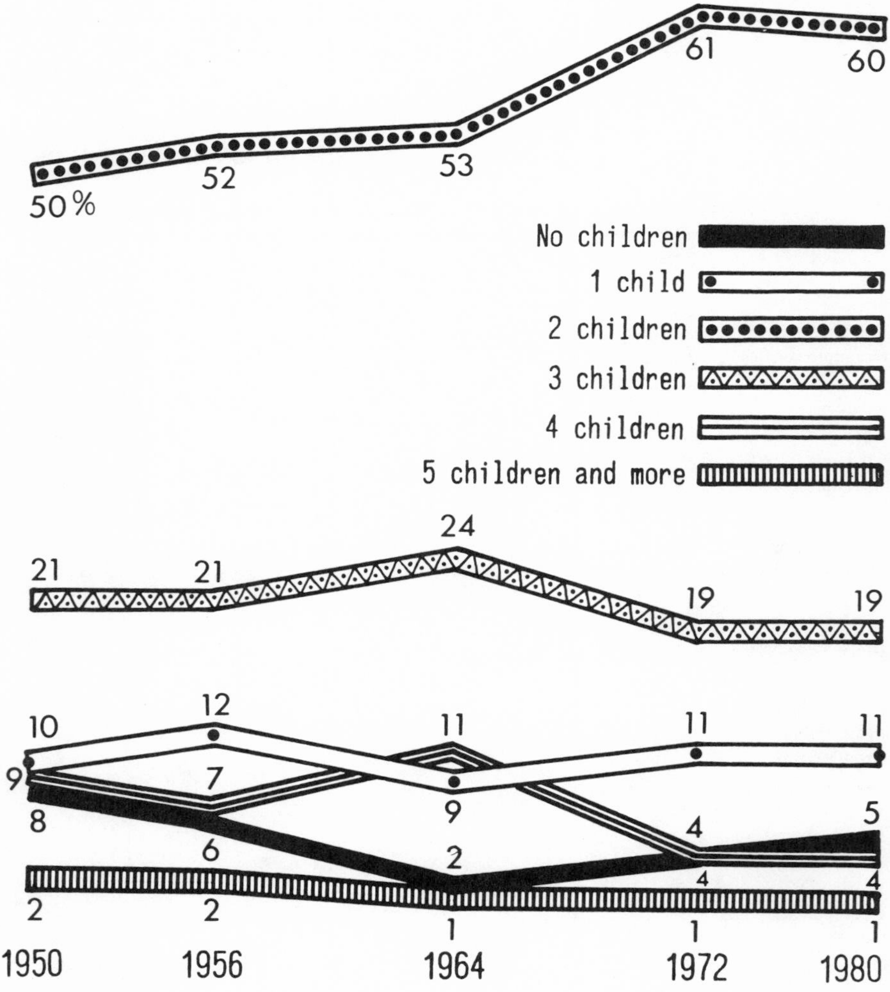

FAMILY-HAPPINESS?

Question: *"Do you feel that one needs a family in order to be truly happy, or is it possible to be just as happy alone?"*

A

	August 1976						
	Need family		Happy alone		Undecided		
	Men	Women	Men	Women	Men	Women	
	%	%	%	%	%	%	
Total men	58	–	36	–	6	–	= 100
Total women	–	58	–	37	–	5	= 100
AGE GROUPS							
16 - 29	39	42	53	50	8	8	
30 - 44	55	51	38	42	7	7	
45 - 59	70	66	27	33	3	1	
60 and over	77	73	18	23	5	4	
MARITAL STATUS							
Single	34	37	57	57	9	6	
Married	65	62	30	33	5	5	
Divorced	40	41	55	53	5	6	
Widowed	75	69	25	29	x	2	

COMMON INTERESTS

Question put to persons who don't live alone (84= 100 percent): *"Although not every person in a household has the same interests, there are some things you often do together with other members of the family. - Which of the items on this list apply to you?"* (L)

D

	Spring 1977						
	Total	Unskilled workers	Skilled workers	Non-manag. employees	Managerial pub. servants	Self-empl., professionals	Farmers
	%	%	%	%	%	%	%
Often watch television together	72	71	78	70	69	67	73
Frequently play games	41	38	43	42	45	36	35
Take care of the household	41	49	44	44	63	40	18
Go visit friends and relatives	40	34	41	41	45	37	40
Often go on hikes and excursions	38	28	38	40	50	39	25
Read a lot at home	35	26	33	37	50	33	27
Frequently go out together	20	15	20	22	27	23	11
Do sports together	18	11	17	19	25	20	10
Sing, play music together	9	7	7	9	14	11	10
	314	279	321	324	388	306	249

MARRIAGE NECESSARY

Question: *"Do you consider the institution of marriage necessary, or do you think it is antiquated?"*

	Married men			Married women		
	1949	1963	1978	1949	1963	1978
	%	%	%	%	%	%
Necessary	90	92	71	92	95	65
Antiquated	3	3	11	3	1	13
Undecided	7	5	18	5	4	22
	100	100	100	100	100	100

	Men aged 20 - 30			Women aged 20 - 30		
	1949	1963	1978	1949	1963	1978
	%	%	%	%	%	%
Necessary	83	87	40	91	90	42
Antiquated	3	3	26	2	x	28
Undecided	14	10	34	7	10	30
	100	100	100	100	100	100

WIVES LESS HAPPY THAN HUSBANDS?

Question: *"Would you say that most marriages in Germany are happy or unhappy?"*

	Married men			Married women		
	1949	1963	1978	1949	1963	1978
	%	%	%	%	%	%
Happy	17	34	36	12	24	29
Neither nor	39	37	40	43	37	48
Unhappy	22	5	7	24	10	6
No opinion	22	24	17	21	29	17
	100	100	100	100	100	100

	Men aged 20 - 30			Women aged 20 - 30		
	1949	1963	1978	1949	1963	1978
	%	%	%	%	%	%
Happy	13	26	27	14	25	14
Neither nor	40	30	35	40	34	48
Unhappy	18	7	12	28	9	10
No opinion	29	37	26	18	32	28
	100	100	100	100	100	100

HAPPINESS WITHOUT MARRIAGE

Question put to married men:
"Do you believe that a man must be married in order to be really happy, or do you not consider this so important?"

"And would you say that a woman must be married in order to be really happy?"

Question put to married women:
"Do you believe that a woman must be married in order to be really happy, or do you not consider this so important?"

"And would you say that a man must be married in order to be really happy?"

	Married men with reference to men			Married women with reference to women		
	1949	1963	1976	1949	1963	1976
	%	%	%	%	%	%
Yes, married	57	58	42	51	45	29
No, not so important	34	29	45	41	41	57
Undecided	9	13	13	8	14	14
	100	100	100	100	100	100
	with reference to women			with reference to men		
Yes, married	62	50	37	41	41	24
No, not so important	21	27	55	40	39	61
Undecided	17	23	8	19	20	15
	100	100	100	100	100	100

	Men aged 20 -30 with reference to men			Women aged 20 -30 with reference to women		
	1949	1963	1976	1949	1963	1976
	%	%	%	%	%	%
Yes, married	44	38	19	48	40	22
No, not so important	47	39	65	44	38	66
Undecided	9	23	16	8	22	12
	100	100	100	100	100	100
	with reference to women			with reference to men		
Yes, married	61	46	27	34	34	16
No, not so important	24	28	55	40	38	69
Undecided	15	26	18	26	28	15
	100	100	100	100	100	100

SATISFIED

Question put to married persons: *"Are you satisfied with your marriage?"*

	Married men			Married women		
	1949	1963	1976	1949	1963	1976
	%	%	%	%	%	%
Yes, very	45	44	31	45	39	33
Yes	44	45	55	35	45	46
No	6	4	6	15	9	8
Undecided	5	7	8	5	7	13
	100	100	100	100	100	100
	Persons between 20 and 30 years of age					
Yes, very	56	46	45	62	43	36
Yes	35	43	54	25	52	58
No	6	5	x	9	3	4
Undecided	3	6	1	4	2	2
	100	100	100	100	100	100

Question put to married persons: *"Which statement applies to you?"* (L)

	November 1957		August 1978	
	Men	Women	Men	Women
	%	%	%	%
My marriage is particularly happy. There has never been even the slightest quarrel	8	10	4	4
Our marriage has so far been happy. We understand each other excellently in everything. There has never been a serious crisis	33	29	32	34
Though we sometimes come up against difficulties in our marriage, we understand each other very well on the whole	43	43	53	48
When one is married one must put up with many things, but in my marriage there are difficulties which make me very unhappy	6	8	7	9
My marriage is rather unhappy. I sometimes think it would be better if we got divorced	1	1	1	2
No decision	9	9	3	3
	100	100	100	100

Question put to married persons: *"Would you tell me how long you've been married?"* (If married more than once, the present marriage)

R

	Married - Less than 2 years	2 -5 years	6 - 10 years	11 - 20 years	More than 20 years	
	%	%	%	%	%	
Married persons total - 1953	7	14	13	25	41	= 100
- 1979	3	12	14	28	43	= 100

TILL DEATH DO US PART

Question: *"When someone gets married today, do you feel that this is a lifetime commitment, or not necessarily?"*

	Lifetime commitment		Not necessarily		No opinion	
	1974	1979	1974	1979	1974	1979
	%	%	%	%	%	%
Total population	56	52	40	42	4	6

July 1979

	Total men	Age groups 16-29	30-44	45-59	60 and over	Total women	Age groups 16-29	30-44	45-59	60 and over
	%	%	%	%	%	%	%	%	%	%
Lifetime commitment	54	46	49	53	61	51	48	49	51	62
Not necessarily	40	47	46	40	32	44	49	48	44	30
No opinion	6	7	5	7	7	5	3	3	5	8
	100	100	100	100	100	100	100	100	100	100

MARRIAGE ON PROBATION

Question: *"If it was possible for a marriage contract to be entered into for a limited period of time and to be continually renewed thereafter, would you consider this a good idea or not?"*

A

	Good idea	Not a good idea	Undecided	
	%	%	%	
Total population - August 1978	27	60	13	= 100
- October 1973	25	61	14	= 100
Men	26	60	14	= 100
Women	24	62	14	= 100
MARITAL STATUS				
Single	35	45	20	= 100
Married	22	65	13	= 100
Divorced	50	37	13	= 100
Widowed	14	75	11	= 100

EQUAL RIGHTS

Question: *"Do you think that in a marriage husband and wife should have equal rights, or should the husband enjoy more rights than his wife?"*

	1954 Jan. %	1973 Oct. %	1979 Nov. %
Should have equal rights	48	74	75
Husband should have more rights	34	13	9
It depends	16	12	14
No opinion	2	1	2
	100	100	100

	November 1979				
	Should have equal rights %	Husband should have more rights %	It depends %	No opinion %	
Total population	75	9	14	2	= 100
Men	70	11	17	2	= 100
Women	80	7	12	1	= 100
MARITAL STATUS					
Single	85	5	8	2	= 100
Married	74	8	16	2	= 100
Divorced	83	6	9	2	= 100
Widowed	61	17	19	3	= 100
AGE GROUPS					
16 - 29	88	4	6	2	= 100
30 - 44	78	7	13	2	= 100
45 - 59	74	9	16	1	= 100
60 and over	61	14	22	3	= 100
EDUCATION					
Elementary	71	11	16	2	= 100
Secondary	83	3	12	2	= 100

MARRIAGE + CHILDREN = HAPPINESS?

Question: "*Which marriages do you think are happiest—those with children or those without, or don't you think that happiness in marriage is dependent upon having children?*"

E

	With children		Without children		Happiness not dependent upon children		No opinion	
	1972	1978	1972	1978	1972	1978	1972	1978
	%	%	%	%	%	%	%	%
Total population	47	56	2	2	44	39	7	3
Total married population	51	59	1	1	42	37	6	3
MEN, married								
under 30	41	67	x	2	53	28	6	3
30-44	50	62	3	2	41	35	6	1
45 and older	61	67	1	1	31	30	7	2
WOMEN, married								
under 30	32	49	x	2	64	47	4	2
30-44	49	51	1	1	46	46	4	2
45 and older	51	57	1	1	43	39	5	3

FONDNESS OF CHILDREN

Question: "*Many people say that the Germans aren't fond of children. Generally speaking, would you agree with this or not agree with it?*"

	November 1978			
	Don't agree	Agree	Undecided	
	%	%	%	
Total population	46	42	12	= 100

A SON

Question: "*If one could determine the sex of one's children, what would you desire, a boy or a girl?*" In case of "both"): "*And if you could only have one child?*"

B

	June 1971				
	Boy	Girl	Either	No opinion	
	%	%	%	%	
Men	50	19	26	5	= 100
Women	29	38	27	6	= 100
AGE GROUPS					
16 - 29	37	32	29	2	= 100
30 - 44	40	30	27	3	= 100
45 - 59	39	30	26	5	= 100
60 and over	41	21	26	12	= 100

Question put to housewives: "Here two mothers are talking about whether a child should be spanked if it is very naughty. With which of the two would you tend to agree?" (x, ill.)

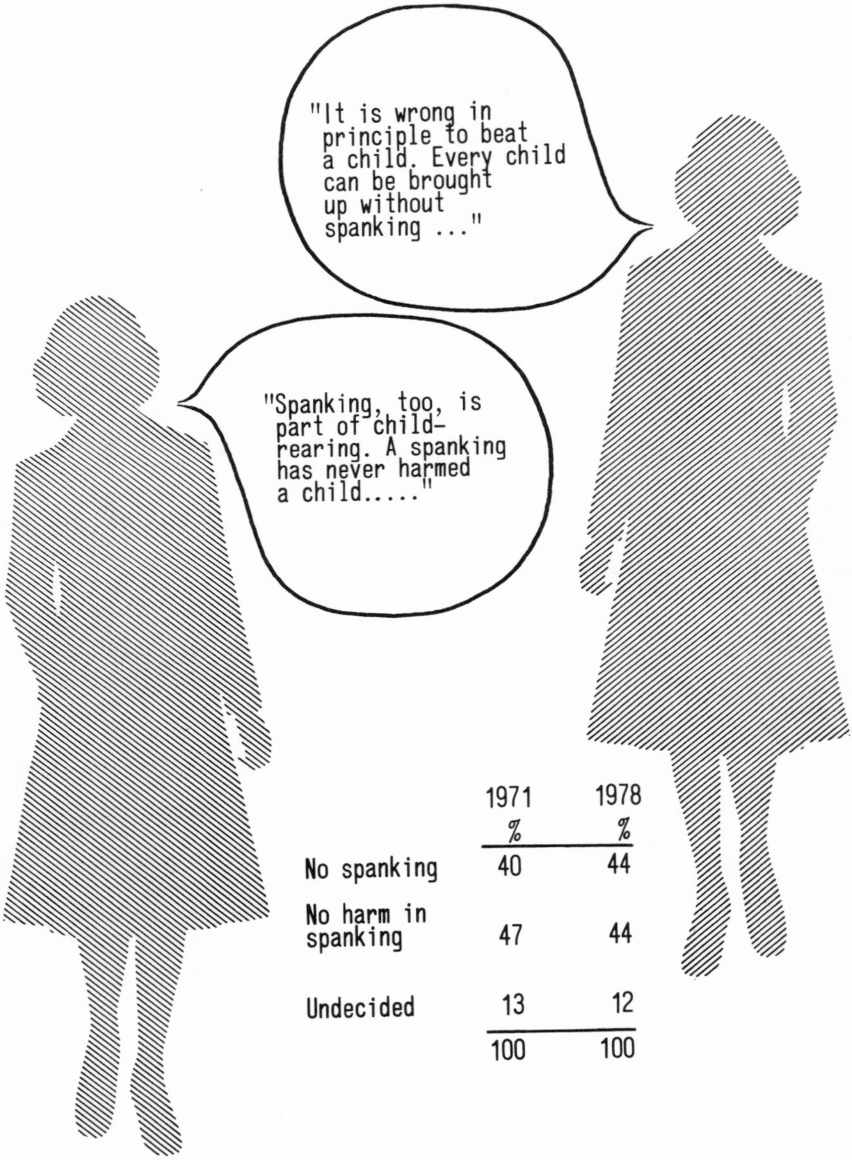

	1971 %	1978 %
No spanking	40	44
No harm in spanking	47	44
Undecided	13	12
	100	100

UPBRINGING

Question: *"Think a moment about the way you were brought up. Would you say your parents were very strict with you, rather strict, hardly ever strict, or not strict at all?"*

	April 1979						
	Total pop.	Men	Women	Age groups 16-29	30-44	45-59	60 and over
	%	%	%	%	%	%	%
Very strict	16	14	18	5	11	21	29
Rather strict	41	43	39	33	43	44	44
Hardly ever strict	28	29	26	42	30	23	14
Not at all strict	15	14	17	20	16	12	13
	100	100	100	100	100	100	100

PRAISE

Question: *"Thinking back to your childhood, did you receive more praise or more criticism?"*

	August 1979			
	Praise	Criticism	Undecided	
	%	%	%	
Total population	28	26	46	= 100
Men	23	28	49	= 100
Women	33	23	44	= 100

HONOR THY FATHER AND THY MOTHER

Question put to women: *"Whom does your child/do your children respect more, your husband or you?"*

Question put to men: *"Whom does your child/do your children respect more, your wife or you?"*

	Parents with children between the ages of 2 and 25 at home					
	Total		Men		Women	
The children have greater respect for-	1965 Sept.	1979 March	1965 Sept.	1979 March	1965 Sept.	1979 March
	%	%	%	%	%	%
Father	54	54	53	56	54	53
Mother	13	18	13	15	14	20
Both equally	33	28	34	29	32	27
	100	100	100	100	100	100

ANTI-AUTHORITARIANISM

Question: *"Have you ever heard of anti-authoritarian education? According to what you know or have heard of it, do you think anti-authoritarian education is good for children, or is it not good?"*

	April 1971				
	Good	Not good	Other response	Never heard of it	
	%	%	%	%	
Total population	18	33	9	40	= 100
Total parents	19	33	11	37	= 100
AGE GROUPS					
16 - 29	30	26	12	32	= 100
30 - 44	19	36	12	33	= 100
45 - 59	14	38	6	42	= 100
60 and over	8	28	6	58	= 100

YOUTH VS. PARENTS

Question: *"Do you think young people have too many rights today or too few, in relation to their parents?"*

A

	August 1979				
	Too many rights	Just right	Too few	Impossible to say	
	%	%	%	%	
Total population	52	30	5	13	= 100
AGE GROUPS					
16 - 29	31	43	14	12	= 100
30 - 44	47	36	3	14	= 100
45 - 59	61	27	1	11	= 100
60 and over	70	15	2	13	= 100

ACHIEVEMENT VS. CHANCE

Question: *"I would like to tell you about a situation and ask your opinion of it:*

A father has two sons who go to school. Over the vacation, one of the two has a chance to go to England as part of an exchange with an English boy, and now the family has to decide which of the two will be the lucky one. Finally, the father says, whoever has the best report card next time can go.

Do you think this father did the right thing, or not?" Addition for half group: *". . . or should they have drawn lots to see who could go?"*

A

	Achievement		Chance	
	1975	1980	1975	1980
	Aug.	March	Aug.	March
	%	%	%	%
Fair	40	44	37	34
Unfair	54	50	50	53
Other answer	6	6	13	13
	100	100	100	100

GOALS FOR LIFE

Question: *"We've put together a list of what children should be provided with for their later life, things they should learn in the home. Which points do you consider especially important?"* (L)

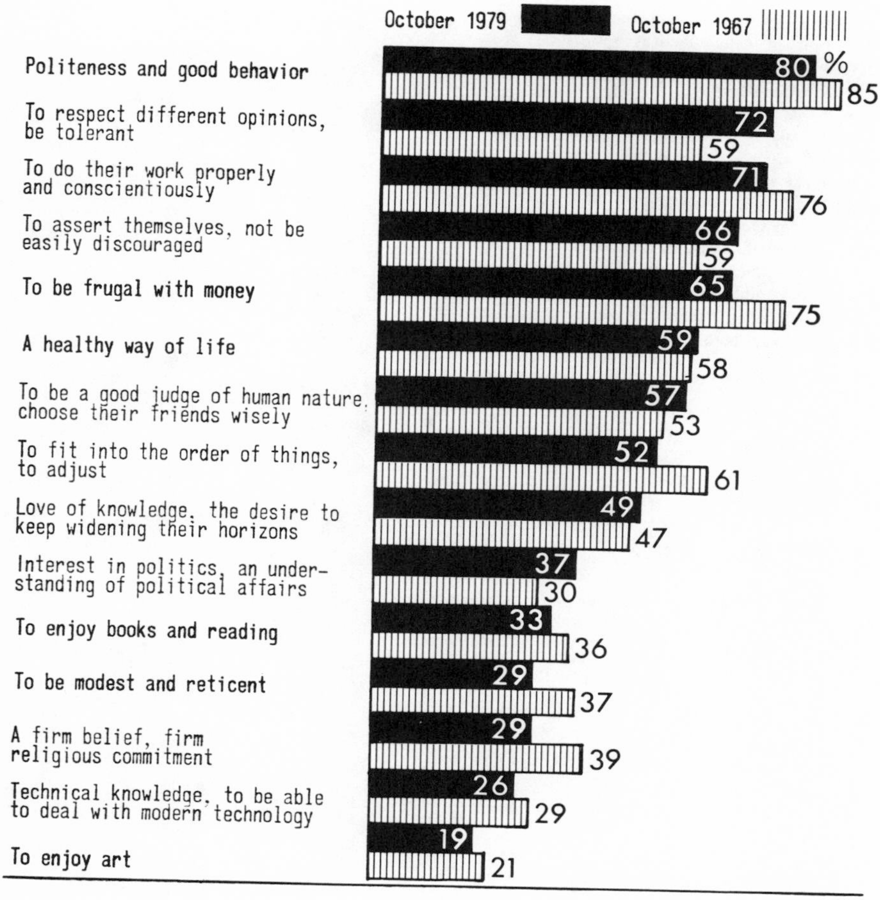

PARENTS WORRY MORE

Question put to fathers and mothers who have children between the ages of 2 and 25: "*When talking to parents, one often hears complaints about the problems they have with their children. Some of these complaints are listed here. Is there anything here that you also worry about or get upset about?*" (C)

	September 1965 %	March 1979 %
They let their things lie around all over the house	45	60
They don't want to go to bed	36	46
They watch too much television	–	43
They are becoming too hard to please, they demand too much	21	43
Their stubbornness, obstinacy	26	35
They don't get up on time in the mornings	22	35
We've already caught them at cheating	23	33
We always have to be after them to get their schoolwork done	20	30
They always talk back	21	24
They waste their money, don't want to save	14	23
One never knows what they're thinking, they don't confide in us	11	17
That they already smoke at their age	11	17
They make a big fuss whenever they have to wash up	11	16
They don't come home at night	13	15
To get them to eat you virtually have to force them	15	15
No matter what I say, they don't obey	11	14
They always sneak food, are always snacking	11	14
Instead of coming home after school they wander around	11	13
They like to drink alcoholic beverages	–	11
They're always bothering us with questions	12	9
None of these	20	8
	354	521

– = not asked in 1965.

HAPPY MEMORIES

Question: "*Would you say that your childhood was happy or not particularly happy?*"

	1958 Dec. %	1968 Nov. %	1974 Aug. %	1979 Aug. %
Happy	60	55	53	58
In some respects	26	30	33	30
Not happy	14	15	14	12
	100	100	100	100

SELF-IMAGE

Question: *"Two men are talking about life.*

One says:

'The fact is that some people are at the top and others are at the bottom and won't get anywhere under present conditions, no matter how hard they try.'

The other says:

'Everybody is master of his fate. Nowadays anybody who really makes an effort can get somewhere.'

Which of the two would you personally tend to agree with?" (X, ill.)

	1955 March %	1963 Nov. %	1975 Aug. %	1978 May %	1980 May %
Everybody master of his fate	53	62	62	63	61
Some at top, others at bottom	35	25	27	26	23
Undecided	12	13	11	11	16
	100	100	100	100	100

	May 1980			
	Everybody master of his fate %	Some at top, others at bottom %	Undecided %	
Total population	61	23	16	= 100
Men	61	24	15	= 100
Women	60	23	17	= 100
AGE GROUPS				
16-29	53	29	18	= 100
30-44	60	23	17	= 100
45-59	62	24	14	= 100
60 and over	67	18	15	= 100
EDUCATION				
Elementary	59	26	15	= 100
Secondary	64	18	18	= 100

SUCCESS

Question: *"In your opinion, what does success depend on to the greatest extent—luck or ability?"*

	Ability	Luck	Both equally	Undecided	
	%	%	%	%	
Total population - September 1970	41	13	44	2	= 100
- June 1972	42	13	43	2	= 100
- March 1974	36	12	50	2	= 100
- February 1978	34	12	52	2	= 100
- November 1980	35	13	50	2	= 100

THE PURPOSE OF LIFE

Question: *"We often ask ourselves what we are living for—what the purpose of life is. What do you consider above all to be the purpose of your life? Could you answer with the help of this list?"* (L)

	November 1978						
	Total pop.	Men	Women	Age groups			
				16-29	30-44	45-59	60 and over
	%	%	%	%	%	%	%
To ensure that my family is provided for	56	62	50	38	65	65	54
To be happy	52	54	51	66	54	47	41
To ensure my children's well-being	47	45	48	30	56	48	51
To achieve something in life, to accomplish something	42	48	37	49	46	39	33
To be able to measure up to my own expectations at any time	42	39	43	41	43	39	41
To enjoy life	37	42	32	56	41	28	20
To get to know the world, to see a lot of the world	35	37	34	54	34	29	24
To be respected by my fellowmen, to have a good reputation	35	34	35	30	35	35	38
To obey my conscience	32	31	34	28	28	33	42
To be liked by others, to be popular	31	29	33	41	28	25	30
To contribute in my own way to the creation of a better society	26	30	23	29	26	25	24
To prove myself in my earthly life in order to be able to face my creator	22	19	26	12	15	23	42
To be able to afford my own house or home	22	28	17	28	25	21	14
To do what God expects me to do	16	14	19	9	8	15	34
To devote all my energies to a particular idea	16	19	14	20	17	15	13
To be entirely at others' disposal, to help others	15	12	18	13	10	14	24
I see no purpose	2	2	2	1	2	3	3
	528	545	516	545	533	504	528

LIFE AN ASSIGNMENT

Question: *"Two people are engaged in conversation.*

The one:

"I consider my life to be an assignment which I am here to carry out and to which I apply my entire energy. I want to accomplish something in life, even if it often proves difficult."

The other:

"I want to enjoy life and avoid any unneccessary exertion. After all, we only live once and the main thing is to make the most of it."

Which one of them do you think has the right attitude?" (X, ill.)

	March 1980			
	Life an assignment	Enjoy life	Undecided	
	%	%	%	
Total population	51	29	20	= 100
Men	50	32	18	= 100
Women	53	27	20	= 100
AGE GROUPS				
16-29	31	43	26	= 100
30-44	46	34	20	= 100
45-59	58	24	18	= 100
60 and over	71	14	15	= 100
EDUCATION				
Elementary	54	27	19	= 100
Secondary	45	33	22	= 100
DENOMINATION				
Protestant	52	28	20	= 100
Catholic	54	26	20	= 100
Other	34	45	21	= 100

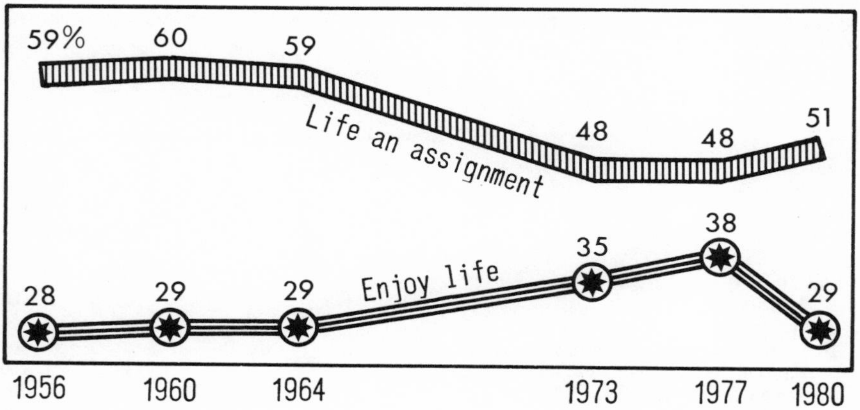

DOUBTS

Question: *"Do you ever get the feeling that life is meaningless?"*

	Never %	Sometimes %	Often %	
Total population - 1964	57	33	10	= 100
- 1973	56	38	6	= 100
- 1978	57	37	6	= 100
Men	63	33	4	= 100
Women	50	41	9	= 100
AGE GROUPS				
16-29	59	35	6	= 100
30-44	60	35	5	= 100
45-59	54	40	6	= 100
60 and over	53	39	8	= 100
DENOMINATION				
Protestant	58	36	6	= 100
Catholic	54	39	7	= 100
Other	52	38	10	= 100

GOOD IDEAS

Question: *"In your own life, do you usually have the chance to put the good ideas you have into effect, or is that frequently not possible?"*

	January 1979			
	Always, almost always %	Usually %	Often not possible %	
Total population	11	41	48	= 100
Men	12	41	47	= 100
Women	10	41	49	= 100
OCCUPATION				
Unskilled workers	5	30	65	= 100
Skilled workers	11	42	47	= 100
Non-managerial employees and public servants	11	45	44	= 100
Managerial employees and public servants	17	45	38	= 100
Self-employeds, professionals	20	46	34	= 100
Farmers	7	41	52	= 100

AN INDICATOR OF SELF-ASSURANCE

Question: *"Would you take a look at this illustration with the large and small weights? You sometimes say of someone that what he says has a lot of weight, meaning how much importance he has. How do you expect you yourself are judged; how would you probably be 'weighted'?"* (ill.)

November 1979

	Total	Age groups 16-29	30-44	45-59	60 and over	Education Elementary	Secondary
	%	%	%	%	%	%	%
Men							
Weight A	6	3	5	10	7	5	7
B	46	43	52	46	43	44	51
C	27	34	24	24	26	27	27
D	6	7	5	4	7	7	4
Impossible to say	15	13	14	16	17	17	11
	100	100	100	100	100	100	100
Women							
Weight A	4	2	5	5	5	4	5
B	37	39	44	38	28	34	44
C	32	37	31	29	31	32	30
D	10	5	5	11	17	12	6
Impossible to say	17	17	15	17	19	18	15
	100	100	100	100	100	100	100

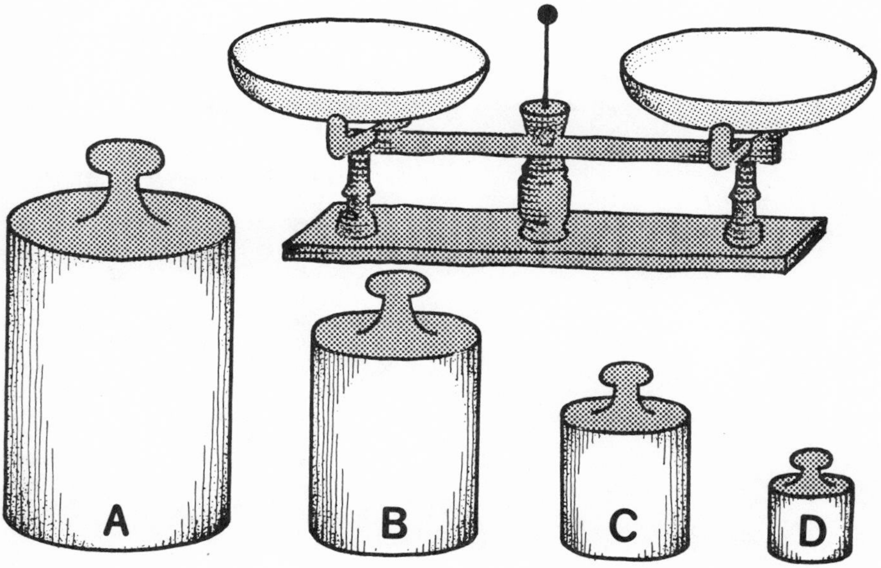

SATISFACTION WITH LIFE

Question: *"Are you generally satisfied with your present life, or do you wish some things were different?"*

	1958 May	1966 May	1973 March	1978 Nov.	Age groups 16-29	30-44	45-59	60 and over
	%	%	%	%	%	%	%	%
Satisfied	45	58	61	67	54	68	63	81
Wish some things were different	52	36	30	30	43	29	34	16
Undecided	3	6	9	3	3	3	3	3
	100	100	100	100	100	100	100	100

STARTING ALL OVER AGAIN

Question: *"If you could live your life all over again, would you live it differently or in exactly the same way?"*

	Much differently	In some respects differently	Exactly the same	Undecided	
	%	%	%	%	
Total population - November 1954	30	32	23	15	= 100
- March 1960	30	38	23	9	= 100
- April 1975	22	46	22	10	= 100

QUITE HAPPY

Question: *"If someone said about you that you are very happy, would he be right or not?"*

	Right	Partly right	Not right	Hard to say	
	%	%	%	%	
Total population - November 1954	28	33	26	13	= 100
- April 1961	27	36	21	16	= 100
- June 1967	28	43	17	12	= 100
- November 1974	30	47	13	10	= 100
- March 1980	30	46	11	13	= 100
Men	30	47	10	13	= 100
Women	30	46	12	12	= 100
AGE GROUPS					
16-29	31	45	9	15	= 100
30-44	35	45	9	11	= 100
45-59	27	47	14	12	= 100
60 and over	26	47	13	14	= 100

FAST-PACED AGE

Question: *"We often hear that we are living in a fast-paced age; we are always in a hurry. What is your situation like? Are you one of those people who never have enough time, or can't you say that of yourself?"*

	1961 Sept.	1976 May	Men	Women	Age groups 16-29	30-44	45-59	60 and over
	Total population							
	%	%	%	%	%	%	%	%
Have enough time	56	58	56	60	54	46	57	80
Never have enough time	44	42	44	40	46	54	43	20
	100	100	100	100	100	100	100	100

EXACTNESS DESIRED

Question: *"Do you generally wear a watch?" - "Does your watch always show the exact time, or does it tend to be somewhat fast or somewhat slow?"*

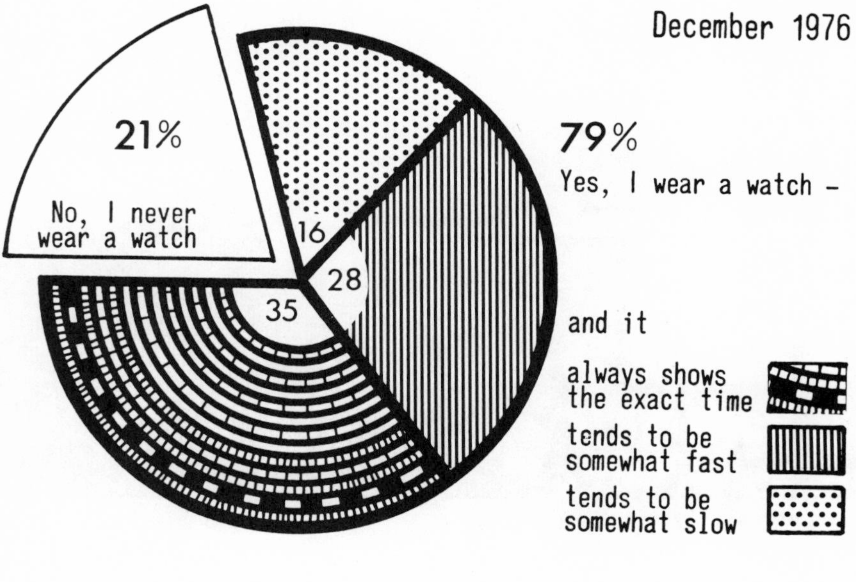

DIFFICULT TIMES

Question: *"Would you say that all in all we live in happy times, or do you have the feeling that we are going through difficult times?"*

	1963 Jan. %	1966 July %	1970 July %	1974 Jan. %	1976 Aug. %
Difficult times	45	42	37	50	43
Happy times	31	40	44	30	35
Undecided	24	18	19	20	22
	100	100	100	100	100

HOW FAST DOES TIME PASS

Question: *"What would you say, how fast does time pass; how fast or how slowly do things change? Could you tell me with the help of this picture? 1 means that time almost stands still, and 7 that it passes extremely quickly. Which number between 1 and 7 would you say is typical of the times we live in?"* (ill.)

"And if you could choose the rate of change, which would you prefer?" (ill.)

July 1975	Almost stands still 1 %	2 %	3 %	4 %	5 %	6 %	Passes extremely quickly 7 %	No reply %	
Perception of reality	x	1	2	8	25	33	30	1	= 100
Desired, ideal	4	12	28	30	17	5	2	2	= 100

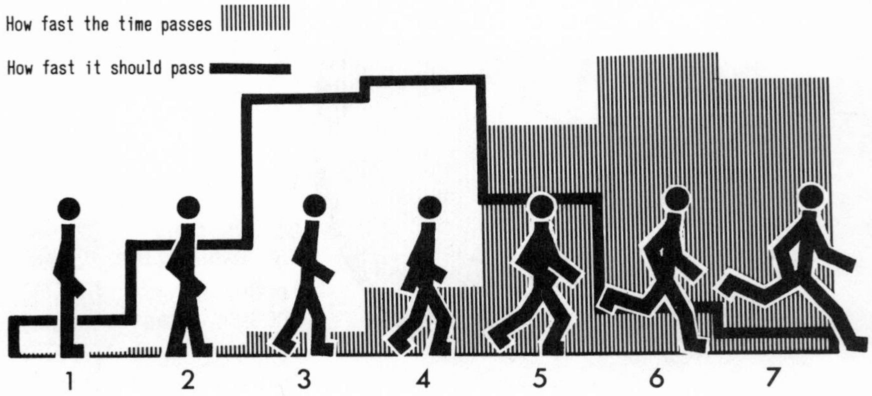

DAY DREAMING

Question: *''Everyone has dreams and often imagines doing something extra special. Have you ever dreamed of doing any of the things on this list? If you are already doing any of these, it doesn't count!''* (L)

	January 1980								
	Total pop.	Men	Women	Age groups 16-29	30-44	45-59	60 and over	Education Elementary	Secondary
I have often imagined-	%	%	%	%	%	%	%	%	%
winning the lottery	64	66	63	68	68	64	56	66	61
taking a trip around the world	53	53	54	64	58	51	40	50	61
working at bringing peace to the world	31	30	31	30	27	30	35	28	36
saving someone's life	26	28	24	28	24	26	24	26	25
escaping the hectic life and moving to a small, out-of-the-way village	22	21	23	24	26	22	16	18	30
preventing a catastrophe	20	23	17	18	21	19	21	20	20
working toward putting through important improvements for others at work	17	22	13	19	21	18	10	17	18
making an important discovery for mankind	16	21	11	20	17	14	11	14	19
being a volunteer worker for development projects in a poor country	15	15	16	22	18	11	8	12	22
actively working for environmental protection	14	17	12	19	15	13	9	11	19
setting up my own business	14	19	10	24	17	11	5	12	18
becoming a famous athlete	12	18	7	21	13	8	4	11	14
being a great artist	11	10	12	16	10	10	9	9	16
working for those on the margins of society	9	7	11	13	11	7	5	6	15
working at a kibbutz	5	3	7	8	8	2	2	3	9
giving a speech at a political assembly	5	7	3	6	6	4	4	4	7
leading a group of freedom fighters	3	4	2	6	3	1	2	3	4
none of these	8	8	9	4	6	8	14	9	6
	345	372	325	410	369	319	275	319	400

SEEING THE WORLD

Question: *"If you could do what you want, what would you most like to see, what would you like to experience? Could you choose the things from this list?"* (Not more than three items) (L)

	April 1977						
	Total	Age groups				Education	
	pop.	16-29	30-44	45-59	60 and over	Elementary	Secondary
	%	%	%	%	%	%	%
A trip around the world	48	52	56	48	32	46	52
Hawaii	25	31	29	22	15	24	25
The ruins of ancient Greece	16	13	18	16	16	12	25
Paris	16	17	14	18	16	17	15
The ancient city of Jerusalem	14	8	13	14	23	15	13
Fly to America	13	14	15	16	9	13	14
Fly in an airplane	12	11	13	13	12	14	8
The Kremlin in Moscow	12	10	11	17	12	11	14
To see the jungle	12	15	15	10	5	11	13
Saint Peter's Cathedral in Rome	11	3	8	13	21	11	9
Travel over the whole of India	10	13	12	8	6	8	15
The casino in Monaco	10	15	10	9	5	10	9
See the American missile-launching site at Cape Canaveral	9	11	12	8	5	10	8
See the pyramids in Egypt	9	9	10	9	8	7	13
Sail across the ocean	8	12	11	5	3	7	11
Fly to the moon	7	13	7	3	4	7	8
Witness the night-life of Las Vegas	7	12	9	6	1	9	4
Take part in a TV show	7	5	6	8	10	8	4
Hollywood	6	11	7	6	1	7	5
A reception with the Federal Chancellor	5	2	4	5	9	5	4
The African desert	5	6	6	5	1	4	7
Visit the VW Plant in Wolfsburg	4	3	4	5	4	5	1
The frozen wastelands of the South Pole	4	6	6	2	2	4	6
Talk to the Federal President	4	2	2	5	10	5	3
Watch a nuclear explosion	3	6	2	2	1	3	3
Hang gliding	3	6	3	1	1	2	5

Question: *"There are various things listed on these cards. Please take a look at them. Which of these are typical of our times, which are characteristic and which are not? Please distribute the cards on this sheet."* (C)

August 1979

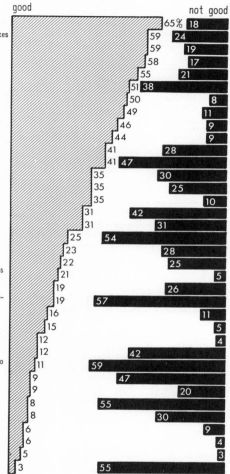

	Typical of our times and – good	not good
Supporting equal rights for men and women	65%	18
The emergence of single-issue movements to redress grievances	59	24
Traveling and getting to know the world	59	19
Having as many enjoyable experiences as possible	58	17
Aid to underdeveloped countries	55	21
If a young girl takes the pill	51	38
To be critical, not to accept anything unthinkingly	50	8
That ordinary people have a say in business, in politics	49	11
That everyone can participate in the things that make life beautiful and interesting	46	9
To feel no prejudice toward other races	44	9
To enjoy sexual relationships	41	28
If a man and a woman live together without being married	41	47
Getting excited about technical achievements	35	30
To have no fears or moral inhibitions when you want to do something that you enjoy	35	25
That social justice may be sought, reduction of inequitable wealth	35	10
To be in favor of abortion	31	42
That instead of simply punishing criminals, a scientific attempt is made to reform them	31	31
Enthusiasm for pop music	25	54
People now control much that was formerly regarded as fate	23	28
The improvement of society by means of scientific planning	22	25
To empathize with others, not to be indifferent toward one's fellowman	21	5
Seeing technical progress as a threat	19	26
If several young people live together in a communal arrangement or a commune	19	57
The ringing of church bells	16	11
To work for others selflessly	15	5
To live a simpler life, be less particular	12	4
That people are restless and want change	12	42
Using all the means available to modern medicine in order to artificially prolong life for those who are terminally ill	11	59
Giving first priority to scientific progress	9	47
Human happiness is basically possible if we use what we know to create it	9	20
Conflicts between the generations	8	55
Even human realitionships and our emotional life are open to a purely scientific explanation	8	30
That new churches are being built	6	9
That you pray before making an important decision	6	4
To let the Bible be your guide in life	5	3
Use of force to accomplish something	3	55

Question: *"There are various descriptions on these cards. Where would you say that's the way I am, or that's the way I think?"* (C)

MEN Spring 79	total %	14–17 years	18–24 years	25–39 years	40–49 years	50–59 years	60 and over
Feel most comfortable at home	56	- 5%	- 5%	± 5%	+ 5%	+ 5%	+ 5%
Get to know people easily	54	± 5%	± 5%	± 5%	+ 5%	± 5%	± 5%
Prefer to follow a routine	48	- 5%	- 5%	- 5%	± 5%	+ 5%	+ 5%
Like to take on responsibilities	39	- 5%	± 5%	+ 5%	+ 5%	± 5%	- 5%
Am careful to live a healthy life	37	- 5%	- 5%	- 5%	± 5%	+ 5%	+ 5%
Am energetic, have no trouble asserting myself	34	- 5%	- 5%	± 5%	+ 5%	± 5%	± 5%
Like to invite friends and acquaintances over	31	- 5%	± 5%	+ 5%	+ 5%	± 5%	- 5%
I sometimes know what lies ahead	31	± 5%	± 5%	± 5%	± 5%	± 5%	± 5%
Like to think about ways of investing money	29	- 5%	± 5%	± 5%	± 5%	± 5%	- 5%
Would like to reduce	23	- 5%	- 5%	± 5%	+ 5%	± 5%	± 5%

Occupation

	total %	Unskilled workers	Skilled workers	Non-managerial employees/ public servants	Managerial employees/ public servants	Self-employeds, profes-sionals	Farmers
Feel most comfortable at home	56	± 5%	± 5%	± 5%	± 5%	- 5%	+ 5%
Get to know people easily	54	- 5%	± 5%	± 5%	+ 5%	+ 5%	- 5%
Prefer to follow a routine	48	± 5%	± 5%	± 5%	± 5%	- 5%	+ 5%
Like to take on responsibilities	39	- 5%	- 5%	± 5%	+ 5%	+ 5%	- 5%
Am careful to live a healthy life	37	- 5%	± 5%	± 5%	± 5%	± 5%	+ 5%
Am energetic, have no trouble asserting myself	34	- 5%	± 5%	± 5%	+ 5%	+ 5%	± 5%
Like to invite friends and acquaintances over	31	- 5%	± 5%	± 5%	+ 5%	± 5%	- 5%
I sometimes know what lies ahead	31	± 5%	± 5%	± 5%	+ 5%	± 5%	± 5%
Like to think about ways of investing money	29	- 5%	± 5%	± 5%	+ 5%	+ 5%	± 5%
Would like to reduce	23	± 5%	± 5%	± 5%	+ 5%	± 5%	- 5%

Legend: Compared to result for total population + 5% = ■ ± 5% = ▨ - 5% = □

Question: *"There are various descriptions on these cards. Where would you say that's the way I am, or that's the way I think?"* (C)

WOMEN Spring 79	total %	14–17 years	18–24 years	25–39 years	40–49 years	50–59 years	60 and over
Feel most comfortable at home	59	□	□	▨	▨	■	■
Get to know people easily	56	▨	■	▨	▨	▨	□
Like to invite friends and acquaintances over	54	▨	▨	■	▨	▨	□
Prefer to follow a routine	52	□	□	□	▨	■	■
Am careful to live a healthy life	45	□	□	□	▨	■	■
Would like to reduce	40	▨	▨	▨	■	■	□
I sometimes know what lies ahead	37	▨	▨	▨	▨	▨	▨
Am energetic, have no trouble asserting myself	32	□	▨	▨	▨	▨	▨
Like to take on responsibilities	27	□	▨	■	▨	▨	□
Like to think about ways of investing money	17	▨	▨	▨	▨	▨	▨

Occupation

	total %	Unskilled workers	Skilled workers	Non-managerial employees/ public servants	Managerial employees/ public servants	Self-employeds, profes-sionals	Farmers
Feel most comfortable at home	59	▨	▨	▨	▨	▨	■
Get to know people easily	56	□	▨	▨	■	■	□
Like to invite friends and acquaintances over	54	□	▨	▨	■	▨	□
Prefer to follow a routine	52	■	▨	▨	□	▨	■
Am careful to live a healthy life	45	▨	▨	▨	■	▨	▨
Would like to reduce	40	▨	▨	▨	▨	▨	▨
I sometimes know what lies ahead	37	▨	▨	▨	■	▨	▨
Am energetic, have no trouble asserting myself	32	□	▨	▨	■	■	▨
Like to take on responsibilities	27	□	□	▨	■	■	□
Like to think about ways of investing money	17	▨	▨	▨	▨	■	▨

BEING ALONE

Question: *''Are you usually alone a lot or not very much?''*

''If you had to be alone frequently without your family or friends, would you be unhappy or not?''

C

	Total		Men		Women	
	1953	1979	1953	1979	1953	1979
	%	%	%	%	%	%
A lot	19	15	10	9	26	21
Average	11	16	10	14	13	17
Not very much	70	69	80	77	61	62
	100	100	100	100	100	100
Would be unhappy	49	56	49	60	49	53
Would not be unhappy	51	44	51	40	51	47
	100	100	100	100	100	100

THE FEELING OF LONELINESS

Question: *''Do you sometimes feel lonely or very alone?''*

	Frequently	Sometimes	Rarely	Never	
	%	%	%	%	
Total population - September 1949	19	26	10	45	= 100
- May 1973	7	22	20	51	= 100
- December 1977	7	18	21	54	= 100
- May 1980	7	24	25	44	= 100

Question: *''Are you afraid that you could be lonely when you're older - would you say . . .''*

	December 1979					
	Often	Sometimes	Never	Am already lonely	Undecided	
	%	%	%	%	%	
Total population	7	37	45	5	6	= 100
Men	4	32	53	3	8	= 100
Women	9	41	38	6	6	= 100
MARITAL STATUS						
Single	4	30	55	3	8	= 100
Married	7	40	45	1	7	= 100
Divorced	8	52	25	10	5	= 100
Widowed	14	26	25	30	5	= 100

NO LUCK

Question: *"There are people who never turn up trumps, who never win, whether they take part in a prize competition or buy a lottery ticket. Whatever they do, they are always unlucky. And there are others who seem to have been born lucky and always win. What about yourself? Would you include yourself among the lucky or the unlucky?"*

	Rather unlucky	Rather lucky	Neither nor	
	%	%	%	
Total population - February 1962	52	10	38	= 100
- September 1976	52	11	37	= 100
- August 1979	45	15	40	= 100

GAMBLING

Question: *"Do you ever buy lottery tickets or participate in the football pools or anything of the sort?"*
D

	Spring 1979 People who play-			
	every week	seldom	never	
	%	%	%	
Total population	44	25	31	= 100
Games of chance comprising -				
Weekly lottery	35	20	45	= 100
TV lottery	7	42	51	= 100
Football pools	5	5	90	= 100
Horse racing	1	4	95	= 100
Dutch lottery	1	6	93	= 100

FATE AND THE STARS

Question: *"Do you believe there is a relationship between man's fate (1975: character) and the stars?"*

	1950 Febr.	1975 Aug.	Men	Women
	%	%	%	%
No	50	62	73	53
Yes	30	24	14	32
Undecided	20	14	13	15
	100	100	100	100

HUMAN RELATIONS

Question: *"Do you feel that more people are spiteful than well-meaning?"*

	1949 March	1953 Nov.	1962 March	1976 June	Age groups 16-29	30-44	45-59	60 and over
	Total population							
	%	%	%	%	%	%	%	%
More well-meaning people	33	40	53	52	53	56	51	46
More spiteful people	46	34	23	16	14	13	16	22
Undecided	21	26	24	32	33	31	33	32
	100	100	100	100	100	100	100	100

TRUSTWORTHINESS

Question: *"Do you believe that most people can be trusted?"*

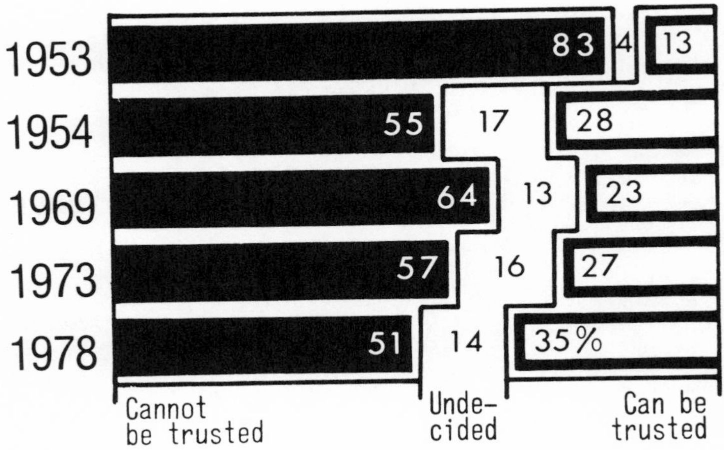

THE YOUNG . . .

Question: *"Do you have a basically favorable or unfavorable impression of young people between the ages of 16 and 25?"*

	1950 June	1960 Aug.	1975 Sept.				
	Total population			Age groups			
				16-29	30-44	45-59	60 and over
	%	%	%	%	%	%	%
Favorable	24	44	62	83	69	53	40
Unfavorable	40	24	16	6	9	22	32
Undecided	36	32	22	11	22	25	28
	100	100	100	100	100	100	100

. . . AND THE OLD

Question: *"Do you have a basically favorable or unfavorable impression of the older generation, of people from about 60 onwards?"*

	1975 Sept.	1979 Sept.				
	Total population		Age groups			
			16-29	30-44	45-59	60 and over
	%	%	%	%	%	%
Favorable	69	68	52	67	75	80
Unfavorable	9	7	13	6	4	3
No opinion	22	25	35	27	21	17
	100	100	100	100	100	100

ACQUAINTANCES

Question: *"Do you have many acquaintances or few?"*

C

		Many	Average amount	Few	
		%	%	%	
Total population	- 1953	45	22	33	= 100
	- 1979	44	36	20	= 100
Men	- 1953	52	20	28	= 100
	- 1979	46	37	17	= 100
Women	- 1953	39	24	37	= 100
	- 1979	39	41	20	= 100

CONFIDANTS

Question: *"When you need advice in a difficult situation and really don't know what to do, would you say you have to come to terms with this on your own, or is there somebody with whom you can discuss everything?"*

C

	Total population		Men		Women	
	1953	1979	1953	1979	1953	1979
	%	%	%	%	%	%
Yes, there's someone	68	79	63	78	71	80
No, there's no one	6	6	6	7	7	5
Don't need anyone	26	15	31	15	22	15
	100	100	100	100	100	100

COMPANY

Question: *"Have you had company in the last two weeks - I mean to say, have neighbors, friends, or relatives visited you in the last two weeks?"* (Yes = 83%) *"Who has visited you in the past two weeks?"*

A

	March 1979				
	Relatives	Neighbors	Colleagues, business friends	Other acquaintances	
	%	%	%	%	
Total population	62	35	20	63	= 180
AGE GROUPS					
16-29	48	22	30	83	= 183
30-44	59	38	22	64	= 183
45-59	71	41	19	53	= 184
60 and over	74	41	7	50	= 172

FAR FROM THE MADDING CROWD

Question: *"Please take a look at these two pictures. Where do you think you would feel more at home, on which beach would you prefer to be, the one above or the one below?"* (ill.) (See following page)

	May 1977			
	The one above	The one below	Undecided	
	%	%	%	
Total population	69	24	7	= 100
Men	70	22	8	= 100
Women	67	26	7	= 100
AGE GROUPS				
16-29	62	32	6	= 100
30-44	73	22	5	= 100
45-59	74	21	5	= 100
60 and over	66	21	13	= 100

PLACES TO MEET

Question: *"When you want to talk to your friends at length, where do you usually meet?"* (L)

C

	At my home %	At a friend's home %	At a pub %	In a park %	At a club %	Never talk to people at length %	
Total population - 1953 ...	68	53	19	16	8	8	= 172
- 1979 ...	82	66	21	11	14	3	= 197

GET-TOGETHERS

Question to men: *"One newspaper recently wrote that these days one hardly ever sees groups of people who meet regularly at a pub. We want to find out whether the newspaper is right or wrong. Do you belong to any such group of regulars?"*

Question to women: *"One newspaper recently wrote that these days women hardly ever meet for a friendly kaffeeklatsch. We want to find out whether the newspaper is right or wrong. Do you personally meet your friends regularly for a chat over a cup of coffee?"*

A

	Belong to regulars - Men %	Women %
Total - May 1955	17	18
Total - October 1977	30	31
OCCUPATION		
Unskilled workers	28	29
Skilled workers	27	37
Non-managerial employees and public servants	29	28
Managerial employees and public servants	29	42
Self-employeds, professionals	35	26
Farmers	59	25
TOWN AND COUNTRY		
Villages	41	28
Small towns	29	31
Medium-sized cities	27	34
Large cities	26	29

CLUB MEMBERSHIP

C

	Total 1953	Total 1979	Men 1953	Men 1979	Women 1953	Women 1979
	%	%	%	%	%	%
Member of at least one organization	53	62	72	76	36	50
- Sports club, athletic club	12	27	22	36	3	20
- Religious and charity organizations	9	11	6	8	12	14
- Labor union	12	10	23	18	3	4
- Other professional organization	9	6	16	10	4	3
- Choral society, musical society	8	6	13	9	3	3
- Riflemen's association, fire brigade	4	5	8	8	x	1
- Civic organization, social club	4	4	7	7	2	2
- Women's club, mother's club	4	4	–	–	8	7
- Garden club	2	3	3	4	1	3
- Veterans and survivors- groups	3	1	4	2	3	1
- Refugee organization	4	1	4	2	4	–
	71	78	106	104	43	58
Not a member of any organization	47	38	28	24	64	50
	100	100	100	100	100	100

CONFORMITY

Question: *"Some people say that we should not be indifferent to what our neighbors think about us and that we should to some extent accommodate ourselves to their wishes. Others say it doesn't matter what the neighbors think; it doesn't interest them in the least. Among which group would you tend to include yourself?"*

	1963	1971	1975	1980	Age groups 16-29	30-44	45-59	60 and over
	Total population							
	%	%	%	%	%	%	%	%
Accommodate oneself to some extent to neighbors' wishes	49	52	49	49	35	45	54	62
Ignore what neighbors think	42	42	43	30	38	32	28	20
Undecided	9	6	8	21	27	23	18	18
	100	100	100	100	100	100	100	100

WOMEN GOING OUT ALONE

Question put to women: *"There are some occasions when you would rather be accompanied by a man, and other occasions where you don't mind going but alone or with a girlfriend. Please take a look at this list. Could you please pick out those occasions where it wouldn't bother you to go out without the company of a man?"* (L)

Question put to men: *"There are occasions when a woman does not need to be accompanied by a man, and others where that's not exactly best. Please take a look at this list. Could you pick out those situations, where you would say that a woman could easily go unaccompanied by a man?"* (L)

	1969 According to-		1978 According to-	
	Women	Men	Women	Men
A woman can go unaccompanied by a man:	%	%	%	%
To the movies	68	72	64	67
To a lecture	65	77	68	72
To an exhibition, a museum	62	77	66	75
On a bus trip	60	65	65	70
To a café	58	57	62	61
To a concert	54	61	58	62
To the theater	52	56	58	60
On a vacation trip	40	42	45	45
To a social gathering, a party at another couple's house	29	34	35	38
Out to eat at a restaurant	27	31	33	32
Dancing	12	16	18	24
To a bar	7	10	12	15
A woman can't (doesn't want to) go anywhere unaccompanied by a man	17	8	7	6
	551	606	591	627

SCALES OF TOLERANCE

Question: *"Here is a list of a great variety of groups of people. Could you please pick out those you would* not *like to work with or live in the same building with?"* (L)

"And which of these wouldn't you mind having among your closest friends? Which of these wouldn't bother you at all?" (L)

	February 1975					
	Persons -					
	tolerated	not tolerated				
	Total	Total	Age groups			
	pop.	pop.	16-29	30-44	45-59	60 and over
	%	%	%	%	%	%
People brought up as orphans	76	2	2	1	2	3
Divorced persons	71	5	3	3	6	11
People with illegitimate children	69	6	2	4	8	11
People brought up as illegitimate children	67	3	2	3	2	4
Students	58	9	5	8	10	14
Couples who live together out of wedlock	57	10	3	5	10	22
People raised in the slums	56	6	5	5	7	8
People with many children	56	14	10	13	13	22
People convicted of a serious traffic offense	52	9	5	7	9	15
People suffering from cancer	49	11	12	10	9	12
Jews	41	16	9	14	20	32
Blacks	37	26	14	22	31	36
People who have attempted suicide	36	17	12	18	17	23
Foreign workers	35	21	12	19	23	30
Children of criminals	32	14	8	12	15	21
Convinced communists	20	50	37	49	55	61
People previously convicted of theft	19	46	32	45	50	59
People who have spent a few months in a home for the mentally ill	19	46	42	45	47	52
People who are frequently drunk	16	54	46	50	58	62
Convinced National Socialists	15	44	36	45	47	47
A woman who earns her money by prostitution	15	55	40	50	63	68
	896	464	337	428	502	613

CUSTOMS AND TRADITIONS

SUNDAY MORNING

Question: *''We would like to find out how people spend their Sunday mornings. If you think back—what did you do last Sunday between about 9 and 12 in the morning? Could you tell me about it, perhaps with the aid of this list?''* (L)

	August 1979						
	Total pop.	Men	Women	Age groups 16-29	30-44	45-59	60 and over
	%	%	%	%	%	%	%
Slept late	45	50	41	67	48	38	25
Cooked, did housework	41	10	66	28	41	46	48
Bathed, took care of myself	34	30	37	39	35	36	26
Read newspapers, magazines, book	24	28	21	24	24	22	29
Attended church	19	14	23	7	12	23	34
Went for a walk, a drive	17	21	15	13	17	17	22
Had a long conversation with someone	17	16	17	19	16	15	16
Spent time with children, played	16	15	17	16	29	12	6
Worked at my hobby	12	17	7	13	11	13	9
Watched television program	11	11	11	11	8	9	15
Rested, didn't do anything	11	12	11	15	8	9	13
Visited friends, relatives	9	9	10	8	8	9	12
Went out for a drink	9	18	1	7	9	10	9
Was at the cemetary	7	4	9	1	3	7	17
Participated in sports	6	8	4	10	6	4	3
Went to watch a sports game	4	8	2	5	4	5	4
Did repairs at home	4	8	2	4	6	5	3
Wrote letters or postcards	4	1	5	3	3	3	6
Listened to morning church service on the radio	4	2	5	1	2	4	7
Had to work for my job, go to work	4	6	2	4	4	4	3
Did other things	7	10	5	9	6	7	4
	305	298	311	304	300	298	311

SUNDAY DINNER

Question: "*Do you usually have a real Sunday dinner with all the trimmings, or wouldn't you say you have a regular Sunday dinner?*"

	October 1977			
	Real Sunday dinner %	Not a regular Sunday dinner %	Usually eat out on Sunday %	
Total population	72	23	5	= 100
OCCUPATION				
Unskilled workers	76	22	2	= 100
Skilled workers	78	18	4	= 100
Non-managerial employees and public servants	66	27	7	= 100
Managerial employees and public servants	61	33	6	= 100
Self-employeds, professionals	75	20	5	= 100
Farmers	86	11	3	= 100

SUNDAY AFTERNOON

Question: "*What about your Sunday afternoons—do you often get together with friends and acquaintances, or do you remain with the immediate family, or are you mostly alone?*"

		November 1977				
		Immediate family %	Friends, acquaintances %	Mostly alone %	It varies %	
Total men		52	27	9	12	= 100
Total women		51	24	14	11	= 100
MARITAL STATUS						
Single	Men	16	64	8	12	= 100
	Women	23	51	13	13	= 100
Married	Men	66	16	5	13	= 100
	Women	66	15	8	11	= 100
Divorced	Men	24	36	36	4	= 100
	Women	32	29	26	13	= 100
Widowed	Men	13	15	60	12	= 100
	Women	34	19	37	10	= 100

Question: *"How do you generally dress on Sundays?"*

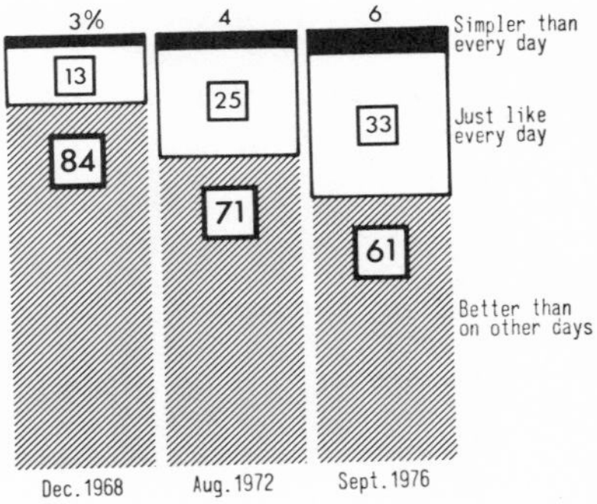

Question: *"From what you've seen, do you think that most people make good use of their leisure time, or would you say that most of them don't really know what to do with it?"*

D

	April 1976						
	Total pop.	Age groups				Education	
		14-29	30-44	45-59	60 and over	Elementary	Secondary
	%	%	%	%	%	%	%
Don't know what to do	47	51	46	45	44	45	52
Sometimes yes, sometimes no	32	30	34	34	31	32	31
Make good use of it	16	15	16	16	16	16	14
No reply	5	4	4	5	9	7	3
	100	100	100	100	100	100	100

Question: *"Do you ever find that time drags on Sundays and public holidays?"*

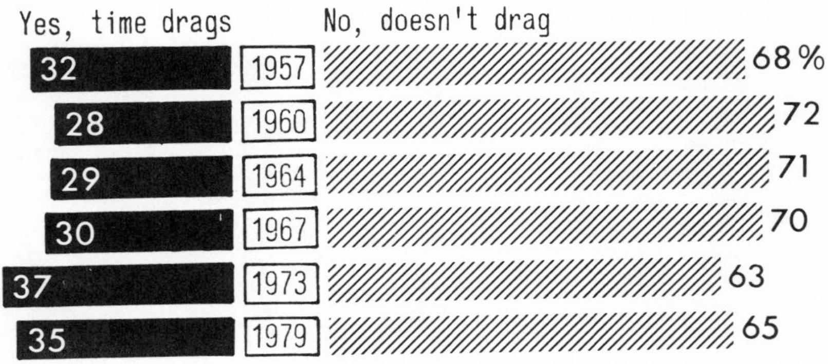

CARNIVAL

Question: *"At carnival time this year, were you ever in a real carnival mood and feeling exuberant, or not?"* (Yes = 53 percent)

Question put to persons who were in carnival mood (53 = 100 percent): *"Did you attend a carnival event this year?"*

	March 1973						
	Total pop.	Men	Women	Age groups			
				16-29	30-44	45-59	60 and over
	%	%	%	%	%	%	%
Yes, attended a carnival event	75	74	76	82	78	65	59

Question put to persons who attended a carnival event (40 = 100 percent): *"Did you wear an actual costume, or did you just dress up a bit, or did you go in plain dress?"*

	March 1973			
	Real costume	Dressed up	Plain dress	
	%	%	%	
Total population	33	39	28	= 100
Men	28	39	33	= 100
Women	39	39	22	= 100

EASTER

Question: *"In many families it is the custom at Easter to hide Easter eggs or sweets, which the children and sometimes the adults have to search for. Was this the case in your family this year, or was nothing hidden?"*

A

	Yes, at home	Yes, in the yard	Yes, during a walk	No	
	%	%	%	%	
Total population - April 1961	36	12	3	53	= 104
April 1971	22	22	3	56	= 103

Question: *"Many families keep to special Easter traditions. Did you yourself do any of the things listed here on Easter or during the days before Easter?"* (L)

	April 1978
	%
Dyed or painted eggs	76
Had an Easter bouquet	51
Visited relatives and friends	47
Went for an Easter walk	45
Made a nest for Easter presents	38
Went to church	35
Hid, looked for Easter eggs, sweets	34
Baked an Easter rabbit, a Paschal Lamb, an Easter cake	16
Went on a vacation trip	13
Made Easter decorations	10
Other	12
	377

CHRISTMAS

Question: *"What does Christmas mean to you - which of these things is it most?"* (L)

D

	1974 Total population	1978 Total population	Age groups 14-29	30-44	45-59	60 and over
	%	%	%	%	%	%
A special family celebration	66	68	64	72	72	65
A time of contemplation	43	47	30	48	52	60
The birth of Christ, a church celebration	44	45	36	44	47	56
An exhortation for peace	38	42	32	41	44	52
An opportunity to give and be given	31	38	41	35	39	38
An opportunity to be good to others	24	31	21	31	35	41
A time for remembrance	31	29	18	24	32	47
A welcome vacation	23	21	33	27	16	6
A time in which I feel especially lonely	8	7	4	4	6	14
None of these	3	3	4	3	2	2
	311	331	283	329	345	381

FAMILY FEAST

Question: *"How are you going to celebrate Christmas Eve - with your family, with friends or acquaintances, or will you be alone?"*

	1974 Total population	1978 Total population	Age groups 16-29	30-44	45-59	60 and over
	%	%	%	%	%	%
With my family	88	86	83	90	90	80
With friends, acquaintances	6	7	10	5	5	8
I'll be alone	4	3	2	2	2	8
Don't know yet	2	6	8	5	4	7
	100	102	103	102	101	103

CHRISTMAS TREE

Question: *"Did you have a Christmas tree last Christmas?"*

	Total population		Protestants		Catholics		Other	
	1965	1979	1965	1979	1965	1979	1965	1979
	%	%	%	%	%	%	%	%
Yes, had a Christmas tree	89	84	90	83	90	87	77	63
No	11	16	10	17	10	13	23	37
	100	100	100	100	100	100	100	100

TRADITIONAL DINNER

Question: *"What did you have for Christmas dinner on Christmas day?"* (O)

A

	January 1977						
	Goose	Turkey	Duck	Hare	Other meat dish	Don't remember	
	%	%	%	%	%	%	
Total population	18	17	9	7	44	10	= 105

MUSIC

Question: *"Do you sing Christmas songs on Christmas Eve, or do you listen to Christmas music?"*

	Listen to Christmas music	Sing Christmas songs	Neither	
	%	%	%	
Total population - November 1974 ..	69	50	9	= 128
- November 1978 ..	75	52	8	= 135

CHRISTMAS SPIRIT

Question *"Do you have the feeling that people are friendlier than usual at Christmastime, or is there no difference?"*

	Total population		Age groups			
	1974 Nov.	1978 Nov.	16-29	30-44	45-59	60 and over
	%	%	%	%	%	%
Yes, friendlier	51	58	53	59	59	62
No difference	39	35	40	35	36	29
Don't know	10	7	7	6	5	9
	100	100	100	100	100	100

Question: *"Some people invite someone who lives alone over for Christmas Eve. Have you ever done that? If yes, when was the last time?"*

	February 1975			
	Last Christmas	Longer ago	Never	
	%	%	%	
Total population	13	13	74	= 100

OFFICIAL ENGAGEMENT

Question: *"Do you think it still appropriate today for young people to get officially engaged, or do you think they should marry without previous engagement?"*

	Official engagement %	No engagement %	Undecided %	
Total population - April 1959	71	16	13	= 100
- September 1976	55	22	23	= 100
- January 1981	53	20	27	= 100

WEDDING BELLS

Question put to married persons: *"Were you married at the registry office only or did you have a church wedding as well?"*

C

	Registry office and church %	Registry office only %	
Married persons - 1953	88	12	= 100
- 1979	82	18	= 100

WEDDING FEAST

Question: *"Many engaged couples no longer want a big wedding feast because it costs a lot of money and the newlyweds get the least enjoyment out of it. Other couples say, however, that their wedding day is the happiest and most wonderful day in the life of a family and will always be remembered as such; it should be celebrated accordingly. What do you find better—a really big wedding feast or only a small one?"*

	1965 Sept. Total population	1976 Sept. Total population	Men	Women	Villages	Small towns	Medium cities	Large cities
	%	%	%	%	%	%	%	%
Only a small feast	55	53	54	53	52	54	51	52
A really big feast	35	35	32	39	36	34	37	35
Undecided	10	12	14	8	12	12	12	13
	100	100	100	100	100	100	100	100

HONEYMOON

Question put to married persons: *"When you got married did you go on a honeymoon, or not?"*

	1959 Total population	1976 Total population	Age groups Under 29	30-44	45-59	60 a.o.	Education Elementary	Secondary
	%	%	%	%	%	%	%	%
Yes	21	36	46	46	30	26	29	55
No	79	64	54	54	70	74	71	45
	100	100	100	100	100	100	100	100

HAPPY BIRTHDAY

Question: *''In many families birthdays are treated as a big occasion. The person concerned receives congratulations, small presents, and the family sits down to a good meal. In other families birthdays are hardly celebrated at all. Do you always celebrate your birthday or not?''*

	Celebrate %	Don't celebrate %	Varies %	
Total population - March 1960	68	16	16	= 100
- September 1976	77	11	12	= 100

BOWS AND CURTSIES

Question: *''Do you like it when little boys are taught to make a bow when they greet grown-ups, or would you say that this is outdated?''*

Question: *''Do you like it when little girls are taught to curtsy when they greet grown-ups, or would you say that this is outdated?''*

Bow -	1968 May %	1978 May %
Outdated	28	57
I like it	65	36
Undecided	7	7
	100	100

Curtsy -	1978 May %
Outdated	54
I like it	39
Undecided	7
	100

GALLANTRY

Question: *''If you see a gentleman greet a lady by kissing her hand - do you think that's a nice custom, or doesn't it appeal to you?''*

	1956 April %	1962 Sept. %	1972 Sept. %	1980 Jan. %	Age groups 16-29 %	30-44 %	45-59 %	60 and over %
Nice custom	29	36	42	45	35	41	47	59
Doesn't appeal to me	48	40	35	32	39	34	32	22
Depends on person and place	10	8	12	13	16	15	10	10
Undecided	13	16	11	10	10	10	11	9
	100	100	100	100	100	100	100	100

KISS ON THE CHEEK

Question: *"Sometimes we see people who are well-acquainted greet each other with a kiss on the cheek. Do you also do this sometimes?"*

"All in all, do you like this custom, or don't you like it so well?"

	September 1980						
	Total pop.	Men	Women	Age groups 16-29	30-44	45-59	60 and over
	%	%	%	%	%	%	%
Yes, do it	35	26	42	42	37	32	28
No	65	74	58	58	63	68	72
	100	100	100	100	100	100	100
Like custom	28	22	33	38	29	22	21
Don't like custom	37	43	31	27	36	43	43
Yes and no	27	25	28	25	27	26	28
Undecided, no reply	8	10	8	10	8	9	8
	100	100	100	100	100	100	100

SUPERSTITION

Question: *"Even if you are not superstitious, please take a look at this list. Which of these things do you think may possibly have some significance - which ones do you yourself pay attention to?"* (L)

	September 1976 %		September 1976 %
Four leaf clover	28	The hoot of the owl means bad luck	9
Chimney sweeps	23	A lamb on the left	8
Number 13	22	When the clock stands still	7
Falling stars	21	Borrowing salt brings bad luck	6
Black cats crossing your path	20	If you stumble go back again	6
Shake your purse when the cuckoo calls	13	Don't lay a knife down with the sharp edge up	5
Spider in the morning	13	Number 7	4
Finding a horseshoe	13	When the door opens by itself	3
Swallow's nest on the house	11	When it rains on a bride's veil	3
Fridays	9	Touch a hunchback	1
None of these			41

EDUCATION AND KNOWLEDGE

Question: "*What would you say is decisive for a person's future conduct—the environment in which he grows up or hereditary factors? Which of these is more important*" (X)

	Environment %	Heredity %	Undecided %	
Total population - December 1954	50	29	21	= 100
- May 1977	67	17	16	= 100
AGE GROUPS				
16-29	77	11	12	= 100
30-44	74	12	14	= 100
45-59	63	20	17	= 100
60 and over	48	29	23	= 100

DIFFERENT APTITUDES

Question: "*There are different opinions about whether boys and girls differ in their aptitudes. What do you think?*" (C, L)

See illustration next page

A

	December 1973					
	Same aptitude		Greater aptitudes attributed to			
			Girls		Boys	
As regards -	Men %	Women %	Men %	Women %	Men %	Women %
Intelligence	81	83	6	9	13	8
Business	70	71	11	12	19	17
Teaching elementary school	78	75	16	19	6	6
Teaching secondary school	70	73	4	5	26	22
The medical profession	64	65	5	4	31	31
Getting along with people	60	59	34	38	6	3
Learning languages	57	63	39	33	4	4
Logical thinking	49	59	5	10	46	31
Natural science	50	51	9	9	41	40
The arts	49	49	47	48	4	3
The legal profession	41	41	1	1	58	58
The engineering profession	16	17	1	1	83	82
Technical work	16	19	2	1	82	80

LA PETITE DIFFERENCE

Question: *"There are different opinions about whether boys and girls differ in their aptitudes? What do you think?"* (C, L)

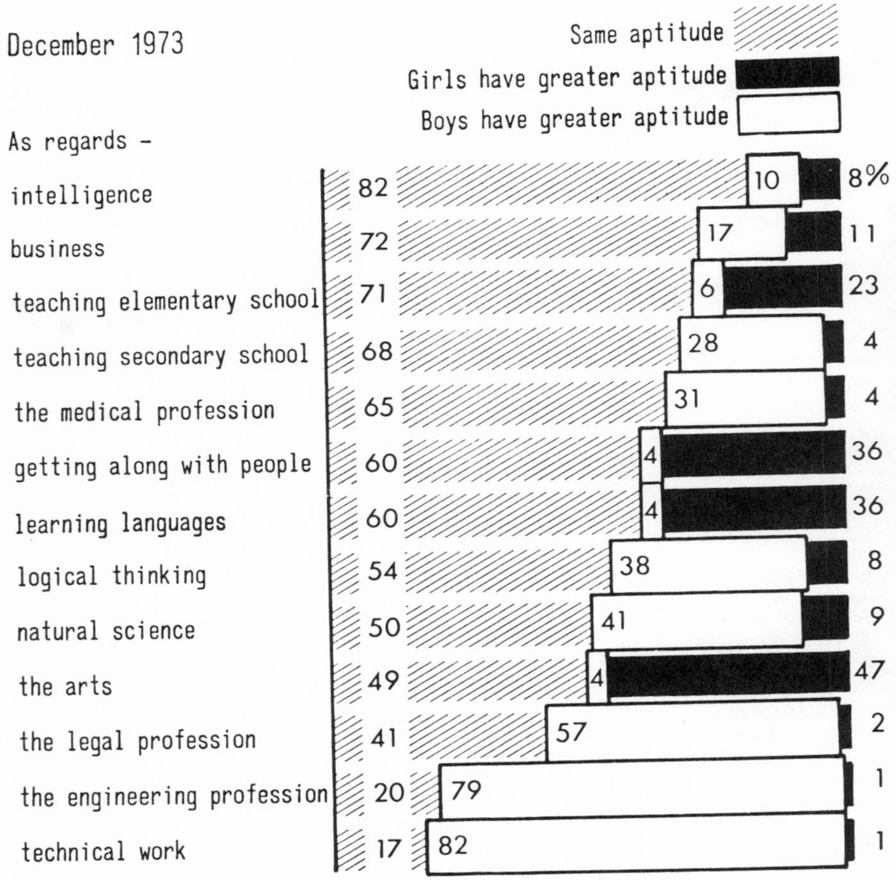

SELF-REALIZATION

Question: *"There are certain people of whom it is often said, 'he would have made a good artist or a good engineer or she would have made a good doctor'. What is meant is that the person concerned has talents and capabilities which he/she did not have the opportunity to develop fully. Think a moment about yourself. Is this also true for your own gifts and talents, or would you say you actually are or have been able to develop all your capabilities fully?"*

	March 1979					
	Capabilities -				Undecided	
	not fully developed		fully developed			
	Men	Women	Men	Women	Men	Women
	%	%	%	%	%	%
Total	42	38	31	28	27	34
AGE GROUPS						
16-29	39	35	24	27	37	38
30-44	48	43	30	29	22	28
45-59	45	45	32	24	23	31
60 and over	35	31	39	30	26	39

PLAYING AN INSTRUMENT

Question: *"Do you play a musical instrument? What do you play?"* (L)

		September 1980
		%
Yes, play an instrument		26
namely:		
Piano	8	
Recorder	7	
Guitar	7	
Harmonica	5	
Accordion	4	
Violin or other stringed instrument	2	
Electric piano, home organ	2	
Trumpet, trombone, saxophone	1	
Organ	1	
Flute, clarinet	1	
Percussion, drums	1	
Harp, zither	1	
Synthesizer	x	
Other instrument	1	
No, play no instrument		74
		100

DRAWING - PAINTING

Question: *"When did you do last any drawing or painting?"*

	During the past 4 weeks	the past 12 months	More than a year ago	
	%	%	%	
Total population - March 1965 ..	16	7	77	= 100
- November 1972	20	14	66	= 100

MODERN AND ANCIENT LANGUAGES

Question: *"Here is a list of various languages. Is there one among them that you can speak or understand fairly well?"* (L)

	1961	1979			Age groups			
	Total population		Men	Women	16-29	30-44	45-59	60 and over
	%	%	%	%	%	%	%	%
English	22	41	45	38	67	47	32	19
French	11	13	13	13	22	13	10	8
Dutch	4	5	6	4	5	6	5	3
Polish	3	2	2	2	1	1	3	4
Italian	2	2	3	2	3	3	2	1
Russian	2	2	3	1	1	1	2	3
Spanish	1	2	3	2	3	3	2	1
Swedish, Danish, Norwegian	1	3	4	3	2	3	1	1
	46	70	79	65	104	77	57	40
None of these	69	52	48	57	30	48	59	72

Question: *"Do you think it is useful for a child (1972: a son) to learn Latin/Greek at school, or do you think the time and effort would be better spent on another subject?"*

A

	Useful		Another subject better		Depends on intended profession		Undecided	
	Greek	Latin	Greek	Latin	Greek	Latin	Greek	Latin
	%	%	%	%	%	%	%	%
Total population - 1957	20	41	49	30	13	17	18	12
- 1972	20	35	62	40	9	15	9	10
AGE GROUPS								
16-29	20	32	64	44	7	16	9	8
30-44	20	36	62	43	11	12	7	9
45-59	17	36	64	38	9	16	10	10
60 and over	22	36	57	32	8	17	13	15
EDUCATION								
Elementary	17	30	65	45	7	14	11	11
Intermediate	27	47	57	26	13	20	3	7
Secondary	32	65	47	17	12	11	9	7

AMERICA - HOW OLD?

Question: ''*America is celebrating a big birthday next year. Do you happen to know how long there's been a United States of America—for 100, 200 or 300 years, or how long?*''

A

	December 1975 100 years %	200 years %	300 years %	Other response %	Don't know %	
Total population	12	46	10	3	29	= 100

CHARLEMAGNE

Question: ''*Do you know roughly when Charlemagne lived?*'' (O)

	Right answers %	Vague answers %	Wrong answers %	Don't know %	
Total population - December 1957	24	8	11	57	= 100
- September 1976	28	6	15	51	= 100

MARTIN LUTHER

Question: ''*Do you know whether Luther lived before or after the Thirty Years' War?*''

A

	Before (right answer) %	After %	Don't know %	
Total population - December 1957	54	18	28	= 100
- September 1976	54	17	29	= 100

NEFERTITI

Question: ''*I have a card with a silhouette on it. Do you by chance know from which country this silhouette is?*'' (ill.) ''*Do you perhaps know who this is?*'' (ill.)

	1957 %	1976 %
Country -		
Egypt	46	66
Other country	8	6
Don't know	46	28
	100	100
Person -		
Nefertiti	29	57
Vague answers	4	2
Don't know	67	41
	100	100

1 + 1 = ?

Question: *"I have a small math problem here that might interest you. What would the correct answer be?"* (L)

1/2 + 5/10 = ?

	1957 Dec. Total population	1976 Aug. Total population	Men	Women	Age groups 16-29	30-44	45-59	60 and over	Education Ele-mentary	Secon-dary
	%	%	%	%	%	%	%	%	%	%
Correct answer (= 1)	75	78	84	73	84	84	76	64	72	92
Incorrect answer, don't know	25	22	16	27	16	16	24	36	28	8
	100	100	100	100	100	100	100	100	100	100

WORLD WAR I

Question: *"Many people are no longer able to remember exactly when World War I ended. Do you know exactly which year that was?"* (O)

	Right answer '1918'	Wrong answer	Don't know	
	%	%	%	
Total population - 1958	87	5	8	= 100
- 1977	72	9	19	= 100

FAIRY TALES

Question: *"Do you think children still should learn about the old German fairy tales today, or are these fairy tales no longer suited to our times?"*

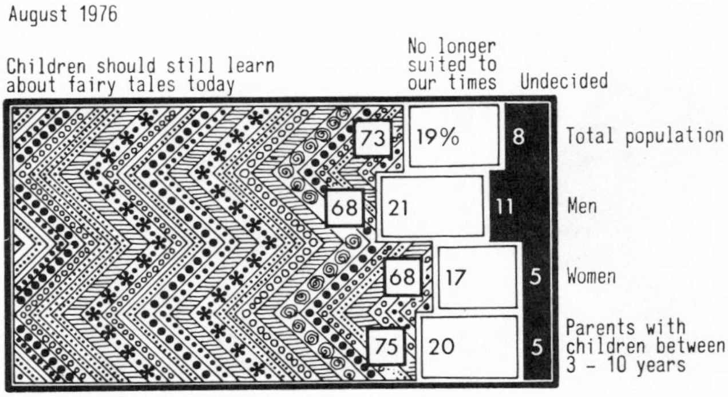

READING BOOKS*

Question: *"Have you read a book within the last 12 months?"*

"How often would you say you have a chance to read a book - would you say. . . ."

	1967/68 Winter %	1973/74 Winter %	1979 March %	1980 Dec. %
Daily	10	11	11	12
Several times a week	19	18	19	21
About once a week	13	12	13	11
About every two weeks	8	6	8	7
Roughly once a month	8	8	9	7
Less frequently	10	12	10	14
Haven't read a book in the last 12 months	32	33	30	28
	100	100	100	100

*see also chapter on MEDIA.

INTEREST IN HISTORY

Question: *"Are you interested in how people lived in earlier times - for example in the Middle Ages, the Stone Age, etc?"*

	Very interested %	Somewhat interested %	Little interest %	Not at all interested %	
Total population - April 1977	20	38	22	20	= 100

TRAVEL BOOKS MOST POPULAR

Question put to people who read books last year: *"Various types of books are listed here. Supposing you won a voucher for 100 Deutschemarks in a prize competition and can now select books to that amount, what kind of books would you buy?"* (L)

	1967 Oct. %	1978 Feb. %
Books about travel, countries, peoples	37	47
Humorous books	32	35
Historical fiction	31	35
Books about contemporary problems, contemporary history, politics	14	33
Modern literature, fiction that is critical of contemporary issues	20	31
Crime fiction	38	28
Family novels	27	28
Biographies, life stories of famous personalities, correspondence	23	26
Books about new discoveries in medicine	16	23
War fiction	17	12
Books about business, the large companies, the executives	9	12
Religious books, books about faith	10	10
	274	320

KNOWLEDGE OF GERMAN WRITERS

Question put to students: *"On these cards are the names of various writers. Could you distribute the cards according to the headings on this sheet for me? Just put aside the cards with names of writers you're not familiar with."* (C, L)

	February 1978				
	University students*				
	Like	Don't like	Familiar with name only	Completely unfamiliar	
German-language writers:	%	%	%	%	
Max Frisch	82	5	8	5	= 100
Heinrich Böll	82	12	3	3	= 100
Bertolt Brecht	81	13	4	2	= 100
Thomas Mann	81	10	7	2	= 100
Friedrich Dürrenmatt	79	6	10	5	= 100
Hermann Hesse	76	10	12	2	= 100
Heinrich Heine	74	9	14	3	= 100
Günter Grass	68	20	8	4	= 100
Siegfried Lenz	67	7	17	9	= 100
Franz Kafka	66	19	11	4	= 100
Günter Wallraff	55	14	20	11	= 100
Ingeborg Bachmann	41	6	29	24	= 100
Peter Handke	41	18	25	16	= 100
Rolf Hochhuth	36	11	24	29	= 100
Hans Magnus Enzensberger	36	10	29	25	= 100
Carl-Friedrich von Weizsäcker	35	14	38	13	= 100
Martin Walser	32	8	29	31	= 100
Karl Jaspers	32	10	41	17	= 100
Peter Weiss	31	7	29	33	= 100
Ludwig Marcuse	28	13	30	29	= 100
Rainer Kunze	28	5	36	31	= 100
Luise Rinser	26	9	35	30	= 100
Werner Bergengruen	23	9	29	39	= 100
Anna Seghers	22	6	34	38	= 100
Sarah Kirsch	18	5	42	35	= 100
Ilse Aichinger	17	4	33	46	= 100
Uwe Johnson	16	6	30	48	= 100
Carl Améry	15	7	39	39	= 100
Gabriele Wohmann	15	5	28	52	= 100
Rudolf Hagelstange	12	6	28	54	= 100
Robert Neumann	8	4	28	60	= 100
Hans Joachim Schädlich	5	3	27	65	= 100

continued

KNOWLEDGE OF FOREIGN WRITERS

	February 1978				
	University students*				
Foreign-language writers:	Like %	Don't like %	Familiar with name only %	Completely unfamiliar %	
Ernest Hemingway	78	9	9	4	= 100
Alexander Solzhenizyn	61	20	15	4	= 100
Jean-Paul Sartre	60	19	16	5	= 100
Albert Camus	56	6	18	20	= 100
John Steinbeck	56	9	19	16	= 100
Henry Miller	44	21	25	10	= 100
Françoise Sagan	42	17	27	14	= 100
James Joyce	39	9	30	22	= 100
Jean Anouilh	37	6	26	31	= 100
Georges Simenon	37	11	23	29	= 100
Eugène Ionesco	32	9	31	28	= 100
Truman Capote	29	9	29	33	= 100
William Faulkner	26	6	34	34	= 100
Marcel Proust	22	4	41	33	= 100
André Gide	20	4	32	44	= 100
Sinclair Lewis	9	6	29	56	= 100

*480 students of all subject areas in the Federal Republic and West Berlin.

HEINRICH BÖLL - GÜNTER GRASS

Question: *Have you ever heard of the German writer Heinrich Böll (half group: Günter Grass) or read a book by him, or are you not familiar with his name?''*

A

	March 1978					
	Familiar with name of -		Have read a book by -		Not familiar with name of -	
	Böll %	Grass %	Böll %	Grass %	Böll %	Grass %
Total population	58	56	31	24	11	20
Men	61	56	31	29	8	15
Women	53	56	33	19	14	25
AGE GROUPS						
16-29	51	56	42	24	7	20
30-44	59	55	35	29	6	16
45-59	65	61	25	20	10	19
60 and over	58	53	21	20	21	27

KNOW LESS ABOUT TREES

Question: *"Most people these days can hardly distinguish the leaves of trees. Would you look at these four leaves and tell me if you know the name of any of them?"* (ill.)

	Oak (2)		Chestnut (1)		Linden (3)		Maple (4)	
	1953	1976	1953	1976	1953	1976	1953	1976
	%	%	%	%	%	%	%	%
Knew	90	81	72	66	63	26	43	49
Did not know	10	19	28	34	37	74	57	51
	100	100	100	100	100	100	100	100

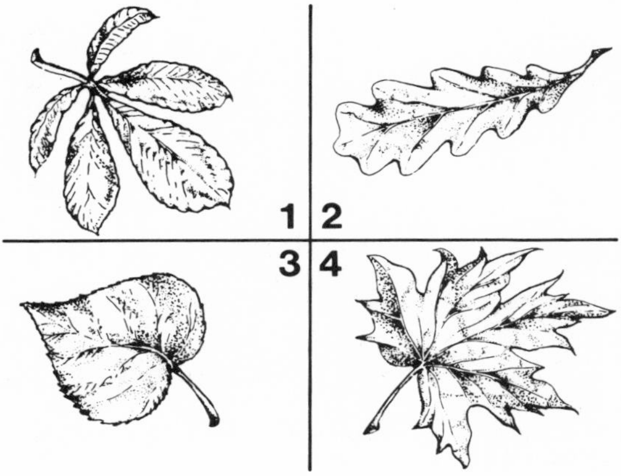

STYLE AND TASTE

Question: *"There are aspects of life in which practically everybody has his personal touch, his own style. Where do you place special value in the realization of your personal wishes and attitudes?"* (L, X)

A

	1972 %	1976 %
In the way my house/apartment is furnished	28	67
The people I associate with	34	61
In what I do during my leisure time	27	60
In the way I dress	27	59
In the way we plan our family life	–	57
In the way I spend my vacation	17	48
In the way I bring up my children	28	47
The newspapers and periodicals I read	20	41
Where I spend my vacation	12	39
In the way I practice my profession	25	38
The doctor I go to	–	37
In the meals that are served at home	9	33
In the area and suburb in which I live	13	31
The stores I shop at	7	31
The model and kind of car I would buy	9	23
The appliances in our household	4	19
	260	691

– = not asked in 1972

YOUNG AND FASHIONABLE

Question: *"When a new style appears on the scene, people have different reactions. Some go right ahead and wear whatever they like of the new style. Others like to wait and see whether the new fashion really becomes popular. Would you include yourself in the first group or the second?"*

D

	Spring 1979						
	Persons who wear the latest fashion right away						
	Total	Age groups					
		14-19	20-29	30-39	40-49	50-59	60 and over
	%	%	%	%	%	%	%
Men	7	12	12	8	5	4	1
Women	14	32	27	16	12	8	4

TIE OR BOW TIE

Question put to men: *"Do you usually wear a tie or a bow tie, or do you so rarely or not at all?"*

D

	Usually wear a tie	Bow tie	Rarely do so	Not at all	
	%	%	%	%	
Men total	26	1	51	22	= 100

CASUAL DRESS

Question: *"When it comes to clothes, everyone has his/her own style. Which of these characteristics best apply to your clothing - how do you usually dress?"* (L, X)

D

	Spring 1979						
	Total	Age groups					
		14-19	20-29	30-39	40-49	50-59	60 and over
	%	%	%	%	%	%	%
MEN							
Comfortable	84	79	83	85	85	85	86
Casual	52	61	63	60	54	45	28
Things that don't go out of fashion	44	26	34	43	50	50	56
Conservative	41	25	28	36	44	50	60
Youthful	23	57	39	21	13	7	6
Elegant	14	14	16	15	14	13	10
Lively colors	12	19	15	10	10	10	8
Figure-flattering, tight-fitting	9	17	15	10	5	3	3
According to the latest fashion	6	8	9	6	5	5	3
Striking, extravagant	1	3	3	1	1	1	x
	286	309	305	287	281	269	260
WOMEN							
Comfortable	77	76	78	77	78	77	76
Casual	49	66	66	59	57	43	25
Things that don't go out of fashion	46	20	31	40	48	56	61
Conservative	40	13	22	31	41	51	60
Youthful	27	70	50	32	23	8	6
Lively colors	23	30	28	27	25	22	15
Elegant	20	19	23	20	22	21	15
According to the latest fashion	11	26	21	13	8	6	3
Figure-flattering, tight-fitting	10	21	18	14	9	6	3
Striking, extravagant	2	4	3	1	2	1	x
	305	345	340	314	313	291	264

INCREASED COLOR CONSCIOUSNESS

Question: *"Which is your favorite color?"* (O)

	1949 Aug. %	1959 April %	1964 Febr. %	1978 Nov. %
Blue	35	31	34	29
Green	16	21	28	22
Red	17	21	19	21
Yellow	3	7	9	7
Brown	6	4	8	12
Black	3	2	6	6
White	x	x	7	5
Other	6	12	19	14
None in particular	14	6	2	2
	100	104	132	118

BEARDS

D

	1972 Total %	1979 Total %	Men, Age groups: 14-19 %	20-29 %	30-39 %	40-49 %	50-59 %	60 and over %
Have a beard	18	26	20	48	38	22	10	10
Have no beard	82	74	80	52	62	78	90	90
	100	100	100	100	100	100	100	100

Question: *"How often do you go to the hairdresser's?"*

D

At least every -	1979 Total women %
14 days	14
4 weeks	27
6 weeks	24
Seldom or never	35
	100

At least every -	1979 Total men %
3 weeks	12
4 weeks	29
6 weeks	34
Seldom or never	25
	100

STANDING OUT IN A CROWD

Question: *"If you had to drive a car that is so unusual in color or shape that a lot of people take a second look at it and you're very conspicuous - would you tend to find this pleasant or unpleasant?"*

	January 1980 Total pop. %	Men %	Women %	Age groups: 16-29 %	30-44 %	45-59 %	60 and over %
Unpleasant	72	70	73	48	69	83	88
Pleasant	28	30	27	52	31	17	12
	100	100	100	100	100	100	100

ELVIS

Question: *"A few weeks ago the American singer Elvis Presley died. Did you hear about this?"* (Yes, heard = 96 percent) *"Do you like his music, or did you use to like it, or was it never really your taste?"*

	September 1977				
	Like Elvis' music	Used to like it	Never really my taste	No opinion	
	%	%	%	%	
Total population	40	16	37	7	= 100

MODERN ARCHITECTURE

Question: *"On the whole, do you like the style of present-day architecture, or not particularly?"*

	June 1976				
	Total	Age groups			
	pop.	16-29	30-44	45-59	60 and over
	%	%	%	%	%
Yes, like it	31	39	32	32	20
Not particularly	52	46	51	52	62
Undecided	17	15	17	16	18
	100	100	100	100	100

GOURMETS

Question: *"If someone said that you are a gourmet, would he be right or wrong?"*

A

	Right	Wrong	Undecided	
	%	%	%	
Total population - September 1978	42	36	22	= 100

Question: *"If you were invited out to dinner and could select a restaurant from this list, which type would you choose?"* (L)

	November 1978						
	Total	Men	Women	Age groups			
	pop.			16-29	30-44	45-59	60 and over
	%	%	%	%	%	%	%
German	42	43	42	22	41	43	68
French	21	18	23	24	23	20	14
Balkan	17	18	16	24	21	17	4
Chinese	13	12	13	16	14	14	5
Italian	9	9	9	17	11	4	x
Austrian	8	8	8	5	8	8	12
Greek	4	4	4	10	3	3	1
Spanish	2	1	2	2	1	3	x
Other	5	7	5	4	3	7	10
	121	120	122	124	125	119	114

LEISURE TIME

	Leisure time per week including Saturday and Sunday 1967 Hrs./Min.	1977 Hrs./Min.
Total population	26.06	30.34
Men	28.54	32.46
Women	23.42	28.35
AGE GROUPS		
16-29	26.18	30.58
30-44	21.54	26.13
45-59	23.54	27.33
60 and over	34.24	38.34
OCCUPATION		
Unskilled workers	24.54	30.53
Skilled workers	28.30	31.03
Non-managerial employees and public servants	27.24	31.03
Managerial employees and public servants	28.12	32.43
Self-employeds, professionals	24.12	26.47
Farmers	16.54	24.53

ACTIVITY VS. RELAXATION

Question: *"If you just generally think about the weekend, about your leisure time - all in all, what is more important to you: to relax as much as possible - to rest - or to do something?"*

	Relax %	Do something %	Both important %	
Total population - January 1977	47	26	27	= 100
- January 1978	42	25	33	= 100
- January 1979	31	29	40	= 100
Men	31	30	39	= 100
Women	32	29	39	= 100
Housewives total	35	23	42	= 100
Total gainfully employed persons	32	29	39	= 100

DISTRACTIONS

Question: "*What do you generally do in your leisure time on the weekend, on Saturdays and Sundays?*" (L)

	1955 Total %	1977 Total %	Men %	Women %
READING, LISTENING, VIEWING				
Watch television	–	69	69	69
Listen to the radio	56	33	32	34
Read the newspaper	39	43	48	39
Go to the cinema	31	11	13	10
Read books	23	29	25	33
Read magazines, etc.	22	29	23	34
Go to sporting events	16	17	29	6
Attend lectures, meetings	3	4	5	3
Visit exhibitions, museums	2	5	5	5
	192	240	244	233
REST, RELAXATION				
Sleep late	37	29	31	27
Enjoy the comforts of home	35	45	37	51
Go to church	34	23	17	28
Take a nap, rest in the afternoon	31	23	21	25
Play with the children	22	27	24	30
Sit and look out the window	18	10	8	11
Write letters	16	15	8	20
Care for pets	12	13	16	10
Occupy myself with my collection of stamps, photographs, etc.	2	7	11	3
	207	192	173	205
SOCIAL LIFE, ENTERTAINMENT				
Visit friends, relatives	33	45	38	50
Go to a restaurant	18	21	26	18
Entertain guests	16	32	27	36
Play cards, chess	15	16	22	12
Go dancing	9	17	18	16
Attend the theater	7	9	7	12
Play music	6	9	9	8
Attend concerts	5	7	6	8
	109	156	153	160

continued

continued

	1955 Total %	1977 Total %	Men %	Women %
IN THE OPEN AIR				
Go for a walk	50	50	44	56
Visit the cemetary	19	19	13	24
Go for a drive with the car, motorcycle	15	29	36	23
Go on an outing (on foot, on bicycle, with a boat)	14	16	17	16
	98	114	110	119
OTHER ACTIVITIES				
Repair things at home	26	30	38	22
Gardening, other yardwork	15	26	31	21
Handicrafts, needlework	13	25	12	36
Sports	6	14	21	7
Photography, painting	6	6	8	4
Job-related studies	5	8	11	4
	71	109	121	94

GOING OUT

Question: *"Here is a list. Could you tell me where you go most often?"* (L)

R

	Total		Men		Women	
	1953 %	1979 %	1953 %	1979 %	1953 %	1979 %
To visit friends and acquaintances	30	60	29	61	30	60
Walks	53	55	53	51	54	59
Weekend trips, hikes, longer trips	20	42	23	47	17	38
To sports events	19	21	33	33	7	12
Club events	14	21	23	29	7	14
To visit neighbors	14	20	13	20	15	20
To church	35	18	29	14	39	20
Concerts, theater	18	15	18	10	17	20
To play cards	7	8	13	14	2	4
To company parties	6	7	8	9	4	6
To the movies	25	6	26	9	23	4
To party meetings, election meetings	2	3	4	4	1	2
None of the above	4	4	3	2	5	6
Don't go anywhere often	7	3	5	3	9	3
	254	283	280	306	230	268

GAMES

Question: *"Various games are listed here. Which of them have you played at some time or other?"* (L)

Board games -	1957 %	1978 %	Card games -	1957 %	1978 %
Parcheesi	81	24	Old Maid	66	5
Mill	74	18	Sixty-six	50	6
Checkers	64	14	Skat	37	24
Chinese checkers	56	10	Quartet	37	4
Dominoes	35	3	Sheephead	33	10
Chess	28	14	Patience	15	5
Roulette	7	2	Bridge	7	1
Backgammon, scrabble	x	1	Canasta	7	9
	345	86		252	64

IF I HAD MORE MONEY . . .

Question: *"If you had more time or money, what would you like to do?"* (L)

C

	1953 %	1979 %
Travel	56	73
Spend time with my family	45	46
Do handicrafts and needlework, paint, make music	29	33
Participate in sports	18	31
Read	28	29
Go to the theater	29	23
Continue my professional education	25	22
Invite neighbors over	10	16
Get involved in political matters	5	13
Watch television	–	13
Take part in church events	11	8
Do more work for my church congregation	9	7
None of the above, no response	10	4
	275	318

COLLECTING

Question: *"There are countless things that you can collect. Could you tell me, with the aid of this list, what you personally collect, whether it be for others or for yourself, simply because you enjoy this activity?"* (L)

	November 1978								
	Stamps %	Coins %	Recipes %	Art objects %	Rocks %	Rare books %	Beer mugs %	Other things %	Don't collect anything %
Total population	82	38	22	19	16	15	13	38	3

PARTICIPATION IN SPORTS

Question: *"Do you participate in sports?"*

D

	Spring 1976 Regularly %	Occasionally %	No %	
Total population	21	29	50	= 100
Men	25	32	43	= 100
Women	18	26	56	= 100
AGE GROUPS				
14-19	49	36	15	= 100
20-29	31	41	28	= 100
30-39	24	38	38	= 100
40-49	18	31	51	= 100
50-59	12	23	65	= 100
60 and over	7	11	82	= 100

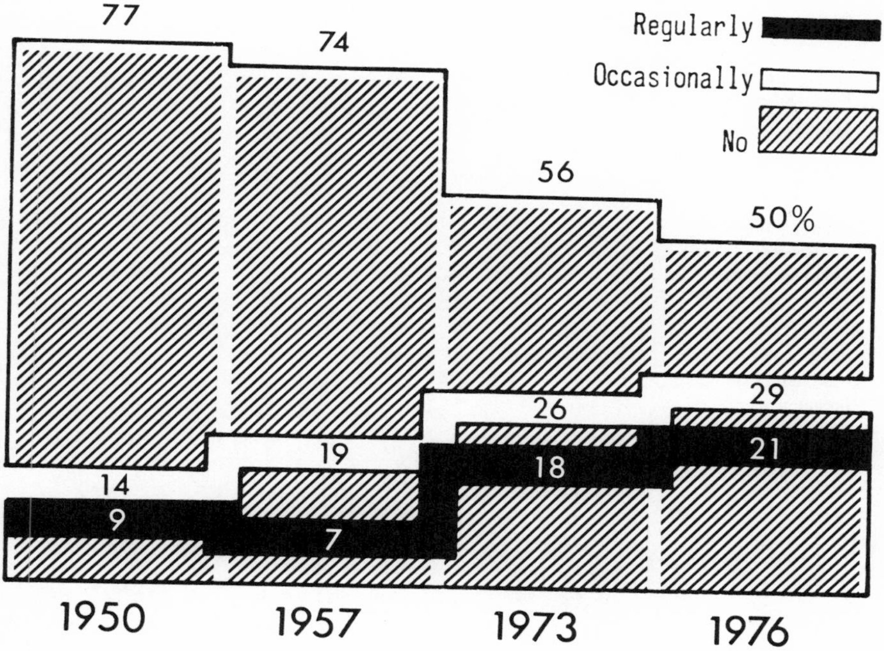

CHOICE OF SPORTS

D

				Spring 1979				
	Total pop.	Men	Women	Age groups				
				14-29	30-39	40-49	50-59	60 and over
	%	%	%	%	%	%	%	%
Swimming								
Frequently	22	23	22	33	24	23	17	11
Seldom	43	47	40	52	56	47	39	20
Never	35	30	38	15	20	30	44	69
	100	100	100	100	100	100	100	100
Physical fitness exercises								
Frequently	14	13	14	18	16	14	12	8
Seldom	33	34	33	43	39	37	29	19
Never	53	53	53	39	45	49	59	73
	100	100	100	100	100	100	100	100
Mountain climbing, hiking								
Frequently	11	11	10	7	11	14	16	11
Seldom	35	35	32	36	40	36	31	24
Never	54	54	58	57	49	50	53	65
	100	100	100	100	100	100	100	100
Track, gymnastics								
Frequently	8	8	7	15	7	6	4	3
Seldom	19	21	17	31	23	19	13	6
Never	73	71	76	54	70	75	83	91
	100	100	100	100	100	100	100	100
Downhill skiing								
Frequently	5	6	4	8	7	6	2	1
Seldom	9	10	7	15	10	9	5	2
Never	86	84	89	77	83	85	93	97
	100	100	100	100	100	100	100	100
Cross-country skiing								
Frequently	3	4	2	4	4	5	3	2
Seldom	7	8	6	9	9	8	7	3
Never	90	88	92	87	87	87	90	95
	100	100	100	100	100	100	100	100
Tennis								
Frequently	4	5	4	6	4	6	2	1
Seldom	7	8	6	13	8	7	3	2
Never	89	87	90	81	88	87	95	97
	100	100	100	100	100	100	100	100

FOR FUN

Question put to people who have participated in sports in the last 12 months: *"Two people are talking about sports here. Which one would you tend to agree with?"* (ill., X)

The one:
"I'd rather participate in sports purely for the fun of it. That's why the whole sports business with its competition and games and tournaments doesn't suit me. But if you don't go along with all that, you don't have a chance."

The other:
"In sports I also want to know how I stand as far as performance goes. That's why I like competition, and why it encourages me to do better. It doesn't mean you have to win a gold medal."

	Women		Men	
	1965	1976	1965	1976
	%	%	%	%
Sports for fun	53	58	45	47
Competitive sports	20	21	32	33
Undecided	27	21	23	20
	100	100	100	100

SOCCER

Question: *"Are you interested in soccer?"*

	February 1977			
	Yes, very much	A little	Not at all	
	%	%	%	
Total population	27	31	42	= 100
Men	45	36	19	= 100
Women	10	27	63	= 100
AGE GROUPS				
16-29	29	35	36	= 100
30-44	30	33	37	= 100
45-59	21	35	44	= 100
60 and over	25	21	54	= 100

ATTENDANCE AT SPORTS EVENTS

D

	Spring 1979							
	Total pop.	Men	Women	Age groups				
				14-29	30-39	40-49	50-59	60 and over
	%	%	%	%	%	%	%	%
Frequently	14	22	7	23	15	13	9	6
Seldom	35	44	27	43	42	39	30	21
Never	51	34	66	34	43	48	61	73
	100	100	100	100	100	100	100	100

HEALTH AND HEALTH CARE

Question: *''In which season of the year do you generally feel the best - in spring, summer, fall or winter?''*

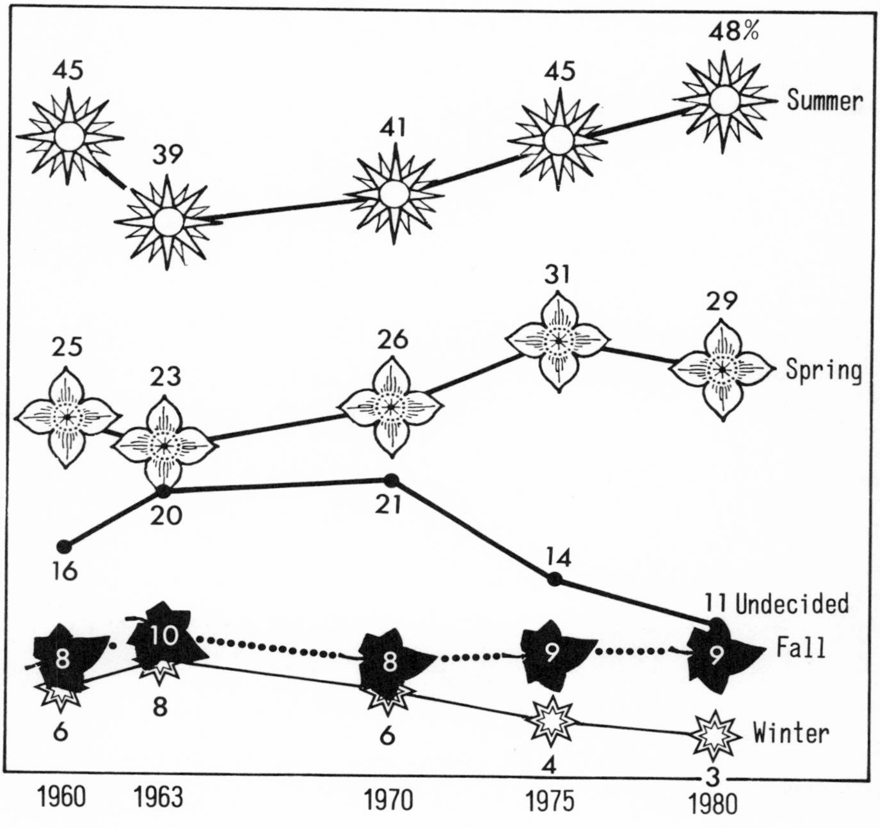

FINE, THANKS!

Question: *"Generally speaking, how would you describe your state of health?"*

	1963 Nov. %	1965 Sept. %	1967 Dec. %	1969 April %	1973 Feb. %	1975 Oct. %	1980 Jan. %
Very good	17	17	17	15	19	18	20
Rather good	37	37	36	38	42	41	41
All right	38	38	39	41	33	35	33
Rather poor	7	7	7	5	4	5	5
Very poor	1	1	1	1	2	1	1
	100	100	100	100	100	100	100

	January 1980					
	Very good %	Rather good %	All right %	Rather poor %	Very poor %	
Total population	20	41	33	5	1	= 100
Men	23	43	29	4	1	= 100
Women	17	40	36	6	1	= 100
AGE GROUPS						
16-29	39	47	12	1	1	= 100
30-44	23	50	24	2	1	= 100
45-59	10	40	43	6	1	= 100
60 and over	5	28	52	13	2	= 100

AVERAGE HEIGHT AND WEIGHT

	April 1979			
	Men		Women	
	cm	kg	cm	kg
Total average	175	77	165	64
AGE GROUPS				
16-20	177	68	166	58
21-29	178	75	166	59
30-39	176	78	166	62
40-49	175	80	166	67
50-59	175	78	165	67
60-70	173	78	164	67
71 and over	170	73	163	67

WEIGHT WATCHING

Question: *"Do you watch your weight?"*

A

	November 1978				
	Persons who watch their weight				
	Total	Age groups			
		16-29	30-44	45-59	60 and over
	%	%	%	%	%
Men	37	30	38	42	42
Women	67	66	69	75	59

NOT CALORIE CONSCIOUS

Question: *"Many people aren't interested at all in how many calories or joule the food they eat has. Do you happen to know how many calories or joule a bar of chocolate has?"*

	October 1979									
	Estimated calories -									
	under 250	250-349	350-449	450-549	550-649	650-749	750-999	1000+	Don't know	
	%	%	%	%	%	%	%	%	%	
Total population	4	4	4	5	4	2	2	2	73	= 100
Men	4	3	4	3	2	1	1	1	81	= 100
Women	4	4	3	7	5	3	2	3	69	= 100

Note: 23.8% of the responses in calories; 1.3% of the responses in joule. 100g of milk chocolate contain on the average 565 calories = 2,366 joule.

NOISE CONSCIOUS

Question: *"Some people say they are bothered by noise, others say that it doesn't bother them or hardly bothers them. Have you been bothered by noise in the last three months or not?"*

	April 1977			
	Bothered by noise	Hardly bothered	Not bothered	
	%	%	%	
Total population	35	35	30	– 100
Men	35	34	31	= 100
Women	36	35	29	= 100
AGE GROUPS				
16-29	26	38	36	= 100
30-44	36	36	28	= 100
45-59	42	31	27	= 100
60 and over	39	34	27	= 100

SLEEP

Question: *"On the average, how many hours do you sleep at night - if you take time to count, what would you say?"*

A

	August 1976						
	Total pop.	Men	Women	Age groups 16-29	30-44	45-59	60 and over
	%	%	%	%	%	%	%
Less than 7 hours	20	20	20	13	18	23	27
7 to 8 hours	32	37	28	35	33	36	24
8 to 9 hours	31	27	35	35	34	27	29
9 to 10 hours	8	7	8	8	7	5	11
10 and more hours	3	2	3	4	2	2	3
Completely differs	6	7	6	5	6	7	6
	100	100	100	100	100	100	100

Question: *"Generally speaking, do you feel that you get enough sleep these days, or do you frequently have the feeling that you don't get enough sleep?"*

	Enough sleep	Can't complain	Not enough sleep	
	%	%	%	
Total population - November 1963	40	32	28	= 100
- March 1979	43	30	27	= 100

EARLY BIRD . . .

Question: *"Usually, one doesn't get up at the same time every day. Could you tell me when you got up this morning?"*

A

	Total population			Monday - Friday Gainfully employed			Not gainfully employed		
	1962	1976	1978	1962	1976	1978	1962	1976	1978
	%	%	%	%	%	%	%	%	%
Before 6:00	26	17	15	33	21	16	16	10	8
6:00 - 6:29	22	21	20	26	25	22	16	15	16
6:30 - 6:59	16	20	18	15	19	20	17	21	17
7:00 - 7:29	14	17	16	10	17	17	20	19	21
7:30 - 8:29	13	15	18	8	9	16	22	21	26
8:30 and later	9	10	13	8	9	9	9	14	12
	100	100	100	100	100	100	100	100	100
Average time of getting up	6:44	6:58	7:17	6:31	6:46	6:57	7:02	7:16	7:30

THREATS TO HEALTH

Question: "*In your opinion, which of these things are especially bad for our health?*" (L)

	March 1979				
	Total	Age groups			
	pop.	16-29	30-44	45-59	60 and over
	%	%	%	%	%
ENVIRONMENT					
Exhaust fumes	66	67	65	66	66
Toxic refuse	63	69	63	64	57
Traffic noise	31	27	33	34	30
Food coloring	30	25	25	35	35
Smoke-filled rooms	22	16	22	24	28
Chemical fertilizer	22	17	20	25	27
Gas fumes at the gas station	13	14	11	11	15
Chlorine in swimming pools	9	11	7	8	11
	256	246	246	267	269
CONSUMPTION					
Vegetables and fruit treated with insecticides	57	52	53	62	61
Fatty food	56	50	56	62	59
Contamination of drinking water	55	61	57	54	48
Hard liquor	51	50	53	52	50
Cigarette smoking	44	45	46	45	41
Eating too much	37	32	38	40	37
Sweets	19	16	18	22	23
Beer	7	7	6	7	9
Coffee	5	3	3	6	9
Wine	4	3	5	5	4
	335	319	335	355	341
LACK OF ACTIVITY					
Sitting around a lot, little activity	52	52	54	54	48
Too much television	12	11	12	11	13
Too much sleep	3	2	2	3	6
	67	65	68	68	67
OTHER					
Tooth decay	13	16	13	14	11
Oral contraceptives	12	9	8	14	18
Synthetic clothing	6	4	4	6	9
	31	29	25	34	38

ILLNESS

Question: *"How often in your life have you been seriously ill up to now? Never, only once or twice, often or very often?"*

	October 1979				
	Never %	Once or twice %	Often %	Very often %	
Total population	38	41	18	3	= 100
Men	42	40	16	2	= 100
Women	36	41	20	3	= 100
AGE GROUPS					
16-29	56	35	8	1	= 100
30-44	49	40	10	1	= 100
45-59	29	45	22	4	= 100
60 and over	17	43	34	6	= 100
OCCUPATION					
Unskilled workers	34	39	24	3	= 100
Skilled workers	39	42	17	2	= 100
Non-managerial employees and public servants	40	41	16	3	= 100
Managerial employees and public servants	37	45	17	1	= 100
Self-employeds, professionals	36	41	20	3	= 100
Farmers	44	37	18	1	= 100

GLASSES

Question: *"Leaving aside normal sunglasses and protective goggles, do you wear glasses all the time or only occasionally?"*

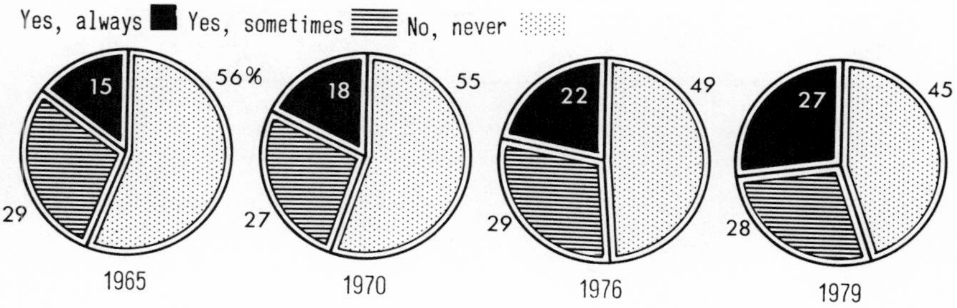

MEDICINES AND DRUGS SOLD OVER THE COUNTER

D

Within the last three months, used medicine for -	1978 %	1980 %
Toothache, headache	25	22
Sore throat	11	10
Disinfection of the mouth and throat	11	9
Cold	11	12
Cough	9	10
Regulation of digestion, constipation	9	10
Nervousness, to calm down	5	7
Backache or arthritis	4	6
Stomach problems or complaints of the gall bladder	4	5
Pimples, acne, blackheads	4	5
Dieting	3	3
Rashes, allergies	–	3
Care of the veins	2	3
Restoring strength	2	4
Counteraction of premature signs of aging	2	3
Stopping smoking	x	1

BAN ON SMOKING

Question: *"Would you be for or against a new law that would generally prohibit smoking at public places of work?"*

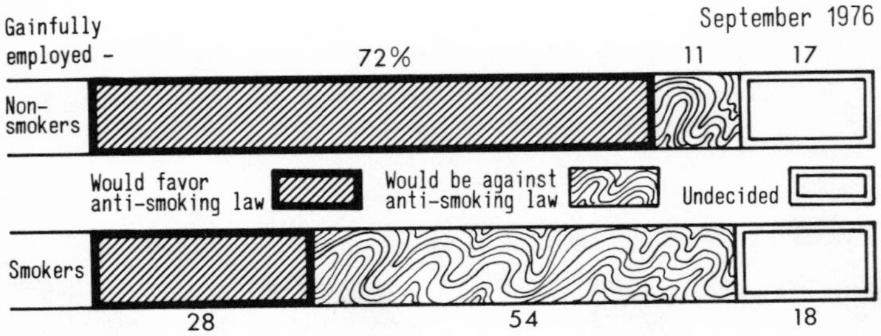

DRUGS AND ALCOHOL

Question: "*What poses more of a threat to youth today, drugs or alcohol?*"

A

	November 1978				
	Total	Age groups			
	pop.	16-29	30-44	45-59	60 and over
	%	%	%	%	%
Alcohol	37	46	39	36	27
Drugs	21	19	19	19	27
Both equally	39	32	40	44	41
Undecided	3	3	2	1	5
	100	100	100	100	100

Question: "*Within your family or among your friends has anyone under 25 taken drugs and as a result become sick or dependent, i.e. unable to lead a normal life or hold a job? Do you know of such a case?*"

	Total pop.		Age group 16-29	
	1972	1978	1972	1978
	%	%	%	%
Yes, know of such a case	9	11	18	22

INCREASED DANGER

Question: "*Do you think that drugs pose more of a threat to young people in Germany than they did a year ago, or is it the same, or has it increased?*"

	Increased danger	The same	Less danger	Don't know	
	%	%	%	%	
Total population - 1972	49	35	15	1	= 100
- 1978	51	33	6	10	= 100

ALCOHOLICS

"*A question about alcoholics and drinkers: In your opinion, which descriptions on this list are appropriate?*" (L)

	1973	1979
	%	%
Weak-willed	77	74
Sick	45	55
Comes from a broken home	44	45
A failure	43	47
Derelict	42	39
Hereditarily predisposed	26	25
Enjoys life	12	9
	289	294

ALCOHOL CONSUMPTION

Question: *"Are you worried about too much alcohol being consumed in West Germany, or don't you find this a cause for concern?"*

	Worried		Not worried		Undecided	
	1973	1978	1973	1978	1973	1978
	%	%	%	%	%	%
Total population	31	56	50	28	19	16
Men	27	48	57	36	16	16
Women	36	63	43	21	21	16
AGE GROUPS						
16-29	25	49	61	34	14	17
30-44	29	59	52	26	19	15
45-59	37	58	46	29	17	13
60 and over	35	59	39	23	26	18

DOUBLE STANDARDS?

Question: *"Some people say that when you go to the doctor with a health insurance certificate, he makes less effort than if you pay the doctor privately. Would you say this is true of most doctors, or would you say it is not true?"*

	True	Not true	Undecided	
	%	%	%	
Total population - April 1958	41	33	26	= 100
- April 1975	44	34	22	= 100

HOSPITALIZATION

Question: *"Have you ever been in the hospital?" ("Not including military hospitals.")*

	Yes, often	Yes, twice	Yes, once	No, never	
	%	%	%	%	
Total population - April 1958	21	14	29	36	= 100
- January 1970	31	17	26	26	= 100
- November 1977	37	18	21	24	= 100

HOSPITALS

Question: *"All in all, do you have a good or bad impression of the hospitals in West Germany?"*

	Good impression %	Neither nor %	Bad impression %	No opinion %	
Total population - January 1970	45	36	10	9	= 100
- November 1977 ...	47	35	7	11	= 100

GOVERNMENT SUBSIDIES

Question: *"Consideration is being given to whether the hospitals are to pay their own way or whether they should receive government subsidies, as the theaters and museums do. Two people are talking about this. Which of them says what you also tend to think?"* (ill.)

A

	November 1977 %
The hospital is of vital importance for all of us. I think the government can perfectly well afford to pay something toward our health and should grant subsidies to help cover the running costs of hospitals	73
I am of a different mind. Hospitals are more careful if they have to manage on the money they take in, just as private businesses must. I don't see why hospitals should receive government subsidies toward their running costs	17
Undecided	10
	100

WHAT MATTERS MOST TO YOU WHEN YOU ARE ILL?

Fall 1974

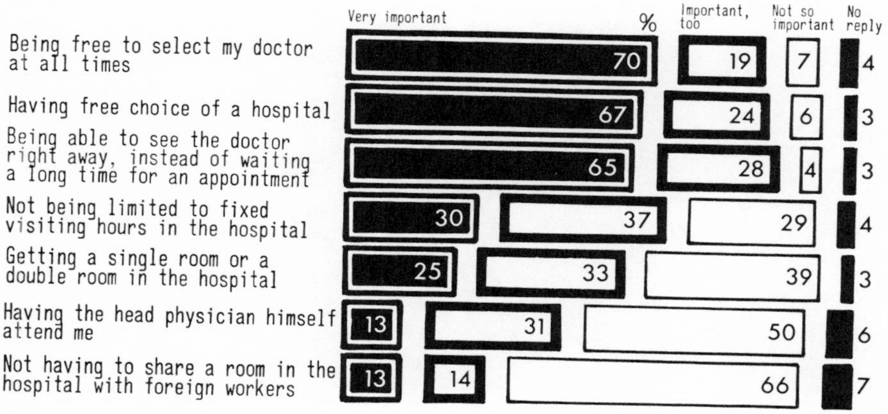

HOSPITALS IN THE COMMON MARKET COUNTRIES AND USA

Country	Hospitals	Beds per 10,000 inhabitants	
	Number	Number	Year
Federal Republic of Germany	3,416	118	1977
Belgium	479	89	1974
Denmark	296	97	1970
France	–	–	–
Great Britain	–	93	1975
Ireland	215	108	1975
Italy	2,189	106	1972
Luxembourg	26	108	1975
Netherlands	–	–	–
For comparison:			
USA	7,336	66	1975

– = no figures available

II. THE NATION

NATIONAL CONSCIOUSNESS

Question: *"When in this century do you feel things have gone best for Germany?"*

	1951 %	1959 %	1963 %	1970 %	1980 %
At present	2	42	63	81	80
Between 1933 and 1939 (Third Reich before World War II)	42	18	10	5	3
Between 1920 and 1933 (Weimar Republic)	7	4	5	2	2
Before 1914 (Kaiser Reich)	45	28	16	5	4
Don't know	4	8	6	7	11
	100	100	100	100	100

DIFFICULTIES

Question: *"Would you tell me what your greatest worries and difficulties are at the moment?"* (O)

	1954 March %	1972 April %	1980 Jan. %
Money worries	46	20	15
Worries connected with work, the job, unemployment	18	13	15
Illness in the family	14	21	19
Worries about housing	12	6	3
Worries about war (1980 including oil crisis and invasion of Afghanistan)	3	1	18
Uncertainty about the future	2	3	11
Other worries	15	14	14
Nothing in particular, no worries	9	33	16
	119	111	111

POSTWAR WORRIES

Question put to persons over 40 years of age: *"Everybody has different memories of the period from 1945 to the end of 1947. Would you read what is written on these cards? Which statements most aptly describe the first few years after the war in Germany, as you experienced them?"*

Question put to persons under 40: *"A question about the first few years after the war. Even though you might still have been a child during the period from 1945 to the end of 1947, or perhaps you hadn't even been born then, you still have some notion of the way things were during that period. Would you read what is written on these cards? Which statements most aptly describe the first few years in Germany after the war, from what you know or have heard about this?"*

	April 1978				
	Total	Age groups			
	pop.	16-29	30-44	45-59	60 and over
	%	%	%	%	%
People had very little to eat	84	89	85	82	81
People were glad to have survived the war and everything	82	78	77	85	90
Relief that the air raids were over	77	74	73	79	82
Hope for a better future	75	74	72	77	79
Bad housing conditions	75	84	75	72	68
Black market, hoarding	74	76	76	74	70
At that time one was content with little	74	64	75	78	80
People were inventive, managed to achieve something with simple means	70	62	68	75	76
Worries about missing relatives	66	76	65	57	63
Uncertainty as to the future	61	61	59	61	63
Lack of fuel	61	62	61	63	62
Relief that the Hitler era was over	59	59	56	56	65
We Germans were hated abroad	58	62	58	56	56
You no longer feared for your relatives	52	43	50	55	59
People were very willing to help one another	50	50	47	52	52
You were happy to be able to say what you thought once again	50	48	44	50	56
Fleeing, homeless	48	61	53	40	35
	1116	1123	1094	1112	1137

continued

continued

	Total pop. %	April 1978 Age groups 16-29 %	30-44 %	45-59 %	60 and over %
Grateful for help from America	47	48	48	44	46
Difficulty in finding a job	45	56	48	38	36
At last one could listen to all the programs one wanted to on the radio	42	43	40	40	46
People had had enough of politics	42	33	38	43	54
Fear of plundering, of being arrested by the occupying powers	35	35	35	35	34
At long last you could lay down your military uniform for good	33	39	32	28	32
The newspapers were no longer so biased	28	26	27	31	29
People felt helpless in the face of their problems	28	30	26	26	29
Delight at being able to see plays and read books again which had been prohibited until then	28	28	26	28	29
Industriousness, desire to learn, thirst for knowledge	27	25	28	33	23
Disillusionment with the Third Reich, old ideals were shattered	27	22	25	29	31
At that time everybody had the chance to get ahead in life	24	23	26	25	22
Annoyance about the injustices connected with de-Nazification	23	17	19	27	31
Enthusiasm for democracy	22	25	21	21	20
Egotism, one only thought of oneself	20	16	18	23	26
Fear of being denounced and spoken ill of to the occupying powers by other Germans	20	21	16	20	23
One got to know lots of kind people	19	12	16	21	29
Loneliness	18	25	17	12	15
	528	524	506	524	555

NOW AND THEN

Question: *"If you think of the problems people (half-group: 'politicians') in West Germany face today and compare them with the problems which were to be surmounted during the postwar years after 1945, do you believe the people ('politicians') had a more difficult time after 1945, or do people ('politicians') have a more difficult time now?"*

A

	February 1980 More difficult- after 1945 %	now %	Impossible to say %	
The people	76	9	15	= 100
The politicians	33	39	28	= 100

NATIONAL PRIDE

Question: *"Are you proud to be German?"*

	1971 Oct. Total population	1976 June	Age groups 16-29	30-44	45-59	60 and over
	%	%	%	%	%	%
Yes	76	71	57	67	78	84
No	11	11	20	12	6	6
Undecided	13	18	23	21	16	10
	100	100	100	100	100	100

UNPOPULAR

Question: *"It is often heard that the Germans are unpopular throughout the world. What do you think is the reason for this?"* (O)

A

	1955	1959	1969	1975	1980
	%	%	%	%	%
Our negative characteristics	45	51	60	62	61
Our positive characteristics	25	19	20	17	22
We are not unpopular	14	10	9	7	9
Other/no reply	16	23	17	21	15
	100	103	106	107	107

GOOD QUALITIES

Question: *"Generally speaking, what do you consider to be the best qualities of the Germans?"* (O)

A

	1952	1962	1972	1978	1980
	%	%	%	%	%
Industry, efficiency	72	71	63	61	66
Tidiness, reliability, thoroughness	21	12	21	23	21
Thrift	x	x	x	9	12
Cleanliness	x	x	10	12	11
Intelligence, inventiveness	9	4	2	4	8
Openness, honesty, sincerity	x	6	7	5	7
Good nature, willingness to help	12	3	2	5	7
Loyalty	11	4	4	3	4
Endurance, tenacity	8	4	2	4	3
Courage, bravery, make good soldiers	7	3	1	2	1
Modesty	3	x	x	1	1
Other qualities	13	12	11	10	11
Don't know	4	14	20	15	15
	160	133	143	154	167

BAD QUALITIES

Question: *"Generally speaking, what do you consider to be the bad qualities of the Germans?"* (O)

A

	1973 %	1975 %	1978 %	1980 %
Bragging, showing-off	12	16	16	12
Materialistic attitude	12	8	10	11
Intolerance, domineering behavior	7	8	10	12
Too industrious, diligent, ambitious	6	8	10	9
Perfectionism	4	5	9	7
Unpleasantly conspicuous abroad	4	3	6	4
No national consciousness	4	3	4	2
Egotism, unwillingness to help others	6	5	4	8
Bad manners, impoliteness	5	4	4	4
Unkind to children	1	1	4	3
Nationalistic, exaggerated national pride	5	2	3	3
Provincial, philistine	2	2	2	1
Unbalanced, inclined to extremes	2	1	2	2
Other replies	13	11	9	13
We have no bad qualities	5	8	6	5
Don't know	24	24	20	17
	112	109	119	113

MORE EFFICIENT?

Question: *"Would you say that we are more efficient and capable than other nations?"*

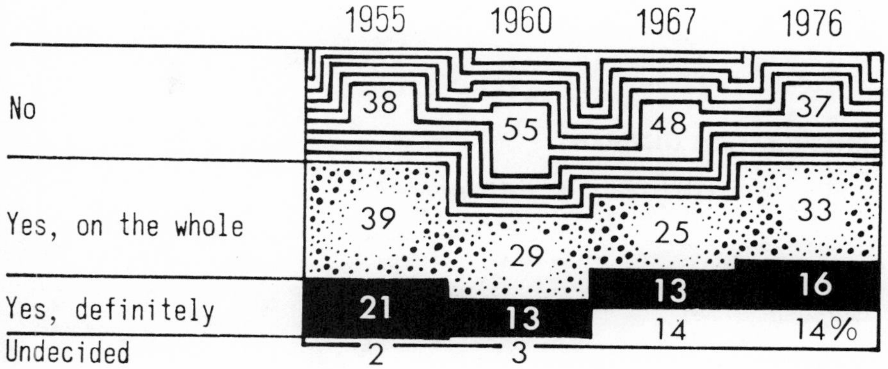

FATHERLAND

Question: *"When you hear the word 'fatherland', does that sound good to you, or do you think it no longer suits our times?"*

	Total population		Age groups 16-29		30-44		45-59		60 and over	
	1975	1981	1975	1981	1975	1981	1975	1981	1975	1981
	%	%	%	%	%	%	%	%	%	%
Sounds good	60	59	41	35	55	54	63	69	82	81
No longer suits our times	38	39	56	61	42	44	35	29	17	17
No reply	2	2	3	4	3	2	2	2	1	2
	100	100	100	100	100	100	100	100	100	100

THE FLAG

Question: *"Do you like it when you see the black-red-gold federal flag somewhere?"* (O)

	1951 May	1961 Oct.	1977 Sept.	Age groups 16-29	30-44	45-59	60 and over
	Total population						
	%	%	%	%	%	%	%
Yes, like it	23	46	47	31	47	47	62
No, don't like it	33	22	30	41	30	30	17
Depends	7	x	4	5	4	6	4
Indifferent	21	21	12	15	12	12	10
Other or no answer	16	11	7	8	7	5	7
	100	100	100	100	100	100	100

PREFER WEST GERMANY

Question: *"In which country of the world would you prefer to live?"*

	West Germany	Another European country	Country outside of Europe	Undecided	
	%	%	%	%	
Total population - 1953	77	10	8	5	= 100
- 1979	72	15	9	4	= 100

ORDERS OF MERIT

Question: *"You will no doubt have heard that the state confers orders on citizens for outstanding service. Are you in principle for or against such orders?"*

	For %	Against %	Undecided %	
Total population - January 1966	43	22	35	= 100
- July 1975	28	40	32	= 100
AGE GROUPS				
16-29	21	44	35	= 100
30-44	24	41	35	= 100
45-59	31	39	30	= 100
60 and over	37	35	28	= 100

GREAT GERMANS

Question: *"Which great German, in your opinion, has done most for Germany?"* (O)

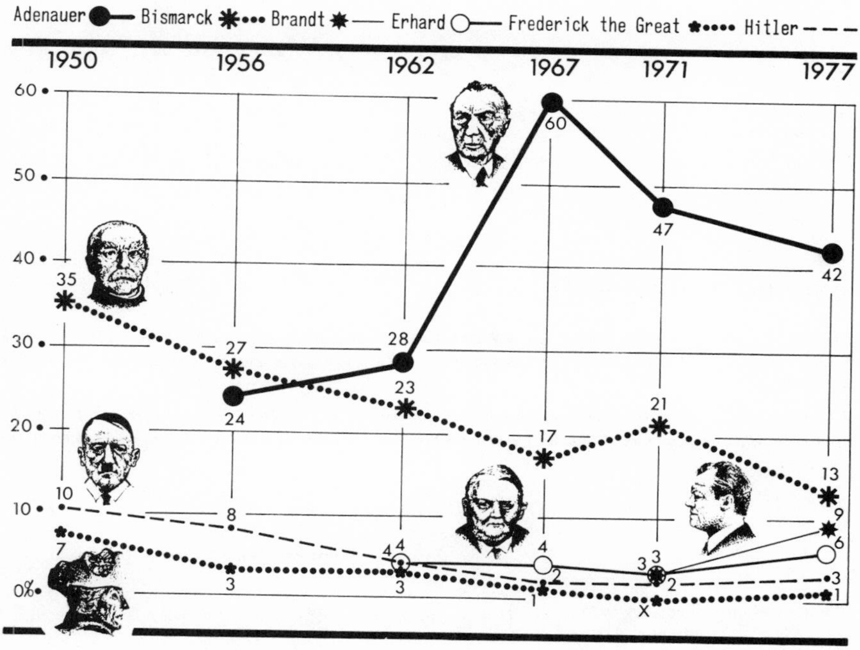

NATIONAL ANTHEM

Question: *"Recently it has been suggested that the national anthem - the Deutschlandlied - should be played every night on all radio stations before they go off the air. Are you for or against this?"*

EE

	August 1976			
	For	Against	Undecided	
	%	%	%	
Total population	31	32	37	= 100
AGE GROUPS				
16-29	23	35	42	= 100
30-44	27	34	39	= 100
45-59	33	31	36	= 100
60 and over	44	25	31	= 100

RETURN TO POWER?

Question: *"Do you believe that Germany will ever again be among the most powerful countries in the world?"*

A

	1955	1965	1972	1975	1980
	%	%	%	%	%
No, don't believe so	48	52	67	62	59
Yes, believe so	25	17	12	18	22
Impossible to say	27	31	21	20	19
	100	100	100	100	100

DECLINING BIRTHRATE

Question: *"In recent years the birthrate in West Germany has declined. More people have died than children have been born. Did you know this, or is this the first time you've heard about it?"* (Yes, knew = 1973 - 70%, 1977 - 90%)

"Opinions about this differ. Some welcome this development while others tend to find it detrimental. Generally speaking, what do you think? Is it a detriment to the future of West Germany if less children are born, or is it not a detriment?"

A

	Detriment	Not a detriment	Undecided	
	%	%	%	
Total population - February 1973	59	24	17	= 100
- August 1978	76	13	11	= 100

THE IMAGE OF A DEMOCRACY

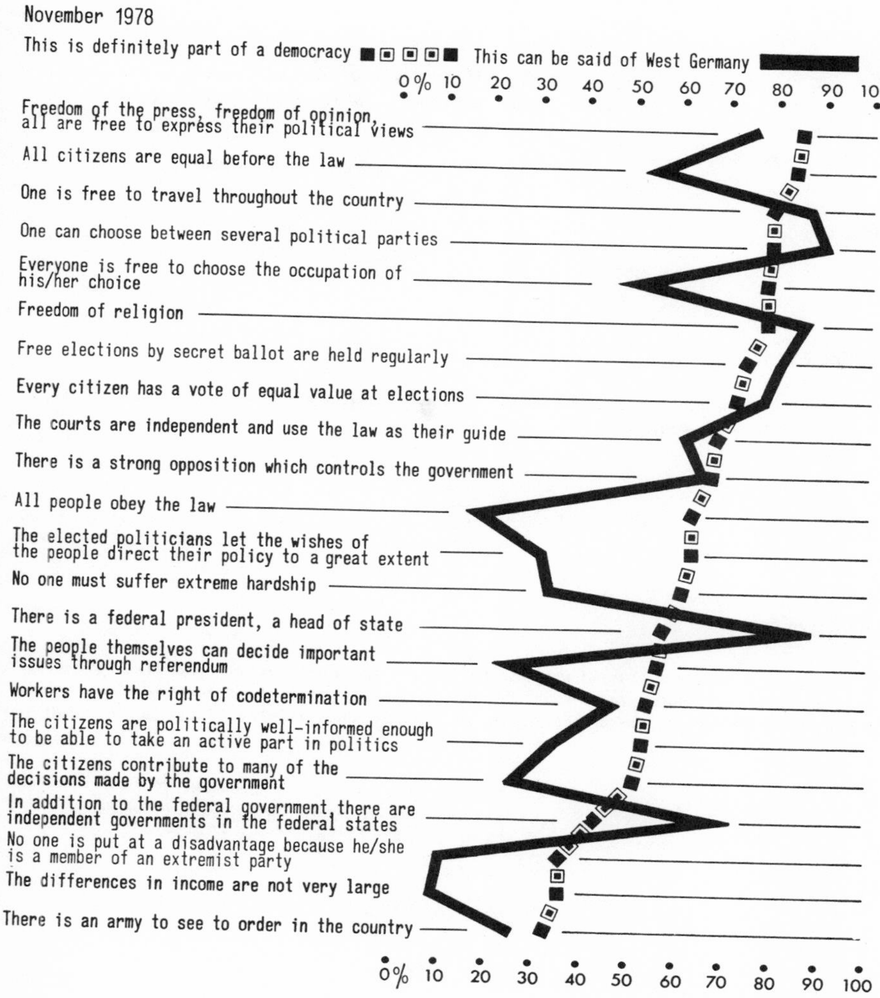
November 1978
This is definitely part of a democracy
This can be said of West Germany
0% 10 20 30 40 50 60 70 80 90 100
Freedom of the press, freedom of opinion, all are free to express their political views
All citizens are equal before the law
One is free to travel throughout the country
One can choose between several political parties
Everyone is free to choose the occupation of his/her choice
Freedom of religion
Free elections by secret ballot are held regularly
Every citizen has a vote of equal value at elections
The courts are independent and use the law as their guide
There is a strong opposition which controls the government
All people obey the law
The elected politicians let the wishes of the people direct their policy to a great extent
No one must suffer extreme hardship
There is a federal president, a head of state
The people themselves can decide important issues through referendum
Workers have the right of codetermination
The citizens are politically well-informed enough to be able to take an active part in politics
The citizens contribute to many of the decisions made by the government
In addition to the federal government, there are independent governments in the federal states
No one is put at a disadvantage because he/she is a member of an extremist party
The differences in income are not very large
There is an army to see to order in the country
0% 10 20 30 40 50 60 70 80 90 100

THE LEGACY OF THE PAST

Question: "*Everything that had been built up between 1933 and 1939, and much more, was destroyed by the war. Would you say that if it weren't for the war, Hitler would have been one of the greatest German statesmen?*"

	No, he would not	Yes, he would	Don't know	
	%	%	%	
Total population - May 1955	36	48	16	= 100
- May 1967	52	32	16	= 100
- November 1978	55	31	14	= 100

HITLER RESURRECTED?

Question: "*Do you think that a man like Hitler could once again come to power in this country, or do you consider this to be out of the question?*"

	Out of the question	Could come to power again	Undecided	
	%	%	%	
Total population - April 1975	58	18	24	= 100
- August 1977	57	23	20	= 100

RESISTANCE

Question: "*You sometimes hear that the German people went along with everything and did not offer enough resistance to Hitler. What is your view - did the population have the opportunity to change anything during the Third Reich, with respect to the concentration camps or the persecution of the Jews, or did it have practically no such opportunity?*"

A

	September 1977			
	There were opportunities - Yes	No	Undecided	
	%	%	%	
Total population	11	68	21	= 100
AGE GROUPS				
16-29	15	47	38	= 100
30-44	17	59	24	= 100
45-59	7	83	10	= 100
60 and over	4	86	10	= 100

THE GENERALS' PUTSCH

Question: *"Do you by any chance know what happened on July 20, 1944* - what took place on that day?"* (O)

Question put to persons who gave correct or vague replies for the events of the 20th of July (62% = 100): *"How should one judge the men of the 20th of July, in your opinion?"*

	April 1970				
	Total pop.	Age groups 16-29	30-44	45-59	60 and over
	%	%	%	%	%
Correct answer*	59	46	62	69	62
Vague replies	4	3	3	3	6
Wrong answers	3	3	2	3	3
Don't know	34	48	33	25	29
	100	100	100	100	100
In favor of the men of the 20th of July	39	29	40	44	44
Against the men of the 20th of July	7	5	10	9	6
Unsure of judgment	7	5	7	9	5
No judgment	10	10	8	10	13
Not informed	37	51	35	28	32
	100	100	100	100	100

*Assassination attempt on Hitler; the generals' putsch.

NATIONAL SOCIALISM OR COMMUNISM?

Question: *"It is often argued that in 1933 Germany could only choose between Communism and National Socialism. Do you consider this argument to be right, or wrong?"*

	Wrong %	May be right %	Absolutely right %	Don't know %	
Total population - June 1956	28	15	22	35	= 100
- August 1962	29	17	22	32	= 100
- May 1979	30	16	18	36	= 100

CRIMINAL REGIME

Question: *"If someone says the National Socialist government was an unjust government, a criminal regime, according to what you know of the Hitler period or what you personally experienced, would you say that is true - it was an unjust government, a criminal regime - or can't one say that?"*

A

	True %	Not true %	Not everything was bad %	Don't know %	
Total population - May 1964	54	28	9	9	= 100
- November 1978	71	21	3	5	= 100

LESSONS FROM THE PAST

Question: *"There are two people here who are talking about what can be learned from the Hitler period. Which of the two comes closest to your opinion?"* (ill.)

A	February 1979 %
"The most important thing that I've learned from the atrocities of the Nazis is that we have to fight against any system that gives the people at the top unrestricted power."	63
"I think that the atrocities of the Nazis only show what criminals the people in power in Hitler's Germany were. I don't think that every dictatorship necessarily results in criminal action."	21
Undecided	16
	100

STATUTE OF LIMITATIONS FOR NAZI CRIMES

Question: *"It is expected that at the end of 1979 the statute of limitations for crimes committed during the Hitler period will come into effect. Have you heard of this?"* (1979: yes, heard of it=91 percent)

"Are you personally for making a clean break with the past or for the continuation of the pursuit of Nazi crimes?" (X)

A	1969 Jan. %	1978 Nov. %	1979 Febr. %	Age groups 16-29 %	30-44 %	45-59 %	60 and over %
Make a clean break	67	62	50	42	48	54	57
Continue pursuit	23	24	36	39	40	32	31
Undecided	10	14	14	19	12	14	12
	100	100	100	100	100	100	100

RUDOLF HESS

A question about Rudolf Hess, who is locked up in the prison for war criminals in Spandau: *"Two people are talking about whether Rudolf Hess should be released or not. Which of the two says more or less what you think?"* (ill.)

The one:
"I think Rudolf Hess should be pardoned now and released from the prison for war criminals. We should be able to show that much humanity nowadays."

The other:
"I am not of that opinion. Rudolf Hess was one of Hitler's most important men in the Third Reich, so humanity and mercy are inappropriate in this case."

A	August 1974 Total pop. %	Age groups 16-29 %	30-44 %	45-59 %	60 and over %
For pardon	69	58	68	76	76
Against pardon	12	12	14	12	11
Undecided	8	8	8	7	6
Never heard of Rudolf Hess	11	22	10	5	7
	100	100	100	100	100

GERMAN PROBLEMS

Question: *"The 1972 Four Power Agreement about Berlin acknowledged that Berlin is* not *a part of the Federal Republic of Germany but that close ties between Berlin and the Federal Republic exist and should be further expanded. Did you know this?"* (Yes, knew it = 65 percent)

Question: *"The GDR would not like the Federal Republic of Germany to have particularly close ties to Berlin. What is your opinion—should these close ties be kept up as they have been in the past, or should an even greater effort be made to make these ties closer?"*

A

	April 1978				
	Keep up ties as in the past	Make greater effort	Give up ties	Undecided	
	%	%	%	%	
Total population	57	34	2	7	= 100

THE BERLIN WALL

Question: *"There is a wall in Berlin which separates East and West Berlin. Do you still know why the wall was built, i.e. what the reason was?"* (O)

	To stop the stream of refugees	Other conjectures	Don't know	
	%	%	%	
Total population - July 1967	66	18	16	= 100
- December 1975	66	16	18	= 100

FINANCIAL AID

Question: *"As you know, West Berlin receives financial aid from the federal government. There is a conflict of opinion as to whether this financial support for Berlin should be increased or not. Some say it is quite senseless to lend even more money to Berlin. Others say that the tougher the situation is, the more aid we have to send the Berliners. What is your opinion?"*

	More aid necessary	More aid senseless	No opinion	
	%	%	%	
Total population - September 1968	49	26	25	= 100
- April 1978	52	22	26	= 100

DON'T FORFEIT BERLIN

Question: *''Ever since the end of the war, Berlin has been the subject of unrest and dispute because it lies in the middle of the GDR (1953: 'Soviet Zone'). What is the solution? Would you say it would be better to forfeit West Berlin so as to end the dispute with the Russians, or do you think it should be retained?''*

A

Berlin should be -	1953 June %	1958 Nov. %	1970 July %	1978 April %
retained	79	78	87	88
forfeited	5	4	5	5
Undecided	16	18	8	7
	100	100	100	100

IMPROVED SITUATION

Question: *''Has the situation of Berlin improved since the Berlin Agreement and the treaties with the German Democratic Republic were concluded, or don't you think so?''*

	Has improved %	Don't think so %	Undecided, no opinion %	
Total population - June 1972	50	27	23	= 100
- April 1978	41	30	29	= 100
PARTY PREFERENCE				
SPD	34	40	26	= 100
CDU/CSU	51	22	27	= 100
FDP	42	26	32	= 100

INCLUDE BERLIN

Question: *''When the Federal Republic negotiates agreements with East Bloc countries, problems always arise because the Federal Republic would like Berlin to be included in these agreements. Two people are discussing the matter here. Which of the two comes closer to what you think?''* (ill.)

	April 1978 %
I think that the Federal Republic is responsible for Berlin and should therefore insist upon Berlin being included in the agreements	67
All or nothing is no position to take in politics. That's why I still find it better to have an agreement that only applies to the Federal Republic than to have no agreement at all	19
Undecided	14
	100

WEST BERLIN WILL REMAIN WITH THE WEST

Question: *"Here are four statements about Berlin. Could you please read them. How would you judge West Berlin's situation at this time - which of these statements best matches your opinion?"* (L)

	1961 October %	1978 April %
I am totally convinced that West Berlin will remain with the West	29	50
I believe that it is more likely that West Berlin will remain with the West	36	37
I have the feeling that we might have to hand over West Berlin to the East	18	6
I am convinced that West Berlin will soon be handed over to the East	6	2
Undecided	11	5
	100	100

Question: *"Have you ever been to Berlin?"*

	1953 Total population %	1978 Total population %	Age groups 16-29 %	30-44 %	45-59 %	60 and over %
Yes, have been to Berlin	45	42	31	45	49	45
No, have not been to Berlin	55	58	69	55	51	55
	100	100	100	100	100	100

AMERICANS WILL HELP

Question: *"Supposing the Berlin conflict resulted in war, do you think the Americans will help us or not?"*

	1975 May		1976 June		1979 September		1980 May	
	Total * %	West Berlin %	Total * %	West Berlin %	Total * %	West Berlin %	Total * %	West Berlin %
Will certainly help	46	75	44	38	50	33	49	51
Perhaps	26	13	28	17	28	39	27	41
Don't think so	16	8	19	37	14	22	13	5
No opinion	12	4	9	8	8	6	11	3
	100	100	100	100	100	100	100	100

* = West Germany, not including West Berlin

Question: *"As you know, West Berlin receives financial aid from the federal government. Views differ about whether financial support for Berlin should be increased or not. Some people say that it does not make any sense to pump more money into Berlin. Others say that the more difficult the situation, the more aid has to be given to the Berliners. What is your view?"*

	More aid %	Doesn't make any sense %	No response %	
Total population - September 1968	49	26	25	= 100
- April 1978	52	21	27	= 100

GERMANY: EAST AND WEST

Question: *"Do you think it is right that West Germany claims to speak for all of Germany, or don't you think that's right?"* (It's right = 61 percent)

"Do you by chance know why West Germany makes this claim, and on what this claim is based?" (O)

	February 1967
	%
The West German government is the only freely elected German government, the East German government has not developed as a result of free elections	32
Although Germany is in fact divided, the other country also belongs with us	13
The West German government is independent and sovereign	5
The West German government represents the greater part of Germany	1
Other reasons	7
Don't know	45
	103

TWO GERMAN STATES

Question: *"In his governmental declaration, Federal Chancellor Brandt mentioned for the first time that there were two states of German nationality. Do you think Brandt was right in saying this, or do you think he acted contrary to German interests?"*

	November 1969				
	Total	Age groups			
	pop.	16-29	30-44	45-59	60 and over
	%	%	%	%	%
Think he was right	43	52	46	40	33
Acted contrary to German interests	31	27	30	32	36
Undecided	26	21	24	28	31
	100	100	100	100	100

SELF-DETERMINATION

Question: "*Could you please read the following sentence from the Basic Law: 'The entire German people are called upon to achieve in free self-determination the unity and freedom of Germany.' What is your opinion: Should this sentence remain in the constitution, or do you think it should be deleted?*" (L)

A

	1973 %	1976 %	1979 %
Should remain	73	72	76
Should be deleted	10	12	10
Undecided	17	16	14
	100	100	100

REUNIFICATION

Question: "*Do you think that East and West Germany will ever be reunited again or not?*" (1966: "*Do you think that you will see the reunification of East and West Germany within your lifetime?*")

A

	Yes			No			Impossible to say		
	1966 %	1970 %	1976 %	1966 %	1970 %	1976 %	1966 %	1970 %	1976 %
Total population	28	18	13	44	50	65	28	32	22
AGE GROUPS									
16-29	30	15	10	37	53	73	33	32	17
30-44	33	20	13	37	50	63	30	30	24
45-59	31	19	10	44	51	69	25	30	21
60 and over	15	18	19	63	46	54	22	36	27

UNITED GERMANY FAVORED

Question: *"I would like to have your opinion on several questions about Germany:**

After World War II, Germany was divided into East and West Germany. If Germany were reunited, would the chances for a lasting peace be more favorable or less favorable?"

Spring 1969	More favorable %	Less favorable %	Would have no effect %	Undecided %	
Total population - USA	45	28	8	19	= 100
- Britain ..	43	30	7	20	= 100
- France ..	42	30	10	18	= 100

"Some people feel that a nation should always have the right to live together as one state; others feel that there are sometimes sound political reasons why a nation should not live together as one state. In the case of the Germans, what is your opinion - should they have the right to live as one state or should they not have this right for political reasons?"

"Many Germans want East and West Germany reunited as one German nation. What is your opinion - should the German demand for reunification be supported or not?"

"If the East and West were reunited, do you think Germany would be too strong a military power?"

"Do you think a reunited Germany would be too strong economically, or don't you think so?"

Spring 1969	USA %	Britain %	France %
The right to live as one state-			
Yes	62	62	70
No	17	21	16
Undecided	21	17	14
	100	100	100
Germany as a military power -			
Too strong	28	44	60
Don't think so	52	39	25
Undecided	20	17	15
	100	100	100

Spring 1969	USA %	Britain %	France %
Support for German demands-			
Yes	56	52	56
No	19	28	25
Undecided	25	20	19
	100	100	100
Germany's economy -			
Too strong	20	46	60
Don't think so	56	31	22
Undecided	24	23	18
	100	100	100

*The Institut für Demoskopie Allensbach conducted this survey together with INRA/New York, Research Services Ltd./London and COFREMCA/Paris in the USA, Great Britain and France.

THE PRICE OF REUNIFICATION

Question: *"As you know, the people in East Germany have less freedom than we do. Supposing there were negotiations on reunification and the Russians demanded that, as the price for reunification, we forgo some of our freedoms. Which of the things on this list could we afford to give up in exchange for reunification?"* (L)

A

	1958 March %	1969 May %
Privacy of correspondence, postal authorities may not open letters	8	12
Right of assembly	7	10
Freedom of the press, newspapers and books are not subject to censorship	6	6
Freedom of alliance, Germany is free to conclude agreements with other countries	6	7
Freedom of vocational choice	4	4
Freedom of speech, everyone is free to express his opinion	4	2
Freedom to choose one's own place of work	3	4
Freedom for all democratic parties	3	3
Free elections by secret ballot	3	3
Freedom to do as one likes with one's property	2	4
None of these	51	56
Undecided	21	9
	118	120

GROWING APART

Question: *"If you think about the two Germanys - the Federal Republic (West Germany) and the German Democratic Republic (East Germany) - would you say that they have grown closer in recent years or have they grown farther apart? What do you feel is true?"*

	The two Germanys have - remained unchanged %	grown closer %	grown farther apart %	undecided %	
Total population - June 1971	45	34	11	10	= 100
- September 1976	31	38	25	6	= 100

HOW MANY EAST GERMANS?

Question: *"What do you estimate the population of East Germany to be?"*

	Correct answer (17 million) %	Overestimate %	Underestimate %	Don't know %	
Total population - July 1967	18	26	18	38	= 100
- December 1975	10	36	16	38	= 100

SED PARTY MEMBERS

Question: *"In East Germany they have the SED, the Socialist Unity Party of Germany, with Erich Honecker* as leader. What percentage of adults in East Germany do you think are party members of the SED?"*

	December 1967 %	December 1975 %
Roughly 10 - 39 percent (correct: 15.5 percent)**	20	13
Roughly 40 - 69 percent	23	23
Roughly 70 - 100 percent	21	32
Impossible to say	36	32
	100	100

*) 1967: Walter Ulbricht
**) July 1974 = 1,907,719 members aged 18 and over.

ONE-PARTY SYSTEM?

Question: *"Do you know if there is just one political party in East Germany, or are there a number of parties?"*

	March 1966 %	December 1975 %
Just one party	51	49
Numerous parties (correct answer)	28	30
Don't know	21	21
	100	100

CONTACT WITH EAST GERMANS

Question: *"Imagine for a moment that you were taking a vacation somewhere on the Black Sea and happen to meet another German. By talking with him you learn that he is from East Germany. What would your first reaction be to that? Please take a look at these cards. Which of these things would you think?"* (C)

	1970 July %	1975 Nov. %	1979 Aug. %
I would be curious and interested in having a conversation with him	71	71	71
I would be pleased	61	57	48
I believe that we as Germans abroad would get along very well	59	54	50
I would suggest that we have a drink together	45	47	40
I don't think I would hear his true feelings because he wouldn't feel safe in expressing them	40	47	44
As a West German, I don't believe that he would like to have me sit at his table because he certainly thinks much differently than we do	13	18	15
I think we wouldn't have much to say to each other	12	16	14
I'd think he was a spy	6	6	6
I would want to get away from him	3	4	4
I would be disappointed	2	3	3
	312	323	295

COMPATRIOT

Question: *"Would you feel that he's a compatriot, or would you not feel any more akin than you would to an Austrian, who speaks the same language?"*

	Compatriot %	No more akin than to Austrian %	Undecided %	
Total population - July 1970	68	20	12	= 100
- November 1975	53	29	18	= 100

TRAVELING TO EAST GERMANY

Question: *"Do you think you will live to see the day when we will be able to travel to East Germany just as easily as to Austria or to Switzerland?"*

	October 1975			
	Don't think so %	Think so %	Undecided %	
Total population	63	20	17	= 100

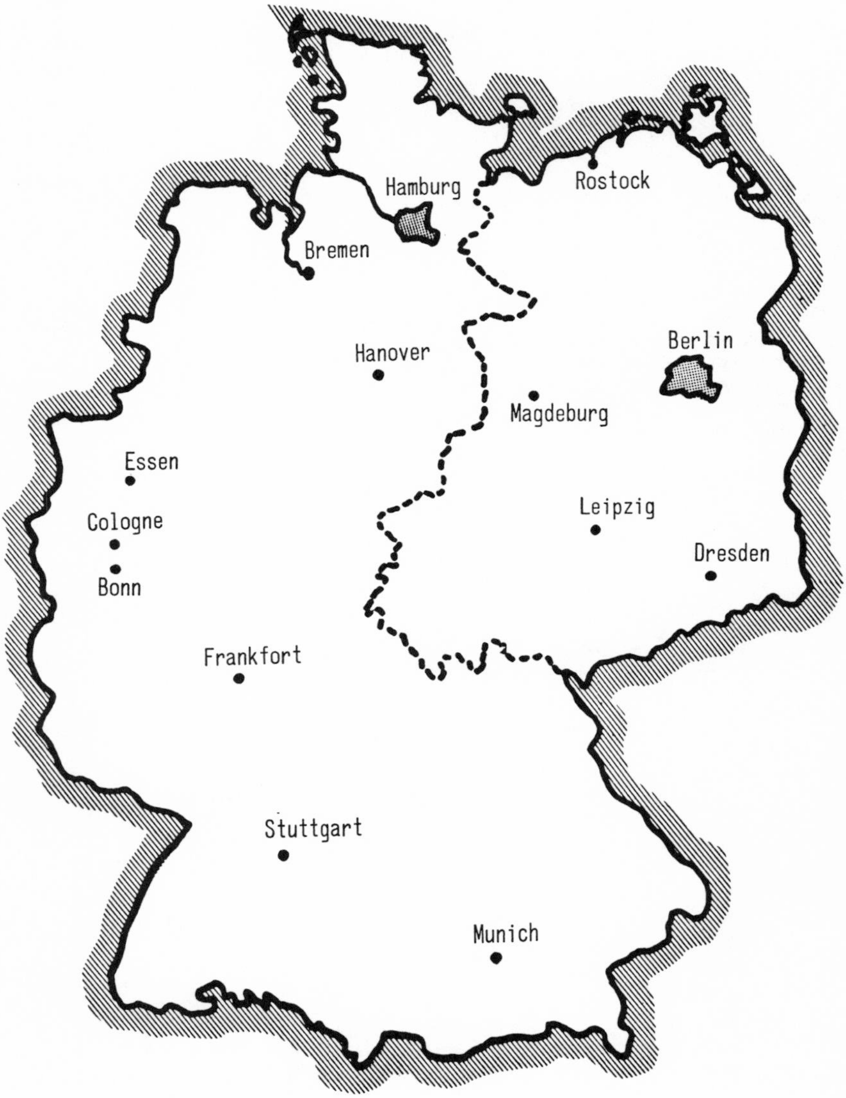
Hamburg
Rostock
Bremen
Berlin
Hanover
Magdeburg
Essen
Cologne
Bonn
Leipzig
Dresden
Frankfort
Stuttgart
Munich

"GERMANY" FAVORED

Question: *"Here is a map of Germany. On the left, you see our area and on the right the other part of Germany. When you speak of our part of Germany - what term do you use?"* (O, ill.)

A

	1966 March	1980 May	Age groups			
	Total population		16-29	30-44	45-59	60 and over
	%	%	%	%	%	%
The Federal Republic	36	26	25	26	25	26
West Germany	29	12	10	11	15	13
Germany	12	34	40	36	30	30
FRG	x	13	16	13	10	10
The West	8	5	3	2	8	5
Here, our part	5	5	4	5	6	6
Federal Republic of Germany	3	4	2	5	5	6
The federal area	2	1	x	x	1	x
Other/no reply	7	5	4	5	4	10
	102	105	104	103	104	106

GDR

Question: *"When you speak of the other part of Germany, what do you call it, what term do you use?"* (O, ill.)

	1966 March	1970 July	1980 May
	%	%	%
The Eastern Zone	48	33	16
East Germany	12	13	6
GDR	11	37	61
The Zone	9	4	3
The other side, from the other side	5	4	7
Central Germany	4	2	x
Soviet occupied zone, Soviet occupied territory, occupied zone	4	2	1
Soviet Zone	3	x	x
Other, no reply	9	9	14
	105	104	108

Based on 2,000 respondents in the Federal Republic of Germany not including West Berlin.

REUNITED?

Question: *"Do you very much wish Germany would be reunified, or is it not so important for you?"*

A

	January 1976			
	Wish it very much	Not so important	Other answer	
	%	%	%	
Total population	61	36	3	= 100
AGE GROUPS				
16-29	44	52	4	= 100
30-44	57	40	3	= 100
45-59	65	30	5	= 100
60 and over	77	20	3	= 100

DESIRED GOVERNMENT ACTIONS

Question: *"Assuming the federal government were doing something from this list. With which of these things would you personally agree?"* (L)

A

	February 1977			
	Total	Party preference		
	pop.	SPD	CDU/CSU	FDP
	%	%	%	%
Reduction of loans to East Germany	50	45	58	43
Bring it to the attention of the UN when East Germany violates human rights	46	44	52	44
Convince friendly countries to work together less with East Germany	21	17	22	18
Restrict the export of our industry to East Germany	19	18	22	19
Allow our border patrols to shoot back when East German soldiers shoot at escapees	19	18	23	16
Expel East German journalists from West Germany	10	7	14	3
Break off all current negotiations with East Germany	7	5	11	5
Expel the East Berlin representatives in Bonn	5	4	7	1
Close Bonn's diplomatic mission in East Berlin	3	2	5	x
None of these, against firmer policy	23	31	17	32
	203	191	231	181

PREREQUISITES FOR REUNIFICATION

Question: "*What do you think of the following suggestion for German reunification? The following demands are prerequisites for reunification:*

- *East Germany must withdraw from the Warsaw Pact, and West Germany from NATO.*
- *There must be guarantees that a reunited Germany will be neutral and unallied.*
- *In a reunited Germany, free elections by secret ballot will determine the social system.* (L)

What is your position? Would you welcome reunification under these conditions or not?"

Question: "*I know it's hard to say, but what's your opinion—do you think the reunification of Germany in the next twenty years is possible under these conditions, or do you think this is unlikely?*"

	June 1979			
Reunification under these conditions is -	Yes %	No %	Undecided %	
welcome	49	26	25	= 100
possible	17	64	19	= 100

CHANGE OF EMPHASIS

Question: "*Which, in your opinion, is the most important question we in West Germany should at present concern ourselves with?*" (O)

Excerpt*)	Reunification %	Berlin problem %	Preservation of peace, East-West détente %	Economic problems %
October 1951	18	x	17	45
January 1955	34	x	16	28
January 1959	45	16	16	15
January 1963	31	11	15	21
January 1967	18	1	4	62
January 1976	1	x	3	74
January 1980	x	x	33	86

*) For further reference see THE GERMANS, vol. I, pp. 214 and 459; vol. II, p. 144.

THE POLITICAL SYSTEM

Question: *"The Basic Law came into being 30 years ago (1968: 20 yrs., 1974: 25 yrs.) under the supervision and control of the Western Powers. Because of this fact, some people think we Germans should create a new Basic Law that better conforms to our needs and interests. However, others say that our present Basic Law has proved its worth and that we don't need a new one. What is your opinion?"*

	1968 Nov. %	1974* May %	1979* April %
No, we don't need a new Basic Law	43	60	68
Yes, we need a new Basic Law	26	20	14
Undecided	31	20	18
	100	100	100

*Survey conducted in West Germany not including West Berlin.

CONSTITUTIONAL AMENDMENT

Question: *"As far as you know, can the Basic Law be amended, or is it not amendable?"*

If yes:
"How do you think the Basic Law can be amended, or rather, who can amend it?"

	1970 March %	1974 May %	1979 April %
Can be amended	62	74	68
namely by			
- the Lower House of Parliament (Bundestag)	–	42	38
- referendum	–	12	9
- the Upper House of Parliament (Bundesrat)	–	9	10
- the government, the Federal Chancellor and the Ministers	–	8	7
- the Federal Constitutional Court	–	7	10
- the Federal President	–	3	1
- other answers, no answer	–	4	4
	62	85	79
Not amendable	11	7	8
Don't know	27	19	24
	100	100	100

- 1970 not investigated

Note: The Basic Law can be amended by a two-thirds majority of the members of both the Upper and Lower House.

CONFUSING SIMILARITIES

Question: *"Various passages from both the Basic Law of the Federal Republic of Germany and the Constitution of the German Democratic Republic are printed on these cards. Obviously it is impossible to know such constitutions in detail, but which of these statements do you suspect come from our Basic Law and which of them come from the Constitution of East Germany? Could you please distribute the cards onto this sheet according to what you think or to where you feel they belong?"* (C)

A

	April 1979		
	Attributed to the constitution of -		
Statements from the Basic Law of the FRG (West Germany)	West Germany %	East Germany %	Don't know %
All persons shall be equal before the law (Article 3.1)	92	2	6
No one may be prejudiced or favored because of his sex, his parentage, his race, his language, his homeland and origin, his faith, or his religious or political opinions (Article 3.3)	89	2	9
No one may be compelled against his conscience to render war service involving the use of arms (Article 4.3)	86	2	12
Persons persecuted on political grounds shall enjoy the right of asylum (Article 16.2)	79	3	18
Illegitimate children shall be provided by legislation with the same opportunities for their physical and spiritual development and their place in society as are enjoyed by legitimate children (Article 6.5)	64	12	24
All state authority emanates from the people. It shall be exercised by the people by means of elections and voting and by specific legislative, executive, and judicial organs (Article 20.2)	57	22	21
Acts tending to and undertaken with the intent to disturb the peaceful relations between nations, especially to prepare for aggressive war, shall be unconstitutional. They shall be made a punishable offense (Article 26.1)	29	37	34
Property imposes duties. Its use should also serve the general public welfare (Article 14.2)	29	52	19
All Germans shall have the right to resist any person or persons seeking to abolish this constitutional order, should no other remedy be possible (Article 20.4)	23	39	38
Land, natural resources and means of production may for the purpose of socialization be transferred to public ownership or other forms of publicly controlled economy by a law which shall provide for the nature and extent of compensation (Article 15)	14	63	23
	562	234	204

continued

continued

A

Statements from the Constitution of the GDR (East Germany)	April 1979 Attributed to the constitution of - West Germany %	East Germany %	Don't know %
Every citizen . . . has the right to express his opinion according to the principles of this constitution . . . the freedom of the press, of radio and of television is guaranteed	86	3	11
Every citizen has the right to a job and the right to choose it freely, according to what is required by society and according to personal qualifications	63	18	19
Every citizen has the right to leisure time and rest	60	14	26
In the interest of the well-being of its citizens, the state and society take care of the protection of nature	39	29	32
The principle "To each according to his abilities, to each according to his achievement" will be put into effect	23	40	37
To do socially useful work is the honored duty of every citizen capable of work. The right to work and the duty to work are one thing	14	64	22
	285	168	147

RESTRICTIONS ON PERSONAL FREEDOM

Question: "*Nobody is completely independent in his private life. Where do you feel that your personal freedom is restricted? By that I mean, which of the items on this list keep you from taking action or making decisions the way you would like to?*" (L)

	Feb. 1979 %
My financial circumstances	46
Lack of time	40
Insufficient opportunities here in town	28
Neighbors you have to be considerate of	27
My wife/my husband doesn't always want what I want	25
Children you have to attend to	22
Friends/relatives you have to be considerate of	20
The administration, the bureaucracy	19
Lack of sufficient education	18
The rules at work	15
Decisions made by my boss, my superior	14
Disadvantages because I'm a man/a woman	12
Etiquette, the prevailing customs	10
My father/my mother doesn't want me to do certain things	9
The police	8
The state, the government	6
The union, the officials	4
The dictates of the church	3

THE RIGHT TO EXPRESS ONE'S OPINION

Question: *"In this country the Basic Law, that is, the constitution, guarantees everybody the right to express his opinion freely. I have here a few questions about this. Please reply with one of the five possible answers."* (L)

	June 1972					
	Yes -		No -			
	definitely	probably	probably not	definitely not	Undecided	
Has one the right to publicly -	%	%	%	%	%	
criticize the Federal Chancellor	68	20	4	2	6	= 100
criticize the Federal President	62	22	6	3	7	= 100
speak out against religion or against Christianity	55	23	9	5	8	= 100
advocate the abolition of the Federal Armed Forces	50	20	12	8	10	= 100
support Communism or the communist world revolution	33	18	18	19	12	= 100
advocate the founding of a new National Socialist Party	26	16	18	27	13	= 100

Question: *"Do you feel that one can express one's political views freely in West Germany, or is it advisable to be careful about what one says?"*

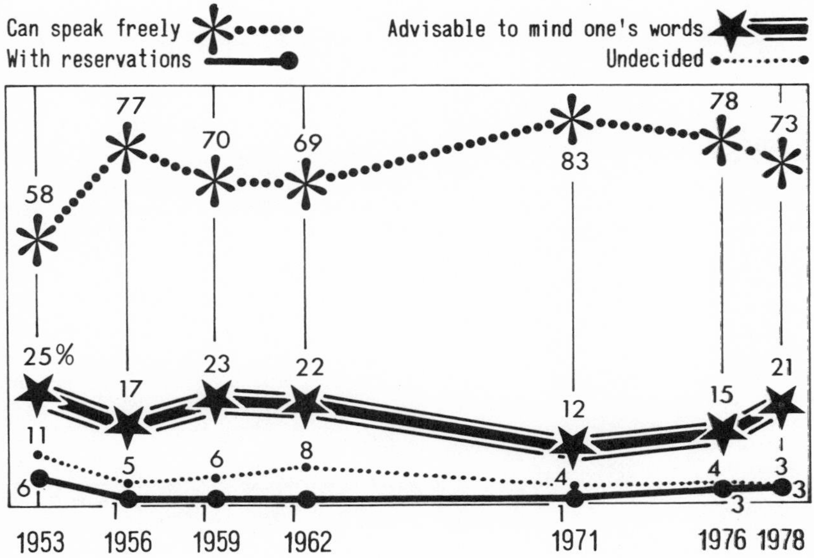

DEMOCRACY BEST FORM OF GOVERNMENT

Question: *"Do you believe that the democracy we have in West Germany is the best form of government, or is there another form of government that is better?"*

	Best form of government %	There is another that is better %	Undecided %		
Total population - October 1967	74	4	22	=	100
- August 1975	74	9	17	=	100
- November 1978	71	11	18	=	100
AGE GROUPS					
16-29	64	17	19	=	100
30-44	74	10	16	=	100
45-59	73	10	17	=	100
60 and over	71	8	21	=	100
PARTY PREFERENCE					
SPD	76	10	14	=	100
CDU/CSU	73	10	17	=	100
FDP	68	11	21	=	100

PARTY SYSTEM

Question: *"Do you think that it is better for a country to have only one political party so that there is as much unanimity as possible, or would it be better to have several parties, so that different opinions may be freely represented?"*

	1950 Sept. %	1956 June %	1960 Aug. %	1967 Oct. %	1972 Sept. %	1978 Nov. %
Several parties	53	45	50	55	54	68
Not more than 2 or 3 parties	x	31	29	26	34	24
One party only	24	11	11	9	8	5
No parties at all	x	2	1	1	x	1
No opinion	23	11	9	9	4	2
	100	100	100	100	100	100

SATISFIED WITH CONDITIONS

Question: *"Are you generally satisfied with conditions here in West Germany, or would you like to see many fundamental changes?"*

	Satisfied %	Changes wanted %	Undecided %	
Total population - May 1970	65	25	10	= 100
- January 1980	65	26	9	= 100
AGE GROUPS				
16-29	63	28	9	= 100
30-44	70	22	8	= 100
45-59	65	28	7	= 100
60 and over	64	26	10	= 100
EDUCATION				
Elementary	66	25	9	= 100
Secondary	64	28	8	= 100
PARTY PREFERENCE				
SPD	76	16	8	= 100
CDU/CSU	60	32	8	= 100
FDP	64	24	12	= 100

REFORM POLICIES

Question: *"On this list, there are three basic points of view about the society in which we live. Which of these comes closest to expressing what you think?"* (L)

A

	May 1979				
	Total	Age groups			
	pop. %	16-29 %	30-44 %	45-59 %	60 and over %
Our society must be changed step by step through meaningful reforms	59	68	60	59	50
Our existing society must be courageously defended against all subversive powers	33	26	35	35	38
Our entire social order must be radically changed by means of revolution	2	3	2	1	1
Undecided	6	3	3	5	11
	100	100	100	100	100

LEADERSHIP

Question: "*Two men are discussing how a country should be governed. Which of these opinions comes closest to your own views?*" (ill., X)

	1955 May %	1960 Aug. %	1967 Feb. %	1978 Aug. %
"I prefer several people to have a say in the management of the country's affairs. Things may be debated again and again, but it is not easy for such a government to misuse its powers"	55	62	61	63
"I'd like to see the people choose the best politician to lead the country and give him all powers of government. He would then be in a position to make clear and swift decisions with the aid of a few experts. There would be less talk and more action"	31	21	27	26
Undecided	14	17	12	11
	100	100	100	100

INFLUENCE OF GROUPS

Question: "*It is often said that there are many cases where the individual is more or less at the mercy of various groups and organizations and can hardly defend himself against them. A number of them are listed here. For which do you tend to have the feeling that one is quite defenseless?*" (L)

	1978 Dec. Total %	1977 Sept. Total %	Age groups 16-29 %	30-44 %	45-59 %	60 and over %
Civil service, administration	57	43	45	44	40	41
Police	39	27	39	25	23	19
Television	37	39	40	43	39	34
Political parties	33	28	33	25	30	25
Newspapers	32	28	35	26	28	23
Illustrated magazines	28	27	29	27	27	23
Labor unions	25	21	21	20	20	23
Schools, teachers	23	20	26	22	20	12
The Church	14	13	19	14	11	7
None of these	12	18	13	17	19	25
	300	264	300	263	257	232

CHARACTERISTICS OF A GOOD DEMOCRAT

Question: *"If it is said that someone is a good democrat, which of these characteristics and attitudes would you suspect apply to this person?"* (C)

	November 1978 %
Votes at every election	83
Is well-informed about politics	75
Abides by the law	74
Is tolerant	65
Speaks up for others	62
Is receptive to new ideas in politics	59
Supports equal opportunity everywhere	57
Reads the political section of the newspaper thoroughly	55
Often takes part in political discussion	53
Closely follows the political programs on television	52
Stands up for his convictions	49
Is against communism	49
Supports codetermination	49
Is politically active	47
Supports a free market economy	46
Is self-assured when dealing with authorities	44
Is active in the community	40
Only votes for the parties represented in parliament	38
Participates in single-issue movements	34
Is politically middle-of-the-road	31
If a party member, always adheres to the majority votes of the party	29
Is member of a party	29
Unselfish	21
Doesn't always vote for the same party	17
Is member of a labor union	16
Tends to be toward the right politically	14
Is a member of many organizations	13
Conservative	12
Is not willing to serve in active military duty	9
Tends to be toward the left politically	6

FREEDOM OR EQUALITY?

Question: *''Here are two people discussing which is more important in the final analysis, freedom or the highest possible degree of equality. Please read through this and tell me which of the two says what you tend to believe.''* (ill., X)

The one:
''I feel freedom and the highest possible degree of equality are both equally important. But if I had to choose between them, personal freedom would be most important to me—that is, for everybody to be able to live and grow in freedom.''

The other:
''Certainly freedom and the highest possible degree of equality are both equally important. But if I had to choose between them, I would find the highest possible degree of equality most important—that is, for nobody to be underprivileged and the social divisions not to be so marked.''

A

	November 1976				
	Total	Age groups			
	pop.	16-29	30-44	45-59	60 and over
Of greatest importance -	%	%	%	%	%
Freedom	61	62	65	61	54
Equality	30	30	30	31	30
Undecided	9	8	5	8	16
	100	100	100	100	100

FREEDOM OR JUSTICE?

Question: *''Here two people are discussing which is ultimately more important, freedom or justice. Would you please read the following texts and tell me which of them comes closest to expressing your opinion?''* (ill., X)

The one:
''I feel both freedom and justice are actually of equal importance. But if I had to decide for one of the two, freedom would be most important to me personally—for each individual to be able to live and grow in freedom.''

The other:
''Certainly both freedom and justice are equally important. But if I had to decide for one of the two, I would choose justice—for no one to be placed at a disadvantage and the social difference not to be so extreme.''

	1979	1976				
	Aug.	Nov.	Age groups			
	Total population		16-29	30-44	45-59	60 and over
Of greatest importance -	%	%	%	%	%	%
Freedom	48	45	45	49	39	45
Justice	34	41	41	37	44	43
Undecided	18	14	14	14	17	12
	100	100	100	100	100	100

EQUALITY

Question: *"Would you personally like to live in a country where, instead of there being poor people and rich people, everyone had pretty much the same amount?"*

	Yes, I would like to	No, I would not like to	Undecided	
	%	%	%	
Total population - March 1955	49	40	11	= 100
- July 1964	37	44	19	= 100
- August 1976	46	42	12	= 100

SOCIALISM

Question: *"When one hears the word socialism all sorts of things might enter one's mind in connection with it. May I read a few to you? And will you please tell me whether, on hearing the word socialism, these things really could come to mind?"*

A

	October 1961		February 1975	
	Yes*	No*	Yes*	No*
	%	%	%	%
Safety from disease and distress	75	12	54	27
Security in old age	73	12	51	27
Prosperity for all	69	15	45	36
Justice	65	15	50	27
Progressive	63	16	44	32
Human dignity	63	21	47	36
Freedom	62	21	43	43
Peace-loving	60	20	49	30
Comradeship	55	20	41	33
Vigorous	35	33	26	38
Labor union boss	30	48	45	39
Levelling mania	29	47	49	28
Soviet zone	28	55	61	27
High social insurance contributions	26	53	43	38
Radical	25	56	39	47
Bureaucratic	22	51	31	38
Compulsion	19	64	41	41
Communism	18	65	49	40
Bleak theory	17	56	31	36
Undemocratic	13	66	28	49
Obsolete	13	68	17	54

* = The figures for "Undecided" may be calculated by subtracting the total of Yes and No figures from 100.

Question: *"Would you vote for or against a government that says it wants to introduce socialism?"*

	1978 Jan. Total population	1980 Sept. Total population	Age groups 16-29	30-44	45-59	60 and over	Party preference SPD	CDU/CSU	FDP
	%	%	%	%	%	%	%	%	%
For	12	9	14	9	7	7	16	2	6
Against	65	66	57	68	70	71	52	86	77
No opinion	23	25	29	23	23	22	32	12	17
	100	100	100	100	100	100	100	100	100

CLASS STRUGGLE

Question: *"Do you consider class struggle to be detrimental or do you think it is necessary?"*

	Detrimental	Necessary	Undecided	Never heard of class struggle	
	%	%	%	%	
Total population - June 1950	45	21	22	12	= 100
- December 1971	32	28	25	15	= 100
- September 1974	42	25	26	7	= 100
- November 1976	41	24	24	11	= 100

CAPITALISM

Question: *"Think about the word capitalism for a moment. Many things might come to mind. May I read a few of them to you? Please tell me in each case whether capitalism could come to mind."*

A

	February 1975 Yes	No	Undecided	
	%	%	%	
Profit	83	8	9	= 100
Entrepreneurial spirit	78	10	12	= 100
Efficiency	76	12	12	= 100
Successful	71	14	15	= 100
Economic crises	69	17	14	= 100
Progress	65	18	17	= 100
Democracy	56	29	15	= 100
Exploitation	53	31	16	= 100
Freedom	52	28	20	= 100
Class struggle	51	29	20	= 100
Prosperity for everybody	44	39	17	= 100
Authoritarian	44	31	25	= 100
Fairness	35	44	21	= 100
War	32	46	22	= 100

COUNTRY OF CHOICE

Question: "*Assuming that you have a choice between these two countries, in which country would you rather live?*" "*And which country is more like West Germany?*"

	November 1978	
	Conditions in -	
	country of choice	West Germany
	%	%
In the one country everyone is fully covered by insurance - for unemployment, accident, old age - for everything. But the taxes are high and there are a lot of government regulations	30	49
In the other country, only the poorer people are cared for; the others are expected to help themselves, at least in part. In this country the taxes are low and the individual can do more for himself/herself and can make his/her own decisions	56	34
Undecided	14	17
	100	100

SECURITY FIRST

Question: "*There are various words printed on these cards. These words are capable of arousing both pleasant feelings and unpleasant feelings in different people. Could you please distribute the cards onto this sheet according to how you feel? If there is any word that you simply cannot decide about, please lay the card aside.*" (C)

A

	February 1976			
	Pleasant	Unpleasant	Undecided	
	%	%	%	
Security	87	6	7	= 100
Germany	81	5	14	= 100
Research	81	7	12	= 100
Progress	81	7	12	= 100
Television	75	15	10	= 100
Future	70	13	17	= 100
The present	67	16	17	= 100
Work	67	19	14	= 100
Society	60	20	20	= 100
Tradition	59	25	16	= 100
School	54	27	19	= 100
The past	42	38	20	= 100
Emancipation	40	39	21	= 100
Politics	36	44	20	= 100
Socialism	24	59	17	= 100

COMMUNISM

Question: *"A lot is said and written about Communism today, but what do people really mean when they talk about Communism? Please read the following statements and then tell me which of them, in your view, are part of the goals and ideas of Communism?"* (C) *(Addition for half-group: "How did Marx and Lenin imagine Communism?") Also, which of these goals do you personally approve of?"* (C)

A

	December 1978		
	Goals and ideas of Communism %	Communism à la Marx and Lenin %	Goals personally approved of %
No private ownership of the means of production, nationalization of industry	78	74	8
The government controls the economy	74	71	11
Abolishment of class differences so that no group is more powerful or more privileged than another	67	73	36
Aim for a world revolution, so all countries can become Communist	67	66	2
Try to convince everyone of the advantages of Communism	65	64	3
The Communist party determines to a great extent how people are to live their lives	64	57	2
Newspaper, radio and television are means of propaganda and are government-controlled	64	58	3
Since everyone earns about the same amount, the differences in income are insignificant	57	62	34
The workers' struggle against the ruling class	55	59	10
Since educating the children is taken over by the state, parents have essentially no control	50	47	2
Religion is the 'opium of the people' and is combatted as such	43	44	3
No more exploitation of man	43	47	58
Social conditions can only be changed by force, through revolution	39	42	1
Workers have the greatest influence on society	38	42	11
Everybody is to work according to his ability and be paid according to his needs	21	21	39
The alienation of people from their work is overcome; everyone has a say at work	13	14	22
Everyone can speak his opinion freely	12	15	60
Freedom for all to live as they see fit	11	15	48
Tolerance toward other views, admit other opinions	9	10	50
	870	881	403

COMMUNISM A GOOD IDEA?

Question: *"Three people are talking about Communism. Would you please read this and tell me which of the three comes closest to what you think?"* (ill.)

A

	December 1978 %
"I think the very idea of Communism is a mistake. And the existing Communist states, which are based on this idea, serve as a deterrent."	47
"I think the idea of Communism is good, but I don't like the way the existing Communist states practice Communism."	35
"I think the idea of Communism is good, and the states which have developed their social systems in accordance with it are certainly superior to the capitalist states."	3
Undecided	15
	100

SUPPORT FOR EXTREMIST PARTIES

Question: *"Supposing a Communist party (Half group: 'a new National Socialist Party') tried to assume power. How would you react? Here are various possibilities."* (L)

A

	Power assumed by -				
	Communist Party		National Socialist Party		
I would -	1972 Aug. %	1974 March %	1953 Nov. %	1962 Aug. %	1972 Sept. %
do all I could to prevent this happening	41	44	25	34	40
be against it but would do nothing in particular	38	40	29	29	39
not care	9	7	20	18	12
welcome it and support it	3	2	5	2	2
welcome it but do nothing in particular to support it	3	3	8	5	5
No reply	9	4	13	12	2
	103	100	100	100	100

FAITH IN DEMOCRACY

Question: *"Think a moment about the host of problems we are faced with as a result of the rapid growth of the world's population, the scarcity of raw materials, food stuffs and sources of energy and the growth of the economy. Do you think we are able to cope with these problems through our democratic form of government with numerous parties in the parliament or do all these problems require a one party system headed by a strong government in the future?"*

	We can manage with our democracy %	A one-party system is required %	Undecided %	
Total population - April 1975	66	18	16	= 100
- November 1978	77	9	14	= 100

PERSONAL COMMITMENT

Question: *"Is there anything, any idea at all that you think is worth committing yourself to completely?"*
Yes: *"What is it? What do you think?"* (O)

A

	May 1966	December 1977
	%	%
Yes, there is something	42	48
namely:		
family	22	22
personal and human freedom	3	7
social ideals	3	2
Germany, my people, my country	2	3
the Christian religion	2	3
peace	2	2
other ideals	3	3
other responses	5	6
No, there is nothing	58	52
	100	100

THE ARMY

Question: *"Do you generally speaking have a good opinion or not such a good opinion of the Federal Armed Forces?"*

	1964 Jan.	1969 June	1971 April	1980 Dec.
	%	%	%	%
Good opinion	36	33	35	47
Yes and no	26	30	25	27
Not such a good opinion	22	24	27	16
No opinion	16	13	13	10
	100	100	100	100

Question: *"Do you believe that people respect a young man who has served in the Army more than someone who has not served, or don't you think so?"*

	August 1968				
	Don't believe so	Is more respected	Depends	No opinion	
	%	%	%	%	
Total population	59	22	15	4	= 100
Men	62	20	15	3	= 100
Women	56	25	14	5	= 100

CONSCIENTIOUS OBJECTORS

Question: *"If you think for a moment about conscientious objectors, are they for the most part people who out of an honest sense of conviction do not want to serve as soldiers, or are most of them simply interested in evading the military service?"*

	August 1968				
	Have honest conviction %	Are evading service %	Undecided %	No opinion %	
Total population	31	45	18	6	= 100
Total men	30	48	18	4	= 100
Men who are or have been in the army	27	47	24	2	= 100
Men who haven't been in the army	30	49	17	4	= 100
Total women	32	42	18	8	= 100

MILITARY VS. ALTERNATIVE SERVICE

Question put to men: *"A law has now been passed to the effect that in the future every person liable for military service will be able to choose freely between military service and alternative service. What is your opinion? Are you basically for or against letting every draftee choose freely between military service and alternative service in the future?"*

	August 1977							
	Total	Age groups				Party preference		
	men %	16-29 %	30-44 %	45-59 %	60 and over %	SPD %	CDU/CSU %	FDP %
For	54	75	57	40	34	68	35	64
Against	38	17	36	49	57	26	56	28
Undecided	8	8	7	11	9	6	9	8
	100	100	100	100	100	100	100	100

UNIVERSAL DRAFT

Question: *"The introduction of a universal draft including women has recently been under discussion. If, in such a case, the women were not required to bear arms but only to perform medical and administrative services, would you favor or oppose this idea?"*

A

	September 1979		
	Total %	Men %	Women %
Oppose	50	43	55
Favor	43	50	37
Undecided	7	7	8
	100	100	100

ISSUES

Question: "*Which, in your opinion, is the most important question we in West Germany should at present concern ourselves with?*" (O)

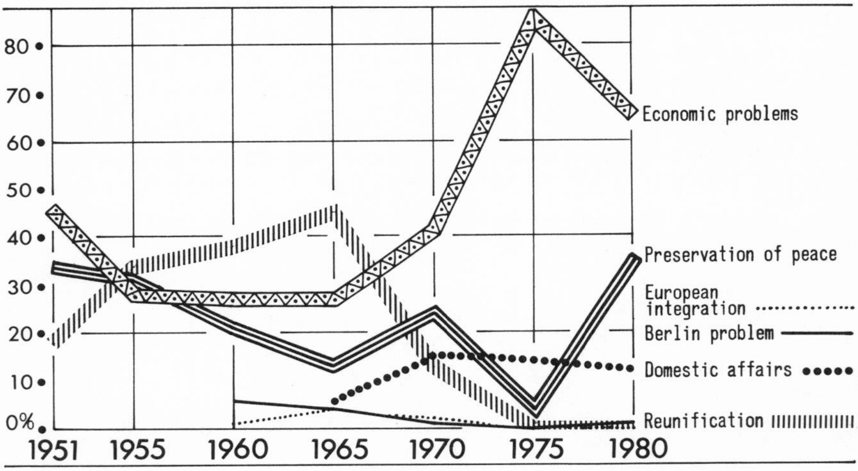

CONTROVERSIAL ISSUES

Question: *"There are some things which even the best of friends have different opinions on. We've written some things down on these cards which we'd like you to read. Where would you say that's really a controversial subject, which even good friends might be at odds about?"* (C) (2 half-groups)

A

	August 1979 %
About Franz Josef Strauss	63
Whether:	
— the death sentence should be re-introduced	63
— most of the unemployed really want to work	60
— it's a good thing to have so many foreigners living in our country	58
— there should be no restrictions on abortion	56
— we should tighten up our penal laws and punish criminals more severely	55
— Communists should be allowed to become teachers	54
— members of the NPD should be allowed to become teachers	49
— it's a good thing for mothers to work	49
— it's bad for children to be spanked now and then	46
— we should continue to feel guilty with regard to Israel	44
— it makes any sense to defend ourselves in case of war	43
— the benefits the unemployed receive are too high	43
— it makes sense to work for German reunification	43
— public servants in West Germany enjoy too many privileges	41
— there should be a speed limit of 100 kilometers on the highways	40
— we're threatened by Russia	37
— the government should do more to regulate parent-child relations by law	33
— exploitation would be eliminated completely by nationalizing the banks, industry and all the means of production	30
— we should work for the political unification of Western Europe	28
— there should be commercial television stations in addition to public ones	23
None of the above	5

MORE REPRESENTATION NEEDED

Question: *"If somebody says that 'Despite the great number of interest groups exisitng today in West Germany there are still lots of people whose interests aren't really represented properly' - would you say this statement is correct or not?"* (Correct = 40%)

"Whom are you thinking of in particular, whose interests aren't really represented properly?" (O) (40% = 100)

"And would you classify yourself as one of those whose interests aren't really represented properly?"

	February 1976				
	Total	Age groups			
	pop.	16-29	30-44	45-59	60 and over
	%	%	%	%	%
Retired people, old people	34	29	29	28	50
The homeless, anomic persons	19	20	23	21	12
Young people, pupils, students, apprentices	19	35	22	13	4
Handicapped persons	18	22	24	12	13
Women: housewives, working mothers, divorced women with children, unmarried mothers, widows	9	8	13	12	3
Blue-collar workers	7	6	9	5	6
The middle class, small-scale businessmen	5	3	4	8	7
Foreign workers, foreigners	5	9	5	4	2
War victims, refugees	4	2	4	4	8
Self-employeds, professionals	2	2	1	x	6
Ordinary citizens	2	3	2	2	2
Farmers	2	2	2	1	1
Unemployed persons	2	4	3	1	x
Other groups	11	13	13	12	6
No reply	10	9	10	12	11
	149	167	164	135	131
Include myself -					
Yes	40	35	37	40	51
No	52	58	56	52	40
No reply	8	7	7	8	9
	100	100	100	100	100

PROMOTION OF THE FAMILY

Question: *"Many proposals have been made recently to promote the family. Some of them are listed here. Which of these seem especially important to you, which ones should politicians work hardest for?"* (L)

B

	November 1979 %
That families with children receive financial support, e.g. in the form of tax breaks, rent subsidies	61
That larger apartments be made available to families with children	58
That more recognition be given to the work involved in being a mother	57
That more centers be set up for children, such as playgrounds, nursery schools, day-care centers	51
That the importance of the family find greater recognition	50
Increased family allowances, so that less mothers have to work	50
Making more part-time jobs available for mothers	43
That families receive a government subsidy for new-born babies	38
That more children be born in West Germany	37
Introduction of a child-raising allowance for gainfully employed and non-working mothers for one or two years after they have a baby	37
That the father, as well as the mother, can be given leave to take care of the baby and can receive a child-raising allowance	28

VOLUNTARY CHARITY GROUPS

Question: *"What do you think - how important are voluntary charity groups for us today?"*

	1960 %	1967 %	1973 %	1979 %
Very important, important	55	57	80	89
Less/not so important	28	26	12	4
Rather superfluous	8	6	1	1
No opinion	9	11	7	6
	100	100	100	100

HELPING WITH CHARITY WORK

Question: *"Could you imagine yourself helping in some way with charity work, that is to say, if you had enough time—or is that out of the question for you?"*

A

	1962 March %	1967 Dec. %	1973 Sept. %	1979 April %
I could imagine helping	49	47	41	37
It's out of the question	47	50	54	59
I already help out on a volunteer basis	4	3	5	4
	100	100	100	100

FINANCING

Question: *"From whom should these organizations* above all *get their money - what do* you *think is* best*?"* (L, only 3 answers)

	1973 Sept. %	1979 April %
From the government, from taxes	76	62
From the church	55	58
From business, from the employers	45	37
Through television lottery	18	37
From private people, through donations and house-to-house collections	21	30
From the labor unions	26	27
Through membership dues	16	25
Through the sale of charity stamps	12	22
	269	298

INFLUENCES

Question: *"Which of the people on this list do you feel exert too great an influence on political life in West Germany today?"*

A

	November 1978 %		November 1978 %
Labor unions	46	Federal constitutional court	21
Multinational industries	36	The Catholic Church	17
TV	34	Scientists, organizers	14
Big banks	30	Farmers' associations	11
German industrialists	29	Conservative politicians	9
The press	29	Former Nazis	9
Government officials, bureaucracy	27	The Protestant Church	6
Leftists in politics	24	The Federal Army, generals	6
Certain student associations	24	None of these	4

THE POLITICAL SPECTRUM

Question: *"How would you describe your own political position? Would you say - ?"*

	November 1978						
	Far left %	Moderately left %	Center %	Moderately right %	Far right %	No reply %	
Total population	1	17	45	27	4	6	= 100
AGE GROUPS							
16-29	3	24	42	21	2	8	= 100
30-44	1	19	45	28	3	4	= 100
45-59	1	12	45	33	4	5	= 100
60 and over	1	10	49	27	8	5	= 100
POLITICAL INTEREST							
Interested	3	23	40	27	5	2	= 100
Not especially	x	12	49	29	3	7	= 100
Not at all	1	8	51	20	6	14	= 100
PARTY PREFERENCE							
SPD	1	35	46	12	1	5	= 100
CDU/CSU	x	1	41	45	9	4	= 100
FDP	1	10	63	22	1	3	= 100

POLITICAL PARTICIPATION

Question: *"Are you interested in politics?"*

	January 1980			
	Yes	Not very much	Not at all	
	%	%	%	
Total population	48	43	9	= 100
AGE GROUPS				
16-29	44	47	9	= 100
30-44	51	43	6	= 100
45-59	53	41	6	= 100
60 and over	44	42	14	= 100
EDUCATION				
Elementary	40	49	11	= 100
Secondary	64	31	5	= 100

	Women						
	1952 June	1960 Jan.	1965 Sept.	1969 Sept.	1973 Feb.	1977 Nov.	1980 Jan.
	%	%	%	%	%	%	%
Yes	11	11	21	27	34	36	33
Not very much	39	41	51	50	46	47	53
Not at all	50	48	28	23	20	17	14
	100	100	100	100	100	100	100

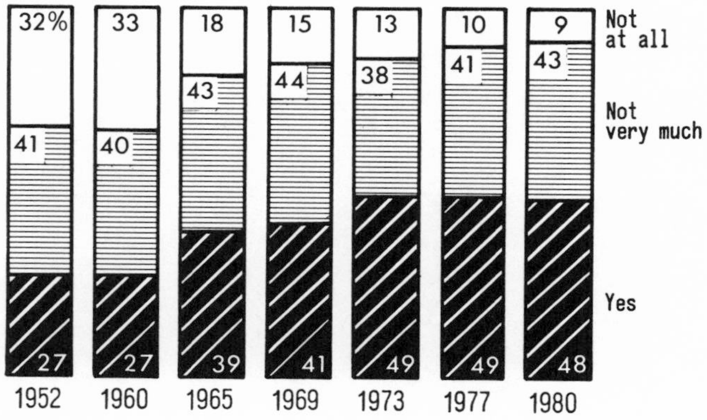

POLITICS MEN'S BUSINESS?

Question: *''You hear so frequently: 'Politics is men's business'. Would you agree with that or not?''*

	Agree		Don't agree		Undecided	
	Men	Women	Men	Women	Men	Women
	%	%	%	%	%	%
June 1966	44	32	42	51	14	17
March 1974	31	28	62	65	7	7

SOURCES OF INFORMATION

Question: *''What is most important to you when you want to form a political opinion - television, radio, newspapers or personal conversations?''* (One response only)

	January 1980							
	Men	Women	Education		Age groups			
			Elementary	Secondary	16-29	30-44	45-59	60 and over
	%	%	%	%	%	%	%	%
Television	48	52	56	40	45	47	56	55
Newspapers	26	18	17	31	22	25	19	19
Personal conversations	16	16	15	18	19	18	14	13
Radio	5	7	6	6	5	5	5	7
Undecided	5	7	6	5	9	5	6	6
	100	100	100	100	100	100	100	100

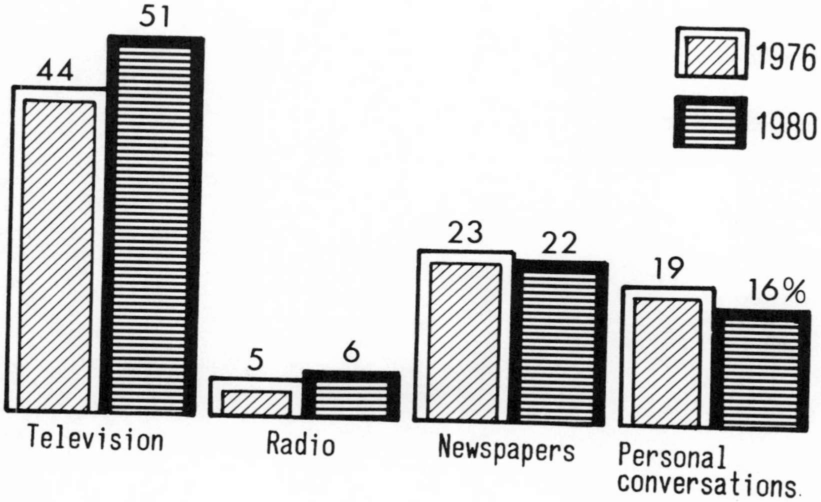

POLITICAL ACTIVITY

Question: *"Various ways of taking part in politics are listed here. Could you tell me which of these apply to you?"* (L)

	1973 Dec. %	1978 Nov. %	Age groups 16-29 %	30-44 %	45-59 %	60 and over %
I vote regularly (federal legislature elections, state legislature elections, local elections)	60	73	60	78	80	75
I keep myself informed about what is happening in politics	55	46	40	49	48	45
There are political issues which I strongly believe in, and I stand up for my convictions when talking to others	33	40	42	45	40	33
I often discuss politics with others	44	39	39	45	36	34
I inform myself in detail on certain political issues	25	31	35	33	28	26
Before the last federal election or at other elections I have supported a specific party/candidate	17	18	11	17	19	25
I sometimes attend lectures, discussions or other events on political issues	11	9	10	11	9	7
I am involved politically in a party, club or association	5	7	7	8	8	5
I get in touch with representatives, authorities, or simply with the public when I have a specific goal I wish to achieve	x	5	3	5	6	4
I sometimes participate in protests, support protest groups	x	3	8	3	1	1
None of these	15	8	13	4	7	11
	265	279	268	298	282	266

Question: *"Do you like a man/woman to be active in politics, or don't you like the idea?"*

A

	Men 1965 %	1971 %	1976 %	1979 %	Women 1965 %	1971 %	1976 %	1979 %
Concerning men -								
Like the idea	47	70	82	70	35	62	70	59
Don't like the idea	16	8	4	5	30	17	9	10
Undecided, depends	37	22	14	25	35	21	21	31
	100	100	100	100	100	100	100	100
Concerning women -								
Like the idea	27	56	62	57	32	68	66	68
Don't like the idea	52	26	16	19	37	20	14	12
Undecided, depends	21	18	22	24	31	12	20	20
	100	100	100	100	100	100	100	100

POLITICS AS A PROFESSION

Question: *"If you had a* son, *would you like him to become a politician, or not?"*

A

	1955 Dec.	1965 Apr.	1976 Sept.	Age groups 16-29	30-44	45-59	60 and over
	Total population						
	%	%	%	%	%	%	%
Would not like it	70	51	43	36	40	46	52
Would like it	9	14	19	13	24	21	18
Undecided	21	35	38	51	36	33	30
	100	100	100	100	100	100	100

Question: *"If you had a* daughter, *would you like her to become a politician, or not?"*

A

	September 1976						
	Total pop.	Men	Women	Age groups 16-29	30-44	45-59	60 and over
	%	%	%	%	%	%	%
Would not like it	40	39	42	33	34	42	54
Would like it	20	18	20	17	23	23	14
Undecided	40	43	38	50	43	35	32
	100	100	100	100	100	100	100

SORE SPOTS

Question: *"Here are a number of points of view. Which of them do you share?"*

	1973 Dec. %
There is more unfairness and inconsiderateness in politics than in many other areas	51
Anyone who wants to achieve something in politics today must belong to a political party or organization	49
There are not enough ways of influencing political decision-making today	43
Political problems are often so complicated today that it is difficult to form judgments	43
Those active in politics often end up with more loss than profit	19
A person with my education and profession can have more of an influence on political decision-making than do many others	5
	210

JOIN A POLITICAL PARTY?

Question: *"Would you be willing to join a political party?"*

	January 1980			
	No	Yes	Already a member	
	%	%	%	
Total population	78	13	9	= 100
Men	70	17	13	= 100
Women	86	9	5	= 100
AGE GROUPS				
16-29	73	21	6	= 100
30-44	73	16	11	= 100
45-59	79	10	11	= 100
60 and over	89	4	7	= 100
EDUCATION				
Elementary	83	10	7	= 100
Secondary	70	18	12	= 100
PARTY PREFERENCE				
SPD	78	13	9	= 100
CDU/CSU	78	12	10	= 100
FDP	82	9	9	= 100

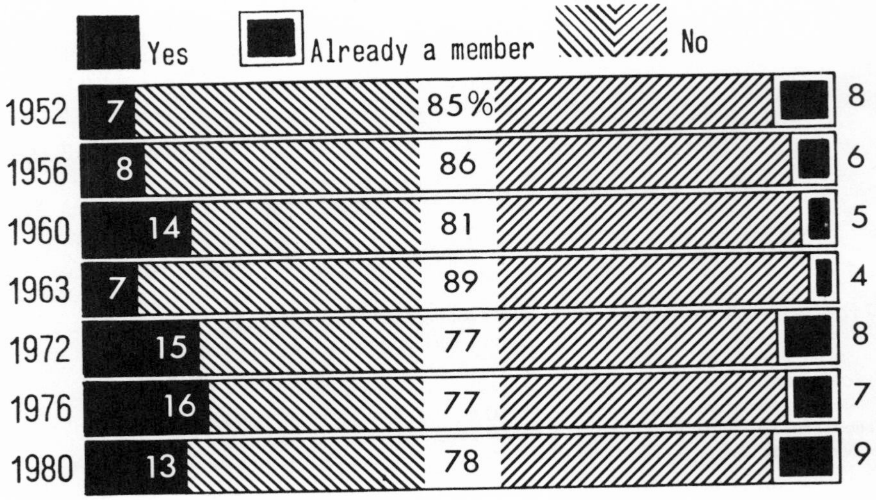

IF OPINIONS DIFFER . . .

Question: *"If you find out about somebody that he thinks completely differently from you on important points, would you continue to trust this person completely or not really?"*

	1956 June	1977 Sept.	Age groups			
	Total population		16-29	30-44	45-59	60 and over
	%	%	%	%	%	%
Trust completely	52	49	54	55	50	35
Would not trust completely	39	35	29	30	35	46
Undecided	9	16	17	15	15	19
	100	100	100	100	100	100

POLITICAL IDEALS

Question: *"Two people are talking about politics here. Which of the two would you tend to agree with?"* (ill., X)

	July 1960	December 1975
	%	%
I think the most important thing is for people to be well off. I've had enough of political ideals and don't want to have anything to do with weltanschauung any more	41	40
I find politics much too materialistic these days. Everyone is only concerned about earning money. What we need are ideals to inspire us	39	39
Undecided	20	21
	100	100

. . . AND IDOLS

Question: *"Here is a list of famous men. Which of them, in your opinion, are models for us today?"* (L)

	January 1974				
	Total pop.	Age groups 16-29	30-44	45-59	60 and over
	%	%	%	%	%
Albert Schweitzer	52	45	55	54	55
John F. Kennedy	45	50	48	45	39
Konrad Adenauer	41	30	38	43	55
Alexander Dubcek	17	19	19	18	11
Willy Brandt	16	17	16	14	16
Kurt Schumacher	15	9	16	19	18
Otto von Bismarck	15	8	12	15	27
Alexander Solzhenitsyn	14	22	13	10	8
Henry Kissinger	13	13	14	12	14
Karl Marx	6	10	5	5	3
Mao Tse-tung	4	6	4	4	1
Che Guevara	3	7	2	1	x
V.I. Lenin	2	3	2	2	1

LAW AND JUSTICE

Question: *"Generally speaking, can we or can we not have complete confidence in German justice, that is, the judges and the courts?"*

	1964 Nov. Total	1974 Jan. Total	1978 Nov. Total	Age groups			
				16-29	30-44	45-59	60 and over
	%	%	%	%	%	%	%
Can have complete confidence	26	32	40	34	39	38	49
Cannot have complete confidence	28	32	26	27	31	26	20
To some extent	30	29	28	32	25	31	26
Undecided	16	7	6	7	5	5	5
	100	100	100	100	100	100	100

CRIME RATE

Question: *"Do you have the impression that the crime rate in Germany is generally increasing, or would you not say so?"*

	April 1975				
	Total pop.	Age groups			
		14-29	30-44	45-59	60 and over
	%	%	%	%	%
Crime is increasing	75	63	73	79	88
Would not say so	18	25	21	14	8
Undecided	7	12	6	7	4
	100	100	100	100	100

Question: *"Is there any district around here, within a radius of, say, one kilometer, where you would not like to go alone at night?"*

	June 1965			October 1975		
	Total	Men	Women	Total	Men	Women
	%	%	%	%	%	%
No, there is none	51	75	29	43	69	20
Yes, there is	43	20	63	51	24	74
Don't know	6	5	8	6	7	6
	100	100	100	100	100	100

STEALING

Question: *"Have you had anything stolen within the last three years, or has this not happened to you within the last three years?"*

	1960 %	1971 %	1975 %	1979 %
Something stolen one or more times	18	24	20	27
Nothing was stolen	82	76	80	73
	100	100	100	100

PORNOGRAPHY

Question: *"Perhaps you know that pornographic publications may not be sold on the open market, that is, descriptions or illustrations that are supposedly sexually stimulating. If it were up to you, would you be for or against the unrestricted selling of pornographic publications?"*

E

	1970 Nov. Total population	1974 April Total population	Men	Women	Age groups 16-29	30-44	45-59	60 and over
	%	%	%	%	%	%	%	%
For	31	29	38	22	46	40	19	8
Against	51	49	38	58	27	38	59	76
Undecided	18	22	24	20	27	22	22	16
	100	100	100	100	100	100	100	100

LAW AGAINST CHILD-BEATING

Question: *"There is a law in Sweden which prohibits parents from beating their children. What is your opinion—would you favor or oppose the passage of such a law in this country?"*

	April 1979 Oppose law %	Favor law %	Undecided %	
Total population	48	31	21	= 100
EDUCATION				
Elementary	50	28	22	= 100
Secondary	44	38	18	= 100

ABORTION

Question: ''*A question about abortion (1973 and 1974: . . . which is prohibited according to § 218 of the penal code): Here are three opinions. Which opinion would you agree with?*'' (L, X)

Opinion 1:
''*Abortion should only be permitted in very specific cases, i.e. when it is recommended by a doctor, or when the socio-economic situation warrants it, or for other pressing reasons.*''

Opinion 2:
''*Every woman should have the basic right to terminate a pregnancy during the first three months.*''

Opinion 3:
''*Abortion should be prohibited again (1973 and 1974: remain prohibited); article 218 should be reintroduced in the original version (1973 and 1974: not be changed).*''

	1 Medical or socio-economic reasons %	2 Basic right %	3 Prohibit according to § 218 %	Undecided %	
Total population - June 1973	41	38	15	6	= 100
- November 1979	50	31	12	7	= 100
Men	48	32	12	8	= 100
Women	53	30	13	4	= 100
AGE GROUPS					
16-29	45	45	4	6	= 100
30-44	48	40	6	6	= 100
45-59	58	24	12	6	= 100
60 and over	51	13	27	9	= 100
DENOMINATION					
Protestant	50	36	7	7	= 100
Catholic	54	21	20	5	= 100
Other/None	34	53	8	5	= 100

Question: ''*I would like to describe a case to you: A young married (half group: unmarried) woman is expecting a child. It has been attested that she is emotionally and economically unable to care for the child, and she has therefore had an abortion. Do you believe that this young woman has made the right decision, or shouldn't she have done this?*''

A

	October 1979			
	Made right decision %	Shouldn't have done this %	Undecided %	
In the case of the -				
married woman	52	28	20	= 100
unmarried woman	53	27	20	= 100

DIVORCE

Question: *"What's your opinion - should divorce be made as easy as possible or as difficult as possible, or should marriage be completely indissoluble?"*

Follow-up question put to persons who say that marriage should be indissoluble: *"Do you mean all marriages, or only if the vows were exchanged in church?"*

C

	Total		Men		Women	
	1953	1979	1953	1979	1953	1979
	%	%	%	%	%	%
Marriage should be indissoluble	32	10	28	7	34	12
- all marriages	27	8	24	6	28	10
- only if vows were exchanged in church	5	2	4	1	6	2
Divorce should be made as difficult as possible	29	28	29	25	29	30
Divorce should be made as easy as possible	14	31	16	38	12	26
Leave it as it is	15	16	18	18	14	15
Don't know	10	15	9	12	11	17
	100	100	100	100	100	100

Question: *"Does the current divorce law make divorce too easy, or too difficult?"*

A

	July 1979				
	Too difficult	Too easy	Just right	Undecided	
	%	%	%	%	
Total population	34	25	10	31	= 100
Men	38	25	9	28	= 100
Women	31	25	10	34	= 100

WIFE FAVORED

Question: *"Do you feel that the current divorce law is more favorable for the husband, for the wife, or is it fair to both?"*

A

	July 1979				
	More favorable for the wife	More favorable for the husband	Fair to both	Undecided	
	%	%	%	%	
Men	60	1	21	18	= 100
Women	42	4	29	25	= 100

WHO PAYS?

Question: *''Nowadays, after a divorce, the breadwinner or the one who earns the most has to pay the other alimony, even if this person is not to be blamed for the broken marriage. Two people are talking about this here. Which of the two would you agree with?''* (ill.)

A

	July 1979 Men %	July 1979 Women %
''I think it's a good thing that the new divorce laws basically protect the financially weaker partner. After all, this person has often given up his/her training and a job just for the sake of the family	39	53
''I think it's a bad thing that according to the new divorce laws the one who did most to earn money for the family is the fool. This person can pay after the divorce as well, whether he/she is to blame for the broken marriage or not	40	30
Undecided	21	17
	100	100

CUSTODY

Question: *''Nowadays, after a divorce, whoever is best able to care for the children overall is granted custody, rather than the parent who was not at fault. Two people are talking about this. Which of the two says what you tend to think?* (ill.)

	July 1979 Men %	July 1979 Women %
''I think it's a good thing that the child's welfare now has priority and the person who is not at fault in the divorce doesn't get custody automatically anymore. After all, this person is not necessarily the better parent.''	56	51
''The idea of giving the child's welfare priority is good, but I think it's unfair for someone who may have done everything to keep the marriage together to have the children taken away on top of everything else.''	29	33
Undecided	15	16
	100	100

RIGHT TO PRIVACY

Question: "*Demands are often made to improve the standard of data protection within the Federal Republic, to guarantee that personal information given in confidence is not passed on to parties for whom it is not destined. Have you ever heard of these demands or have you not?*" (Yes, heard of it = 76 percent)

"*Who do you think is most interested in getting a hold of personal data, from whom must one be most protected? Could you tell me with the help of this list?*" (L)

A

	October 1978 %
Insurance companies	54
Businesses which advertise a lot	50
Political parties and groups	49
Commercial representatives	48
Employers, professional superiors	47
Mail-order firms	43
Internal Revenue Service	42
Banks	41
Police	36
Government agencies	33
Law courts	29
Civic and municipal administration, city hall	25
Employment office	19
The Church	13
Friends, acquaintances, neighbors	12
Distant relatives	9
Close family members	7
No reply	4
	561

STUDENT DEMONSTRATIONS

Question: "*There are different opinions about student demonstrations; some of them are listed here. Which of them do you agree with?*" (L)

A

	July 1967 %
At best, students should demonstrate when university problems are at issue	42
Students definitely should be allowed to demonstrate about political issues	26
Students shouldn't demonstrate at all	20
Undecided	12
	100

A SMALL GROUP

Question: *"Do you believe that many students back the unrest and demonstrations, or is it only a rather small group?"*

A

	July 1967 Rather small group	Many	Don't know	
	%	%	%	
Total population	53	30	17	= 100

	Correct answer	Vague/incorrect answer	Don't know	
	%	%	%	
Total population - December 1968	14	5	81	= 100

Question: *"A few years ago there was the APO, the extra-parliamentary opposition, led by leftist students with Rudi Dutschke at the head. Do you remember the APO or Rudi Dutschke?"* (Yes = 74%)

"If Rudi Dutschke and other supporters of the former APO were to found a new leftist party, would you be in favor of this or not?"

	Favor leftist party - yes	no	Undecided	APO unknown	
	%	%	%	%	
Total population - February 1976	4	64	6	26	= 100

THE RIGHT TO DEMONSTRATE

Question: *"There has been a lot said in recent months concerning the rights and freedoms accorded by the Basic Law. Here are two people discussing the matter. With which of the two would you tend to agree?"* (ill.)

	May 1969
	%
"The recent student unrest has once again proved that our Basic Law often allows for too much freedom. When peace and order are at stake, some of these freedoms such as the right to demonstrate should be curtailed."	53
"The freedoms accorded by the Basic Law must not be curtailed due to such unrest. These rights must under all circumstances continue to be upheld even if some people should misuse them."	39
Undecided	8
	100

BAADER-MEINHOF GROUP

Question: *"Have you ever heard the names Baader, Meinhof or Mahler - they belong to a group that had something to do with department store arson?"* (Yes, heard of them = 82 percent)

"Two people are talking about this group here. Which of the two would you tend to agree with?"* (ill.)

The one:

"The people in this group may have acted out of political conviction in the beginning, but now they have lowered themselves to becoming simple criminals."

The other:

"Even though I am not in agreement with many of the things this group has done, I am convinced that even now they are acting out of political conviction."

A

	March 1971				
	Criminals	Political fighters	Undecided	Never heard of them	
	%	%	%	%	
Total population	51	18	13	18	= 100
AGE GROUPS					
16-29	51	25	10	14	= 100
30-44	50	18	19	13	= 100
45-59	59	14	10	17	= 100
60 and over	41	13	16	30	= 100

*The so-called Baader-Meinhof group was the most prominent terrorist group in West Germany.

SHELTER FOR TERRORISTS?

Question: *"Some of the members of this group are still being pursued by the police. Assuming that someone from this group would ask you for shelter for the night—would you take him/her in for one night or wouldn't you do this?"*

A

	March 1971				
	Would not do it	Would take him/her in	Undecided	Never heard of group	
	%	%	%	%	
Total population	68	5	9	18	= 100
AGE GROUPS					
16-29	65	10	11	14	= 100
30-44	75	7	5	13	= 100
45-59	69	3	11	17	= 100
60 and over	63	1	6	30	= 100

HUNGER STRIKE

Question: "*A member of the Baader-Meinhof group, Holger Meins, recently died in custody while awaiting trial. He was on a hunger strike and had refused all food. Have you heard of this case?*" (Yes, have heard 97%)

"*Two people are talking about the way the prison authorities behaved in this case. With whom would you be more likely to agree?*" (ill., X)

	December 1974
	%
"When a prisoner goes on a hunger strike, he is quite aware of the danger he's getting into. The authorities did try to feed him artificially and, if something went wrong in spite of that, they cannot be blamed."	77
"I think things should never have reached the point where Holger Meins could die in prison. The authorities failed to do their job; they should have seen to it that Meins didn't starve."	13
Undecided	10
	100

FORCED NUTRITION

Question: "*Are you in favor of or opposed to artificially feeding prisoners against their will who are on a hunger strike?*"

	February 1975			
	Against forced nutrition	For forced nutrition	Undecided	
	%	%	%	
Total population	67	25	8	= 100

FAIR TRIAL

Question: "*The trial in Stammheim of the terrorists Baader, Ensslin and Raspe was concluded a short time ago. What is your opinion: All in all, would you say that it was a fair trial, that is to say, were the defendants and their attorneys given every chance to defend themselves, or were they hindered in this?*"

A

	May 1977						
	Total	Education		Age groups			
	pop.	Elementary	Secondary	16-29	30-44	45-59	60 and over
	%	%	%	%	%	%	%
Fair trial	60	58	64	58	64	58	60
Defense was hindered	10	7	16	14	10	8	7
Impossible to say	30	35	20	28	26	34	33
	100	100	100	100	100	100	100

THE SCHLEYER ABDUCTION

Question: *"If you think about what you've heard and read about the Schleyer kidnapping—did the federal government take resolute and deliberate action, or don't you think so?"*

	September 1977 Resolute and deliberate %	Don't think so %	Undecided, no response %	
Total population	48	27	25	= 100

Question: *Do you think there will be a rash of such kidnappings in the near future?"*

	Yes %	No %	Undecided %	
Total population - September 1977	90	2	8	= 100

WHO IS TO BLAME?

Question: *"Speaking in general, what do you think is the reason and who is to blame for the fact that acts of terrorism like the Schleyer kidnapping occur more frequently these days than they used to? Which of the views that are listed here would you include too?"* (L)

	Sept. 1977 %
The government did not intervene soon enough to fight the terrorists and their sympathizers	53
We neglected to put through necessary reforms at a time when the present terrorists were not yet so radical	40
The more terrorists there are in our prisons, the more others there will be who will commit new acts of terrorism to blackmail us into releasing the imprisoned	39
Our whole political climate is at fault because there's always just talk about the problems and no action	31
There is an international wave of violence which has spread into our country too	30
The terrorists want the battle against them to turn our constitutionally governed state into a police state and hope this will give them new supporters	25
Other/no response	3
	221

SUPPORT

Question: *"Do terrorist sympathizers come from all walks of life or do particular groups feel closer to the terrorists?"* If Yes: *"From which group do you think the most support comes?"* (L)

	November 1977 %
Yes, sympathizers come from certain groups	43
namely, -	
Students	38
Lawyers	32
Communists	23
University professors	18
Writers	12
Rightists, former Nazis	10
Members of the Young Socialists	9
Teachers	8
Artists, actors	7
Journalists	7
Certain groups in the Social Democratic Party	6
Labor unions	2
Certain groups in the Free Democratic Party	2
Certain groups in the Christian Democratic Union	x
None of these	1
No, they don't come from certain groups	57
	100

WHAT IS A SYMPATHIZER?

Question: *"These days you hear a lot in the newspapers and on television about the so-called group of sympathizers, but the question is—what is a sympathizer? I will give you some examples. Please tell me which qualify as sympathizers."* (L)

Someone who -	1977 Nov. %
gives shelter in his home to a terrorist	95
recognizes a terrorist but doesn't notify the police	73
spends money on terrorists as in helping to pay the dental bills for Gudrun Ensslin	68
helps ease conditions for terrorists	67
feels sorry for terrorists, feels they are driven to their crimes out of desperation	56
agrees with the terrorists' criticism of society	36
feels that legal counselors should have the right to visit the terrorists in prison at all times	29
does not want the death penalty introduced for terrorists	18
None of the above	2
	444

BRANDED

Question: *"With which of the following statements would you agree?"* (L, X):

The one:

"I think it is right for those who have shown some understanding for terrorist actions to be confronted with being called 'sympathizers' now."

The other:

"I think it is terrible for those who have shown even the slightest bit of understanding for the terrorists to now be branded as 'sympathizers'—this kind of a manhunt is intolerable."

	November 1977			
	Total	Party preference		
	pop.	SPD	CDU/CSU	FDP
Those having shown understanding -	%	%	%	%
are sympathizers	53	46	65	45
are not sympathizers	28	38	17	32
No opinion	19	16	18	23
	100	100	100	100

THE THREAT OF TERRORISM

Question: *"To what extent do you feel the government is threatened by terrorism? Could you tell me according to this illustration; the lowest box means that the government is hardly threatened. What is your opinion; which box would you choose?"* (ill.)

		1977*	1977*	1977**	1977**	1978	1979
		Sept.	Oct.	Nov.	Nov.	Feb.	July
		%	%	%	%	%	%
Severely threatened	A	30	37	33	34	35	29
	B	37	37	37	38	39	37
	C	23	21	17	20	19	25
Hardly threatened	D	10	5	13	8	7	9
		100	100	100	100	100	100

*) Question: *"How do you see the situation now after the kidnapping of Schleyer and the murders in Cologne . . ."*

**) Question: *"How do you see the situation now after the kidnapping of Schleyer and the freeing of the hostages from the airplane in Mogadishu . . ."*

REJECT USE OF VIOLENCE

Question: *"Three people are discussing whether violence may be acceptable in certain situations. Which of them says what you tend to think?"* (ill.)

	November 1978 %
"I reject the use of violence, whether applied to persons or property. In my opinion, no political goal can justify the use of violence."	70
"The use of violence directed at persons can never be justified. The use of violence directed at property is different; I think it is perfectly permissible in certain situations."	16
"When important political goals are to be met, I think the use of violence directed at property and people is permissible."	7
Undecided	7
	100

DO A GOOD JOB?

Question: *"Do you think that the police do a good job of seeing to our security and keeping order in West Germany, or do you think that more has to be done in this area?"*

B

	More must be done %	Do a good job %	No opinion %	
Total population - June 1971	69	22	9	= 100

SHOOT TO KILL?

Question: *"Deliberations are in progress as to whether the police should be allowed to shoot a criminal with aim to kill if this criminal is armed and the danger exists that he might shoot others. Have you heard about this?"* (Yes, have heard = 64%)

"According to your notions of justice, would such a deliberate shot, in cases where other people's lives are in danger, be compatible with the principles of our constitutional system, or would it not?"

A

	Compatible %	Incompatible %	Undecided %	
Total population - August 1975	56	29	15	= 100

Question: *"If it were up to you to decide, would you be in favor of the police being allowed to shoot a criminal with aim to kill if other lives are in danger, or would you not favor this?"*

A

	August 1975				
	Total pop. %	Age groups 16-29 %	30-44 %	45-59 %	60 and over %
In favor	63	55	63	65	71
Not in favor	24	30	25	22	17
Undecided	13	15	12	13	12
	100	100	100	100	100

POLICEMEN WANTED

Question: *"What is your impression—in West Germany do we have too many or too few policemen?"*
B

	Too few %	Just right %	Too many %	No opinion %	
Total population - October 1972	64	19	4	13	= 100

LIMITATION OF PERSONAL RIGHTS

Question: *"If, as part of the fight against terrorism, the influence of the government and of the police must be strengthened, would you accept a limitation of your personal rights by measures such as surveillance and the searching of houses, or would you refuse this?"*

	1975 May	1977 May	1978 Nov.	Age groups			
	Total population			16-29	30-44	45-59	60 and over
	%	%	%	%	%	%	%
Accept	69	62	53	42	57	56	55
Refuse	21	26	36	47	35	35	28
Undecided	10	12	11	11	8	9	17
	100	100	100	100	100	100	100

FREEDOM NOT RESTRICTED

Question: *"Do you have the feeling that your personal freedom or occupational freedom has been restricted over the last five years through government measures or laws, or wouldn't you say so?"*

	Not restricted %	Restricted %	No reply %	
Total population - June 1976	84	9	7	= 100

A JOB BAN FOR EXTREMISTS

Question: *"There has recently been a lot of discussion as to whether a person belonging to an extremist party should be employed as a public servant. Have you heard about this?"* (Yes = 67 percent)

"Here are two people discussing the matter. Please read it through and tell me with which of them you would tend to agree." (ill.)

	1973 Sept. %
"The state demands a special degree of loyalty from a public servant. But whoever belongs to an extremist political party cannot be expected to support the basic order of free democracy."	52
"If somebody is a member of an extremist political party, that surely doesn't mean to say he is an opponent of the basic order of free democracy. Members of the German Communist Party and the National Democratic Party can make just as good public servants as members of other parties." ..	27
Undecided	21
	100

INVESTIGATION PROCEDURES APPROVED

Question: *"Followers of extremist parties such as Communists or NPD followers and people who support the goals of these parties are not easily allowed to become public servants in West Germany. Two people are talking about these so-called 'job bans'. Which of the two would you tend to agree with?"*

The one:
"I think it is right to investigate those Communists and National Democrats who want to become public servants, to see whether they basically support our government and our legal system. Only then should such people be allowed to become public servants."

The other:
"I am against such investigations and job bans. In my opinion, our free democratic order is not endangered by having a few people of the radical left or right in government service."

	1979 Feb.	1978 Nov.	1976 June	Party preference		
	Total population			SPD	CDU/CSU	FDP
	%	%	%	%	%	%
For the investigations	62	70	64	53	85	56
Against the investigations	24	21	21	31	9	31
Undecided	14	9	15	16	6	13
	100	100	100	100	100	100

CAPITAL PUNISHMENT

Question: *"Are you in principle opposed to or in favor of the death penalty?"*

	January 1980			
	Opposed %	In favor %	Undecided %	
Total population	55	26	19	= 100
AGE GROUPS				
16-29	66	16	18	= 100
30-44	59	24	17	= 100
45-59	54	29	17	= 100
60 and over	42	37	21	= 100
EDUCATION				
Elementary	50	29	21	= 100
Secondary	66	20	14	= 100
PARTY PREFERENCE				
SPD	59	23	18	= 100
CDU/CSU	45	34	21	= 100
FDP	69	16	15	= 100
DENOMINATION				
Protestant	53	27	20	= 100
Catholic	55	27	18	= 100
Other/none	68	20	12	= 100

Question: *"Are you in principle opposed to or in favor of the death penalty?"*

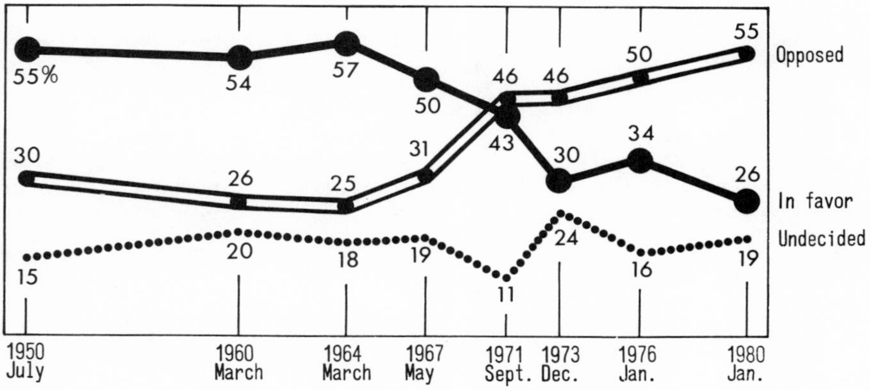

THE FEDERAL PRESIDENT, THE BUNDESRAT, PARLIAMENT

Question: *"Do you think the Federal President should have a greater influence on political life than he has had up to the present or should he have less influence; or do you think he has just the right amount of influence on political life?"*

	Heuss 1953 Jan. %	Lübke 1955 Jan. %	Scheel 1976 Dec. %
More influence	21	17	21
Less influence	5	3	7
Just right	41	56	57
No opinion	33	24	15
	100	100	100

Question: *"How do (did) you like President . . . . ?"*

	Very much %	Well %	Somewhat %	Little, not at all %	No opinion %	
Heinrich Lübke (1959-1969)						
1962 - September	18	51	18	7	6	= 100
1964 - July	11	40	22	19	8	= 100
1967 - July	13	25	25	30	7	= 100
Gustav Heinemann (1969-1974)						
1974 - July	27	50	14	7	2	= 100
Walter Scheel (1974-1979)						
1974 - July	21	52	19	5	3	= 100
1976 - December	16	54	21	6	3	= 100
1978 - September	22	53	18	4	3	= 100
1979 - June	36	47	11	3	3	= 100
Karl Carstens (since 1979)						
1979 - June	7	29	22	26	16	= 100
1980 - February	8	37	29	16	10	= 100
1981 - January	13	39	25	16	7	= 100

THE IDEAL FEDERAL PRESIDENT

Qualities which "a good federal president should have"

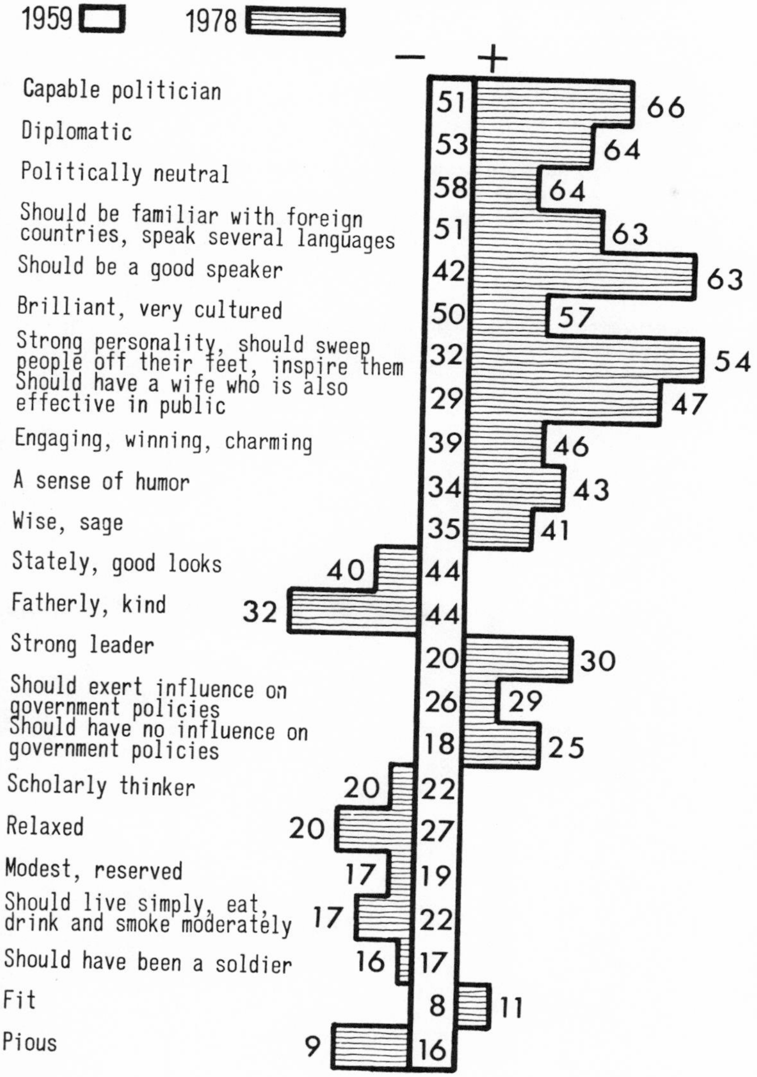

BUNDESRAT MEMBERS

Question: *"Do you happen to know who the Bundesrat consists of, who its members are?"* (L)

A

	1976 Nov. %	1978 Dec. %
Members of the individual state governments	45	32
Minister-presidents of the individual states	31	27
In part, members of the federal parliament, in part members of the federal states	17	15
Experts who are consultants to the federal government	6	5
Representatives of the parties, unions, churches, syndicates	4	4
Don't know	19	22
	122	105

Note: In the West German government system, the Bundesrat largely serves the function of a second legislative chamber. Its members consist of appointed representatives of the state governments.

THE BUNDESRAT

Federal State	Governing Party 1980	Number of votes in the Bundesrat
Baden-Württemberg	CDU	5
Bavaria	CSU	5
Berlin	SPD	4 (only advisory)
Bremen	SPD	3
Hamburg	SPD	3
Hesse	SPD	4
Lower Saxony	CDU	5
North Rhine-Westphalia	SPD	5
Rhineland-Palatinate	CDU	4
Saarland	CDU	3
Schleswig-Holstein	CDU	4
		45

FUNCTION OF BUNDESRAT

Question: *"In Bonn there is the Bundesrat, in addition to the parliament. Do you know what the Bundesrat's function is—what is it responsible for?"* (O)

A

	1976 Nov. %	1979 Jan. %	1980 Nov. %
Correct responses	25	19	21
Vague but not incorrect responses	32	36	28
Incorrect responses	5	3	4
Don't know	38	34	34
Never heard of the Bundesrat	x	8	13
	100	100	100

FEDERALISM OR CENTRALISM?

Question: *"What would you say if all state legislatures and all state governments were dissolved and all laws and political decisions came from Bonn? What do you think of this suggestion?"*

A

	1974 December %	1975 December %	1976 December %	1978 November %	1980 November %
Very good	6 } 17	5 } 15	5 } 14	3 } 10	3 } 9
Good	11	10	9	7	6
Not bad	9	8	8	8	8
Not good	38 } 55	42 } 62	39 } 60	48 } 71	41 } 63
Very bad	17	20	21	23	22
No opinion	19	15	18	11	20
	100	100	100	100	100

	Total pop. %	November 1978 Regional distribution* Northern Germany and West Berlin %	North-Rhine Westphalia %	Rhine-Main/ Southwest %	Bavaria %
Centralists**	10	11	11	10	8
Federalists**	71	68	70	73	72

* see also page 6

** defined by the categories "very good" and "good" or "not good" and "very bad" respectively.

DO WE NEED A PARLIAMENT?

Question: *"Taking a practical point of view, do you think we need a parliament in Bonn and representatives, or could we manage without?"*

	1956 June %	1962 July %	1972 Sept. %	1978 Nov. %
Need parliament	69	69	82	83
Can manage without	10	13	6	7
Undecided	21	18	12	10
	100	100	100	100

Generations in comparison

	June 1956 Age groups				November 1978 Age groups			
	16-29 %	30-44 %	45-59 %	60 and over %	16-29 %	30-44 %	45-59 %	60 and over %
Need parliament	63	72	70	71	81	88	83	76
Can manage without	9	11	9	8	6	5	7	10
Undecided	28	17	21	21	13	7	10	14
	100	100	100	100	100	100	100	100

MIXED FEELINGS

Question: *"Do you have a favorable or unfavorable impression of the way parliament has handled its work so far?"*

A

	1950 Jan. %	1956 June %	1962 July %	1964 Sept. %	1972 Sept. %	1978 Nov. %
Favorable	21	29	34	30	34	39
Unfavorable	32	19	15	21	27	18
Undecided	24	27	31	25	27	31
Don't know	23	25	20	24	12	12
	100	100	100	100	100	100

	November 1978 Age groups			
	16-29 %	30-44 %	45-59 %	60 and over %
Favorable	36	42	41	36
Unfavorable	19	19	19	16
Undecided	31	29	30	33
Don't know	14	10	10	15
	100	100	100	100

ABILITIES OF REPRESENTATIVES

Question: "*Do you believe that one must have great abilities to become a parliamentary representative in Bonn?*"

	1951 May %	1955 May %	1959 May %	1961 Oct. %	1964 Sept. %	1972 Sept. %	1978 April %
Yes	39	46	58	61	54	63	55
No	40	39	27	22	28	23	32
Undecided	21	15	15	17	18	14	13
	100	100	100	100	100	100	100

WHOM DO THEY SERVE?

Question: "*Do you feel that the parliamentary representatives in Bonn first and foremost represent the interests of the people, or do they have other interests that are more important to them?*"

	1951 April %	1953 April %	1957 Aug. %	1964 Dec. %	1972 Aug. %	1978 Nov. %
Interests of the people	25	39	36	51	43	55
Personal, private interests	32	20	20	11	20	15
Party interests	14	13	9	7	3	3
Other interests	11	8	6	8	5	9
Don't know	23	24	31	23	31	18
	105	104	102	100	102	100

GETTING IN TOUCH

Question: "*If you wrote a letter to your parliamentary representative, what do you think would happen to it?*"

	1951 April %	1953 April %	1957 Aug. %	1959 May %	1962 Aug. %	1964 Sept. %	1972 Sept. %	1978 Nov. %
Would be read by the representative	32	48	49	41	47	42	56	55
Would not be read by him, would not reach him	49	35	30	27	22	21	23	22
Don't know, depends	19	17	21	32	31	37	21	23
	100	100	100	100	100	100	100	100

ADHERE TO THE MAJORITY OPINION . . .

Question: "*If there's a vote on a bill in parliament and you know that the majority of the population is* for *it—what, in your opinion, should a representative do who thinks it's a* bad *bill? Should he vote according to what* he/she *thinks is right, or should he/she go by what the majority of the population thinks?*"

A

	August 1977			
	Do what he/she thinks is right	Majority opinion	Undecided	
	%	%	%	
Total population	38	54	8	= 100
AGE GROUPS				
16-29	41	50	9	= 100
30-44	40	53	7	= 100
45-59	34	59	7	= 100
60 and over	34	56	10	= 100
PARTY PREFERENCE				
SPD	41	54	5	= 100
CDU/CSU	35	56	9	= 100
FDP	43	51	6	= 100

. . .OR TO THE PARTY LINE

Question: "*When there's a vote on a bill in parliament, what should a representative do if* he/she *thinks the bill is* good, *but the party is* against *it? Should the representative do what he/she thinks is right and vote for it, or should he/she reject it in accordance with the party line?*"

A

	August 1977			
	Do what he/she thinks is right	Do as party wishes	Undecided	
	%	%	%	
Total population	74	17	9	= 100
AGE GROUPS				
16-29	79	13	8	= 100
30-44	76	17	7	= 100
45-59	70	18	12	= 100
60 and over	68	21	11	= 100
PARTY PREFERENCE				
SPD	74	18	8	= 100
CDU/CSU	74	18	8	= 100
FDP	80	16	4	= 100

THE FEDERAL CHANCELLOR AND THE GOVERNMENT COALITIONS

Question: *''Do you approve of the Federal Chancellor's policies or not?''*

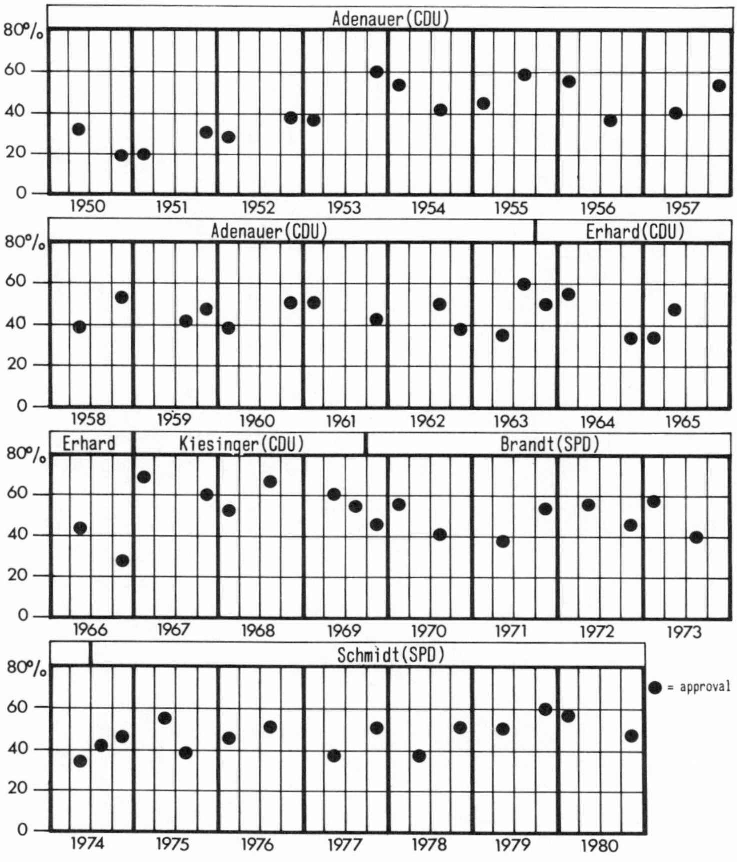

• highest and lowest values for the respective year, in the quarter in which they appeared.

WILLY BRANDT
FEDERAL CHANCELLOR FROM 1969-1974

Question: *"I have some cards here with characteristic traits - could you please look them over and lay out those with characteristics which you feel apply to Brandt?"* (C)

E

	1972 Oct. Total population	1974 March Total population	Party preference SPD	Party preference CDU/CSU	Party preference FDP
	%	%	%	%	%
Social-minded	61	48	70	31	64
Ambitious	51	39	38	42	41
Politically far-sighted	45	32	63	10	36
Great self-control	45	40	56	27	47
Energetic, firm will	44	27	43	15	30
Cautious, prudent, careful	44	43	56	34	51
Modern, progressive	43	25	46	12	26
Tolerant	40	35	56	20	44
Fair	39	39	66	20	53
Honest, upright	39	36	63	17	43
Radiates confidence and success	37	22	44	9	24
Willing to make decisions	36	17	28	11	20
Incorruptible	36	35	58	19	43
Active, always has new ideas	35	18	28	12	17
Warm-hearted	28	23	37	13	23
Kind, fatherly	28	28	43	18	32
Strong leader	24	13	24	7	11
Hard, uncompromising	23	10	11	10	8
Charming, winning	22	18	30	12	22
Robust	21	14	14	15	14
Vivacious, spirited	20	8	15	4	7
Cuts across party divisions	20	13	20	9	17
Cool, reserved	14	12	7	18	11
Christian, devout	6	4	6	3	4
	801	599	922	388	688

HELMUT SCHMIDT
FEDERAL CHANCELLOR AS OF MAY 1974

Question: *"I have some cards here with characteristic traits. Could you please look them over and lay out those with characteristics which you feel apply to Schmidt?"*

A

	1974 July	1978 Nov.	Party preference		
	Total population		SPD	CDU/CSU	FDP
	%	%	%	%	%
Energetic, firm will	69	69	79	66	83
Ambitious	68	66	64	72	71
Politician with acumen and a consistent course	46	61	81	45	73
Brilliant speaker	50	57	63	51	62
Tough toward his opponents	50	53	56	55	57
Social-minded	41	51	67	40	56
Willing to make decisions	48	47	59	41	61
Politically far-sighted	39	47	66	33	62
Strong leader	42	46	52	41	49
Courageous	41	45	58	36	58
Inspires confidence	39	44	64	27	52
Great self-control	39	43	55	35	40
Makes convincing arguments	–	43	62	28	57
Radiates confidence and success	39	40	56	28	42
Modern, progressive	42	40	52	31	49
Good-looking	–	39	43	38	43
Fair	32	38	55	25	52
Vivacious, spirited	37	35	48	24	45
Incorruptible	35	33	45	24	35
Honest, upright	29	32	47	17	41
Tolerant	28	32	44	22	38
Cool, reserved	30	30	23	41	23
Has good advisors	26	29	38	23	26
Has too little support in his party	–	26	19	34	28
Arrogant	–	26	14	38	20
Cautious, prudent, careful	19	25	28	20	22
More conservatively minded	17	19	16	22	17
Christian, devout	3	6	8	6	4
Young, fresh	–	6	6	5	7
	909	1128	1368	968	1273

– = not asked

HELMUT SCHMIDT
POPULARITY DURING HIS POLITICAL CAREER

		Good opinion* Total population %
Minister of Defense October 1969 - July 1972	October - 1969	64
	November - 1970	63
	March - 1971	64
	February - 1972	72
Minister of Economics, Minister of Finance July 1972 - December 1972	August - 1972	67
Minister of Finance December 1972 - May 1974	February - 1973	62
	December - 1973	52
	April - 1974	47
Federal Chancellor As of May 1974	July - 1974	67
	April - 1975	68
	May - 1976	71
	November - 1977	75
	November - 1978	76
	March - 1979	79
	March - 1980	74
	July - 1980	69

*Determined by the question ''*Do you tend to have a good or not so good opinion of. . .?*''

see also page 205

CHANGING VIEWS

Question: *"Do you approve of the Federal Chancellor's policies or not?"*

	February 1980 Approve %	Don't approve %	Undecided %	
AGE GROUPS				
16-29	60	15	25	= 100
30-44	62	18	20	= 100
45-59	59	23	18	= 100
60 and over	54	23	23	= 100
OCCUPATION				
Unskilled workers	61	18	21	= 100
Skilled workers	62	15	23	= 100
Non-managerial employees and public servants	59	18	23	= 100
Managerial employees and public servants	57	26	17	= 100
Self-employeds, professionals	51	29	20	= 100
Farmers	44	29	27	= 100
PARTY PREFERENCE				
SPD	90	1	9	= 100
CDU/CSU	33	41	26	= 100
FDP	70	7	23	= 100

	March 1981 Approve %	Don't approve %	Undecided %	
Total population	42	31	27	= 100
AGE GROUPS				
16-29	41	26	33	= 100
30-44	41	33	26	= 100
45-59	42	34	24	= 100
60 and over	43	30	27	= 100
OCCUPATION				
Unskilled workers	43	25	32	= 100
Skilled workers	45	28	27	= 100
Non-managerial employees and public servants	43	30	27	= 100
Managerial employees and public servants	43	30	27	= 100
Self-employeds, professionals	28	43	29	= 100
Farmers	22	58	20	= 100
PARTY PREFERENCE				
SPD	78	5	17	= 100
CDU/CSU	18	58	24	= 100
FDP	52	15	33	= 100

MEMBERS OF THE FEDERAL CABINET SINCE 1966

1965 federal election			
Great Coalition - CDU/CSU and SPD, 1966-69	Federal Chancellor	Kurt Georg Kiesinger	(CDU)
	Foreign Minister	Willy Brandt	(SPD)
	Minister of Economics	Karl Schiller	(SPD)
	Minister of Finance	Franz Josef Strauss	(CSU)
	Minister of Defense	Gerhard Schröder	(CDU)
1969 federal election			
Social-liberal coalition - SPD and FDP, 1969-72	Federal Chancellor	Willy Brandt	(SPD)
	Foreign Minister	Walter Scheel	(FDP)
	Minister of Economics	Karl Schiller	(SPD)
	Minister of Finance	Alex Moeller	(SPD)
	Minister of Defense	Helmut Schmidt	(SPD)
1972 federal election			
Social-liberal coalition - SPD and FDP, 1972-76	Federal Chancellor	Willy Brandt	(SPD)
	Foreign Minister	Walter Scheel	(FDP)
	Minister of Economics	Hans Friderichs	(FDP)
	Minister of Finance	Helmut Schmidt	(SPD)
	Minister of Defense	Georg Leber	(SPD)
Resignation of Federal Chancellor Willy Brandt in May 1974			
	Federal Chancellor	Helmut Schmidt	(SPD)
	Foreign Minister	Hans-Dietrich Genscher	(FDP)
	Minister of Economics	Hans Friderichs	(FDP)
	Minister of Finance	Hans Apel	(FDP)
	Minister of Defense	Georg Leber	(SPD)
1976 federal election			
Social-liberal coalition - SPD and FDP, 1976-80	Federal Chancellor	Helmut Schmidt	(SPD)
	Foreign Minister	Hans-Dietrich Genscher	(FDP)
	Minister of Economics	Otto Graf Lambsdorff	(FDP)
	Minister of Finance	Hans Matthoefer	(SPD)
	Minister of Defense	Hans Apel	(SPD)
1980 federal election			
Social-liberal coalition - SPD and FDP, 1980-	Federal Chancellor	Helmut Schmidt	(SPD)
	Foreign Minister	Hans-Dietrich Genscher	(FDP)
	Minister of Economics	Otto Graf Lambsdorff	(FDP)
	Minister of Finance	Hans Matthoefer	(SPD)
	Minister of Defense	Hans Apel	(SPD)

POPULARITY OF THE MINISTERS

Foreign Ministers

Willy Brandt December 1966 - October 1969	Good opinion* %
December - 1966	43
July - 1967	51
November - 1968	66
September - 1969	58
Walter Scheel October 1969 - May 1974	
October - 1969	38
November - 1970	54
March - 1971	57
February - 1972	72
February - 1973	72
April - 1974	78
Hans-Dietrich Genscher As of May 1974	
July - 1974	54
April - 1975	47
May - 1976	60
November - 1977	67
November - 1978	63
March - 1979	62
March - 1980	62
July - 1980	62

Ministers of Defense

Gerhard Schröder December 1966 - October 1969	Good opinion* %
December - 1966	33
July - 1967	39
November - 1968	48
September - 1969	48
Helmut Schmidt October 1969 - July 1972	
October - 1969	64
November - 1970	63
March - 1971	64
February - 1972	72
Georg Leber July 1972 - February 1978	
August - 1972	55
February - 1973	50
July - 1974	47
November - 1975	52
May - 1976	54
November - 1977	49
Hans Apel As of February 1978	
November - 1978	49
December - 1979	44
March - 1980	43
July - 1980	40

*Determined by the question *''Do you tend to have a good or not so good opinion of . . . ?''*
see also page 205

MINISTER OF ECONOMICS

Question: *"Do you agree with the economic policy of Friderichs - the present Minister of Economics—or are you not in agreement?"*

	August 1977				
	Agree %	Don't agree %	Undecided %	No reply %	
Total population	32	27	27	14	= 100
OCCUPATION					
Unskilled workers	30	25	25	20	= 100
Skilled workers	29	26	31	14	= 100
Non-managerial employees and public servants	34	30	25	11	= 100
Managerial employees and public servants	39	26	26	9	= 100
Self-employeds, professionals	28	33	29	10	= 100
Farmers	27	23	28	22	= 100
PARTY PREFERENCE					
SPD	43	18	26	13	= 100
CDU/CSU	23	38	27	12	= 100
FDP	46	19	24	11	= 100

Question: *"As you know, Otto Graf Lambsdorff has become the new Minister of Economics after Friderichs. Are you confident that Graf Lambsdorff will be a good minister of economics or are you not so confident?"*

	November 1977				
	Confident %	Not confident %	Undecided %	No opinion %	
Total population	25	8	28	39	= 100
OCCUPATION					
Unskilled workers	13	5	28	54	= 100
Skilled workers	22	5	32	41	= 100
Non-managerial employees and public servants	29	8	29	34	= 100
Managerial employees and public servants	34	10	26	30	= 100
Self-employeds, professionals	34	12	24	30	= 100
Farmers	20	10	22	48	= 100
PARTY PREFERENCE					
SPD	30	6	26	38	= 100
CDU/CSU	28	9	31	32	= 100
FDP	36	7	21	36	= 100

THE ADMINISTRATION

Question: *''There are various offices and institutions which have importance for political decision-making in West Germany. A few of them appear on these cards. Could you please distribute the cards on these 5 strips according to whether you tend to think well of the institution or are inclined to think poorly of it? Please simply lay aside cards for offices and institutions you are not familiar with.''* (C)

''How much of an influence do you think these offices and institutions have on political events in West Germany? Please answer this question by distributing the cards on these strips.'' (C)

January 1979

	Personal opinion -						
	Very good	Good	Good and bad	Rather poor	Very poor	No opinion	
	%	%	%	%	%	%	
Federal Constitutional Court	12	30	34	10	3	11	= 100
Federal President	43	39	12	2	1	3	= 100
Bundestag	12	38	37	7	1	5	= 100
Bundesrat	8	33	39	6	1	13	= 100
Federal government	17	35	35	8	2	3	= 100
Governments of the federal states	8	29	49	5	1	8	= 100
Armed Forces	9	34	34	13	6	4	= 100
Central Bank	9	35	34	7	1	14	= 100

	Political influence -						
	Very strong	Strong	Medium	Limited	Very limited	No opinion	
	%	%	%	%	%	%	
Federal Constitutional Court	17	31	26	13	5	8	= 100
Federal President	19	21	25	23	9	3	= 100
Bundestag	47	36	9	2	2	4	= 100
Bundesrat	28	38	19	4	1	10	= 100
Federal government	68	23	4	x	1	4	= 100
Governments of the federal states	22	41	24	5	1	7	= 100
Armed Forces	8	17	27	27	16	5	= 100
Central Bank	12	27	29	15	7	10	= 100

OF PERSONAL IMPORTANCE

Question: *"If you think of your personal life, do these offices and institutions tend to take on importance or do they not? Could you distribute the cards on this sheet accordingly?"* (C)

	December 1978			
	For my personal life -			
	rather important	rather unimportant	of no concern	
	%	%	%	
Federal government	74	12	14	= 100
Federal Parliament	61	18	21	= 100
Governments of the federal states	56	21	23	= 100
Bundesrat	45	25	30	= 100
Federal Constitutional Court	40	22	38	= 100
Central Bank	40	23	37	= 100
Federal President	37	34	29	= 100
Federal Army	35	24	41	= 100

OFFICE FOR THE PROTECTION OF THE CONSTITUTION

Question: *"Are you aware that we have a Federal Office for the Protection of the Constitution, or is this the first time you have heard of it?"*

"Do you have a good opinion of the Federal Office for the Protection of the Constitution overall, or do you not have a good opinion of it?"

A

	September 1978				
	Good opinion	Not such a good opinion	Undecided	First time I've heard of it	
	%	%	%	%	
Total population	38	19	37	6	= 100

RED TAPE

Question: *"Many people say that there is too much bureaucracy in Germany. Has bureaucracy ever annoyed you?"*

	1950 Jan.	1958 Nov.	1964 Dec.	1978 July
	%	%	%	%
Yes	78	66	69	64
No	22	34	31	36
	100	100	100	100

CORRUPTION?

Question: *"Do you feel that civil servants in Germany are, generally speaking, unimpressionable and incorruptible?"*

	No, not incorruptible %	Yes, incorruptible %	Undecided %	
Total population - January 1950	59	21	20	= 100
- November 1958	44	35	21	= 100
- December 1964	29	49	22	= 100
- October 1974	42	35	23	= 100
- July 1978	41	39	20	= 100
Men	44	39	17	= 100
Women	40	39	21	= 100
AGE GROUPS				
16-29	49	34	17	= 100
30-44	43	38	19	= 100
45-59	39	39	22	= 100
60 and over	35	46	19	= 100
OCCUPATION				
Unskilled workers	42	34	24	= 100
Skilled workers	49	30	21	= 100
Non-managerial employees and public servants	42	45	13	= 100
Managerial employees and public servants	31	55	14	= 100
Self-employeds, professionals	41	34	25	= 100
Farmers	38	27	35	= 100

Question: *"Do you have the impression that too much is regulated by laws and statutes, or do you think that the laws and ordinances are all necessary?"*

A

	July 1978 %
Too many laws and ordinances	50
All are necessary	35
Impossible to say	15
	100

Question: *"Do you consider the number of public offices and agencies in the Federal Republic to be just right, or do you feel there are too many?"*

A

	July 1978 %
Too many	65
Just right	21
Undecided	14
	100

PROTEST AGAINST UNJUST ACTION

Question: *''What would you do if an administrative agency acted unjustly in a matter that concerns you? Do you think that there would be a point in protesting or not?''*

''How would you protest, what would you do?'' (O)

	Would protest	No point in protesting	Undecided	
	%	%	%	
Total population - January 1950	52	37	11	= 100
- November 1958	53	33	14	= 100
- December 1964	51	32	17	= 100
- November 1978	70	22	8	= 100
AGE GROUPS				
16-29	76	17	7	= 100
30-44	76	18	6	= 100
45-59	67	24	9	= 100
60 and over	61	30	9	= 100
EDUCATION				
Elementary	65	25	10	= 100
Intermediate	77	19	4	= 100
Secondary	87	8	5	= 100

A

	November 1978			
	Total	Education		
	pop.	Elementary	Intermediate	Secondary
Ways of protesting -	%	%	%	%
Generally: lodge complaints, raise objections	34	31	37	40
Take legal action, go to court	18	18	15	25
Go through official channels to the top, go to the nearest authority	13	10	17	20
Go to the public (the press)	2	1	4	8
Turn to representatives, political parties	1	1	1	4
Other/no answer	6	5	6	10
I would not protest	30	35	23	13
	104	101	103	120

DO THE POLITICIANS LISTEN?

Question: *"You often hear the following opinion: 'Although we all have the chance to vote periodically, the politicians basically don't pay any attention to this; they just do as they like.' Would you say this is completely true, true in part or not true?"*

	1970 May	1976 Feb.	1978 Nov.	Age groups			
	Total population			16-29	30-44	45-59	60 and over
	%	%	%	%	%	%	%
Completely true	22	19	13	13	11	12	18
Partly true	52	59	64	67	67	64	59
Not true	14	15	18	15	20	18	17
Undecided	12	7	5	5	2	6	6
	100	100	100	100	100	100	100

IS THE CITIZEN POWERLESS?

Question: *"Do you have the feeling that we as citizens have an influence on the decisions of the federal government, or are we powerless?"*

Follow-up question put to those who feel we have influence: *"In your opinion, is the citizens' influence strong enough, or is it insufficient?"*

	1975 May	1976 March	1977 Sept.	1978 Nov.
	%	%	%	%
We are powerless	55	54	51	48
We have influence	23	29	31	29
- insufficient	13	19	21	18
- sufficient	8	8	7	9
- undecided	2	2	3	2
	23	29	31	29
Undecided	22	17	18	23
	100	100	100	100

STATE-OWNED INSTITUTIONS

A question now about state-owned institutions such as the post office, railway, hospitals, etc.: *"Do you think they are operated best and most inexpensively as state-owned enterprises, or would they be run better and more cheaply if they were private enterprises?"*

A

	September 1975 %
Best and most inexpensively as state-owned enterprises	40
Better and more cheaply as private enterprises	37
No difference	11
Undecided	12
	100

VIEWS ON CIVIL SERVANTS

Question: *"Here on this list are some opinions about civil servants and administration in general. Which of them would you agree with?"* (L)

	1978 Nov. %
Praise:	
Most public servants are helpful and polite	37
As citizens, we have sufficient opportunities to defend ourselves against the decisions of the public agencies	26
At our public agencies no one is given preference or disadvantaged - everyone receives his/her due	17
	80
Criticism:	
They make things much too complicated, it takes much too long	83
Because public agencies often give poor information, many people are not able to take advantage of the benefits and allowances that they actually are entitled to	62
Most officials stubbornly follow the book and don't consider the individual	61
There are too many public servants, the administration is blown out of proportion	58
The administrative decisions far too seldom take into consideration the interests of the citizens	42
As a citizen, one is powerless against public agencies	37
	343

POLITICAL PARTIES AND POLITICIANS

Question: *"Do you think that the most capable people tend to go into politics nowadays, or do you think the really good people tend to be in other areas, for example in business or at the universities?"*

	January 1978			
	In business, at the universities	In politics	Impossible to say	
	%	%	%	
Total population	55	9	36	= 100

COMPETENT POLITICIANS

Question: *"In your opinion, which party has more competent, able politicians - the CDU, the SPD or the FDP?"* (X)

	CDU	SPD	FDP	No difference	Undecided	
	%	%	%	%	%	
Total population - March 1974	29	20	9	27	15	= 100
- August 1975	30	28	4	25	13	= 100
- September 1976	35	30	8	19	11	= 103

MORE CHANGE THAN NECESSARY

Question: *"Do you think the politicians change more in our country than is really necessary, too little, or just the right amount?"*

	July 1977				
	More than necessary	Too little	Just right	Don't know	
	%	%	%	%	
Total population	33	28	17	22	= 100
PARTY PREFERENCE					
SPD	24	31	25	20	= 100
CDU/CSU	42	27	11	20	= 100
FDP	27	37	21	15	= 100

SALIENCE OF ISSUES

Question: *"There are various political demands here. Which of them do you personally find especially important?"* (C)

If 'important': *"Where does the SPD do a good job? The CDU/CSU? The FDP?"*

March 1979

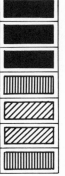

	Especially important	Does a good job		
		SPD	CDU/CSU	FDP
Economic policy, environmental protection				
Overcoming unemployment	[solid]	0	0	0
Sufficient jobs for young people leaving the schools and universities	[solid]	0	0	0
Providing for an environment that is a better place to live	[solid]	0	0	0
Improving occupational training for youth	[vertical lines]	0	0	0
Seeing to it that employers gain confidence, invest more money in their companies	[diagonal hatching]	0	+	0
Preventing the unions from setting the tone and acquiring more power than the government	[diagonal hatching]	–	+	–
Preventing the GDR kind of socialism from taking over here	[vertical lines]	–	+	–
Social policy, family policy				
Assurance of pensions	[solid]	0	0	–
Preventing an increase in wage/salary deductions for taxes, medical insurance and social security	[vertical lines]	0	0	0
Promoting families with children	[vertical lines]	0	0	0
Slowing down the decline of the birthrate, ensuring that more children are born	[diagonal hatching]	0	0	0
Achieving equal rights for women in all spheres	[diagonal hatching]	+	–	0
Decreasing social differences, ensuring that everyone has pretty much the same amount	[diagonal hatching]	+	–	–

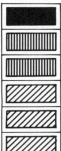

Demanded by -

- [solid] - more than 55 percent of the total population
- [vertical lines] - 45 - 55 percent
- [diagonal hatching] - less than 45 percent

In comparison to the other parties

- + = positive profile (+ 10 percent)
- 0 = no profile (± 10 percent)
- – = negative profile (-10 percent)

March 1979

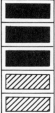

	Especially important	Does a good job: SPD	CDU/CSU	FDP
Terrorism, domestic security				
Effective measures to combat the terrorists	more than 55 percent	0	0	−
Keeping political goals from being achieved by means of violence and terror	more than 55 percent	0	0	−
Combating crime more effectively	more than 55 percent	0	0	0
Preventing radicals from being employed in public service	less than 45 percent	−	+	−
No cooperation with Communist groups in West Germany	less than 45 percent	−	+	0
Protection of personal freedom				
Preserving personal freedom, less government regimentation	more than 55 percent	0	0	0
Right to privacy, preventing misuse of personal data	45 - 55 percent	0	0	0
That children are not influenced in a certain political direction in school	45 - 55 percent	−	+	0
That everyone who has the Abitur is able to study the field of his choice	less than 45 percent	0	0	0
External security, East-West policy				
Preventing Communist influence from gaining ground in Europe	45 - 55 percent	−	+	−
Not yielding too much to the East, no agreement without a quid pro quo	45 - 55 percent	−	+	−
Strengthening NATO and the Armed Forces to prevent Russian military advantage	less than 45 percent	0	0	0
Continuing to compromise with the East in the future, to strengthen the reconciliation	less than 45 percent	+	−	0
Relations with the GDR, reunification				
People living in the two parts of Germany getting closer to each other again	less than 45 percent	+	−	−
Taking steps to ensure the protection of human rights in the GDR too	less than 45 percent	0	0	0
Unification of Europe				
Encouraging the European countries to join together in a United Europe	less than 45 percent	0	0	0

Demanded by -

- [solid black box] - more than 55 percent of the total population
- [vertically striped box] - 45 - 55 percent
- [hatched box] - less than 45 percent

In comparison to the other parties

- + = positive profile (+ 10 percent)
- 0 = no profile (± 10 percent)
- − = negative profile (−10 percent)

PARTIES REPRESENT THE PEOPLE

Question: *''Here are two people discussing the three most important political parties in the Federal Republic, the CDU/CSU, the SPD and the FDP. Which of the two says what you yourself believe?''* (ill.)

	November 1978
	%
''I find that these three parties by and large represent the various interests of the population. For this reason, one should vote for one of these parties in elections.''	75
''I think these parties no longer really represent the interests of the population in certain important matters. For this reason, one should no longer actually vote for them.''	13
Undecided	7
No reply	5
	100

RANKING THE POLITICAL PARTIES

Question: *''The names of the parties which have political importance are listed on these cards. These parties certainly don't all appeal to one equally. Could you please group these three cards according to how much these parties appeal to you?''* (C)

	July 1979									
	Total	Men	Women	Age groups				Party preference		
Most appealing				16-29	30-44	45-59	60 and over	SPD	CDU/CSU	FDP
(Rank 1):	%	%	%	%	%	%	%	%	%	%
CDU/CSU	45	42	48	34	42	48	56	3	95	8
SPD	44	48	40	54	47	39	35	94	2	11
FDP	8	7	9	8	9	10	6	2	1	78
None of these	3	3	3	4	2	3	3	1	2	3
	100	100	100	100	100	100	100	100	100	100
Rank combinations:										
CDU/CSU/FDP/SPD	24	22	25	17	21	25	32	1	53	5
SPD/FDP/CDU/CSU	34	39	29	42	36	31	26	76	x	9
FDP/SPD/CDU/CSU	6	5	7	7	6	8	3	2	1	65
CDU/CSU/SPD/FDP	20	19	21	16	21	22	23	3	40	3
SPD/CDU/CSU/FDP	10	9	11	11	11	9	9	18	2	2
FDP/CDU/CSU/SPD	2	1	2	1	2	2	2	x	1	13
No answer	4	5	5	6	3	3	5	x	3	3
	100	100	100	100	100	100	100	100	100	100

ASSOCIATIONS

A

December 1975

When you hear this,* you think of -

Based on reason	SPD %	CDU/CSU %
Worker	83	25
Reforms	76	46
High taxes	69	40
Progressive	66	50
Freedom	65	67
Capable politicians	59	58
Achievement	58	59
Bourgeois	57	68
Success	48	53
Middle-of-the-road party	46	53
Bureaucracy	46	46
Prosperity for everybody	45	40
Nepotism	44	31
Friendliness	40	44
Lack of unity	40	45
Waste	39	19
Liberal	31	31
Egalitarianism	28	13
Bribery	24	21
Entrepreneurs	21	81
Radical	19	11
The meaning of life	19	20
Security	18	26
Communists	16	2
Happiness	15	16
	1072	965

June 1975

CDU/CSU %	SPD %	*Based on feelings*
76	2	Prayerbook
47	14	Lion's roar
41	9	German oaks
32	20	Army barracks
27	19	Beer
26	6	Sofa with velvet cushions
25	6	Museum director
25	14	Grey flannel suit and tie
24	6	Chandelier
24	10	Champagne
20	8	Horse and buggy
19	8	Autograph book
18	16	Airline captain
18	11	Slippers
17	27	Wasting money
17	47	Pensioner
16	49	Party membership card
11	20	Industrious bees
7	54	Student
5	48	Turtleneck sweater
495	394	

*These words were read aloud to the respondents.

SOCIAL DEMOCRATS AND COMMUNISTS

Question: *"The SPD is sometimes reproached for working too closely with the Communists, for not demonstrating clearly enough that its goals in politics are very different from those of the Communists. Do you think this reproach is justified, or is it not justified?"*

	August 1975			
	Total	Party preference		
	pop.	SPD	CDU/CSU	FDP
	%	%	%	%
Reproach justified	29	11	53	17
Yes and no	21	16	24	23
Not justified	39	66	15	53
Don't know	11	7	8	7
	100	100	100	100

THE YOUNG SOCIALISTS

Question: *"Could you please read this about the youth organization of the SPD, the Young Socialists. Whom would you tend to agree with here?"* (ill.)

A

	June 1976			
	Total	Party preference		
	pop.	SPD	CDU/CSU	FDP
	%	%	%	%
"I fear that the Young Socialists are gaining too much influence on the policies of the SPD and that, as a result, the SPD is gradually becoming more radical."	41	20	65	36
"I don't believe that. The Young Socialists are only a minority. The great majority in the party is sticking to present policies."	45	70	24	58
Undecided	14	10	11	6
	100	100	100	100

NO JOINT EFFORTS

Question: *"Do you approve of it when the SPD occasionally works together with Communist parties and groups, or should it under no circumstances do so?"*

C

	September 1980			
	Approve	Under no circumstances	Undecided	
	%	%	%	
Total eligible voters	13	72	15	= 100
AGE GROUPS				
18-29	21	58	21	= 100
30-44	15	71	14	= 100
45-59	11	75	14	= 100
60 and over	4	81	15	= 100
PARTY PREFERENCE				
CDU/CSU	5	88	7	= 100
SPD	19	60	21	= 100
FDP	19	66	15	= 100

SPD: INNER-PARTY STRIFE?

Question: *"Do you think there is agreement or disagreement within the SPD, generally speaking?"*

A

	1976 Aug.	1977 Nov.	1978 Jan.	1980 May	1980 Aug.
	%	%	%	%	%
Agreement	40	37	45	44	43
Disagreement	40	41	43	27	26
Impossible to say	20	22	12	29	31
	100	100	100	100	100

	March 1981			
	Total	Party preference		
	pop.	SPD	CDU/CSU	FDP
	%	%	%	%
Agreement	23	46	9	23
Disagreement	55	30	76	58
Impossible to say	22	24	15	19
	100	100	100	100

THE FREE DEMOCRATS

Question: "*Two people are talking here about the FDP. Which of the two would you tend to agree with?*" (ill.)

A

	1975 Oct.	1977 July	Party preference		
	Total population		SPD	CDU/CSU	FDP
	%	%	%	%	%
"I think that the FDP does have a different point of view than the SPD on important matters. So it is a good thing that there is an FDP."	59	55	58	51	83
"I think that the FDP basically wants exactly the same things the SPD does. So from my point of view there is no need for the FDP."	24	23	23	31	3
Undecided	17	22	19	18	14
	100	100	100	100	100

LEGITIMATION

Question: "*Two people are talking here about the FDP. Would you please read this and tell me which of the two says pretty much what you also think?*" (ill.)

A

	1977 July	1980 Aug.
	%	%
"As a third party, the FDP is still important nowadays. As a government party it can keep the big parties, i.e. the CDU/CSU and the SPD, from establishing their policies completely."	49	57
"I don't think it is necessary to have the FDP. The strongest party should be able to establish its policies completely without having brakes applied by a small party."	33	23
Undecided	18	20
	100	100

THE CHRISTIAN DEMOCRATS IN OPPOSITION

Question: *"Would you please read what these two people are saying? Whom would you tend to agree with?"* (ill.)

The one:

"I think it is the opposition's job not just to criticize the government but to make its own suggestions. That is the only way it can prove that it is capable and seriously interested in solving our problems. Otherwise it is difficult to take the opposition seriously."

The other:

"I am of a different opinion. It is enough for the opposition to state clearly what it doesn't like about the government's measures. If it has good ideas to offer, the government will either appropriate them and present them as its own policies or the suggestions will be attacked, without the opposition having the chance to demonstrate that this would have been a good solution."

		May 1977		
	Total	Party preference		
	pop.	SPD	CDU/CSU	FDP
	%	%	%	%
The opposition should make its own suggestions	74	90	65	82
The opposition only has to criticize	16	5	26	12
Undecided	10	5	9	6
	100	100	100	100

THE LEADERS OF THE OPPOSITION AND THEIR POPULARITY

		Good opinion* Total population %
Rainer Barzel - CDU October 1969 - February 1973	October - 1969	42
	November - 1970	36
	March - 1971	42
	February - 1972	41
	February - 1973	35
Karl Carstens - CDU May 1973 - December 1976	December - 1973	38
	July - 1974	38
	April - 1975	34
	May - 1976	37
Helmut Kohl - CDU As of December 1976	November - 1977	53
	November - 1978	50
	March - 1979	48
	March - 1980	44

*Determined by the question *"Do you tend to have a good or not so good opinion of . . .?"*

see also page 205

CDU/CSU: INNER-PARTY STRIFE?

Question: *''Do you think there is agreement or disagreement within the CDU/CSU, generally speaking?''*

A

	1976 Aug. %	1977 Nov. %	1978 Jan. %	1979 April %	1980 May %	1980 Aug. %
Agreement	47	41	45	30	41	38
Disagreement	29	41	42	51	32	35
Impossible to say	24	18	13	19	27	27
	100	100	100	100	100	100

	March 1981			
	Total pop.	Party preference		
		SPD	CDU/CSU	FDP
	%	%	%	%
Agreement	54	30	84	43
Disagreement	25	43	8	33
Impossible to say	21	27	8	24
	100	100	100	100

Question: *''One question is how the CDU and the CSU can get more votes in the federal elections - by appearing together or by the CSU separating from the CDU as a so-called fourth party. Which course do you think would produce more votes for the CDU/CSU?''*

Q

	May 1977			
	Total pop.	Party preference		
		SPD	CDU/CSU	FDP
	%	%	%	%
Appearing together	55	48	64	62
CSU as a fourth party	26	34	21	14
Don't know	19	18	15	24
	100	100	100	100

MORE INFLUENCE FOR STRAUSS?

Question: *''Do you think it would be a good thing or not such a good thing if Franz Josef Strauss gained more influence on our political life?''*

E

	April 1975				
	Total pop.	Regional distribution			
		Northern Germany and West Berlin	North-Rhine Westphalia	Rhine-Main/ Southwest	Bavaria
	%	%	%	%	%
Not a good thing	55	59	61	51	44

COMPETITORS

Question: *"Could you please look over these cards and lay out those with characteristics which you feel apply to Helmut Kohl?"* (C)

Question: *"What kind of impression do you have of Franz Josef Strauss as a person? In your opinion, which of these descriptions fit Strauss?"* (C)

Comparison of characteristics	Franz Josef Strauss November 1979 %	Helmut Kohl November 1976 %
Energetic, gets what he wants	64	30
Strong leader	57	12
Brilliant speaker	56	28
Politician with acumen and a consistent course	38	35
Courageous	36	26
Tends to be conservative-minded	36	43
Confident, radiates success	18	28
Honest, upright	13	36
Inspires confidence	9	41
Modern, progressive	8	19
Incorruptible	8	25
Has a social conscience	8	26
Liberal, tolerant	4	27

Question: *"If Strauss weren't the candidate for chancellor, who do you think would probably be the best CDU/CSU candidate for chancellor; who would produce the most votes?"* (L)

	August 1980			
	Total eligible voters	Party preference		
		SPD	CDU/CSU	FDP
	%	%	%	%
Ernst Albrecht	28	28	30	27
Gerhard Stoltenberg	17	14	21	12
Helmut Kohl	13	13	16	6
Kurt Biedenkopf	6	6	5	9
Alfred Dregger	2	1	4	3
None of the above	14	17	8	13
Undecided	20	21	16	30
	100	100	100	100

THE MINOR PARTIES

Question: *"The National Democratic Party of Germany did not make it into the Bundestag. Are you personally pleased about this, or would you have preferred to see the NPD in the Bundestag?"*

	November 1969			
	Pleased that the NPD isn't in the Bundestag	Would have preferred to see the NPD in the Bundestag	Undecided	
	%	%	%	
Total population	80	6	14	= 100

PROHIBIT COMMUNIST PARTY?

Question: *"There is a Communist party, the DKP, here in West Germany; did you know this?"* (Yes, I knew - 88 percent)

"In your opinion, should the DKP be prohibited or should it not be prohibited?"

	September 1973			
	Should not be prohibited	Should be prohibited	Undecided	
	%	%	%	
Total population	43	39	18	= 100

PROLIFERATION OF PARTIES?

Question: *"Supposing there were an additional conservative party in the Federal Parliament other than the three parties represented there, do you think this would be a good thing or not such a good thing?"*

"Supposing there were even more smaller parties besides the FDP in the Federal Parliament, do you think this would be a good thing or not such a good thing?"

A

	November 1978			
	Would be a good thing	Would not be such a good thing	Undecided	
	%	%	%	
Additional conservative party	21	62	17	= 100
More smaller parties	20	64	16	= 100

ENVIRONMENTALIST PARTY

Question: *"The 'Greens' and other environmental protection groups would like to join together to form a national party, in order to be able to run in the 1980 federal election. Did you know this, or is this the first time you've heard of it?"* (Knew=74 percent)

"Could you imagine voting for this party at a federal election - or not?"

A

	November 1979				
	Could imagine voting for it	Don't think so	Impossible to say	Not in favor	
	%	%	%	%	
Total population	15	37	10	38	= 100

THE FEDERAL ELECTIONS

VIEWS ON THE LEADERS

Question: *"Could you please distribute these cards with the names of politicians you have already heard of (selection by a previous question) on this sheet, according to whether you have a good opinion of the politician or not such a good opinion?"* (L, C)

		Good %	Not so good %	Neither nor %	Name unknown %	
SPD - Politicians						
Helmut *Schmidt*						
Federal Chancellor	1979 - December	76	16	8	x	= 100
	1980 - July	69	19	11	1	= 100
Willy *Brandt*						
Party Chairman of the SPD	1979 - December	38	49	11	2	= 100
	1980 - July	39	46	13	2	= 100
Hans *Apel*						
Minister of Defense	1979 - December	44	25	19	12	= 100
	1980 - July	40	23	24	13	= 100
Herbert *Wehner*						
Chairman of the Parliamentary Group	1979 - December	26	57	12	5	= 100
	1980 - July	24	58	13	5	= 100
Egon *Bahr*						
Organizational Manager of the Party	1979 - December	25	43	19	13	= 100
	1980 - July	21	45	18	16	= 100
FDP - Politicians						
Hans-Dietrich *Genscher*						
Foreign Minister and Party Chairman	1979 - December	61	20	15	4	= 100
Party Chairman	1980 - July	62	18	16	4	= 100
Otto *Graf Lambsdorff*						
Federal Minister of Economics	1979 - December	38	22	22	18	= 100
	1980 - July	35	24	24	17	= 100

VIEWS ON THE LEADERS

Question: *"Could you please distribute these cards with the names of politicians you have already heard of (selection by a previous question) on this sheet, according to whether you have a good opinion of the politician or not such a good opinion?"* (L, C)

		Good %	Not so good %	Neither nor %	Name unknown %	
CDU/CSU Politicians						
Franz Josef *Strauss* Party Chairman of the CSU, CDU/CSU candidate for Chancellor, Minister-President of Bavaria	1979 - December	36	52	10	2	= 100
	1980 - July	34	55	10	1	= 100
Helmut *Kohl* Party Chairman of the CDU and Chairman of the Parliamentary Group	1979 - December	41	44	12	3	= 100
	1980 - July	45	37	15	3	= 100
Ernst *Albrecht* Minister-President of Lower Saxony	1979 - December	50	26	14	10	= 100
	1980 - July	49	21	17	13	= 100
Gerhard *Stoltenberg* Minister-President of Schleswig-Holstein	1980 - July	48	22	19	11	= 100
Walter Leisler *Kiep* Minister of Finance in Lower Saxony	1979 - December	34	16	18	32	= 100
	1980 - July	39	13	20	28	= 100
Kurt *Biedenkopf* Acting Party Chairman of the CDU	1979 - December	31	33	20	16	= 100
	1980 - July	34	30	22	14	= 100

Question: *"Do you believe that Strauss is the best candidate for chancellor for the CDU/CSU, or do you think that the CDU/CSU could get better results in the federal election with a different candidate?"*

	August 1980				
	Eligible voters total	Party preference			
		SPD	CDU/CSU	FDP	Environmentalists
	%	%	%	%	%
Different candidate better	61	77	40	69	80
Strauss the best candidate	20	6	39	4	3
Undecided	19	17	21	27	17
	100	100	100	100	100

CONTENDERS

Question: *"Who would you prefer to have as Chancellor—Strauss or Schmidt?"* (X)

	1979						1980					
	March	July	Sept.	Oct.	Nov.	Dec.	Jan.	Feb.	March	May	July	August
	%	%	%	%	%	%	%	%	%	%	%	%
Schmidt ..	65	60	56	59	57	54	55	54	55	56	54	56
Strauss ...	19	23	26	25	25	26	29	28	27	24	27	25
Undecided	16	17	18	16	18	20	16	18	18	20	19	19
	100	100	100	100	100	100	100	100	100	100	100	100

	July 1980			
	Schmidt %	Strauss %	Undecided %	
Total population	54	27	19	= 100
Men	56	29	15	= 100
Women	53	25	22	= 100
AGE GROUPS				
16-29	63	18	19	= 100
30-44	59	26	15	= 100
45-59	54	31	15	= 100
60 and over	43	32	25	= 100
OCCUPATION				
Unskilled workers	57	23	20	= 100
Skilled workers	60	22	18	= 100
Non-managerial employees and public servants	60	23	17	= 100
Managerial employees and public servants	53	28	19	= 100
Self-employeds, professionals	38	40	22	= 100
Farmers	16	61	23	= 100
REGIONAL DISTRIBUTION				
Northern Germany with West Berlin	60	22	18	= 100
North-Rhine Westphalia	63	21	16	= 100
Rhine-Main/Southwest	49	28	23	= 100
Bavaria	42	39	19	= 100

HELMUT SCHMIDT - FRANZ JOSEF STRAUSS

Question: *''What is your impression of Helmut Schmidt (half group)/ Franz Josef Strauss (half group) as a person? In your opinion, which of these descriptions apply?''* (C)

	February 1980	
	Helmut Schmidt	Franz Josef Strauss
	%	%
Politician with acumen and a consistent course	60	43
Knowledgeable in many fields	51	60
Appeals to all population groups	47	14
Brilliant speaker	47	64
Appealing	45	14
Inspires confidence	41	14
Social-minded	40	14
Close to the trade unions	38	3
Politically far-sighted	36	34
Radiates confidence and success	31	20
Honest, upright	29	15
Liberal, tolerant	22	9
Incorruptible	20	14
Arrogant	18	25
Has a sense of humor, happy person	18	30
Doesn't always think before he speaks	13	49
Always has new ideas	14	21
Cold, calculating	13	24
Shrewd, cunning	10	43
Is a good head of family	10	21
Power-hungry	8	38
Has a positive attitude toward employers	8	32
Christian	5	39
Lacks self-control	3	49
	627	689

TOPICS

Question put to gainfully employed persons: *''What are the most important topics for you in this election campaign?''* (L)

	September 1980 %
Unemployment	75
Rising prices	60
Secure energy supply	57
Secure old age pensions	55
Family policy	50
Environmental protection	48
Combatting crime	45
Reduction of the national debt	36
Ostpolitik	32
Military balance	28

WILL AFGHANISTAN AFFECT THE ELECTION?

Question: *''It is probably hard to say, but what do you think—Will the events in Afghanistan have an effect on the coming Bundestag election this fall, or don't you think that they'll have any influence?''*

	January 1980				
	Eligible voters total %	Government supporters %	Supporters of the opposition %	Education Elementary %	Education Secondary %
Will have an effect	32	26	43	29	36
No influence	53	61	44	56	50
Undecided	15	13	13	15	14
	100	100	100	100	100

Question: *''Here are two people discussing voting. Which of the two comes closer to your opinion?''* (ill., X)

C

	September 1980				
	Total eligible voters %	Party preference SPD %	CDU/CSU %	FDP %	Environmentalists %
''If I don't like the leaders of a party, I would never vote for this party, even if it had a good platform.''	24	30	17	28	29
''For me, a party's platform is the most important thing. If I like a party's political line, I vote for it even when I don't especially like the party leaders.''	60	54	67	61	49
Undecided	16	16	16	11	22
	100	100	100	100	100

VOTING IS IMPORTANT

Question: *"We recently asked people what 'voting' meant to them. I'll read you a few of the answers we were given. For each one, would you tell me if you agree?"*

	August 1980			
	Eligible voters			
	Applies %	Doesn't apply %	Undecided %	
Voting is important to me because I want to support the party of my choice	77	10	13	= 100
I like to vote; it gives me the feeling of really taking part in determining what our next government will be like	63	21	16	= 100
I feel that one should still vote when one is not 100 percent in agreement with any of the parties	62	19	19	= 100
I would have a bad conscience if I didn't vote	48	43	9	= 100
I think that one should only vote if one is really sure about a party	38	45	17	= 100
My friends and acquaintances wouldn't understand if I didn't vote	31	48	21	= 100
I think it would be best if everyone were legally required to vote. No one should shirk this responsibility	23	65	12	= 100
Voting does not mean a lot to me, but maybe just because it's customary and not much trouble I always do it anyway	22	67	11	= 100
I think one should only vote if one really believes in one of the leading candidates	21	63	16	= 100
I think that it's good when people sometimes don't go to vote in order to show that they don't feel that any of the parties is really right for them	20	67	13	= 100
Voting is really only eyewash; as a citizen we really don't have any say	19	64	17	= 100
I'm not especially interested in politics and find voting rather a nuisance	10	77	13	= 100

MAKING A COMMITMENT

Question: *"If you were asked whether you would do something for the party you favor -do you find anything on these cards that you would do for the party that you think is best?"* (C)

	September 1980			
	Party preference			
Would -	SPD %	CDU/CSU %	FDP %	Environmentalists %
participate in a meeting of this party	43	47	44	70
attach a sticker to my car	32	23	25	57
get up at a party meeting and say something I think is important during the discussion	25	24	25	51
wear a pin, a button	24	17	16	45
help distribute campaign literature	19	16	11	41
take part in a street-corner discussion and speak up for this party	18	15	14	52
take this party's position at meetings of other parties too	18	14	13	32
put up posters for this party	14	10	8	43
give money to this party's campaign fund	12	15	12	16
put up this party's poster on my house or in my window	7	7	2	25
ring doorbells and discuss points in favor of this party with people	4	3	4	11
None of these	37	41	43	17
	253	232	217	460

	Age groups			
Would -	16-29 %	30-44 %	45-59 %	60 and over %
participate in a meeting of this party	44	47	44	32
attach a sticker to my car	39	27	27	11
get up at a party meeting and say something I think is important during the discussion	25	29	26	15
wear a pin, a button	25	21	19	12
help distribute campaign literature	21	18	16	10
take part in a street-corner discussion and speak up for this party	24	16	15	11
take this party's position at meetings of other parties too	20	17	16	8
put up posters for this party	17	12	10	5
give money to this party's campaign fund	8	13	16	13
put up this party's poster on my house or in my window	8	6	7	4
ring doorbells and discuss points in favor of this party with other people	4	5	2	3
None of these	35	38	38	58
	270	249	236	182

WHO WOULD YOU VOTE FOR?

Question: *"If the federal election were held next Sunday, which party would you vote for?"* (L)

See also illustration on pages 214, 215

C

Eligible voters with concrete party preference*

	SPD			CDU/CSU		
	1950 %	1965 %	1980 %	1950 %	1965 %	1980 %
Total population	32	47	42	26	43	47
Men	38	54	44	21	35	45
Women	27	41	40	31	49	48
AGE GROUPS						
18-29	32	50	50	24	41	31
30-44	36	51	45	21	40	44
45-59	29	49	39	30	39	53
60 and over	24	37	34	41	54	58
EDUCATION						
Elementary	36	51	44	28	41	48
Secondary	20	34	37	24	48	45
OCCUPATION						
Unskilled workers	44	58	49	22	35	42
Skilled workers		59	51		33	39
Non-managerial employees and public servants	26	38	43	27	51	45
Managerial employees and public servants		41	35		48	47
Self-employeds, professionals	12	29	22	27	50	68
Farmers	12	21	13	39	67	79
REGIONAL DISTRIBUTION						
Northern Germany	27	45	41	28	44	45
North-Rhine Westphalia	34	51	48	29	41	40
Rhine-Main/Southwest	35	50	40	22	39	48
Bavaria	27	36	35	24	50	57
DENOMINATION						
Protestant	35	56	49	18	32	38
Catholic	28	35	33	40	57	60
Other	34	58	47	5	27	28

*) n = 4,000 respondents in January/February of the respective year.

continued

continued

Question: *"If the federal election were held next Sunday, which party would you vote for?"* (L)

See also illustration on pages 214, 215

C

Eligible voters with concrete party preference*

	FDP			Others		
	1950	1965	1980	1950	1965	1980
	%	%	%	%	%	%
Total population	17	7	7	25	3	4
Men	16	7	6	25	4	5
Women	18	7	8	24	3	4
AGE GROUPS						
18-29	21	7	7	23	3	12
30-44	17	6	7	26	4	4
45-59	17	8	7	24	4	1
60 and over	10	6	7	25	3	1
EDUCATION						
Elementary	11	5	6	25	3	2
Secondary	33	14	11	23	4	7
OCCUPATION						
Unskilled workers	8	3	6	26	4	3
Skilled workers		5	5		3	5
Non-managerial employees and public servants	27	8	7	20	3	5
Managerial employees and public servants		9	13		2	5
Self-employeds, professionals	32	18	7	29	3	3
Farmers	22	9	7	27	3	1
REGIONAL DISTRIBUTION						
Northern Germany	13	8	8	32	3	6
North-Rhine Westphalia	16	6	8	21	2	4
Rhine-Main/Southwest	26	9	7	17	2	5
Bavaria	16	5	5	33	9	3
DENOMINATION						
Protestant	23	9	9	24	3	4
Catholic	8	5	4	24	3	3
Other	31	6	11	30	9	14

*) n = 4,000 respondents in January/February of the respective year.

Question: *"If the federal elections were held next Sunday, which party would you vote for?"* (L)

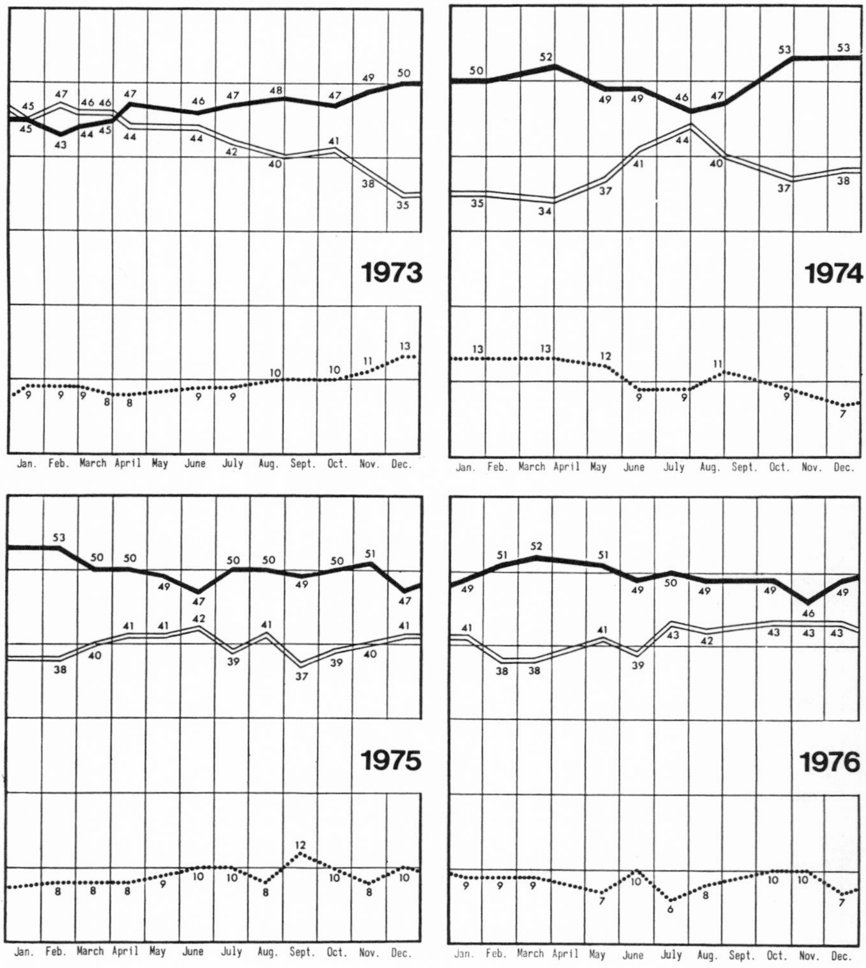

Question: *"If the federal elections were held next Sunday, which party would you vote for?"* (L)

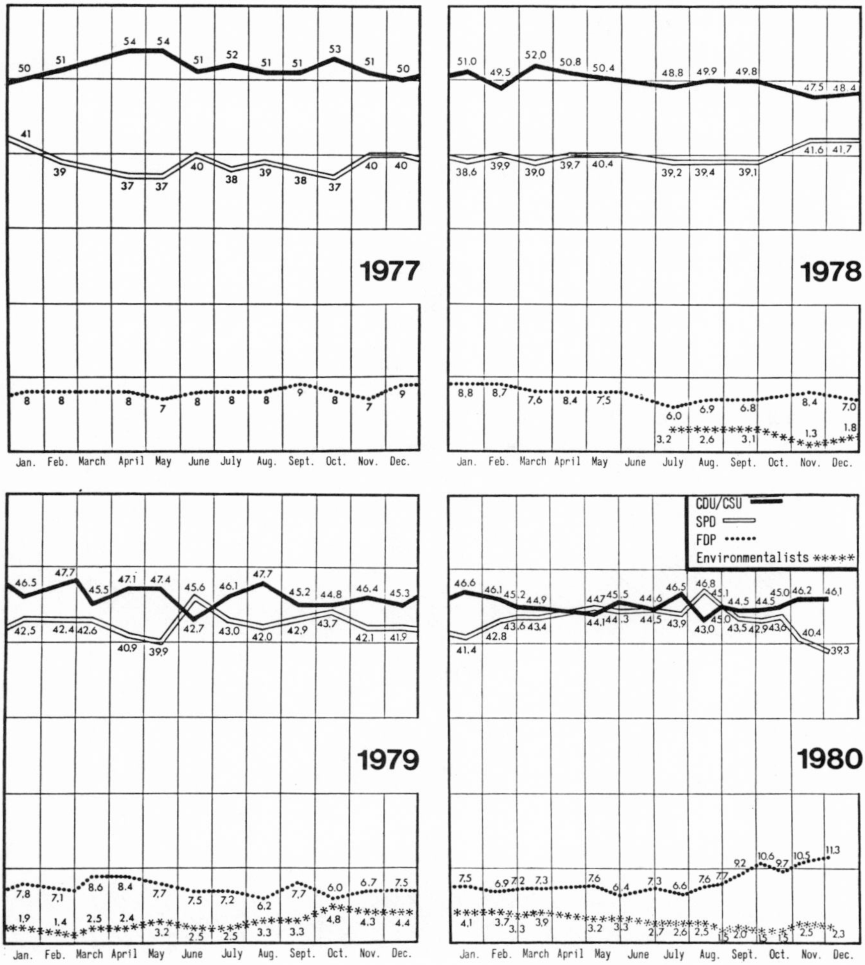

AWARE OF POLLING RESULTS?

Question: *"Do you happen to have recently heard or read which party got more votes in the polls?"*

	No %	Yes %		
Total population - August 1957	73	27	=	100
- September 1980	54	46	=	100

VOTER TURNOUT IN FEDERAL ELECTIONS

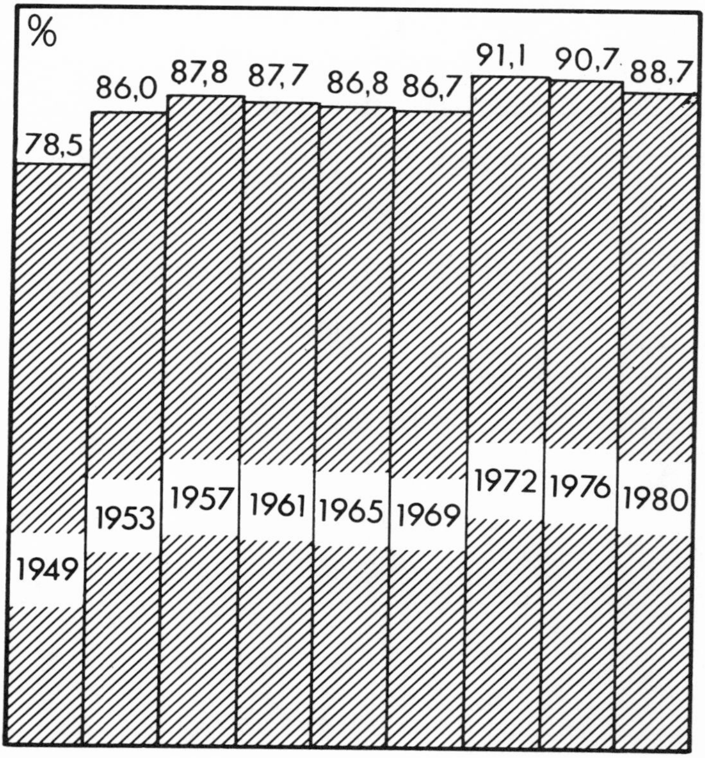

1949 and 1953
without Saarland

IN THE FEDERAL REPUBLIC OF GERMANY, VOTING IS NOT MANDATORY.

PERCENTAGE OF VOTES FOR PARTIES OTHER THAN SPD, CDU/CSU, FDP, IN THE FEDERAL ELECTIONS SINCE 1965

	1965 %	1969 %	1972 %	1976 %	1980 %
NPD - Nationaldemokratische Partei Deutschlands (National Democratic Party of Germany)	2.0	4.3	0.6	0.3	0.2
DFU - Deutsche Friedensunion (German Peace Union)	1.3	-	-	-	-
ADF - Aktion Demokratischer Fortschritt (Campaign for Democratic Progress)	-	0.6	-	-	-
DKP - Deutsche Kommunistische Partei (German Communist Party)	-	-	0.3	0.3	0.2
BP - Bayernpartei (Bavarian Partei)	-	0.2	-	-	-
EFP/EP - Europaeische Foederalistische Partei/Europa Partei (European Federalist Party/Europe Party)	x	0.2	0.1	-	-
AUD - Aktionsgemeinschaft Unabhaengiger Deutscher (Society of Independent Germans)	0.2	-	-	0.1	-
CVP - Christliche Volkspartei (Christian People's Party)	0.1	-	-	-	-
BHE - Gesamtdeutscher Block/Gesamtdeutsche Partei (All-German Bloc/All-German Party)	-	0.1	-	-	-
UAP - Unabhaengige Arbeiter Partei (Deutsche Sozialisten) (Independent Workers' Party - German Socialists)	x	x	-	0.1	-
KPD - Kommunistische Partei Deutschlands (Communist Party of Germany)	-	-	-	0.1	-
KBW - Kommunistischer Bund Westdeutschland (Communist League of West Germany)	-	-	-	0.1	-
FSU - Freisoziale Union - Demokratische Mitte (Free Social Union - Democratic Middle)	x	x	x	-	x
AVP - Aktionsgemeinschaft Vierte Partei (Fourth Party Society)	-	-	-	x	-
CBV - Christliche Bayerische Volkspartei (Christian Bavarian People's Party)	-	-	-	x	-
EAP - Europaeische Arbeiterpartei (European Workers' Party)	-	-	-	x	-
5%-Block-Partei (5% Bloc Party)	-	-	-	x	-
GIM - Gruppe Internationaler Marxisten (International Marxists' Group)	-	-	-	x	-
RFP - Recht und Freiheit Partei (Justice and Freedom Party)	-	-	-	x	-
VL - Vereinigte Linke (United Left)	-	-	-	x	-
BUP - Buergerpartei (Citizens Party - Anti-tax Party)	-	-	-	-	x
GRUENE - Die Gruenen (The Green Party - Environmentalists)	-	-	-	-	1.5
V - Volksfront (The People's Front)	-	-	-	-	x
	3.6	5.4	1.0	1.0	2.0

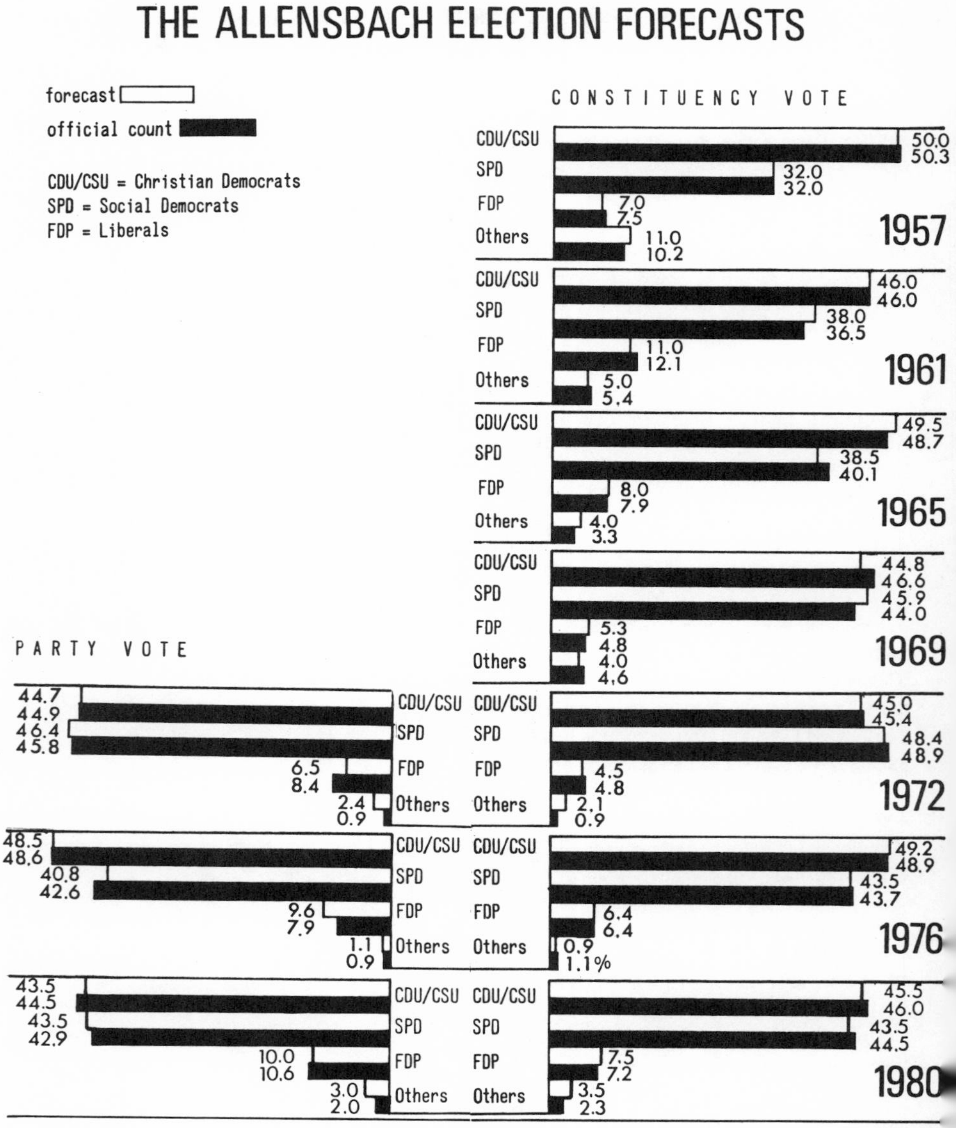

For seven consecutive federal elections, the Institut fuer Demoskopie Allensbach published a forecast before the official count. In 1957 and 1961, the prognoses were published in the Frankfurter Allgemeine Zeitung, a national daily. In all subsequent elections, they were broadcast on TV on Election Day immediately after the polling stations closed. Forecasts were based on omnibus surveys and quota sampling with approximately 2,000 respondents. Interviewing was completed six days before the election in the years from 1957 through 1969, five days before in 1972, four days before in 1976, and two days before in 1980.

III. THE SOCIAL CONTEXT

RELIGION AND THE CHURCH

GOD

Question: "*There are certainly different conceptions of God. Which point of view on this list is most like your own?*" (L)

C

	March 1974 %
You can explain nature scientifically but you cannot explain the way everything has come into being. Therefore there must be a creator, because man cannot have created himself	50
God is present everywhere in nature and becomes visible to us in its wondrous laws	38
Man's mind and soul elevate him above the level of crude nature. God is the symbolic expression of man's opportunity to strive for the Good and Perfect	32
God is the master of the world, our fate is in his hands. Whoever does not live in accordance with his commands will be punished at the Last Judgment	25
There is no God. Both worldly and natural events can be explained scientifically	11
No reply	2
	158

THE MEANING OF LIFE

Question: "*We sometimes ask ourselves what we're living for—what the meaning of life is. Where do you mainly find the meaning of your life? Could you tell me with the aid of this list?*" (L)

	Total population		Protestants		Catholics	
	1974 %	1979 %	1974 %	1979 %	1974 %	1979 %
In -						
helping to create a better society	46	25	48	24	43	24
proving myself in this life, so that I can face my creator	26	20	21	15	35	29
being able to have a home of my own, becoming a home owner	26	19	25	19	30	19
being available for others, helping others	24	15	23	14	28	16
working as hard as I can for a certain idea	23	15	26	15	20	15
doing what God expects of me	21	17	17	12	28	25
	166	111	160	99	184	128

RELIGIOUS BELIEFS OF OUR TIME

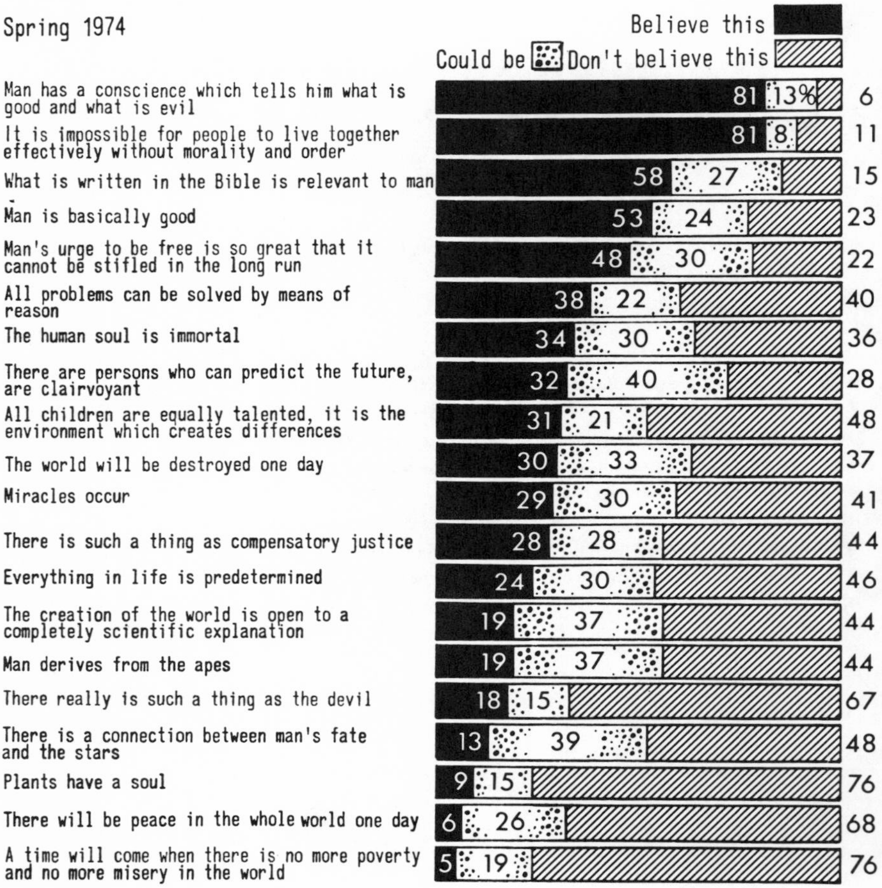
Spring 1974
Believe this
Could be
Don't believe this
Man has a conscience which tells him what is good and what is evil 81 13% 6
It is impossible for people to live together effectively without morality and order 81 8 11
What is written in the Bible is relevant to man 58 27 15
Man is basically good 53 24 23
Man's urge to be free is so great that it cannot be stifled in the long run 48 30 22
All problems can be solved by means of reason 38 22 40
The human soul is immortal 34 30 36
There are persons who can predict the future, are clairvoyant 32 40 28
All children are equally talented, it is the environment which creates differences 31 21 48
The world will be destroyed one day 30 33 37
Miracles occur 29 30 41
There is such a thing as compensatory justice 28 28 44
Everything in life is predetermined 24 30 46
The creation of the world is open to a completely scientific explanation 19 37 44
Man derives from the apes 19 37 44
There really is such a thing as the devil 18 15 67
There is a connection between man's fate and the stars 13 39 48
Plants have a soul 9 15 76
There will be peace in the whole world one day 6 26 68
A time will come when there is no more poverty and no more misery in the world 5 19 76

WHAT IS SACRED?

Question: *"Could you please take a look at these cards? Where would you say, 'I won't stand for having this taken away,' 'this is sacred to me?"* (C)

A

	July 1978
	%
Christmas in the family	73
Having my personal freedom, being able to make decisions on my own	70
For parents to be able to educate children as they see fit	61
For the family, the relatives to stick together	60
Keeping a promise that's been given, no matter what	60
Being able to live in a free society	60
Doing my duty	46
For Sunday to be a day of rest, not a working day	45
Christian baptism	41
The fact that I'm German	40
Being able to go on vacation regularly	35
Loving the place I come from	35
My ideals	31
The Lord's Prayer	27
Being able to drive my own car anytime	27
Finishing work on time, being able to stop punctually	25
Being able to watch television undisturbed in the evenings	24
Doing my part for progress and a better society	23
Attending church	22
The crucifix	17
Dressing in style	16
The New Testament	15
The procession	7
A pilgrimage	7
None of the above	3
	870

GOOD INTENTIONS

Question: *"It is often hard to put into words, but is there anything on this list which you resolve to do at present?"* (L)

	1961 March %	1979 March %
Not to get annoyed	43	41
Not to put off unpleasant things but to tackle them right away	31	34
To do more walking	31	32
To take life less seriously	26	32
To eat less	25	29
To go in for more sports	13	27
To be less nervous	26	26
To be more economical, to be more careful with money	25	24
To do more for my education, to broaden my knowledge	22	23
To be more energetic, not to be too passive	15	22
To understand others better, to put myself in their position	21	21
To smoke less	19	20
To place more blame on myself and less on others	22	19
To eat less sweets	16	18
To get up earlier in the morning	20	15
To be more diplomatic, to handle things more skillfully	13	16
To keep better control of myself, not to let myself go so much	14	13
To be more friendly to others, to be less curt	19	13
To be less reserved, to be more self-confident	12	13
To be less happy-go-lucky and think more about life's purpose	15	13
To go to church more often	15	10
Not to talk so much	18	10
To sleep more	20	12
To be more punctual	11	9
To always tell the truth	10	8
To drink less coffee	13	8
To join in activities with other people	–	20
To drink hardly any liquor	–	14
To think more of others and be less egotistic	–	8
To drink less beer or wine	–	7
	515	557

- = not asked

THE TEN COMMANDMENTS

Question: *"Are the 10 Commandments of the Bible still valid for you?"*

	July 1978					
	Still valid %	Outdated %	Yes and No %	No opinion %		
Total population	48	14	29	9	=	100
Men	42	16	32	10	=	100
Women	53	13	26	8	=	100
AGE GROUPS						
16-29	27	22	39	12	=	100
30-44	46	15	30	9	=	100
45-59	54	13	25	8	=	100
60 and over	67	7	21	5	=	100
EDUCATION						
Elementary	48	14	28	10	=	100
Secondary	48	15	31	6	=	100
DENOMINATION						
Protestant	44	13	32	11	=	100
Catholic	55	13	27	5	=	100
Other	27	36	24	13	=	100

READING THE BIBLE

Question: *"Do you sometimes read the Bible - the Old Testament or the New - aside from during church services, that is?"*

	Frequently %	From time to time %	Seldom %	Never %		
Total population - 1966 April	5	15	17	63	=	100
- 1978 July	4	11	22	63	=	100
Men	2	9	19	70	=	100
Women	5	13	25	57	=	100
AGE GROUPS						
16-29	1	5	15	79	=	100
30-44	3	7	24	66	=	100
45-59	3	13	22	62	=	100
60 and over	9	19	29	43	=	100
DENOMINATION						
Protestant	3	9	23	65	=	100
Catholic	5	14	24	57	=	100
Other	6	6	9	79	=	100

RELIGION OUTDATED

Question: *"Do you think religion can provide an answer to most of the problems of our day, or is it too outmoded and out-of-date?"*

	Total population		Denomination			
			Protestants		Catholics	
	1975	1980	1975	1980	1975	1980
	%	%	%	%	%	%
Can provide an answer	29	33	23	26	36	46
Outmoded	52	48	55	53	46	37
No opinion	19	19	22	21	18	17
	100	100	100	100	100	100

	January 1980							
	Men	Women	Age groups				Education	
			16-29	30-44	45-59	60 and over	Elementary	Secondary
	%	%	%	%	%	%	%	%
Can provide an answer	29	37	21	26	37	51	35	31
Outmoded	53	43	61	55	44	30	45	52
No opinion	18	20	18	19	19	19	20	17
	100	100	100	100	100	100	100	100

TAKING AN OATH

Question: *"As you know, the wording of an oath is 'I swear to this, so help me God'. But you can also just say 'I swear to this'. Assuming you had to take an oath, which wording would you choose?"*

A

	I swear to this, so help me God	I swear to this	Other, no reply	
	%	%	%	
Total population - January 1971	63	35	2	= 100

RELIGIOUS EDUCATION

Question: *"Do you believe it is important for children to receive a religious education, or do you think it really doesn't make any difference or may even have a bad influence?"*

	February 1979				
	Important	No difference	Bad influence	Undecided	
	%	%	%	%	
Total population	51	34	5	10	= 100
DENOMINATION					
Protestant	44	39	4	13	= 100
Catholic	65	26	2	7	= 100

UPBRINGING

Question: *"Would you say your upbringing was very religious, or did your parents not really relate to religion?"*

	February 1979							
	Very religious		Moderately		Didn't relate		Yes and no	
	Protes-tants %	Catho-lics %	Protes-tants %	Catho-lics %	Protes-tants %	Catho-lics %	Protes-tants %	Catho-lics %
Total	16	44	40	37	35	14	9	5
Men	13	38	38	41	39	17	10	4
Women	19	48	41	33	32	12	8	7
AGE GROUPS								
16-29	10	29	34	39	46	24	10	8
30-44	10	34	40	43	40	16	10	7
45-59	15	42	43	40	35	15	7	3
60 and over	30	69	44	23	18	4	8	4
EDUCATION								
Elementary	18	44	41	36	33	14	8	6
Secondary	14	39	38	40	38	16	10	5

DIFFICULT TO BELIEVE

Question: *"There are many reasons why people find it difficult to believe in the Christian message today. These cards list several reasons. Would you please lay out all of those which represent your own view?"* (C)

	August 1979		
	Total population %	Denomination Protestant %	Catholic %
People want to live as they please, without having a bad conscience in doing so	53	50	57
Churches have too often stood by the ruling classes, the property owners, or rather, the strong and not the weak	47	47	43
The church doesn't talk the language of our time	46	48	40
Natural science explains the world very differently than Christianity does	42	44	38
Christianity has failed; people have not become better human beings and there continue to be wars	40	45	31
The present time proves that even without the Christian belief people are obliging, honest and conscientious	37	40	32
There are very few believing Christians and if you are one, you're almost an outsider	31	32	29
The church does not stand up for social justice	25	26	21
None of these	10	10	11

OBLIGATIONS OF A CHRISTIAN

Question: *"Two people are talking here about the obligations of a Christian. Which of the two says what you also tend to think?"* (ill.)

	August 1979		
	Total	Denomination	
	pop.	Protestant	Catholic
	%	%	%
"I think it's a Christian's obligation to try to change society and to fight against anything he, as a Christian, thinks is wrong and unjust."	21	18	24
"I take a different position. A Christian isn't a reformer; his task is simply to work on improving himself and to live a Christian life."	60	63	61
Undecided	19	19	15
	100	100	100

TEST-TUBE BABY

Question: *"In England a woman recently gave birth to a baby that had been produced artificially. Have you ever heard about this so-called test-tube baby?"* (yes = 93 percent)

"Here are two people discussing the subject. Which of the two says what you yourself tend to think?" (ill., X)

	August 1978		
	Total	Denomination	
	pop.	Protestant	Catholic
	%	%	%
I approve of a couple choosing this artificial method if they could not otherwise have any children. I am in favor of making full use of scientific progress.	43	40	49
I believe that if a couple cannot have children by natural means, they should accept the fact and not have their own children. This artificial method is taking it too far.	43	49	36
Undecided	14	11	15
	100	100	100

COMMUNISM AND CHRISTIAN BELIEF

Question: *"Can a devout Christian also be a Communist, or are Christian faith and communist ideology incompatible?"*

C

	Total population		Denomination			
			Protestant		Catholic	
	1959	1974	1959	1974	1959	1974
	%	%	%	%	%	%
Incompatible	70	57	68	55	74	60
Can also be a Communist	12	28	13	31	10	25
Undecided	18	15	19	14	16	15
	100	100	100	100	100	100

INTERESTS

Question: *"If you read over the following, which of these things would you say really interest you, which would you like to find out more about or which would you like to do yourself?"* (L)

C

	August 1979 %
Being together with other people in order to forget everyday troubles and worries	45
Experience a thrilling football game	31
Learning to control your body through exercises in concentration, autogenic training	28
Being present when something special is going on somewhere	25
Classical music (Bach, Beethoven, etc.)	22
Astrology, the relationship between the stars and human fate	17
Yoga	16
Acupuncture	16
Pop festival, pop music	14
Meditation: thinking about oneself in a group, submerging oneself completely in oneself	12
Encounter groups	9
Working for a political party	9
Personal meditation, reflecting on a sentence or a chapter from the Bible	7
Working for a labor union	6
Achieving a happy state of mind through drugs	3
Salvation Army	2
Jehovah's Witnesses	1
None of these	12

PERSONAL ASSESSMENT

Question put to Protestants and Catholics: *"Where would you place yourself on this list—which statement would apply?"* (L)

	August 1979	
	Protestants %	Catholics %
I consider myself a Christian, but the church doesn't mean much to me	34	28
I am a believing member of my church and I follow its doctrine	14	42
I have my own beliefs, my own philosophy of life, completely independent from the church	20	10
I don't know what I should believe in. That's why I'd rather leave such questions open	12	6
I live and work. Everything else takes care of itself - I don't need any beliefs	8	4
I would like to believe but I am uncertain about so many things	6	6
Belief means nothing to me. Instead I concentrate on the problems of this world and the problems of my fellow human beings	5	2
No answer	1	2
	100	100

PROVIDENCE

Question: *''Do you believe that everything in each individual's life is pre-determined, or don't you believe so?''*

	May 1979			
	Don't believe so	Believe so	Undecided	
	%	%	%	
Total population	54	30	16	= 100
AGE GROUPS				
16-29	63	20	17	= 100
30-44	59	25	16	= 100
45-59	50	34	16	= 100
60 and over	43	41	16	= 100
DENOMINATION				
Protestant	55	29	16	= 100
Catholic	51	32	17	= 100
Other/None	66	24	10	= 100

TRANSMIGRATION OF SOULS

Question: *''Have you ever heard tell of the transmigration of souls, meaning that after death the human soul supposedly moves into another body? - Do you think this is possible, or don't you believe in it?''*

	Don't believe in it	Possible	Undecided, Never heard of it	
	%	%	%	
Total population - January 1966	48	11	41	= 100
- December 1977	57	16	27	= 100

DO PLANTS OR ANIMALS HAVE A SOUL?

Question: *''Many people say that animals also have a soul—that they experience pleasure and suffering and can laugh and cry. Do you think this is true, or not?''*

Question: *''Many people say that plants also have a soul. Do you think so too, or not?''*

A

	Animals		Plants
	July 1959	October 1977	October 1977
	%	%	%
Yes, think so	69	69	24
No, don't think so	28	28	63
Undecided	3	3	13
	100	100	100

DESTRUCTION OF THE WORLD

Question: *"Do you think the world will be destroyed one day, or do you think the world will go on existing forever?"*

	May 1979			
	Will be destroyed %	Will go on existing %	Undecided %	
Total population	38	32	30	= 100
Men	38	33	29	= 100
Women	37	31	32	= 100
AGE GROUPS				
16-29	37	31	32	= 100
30-44	35	34	31	= 100
45-59	38	30	32	= 100
60 and over	41	31	28	= 100
DENOMINATION				
Protestant	31	35	34	= 100
Catholic	44	28	28	= 100
Other/None	44	30	26	= 100

LIFE AFTER DEATH

Question: *"Do you believe there is any form of life after death?"*

	Yes %	No %	Impossible to say %	
Total population - April 1956	42	34	24	= 100
- March 1964	38	37	25	= 100
- January 1971	35	42	23	= 100
- November 1975	36	40	24	= 100
- January 1980	41	35	24	= 100
Men	34	41	25	= 100
Women	46	29	25	= 100
AGE GROUPS				
16-29	36	36	28	= 100
30-44	37	37	26	= 100
45-59	38	37	25	= 100
60 and over	50	28	22	= 100
DENOMINATION				
Protestants	33	39	28	= 100
Catholics	52	27	21	= 100
Other/None	28	47	25	= 100

PUNISHMENT

Question: *"Some people fear that we will be punished after death for the wrong we have done. Does this thought occur to you sometimes, often, or not at all?"*

	April 1975					
	Often	Sometimes	Never	No reply		
	%	%	%	%		
Total population	7	27	57	9	=	100
Men	5	24	63	8	=	100
Women	10	29	52	9	=	100
AGE GROUPS						
14-29	5	21	63	11	=	100
30-44	5	26	62	7	=	100
45-59	8	27	57	8	=	100
60 and over	13	33	45	9	=	100

THINKING ABOUT DEATH

Question: *"Have you ever thought about your own death? Would you say frequently, sometimes, seldom, or never?"*

	April 1975				
	Total	Age groups			
	pop.	14-29	30-44	45-59	60 and over
	%	%	%	%	%
Frequently	19	10	10	15	42
Sometimes, seldom	53	46	59	62	46
Never	25	41	28	20	10
No reply	3	3	3	3	2
	100	100	100	100	100

EUTHANASIA

Question: *"The medical profession today is already so advanced that the lives of terminally ill people can often be considerably prolonged by various medical means. There are differing opinions on this matter. With which of the following points of view would you agree?"*

The one:

"Doctors should prolong the life of a terminally ill person at all costs - regardless of the expense involved in the care and treatment and the medical equipment and medicine, and even if it involves great pain for the patient."

The other:

"At all costs - that goes too far. There are limits to the pain one can inflict upon someone, and there are also limits on the medical expenses in such a case."

	June 1977				
	Total	Denomination		Persons who have been -	
	pop.	Protestant	Catholic	present at a death	not present at a death
Prolong life -	%	%	%	%	%
at all costs	14	12	17	18	9
within limits	77	81	73	73	83
Undecided	9	7	10	9	8
	100	100	100	100	100

Question: *"When the terminally ill are no longer able to decide for themselves, who do you feel should make the decision as to whether their lives should be prolonged or whether their suffering should be shortened?"*

B

	June 1977
	%
The relatives	54
The attending physicians	35
A group of physicians that are there for such cases	27
A combination of physicians, lawyers and clergymen	10
A combination of physicians and clergymen	8
A combination of physicians and lawyers	5
Other/No answer	9

Question: *"Could you please read the following statement. Would you agree or disagree?"* (L)

'A seriously ill patient in the hospital should have the right to choose to die and to demand that the doctor give him/her an injection for this purpose.'

B

	1973	1977	Age groups			Denomination		Persons who have been -	
	June	June	16-29	30-59	60 and over	Protestant	Catholic	present at	not present
	Total population							a death	at a death
	%	%	%	%	%	%	%	%	%
Agree	53	55	63	56	48	57	52	52	59
Disagree	33	29	25	26	39	27	33	31	27
Undecided	14	16	12	18	13	16	15	17	14
	100	100	100	100	100	100	100	100	100

CHARACTERISTICS OF A CHURCH GOER

Question: *"If all you know about someone is that he goes to church regularly (half group: never), what kind of a person would you say he is? Which of these characteristics would you expect this person to have?"* (C)

	March 1979 Goes to church- regularly %	never %
Eager to help, a good person	44	12
Friendly, polite	32	11
Honest	31	25
Old-fashioned, conservative	30	4
Happy	28	10
Politically on the right	28	4
Agreeable, easy to get along with	27	10
Social-minded	25	11
Inspires confidence	23	9
Tolerant	20	21
Likable	18	14
Self-confident	18	31
Provincial	17	3
Open-minded	17	16
Fanatical	15	10
Narrow-minded	12	13
Authoritarian	9	8
Well-read	9	9
Intelligent	8	14
Enterprising, active	6	11
Politically active, interested	6	13
Progressive	5	16
Successful	4	11
Egotistical	4	14
Politically on the left	2	25
None of these	20	34

COMMUNION

Question: *"Please answer the next question only if it doesn't bother you. Do you take communion once a year, more often, or less often?"*

	Catholics		Protestants	
	1953 %	1979 %	1953 %	1979 %
Once or more weekly	3	11	x	x
1-3 times monthly	11	11	1	2
Once or more yearly	52	26	40	26
Less frequently	12	23	25	32
Not since my youth	9	16	20	29
Don't take it	2	6	3	6
No reply	11	7	11	5
	100	100	100	100

REGULAR CHURCH ATTENDANCE

	1963 %	1967/69 %	1973 %	1976 %	1980 %
Protestants					
Total	15	10	7	8	8
Men	11	8	5	5	4
Women	17	13	8	11	11
AGE GROUPS					
16-29	11	6	2	3	2
30-44	10	6	4	4	5
45-59	16	11	7	5	8
60 and over	24	22	14	21	18
PARTY PREFERENCE					
SPD	9	6	4	6	7
CDU/CSU	23	18	12	11	11
FDP	16	15	5	5	9
TOWN AND COUNTRY					
Villages	25	19	11	14	11
Small towns	15	10	8	8	10
Medium cities	14	9	6	6	8
Large cities	9	7	4	8	6
Catholics					
Total population	55	48	35	34	31
Men	48	42	28	25	24
Women	61	53	41	42	37
AGE GROUPS					
16-29	52	40	19	21	16
30-44	51	42	30	27	20
45-59	56	53	41	41	36
60 and over	64	62	54	51	51
PARTY PREFERENCE					
SPD	27	28	16	19	14
CDU/CSU	74	66	53	45	46
FDP	37	27	20	21	16
TOWN AND COUNTRY					
Villages	68	63	52	43	40
Small towns	58	50	40	39	32
Medium cities	51	42	28	33	30
Large cities	42	37	24	25	23

*Number of respondents: 1963=11,000 Protestants, 8,500 Catholics; 1967/69=10,700 Protestants, 8,400 Catholics; 1973=4,000 Protestants, 3,400 Catholics; 1976=1,000 Protestants, 850 Catholics; 1980=1,980 Protestants, 1,740 Catholics.

DOES THE CHURCH FIT IN WITH OUR TIMES?

Question: *"In your opinion, how well does the church fit in with our times? I have a scale here. Ten would mean it fits in very well and 0 would mean it doesn't fit in with our times at all. Which rung between 0 and 10 would you choose?"* (ill.)

A

	Total population 1974	Total population 1979	Protestants 1974	Protestants 1979	Catholics 1974	Catholics 1979
	%	%	%	%	%	%
10 - Fits in very well with our times	14	12	12	7	18	21
9	3	3	2	2	6	5
8	10	11	9	9	13	16
7	8	8	7	9	10	9
6	8	9	9	9	8	8
5	25	20	28	24	24	18
4	8	7	10	8	6	5
3	7	9	8	10	5	7
2	5	8	5	9	3	5
1	2	4	2	4	1	1
0 - Doesn't fit in with our times at all	7	6	6	4	3	4
Undecided, no opinion	3	3	2	5	3	1
	100	100	100	100	100	100
Average	5.6	5.4	5.4	5.1	6.4	6.4

Question: *"There are several demands on this list. Which of these would you also favor?"* (L)

A

	October 1974
	%
That non-denominational schools be established everywhere and no child be forced to go to a denominational school	45
That churches be treated like other non-profit societies and receive no special privileges	35
The church tax should no longer be collected by the internal revenue service, together with income taxes, but by the churches themselves	34
That you should no longer have to state your religion when filling out official forms	30
Children who don't take part in religion classes should be offered the choice of another similar field	29
Ministers, such as army chaplains or prison chaplains, should in future be employed and paid by the churches themselves rather than by the state	28
Withdrawal from church membership should be made easier	23
No more crucifixes in schoolrooms, courtrooms or other public buildings	23
No more school prayers in the schools	22
None of these	30
	299

TAKING A POSITION

Question: *"There are various opinions about which issues the church should take a position on, and which it had best stay away from. I have a list here. Could you please read it and tell me which problems the church should take a stand on, i.e. where you think it is important that the church make its position clear."* (L)

A

It is important that the church take a position on -	July 1978 %
Problems of the disadvantaged, for example the elderly, those alone, those handicapped	50
Euthanasia, medical help in dying for the terminally ill	45
Protection, support of the family	40
Aid to developing countries	38
Politics of peace, disarmament	36
Marriage law reform, divorce law reform	36
Abortion	35
Problems of the foreign workers in Germany	29
Expansion of social security, such as improvement of old-age pensions for women, medical care, improvement of benefits for accident victims	26
Violence in television, movies, newspapers	25
Pornography; to what extent should unrestricted presentations on television, in magazines and in advertising be allowed	25
Domestic security, combating crime and terrorism	20
Environmental protection	16
Educational aims, what children should learn in school	14
Being economical, consuming less	13
Ostpolitik, the relationship with East bloc countries	9
Continuing education	8
Well-balanced coverage in television, radio, newspapers and magazines	8

ONE CHRISTIAN CHURCH

Question: *"Supposing the Protestant and Catholic churches were able to agree on all important issues and were to join into one single Christian church, would you favor or oppose the existence of only one Christian church in the future?"* (X)

"Apart from whether one is for or against the union of the two churches, do you believe that such a union is possible at all, or do you believe that the churches will not agree anyhow?"

	Personally — Favor	Oppose	Undecided		February 1967 Churches will not agree	Union possible	Impossible to say	
	%	%	%		%	%	%	
Total population	62	14	24	= 100	45	33	22	= 100
Protestants	60	16	24	= 100	51	28	21	= 100
Catholics	71	12	17	= 100	38	41	21	= 100

CONCESSIONS

Question put to Protestants/Catholics: *"The unification of the two churches would, of course, require concessions to be made on both sides. How do you feel about this? For example, would you agree to the introduction of confession in confessionals for all Christians?" (Catholics: "For example, would you agree to the abolishment of confession in confessionals?")*

A

	February 1967			
	Would agree %	Would not agree %	Undecided %	
Protestants	9	80	11	= 100
Catholics	67	22	11	= 100

HOW THE CHURCHES VIEW EACH OTHER

Question put to Protestants/Catholics: *"There are various things printed on these cards which one hears said about the Catholic (Protestant) church. What would you say as well, what is true in your opinion?"* (C)

A

	February 1967	
	What Protestants say about the Catholic church %	What Catholics say about the Protestant church %
Has too much power	62	6
Always begging for money, even though it has millions at its disposal	48	12
Believes that it alone is able to interpret the Bible correctly	42	26
Always wants to convert others	41	7
Treats its faithful like little children who cannot be counted on to have independent thoughts	41	5
Applies pressure to politicians	40	6
Opposed to any modern conception of life	35	5
Encourages hypocrisy and bigoted attitudes and thus repels others	31	3
Has not got a clear enough political standpoint, always takes the current ruling head of state as its point of orientation	13	10
Vague in matters of faith; one says one thing, another says another	12	26
Destroys the basis of faith with all its talk about modern Christianity	11	13
Adheres too little to traditional religious truths	10	19
Gives its faithful too little support and direction	7	24
Its church services are too simple and not ceremonious enough	5	44
None of these	12	29
	410	235

PRECONCEPTIONS

Question put to Protestants/Catholics: *"Some people say there are certain characteristics which one frequently finds in Catholics (Protestants). A variety of them are printed on these cards. Naturally, it's difficult to generalize, but which of these characteristics do you think are typical of Catholics (Protestants)?"* (L)

	February 1967	
	What Protestants say about Catholics	What Catholics say about Protestants
	%	%
Stick together	48	27
Think they have a lease on religious truth	45	12
Sanctimonious	42	4
Blind believers	36	5
Believe that only they can understand and interpret the Bible correctly	32	28
Act like judges of morality	31	3
Pious, devout	30	11
Insincere	28	4
Morally strict	27	7
Full of prejudices	22	9
Narrow-minded	19	8
Subservient	19	4
Obstinate	17	8
Calculating	17	7
Arrogant, conceited	16	10
Old fashioned	16	4
Ambitious, go for the highest positions	15	9
Efficient in business, always after money	14	8
Self-righteous	14	9
Petty	11	5
The majority don't even go to church	11	42
Self-conscious	9	16
Politically clever	7	9
Well-bred	4	10
Successful in life	4	11
Cosmopolitan	3	23
Don't want to conform, have no discipline	3	7
Fair, just	3	12
None of these	20	34
	563	346

CATHOLICS' VIEW OF THE CATHOLIC CHURCH

Question put to Catholics: *''There are different opinions about the Catholic church, some of them positive, others negative. May I ask first what you like about the Catholic church, what you think is good? Could you tell me with the help of this list?''* (L)

''Could you tell me what bothers you about the church?'' (L)

Positive:	Catholics 1979 %
It gives you a feeling of community	41
It keeps alive traditions and cultural values	41
I'm simply glad that there is a church and that we can find Christ and each other there	35
It provides a framework for educating children in a way I approve of	32
It does a lot for the family	30
The fact that the church doesn't necessarily go along with change	27
I find a spiritual home there	27
Its capacity for regeneration and change	27
It speaks for the weak and oppressed	23
It's the place where you find out what you're living for	22
It makes serious appeals to the politicians	21
You find the divine secret there	19
The church tells me how I should live	18
Don't think anything is positive	15
	378

Negative:	Catholics 1979 %
Its position on contraception	46
The church is too rich, has too much money	43
Its position on other sexual questions	34
The traditional forms of piety	33
It insists too much on tradition	33
The fact that the government collects a church tax	28
The church doesn't practice what it preaches	26
It does too little for the poor and weak	23
It makes excessive moral demands on the individual	22
It meddles too much in politics	19
The church doesn't often enough take a clear and definite position	18
The church is too closely connected with the government	12
The church adjusts too much to the times	9
You don't find a spiritual home or a community in the church	7
Nothing bothers me	16
	369

POPE JOHN PAUL II

Question: *"What do you think of the present pope?"*

Question: *"This time a Polish cardinal and* not *an Italian was elected pope. Do you think this is good or not?"*

Question: *"Do you think that the new pope will greatly change the Catholic church, or do you think it will pretty much stay the same?"*

Question: *"Do you think that the new pope will succeed in eliminating discrimination against Christians in the Eastern bloc, or won't he succeed?"*

	1980 Jan.	1978 Nov.			
	Total population		Protestants	Catholics	Others
Pope John Paul II is -	%	%	%	%	%
Excellent	19	19	13	28	11
Good	45	51	52	52	36
Rather good	16	10	10	10	13
Not so good	5	1	1	x	2
Not at all good	3	1	1	x	4
No opinion	12	18	23	10	34
	100	100	100	100	100
Good that the pope is not an Italian		79	76	83	75
Not good		2	3	2	1
Indifferent		15	16	13	19
No opinion		4	5	2	5
		100	100	100	100
Will change the Catholic church		27	26	30	22
Will pretty much stay the same		53	50	54	55
Undecided		20	24	16	23
		100	100	100	100
Will succeed in eliminating discrimination		26	24	30	18
Don't think so		37	36	37	46
Undecided		37	40	33	36
		100	100	100	100

Question: *"Pope John Paul II has been in office for a while now already. According to what you have heard about him up till now, is Pope John Paul II a progressive pope or is he more conservative?"*

	October 1980			
	Progressive	More conservative	Undecided	
	%	%	%	
Total population	48	30	22	= 100
DENOMINATION				
Protestant	46	28	26	= 100
Catholic	55	31	14	= 100
Other/none	30	39	31	= 100

THE SEXES

Question: *"If you were to be born again, would you rather be a man or a woman?"*

	February 1976					
	Men total	Women total	Age groups of women 16-29	30-44	45-59	60 and over
Would rather be a -	%	%	%	%	%	%
man	82	24	21	29	24	22
woman	6	63	67	61	62	64
Undecided	12	13	12	10	14	14
	100	100	100	100	100	100

EASIER FOR MEN

Question: *"Who generally has an easier time of it, men or women?"*

	Easier for - Men	Women	Equally hard for both	Undecided	
	%	%	%	%	
Total population - August 1979	44	17	33	6	= 100
- March 1979	38	19	37	6	= 100
Men	26	28	41	5	= 100
Women	49	12	35	4	= 100
OCCUPATION					
Unskilled workers	39	20	36	5	= 100
Skilled workers	33	22	40	5	= 100
Non-managerial employees and public servants	42	18	36	4	= 100
Managerial employees and public servants	37	16	40	7	= 100
Self-employeds, professionals	36	23	37	4	= 100
Farmers	43	11	38	8	= 100

WOMEN MORE INDEPENDENT TODAY

Question: *"One often hears that women today are more independent, more self-assured than they used to be and that they no longer simply listen to what men say; instead they have their own opinion. What is your impression—do you also find this to be true, or can't you say that?"*

"Do you approve of this or do you disapprove?"

	Total population		Men		Women	
	1972 June	1979 Nov.	1972 June	1979 Nov.	1972 June	1979 Nov.
	%	%	%	%	%	%
I also find this to be true	82	78	80	76	83	79
- I approve	68	63	60	54	75	72
- I disapprove	6	4	8	7	5	1
- Hard to say	8	11	12	15	3	6
You can't say that	12	14	13	15	11	14
Undecided	6	8	7	9	6	7
	100	100	100	100	100	100

FRAU OR FRAEULEIN?

Question: *"It has been suggested that in public all unmarried women over 30 should be addressed as 'Frau' (Mrs.) and no longer as 'Fraeulein' (Miss). Would you be for or against this?"*

	September 1976			
	For	Against	Undecided	
	%	%	%	
Total women	75	8	17	= 100
Total men	65	12	23	= 100

MARRIED NAME

Question: *"Up to now, women have taken their husband's name at marriage. A bill is now being considered which would permit you to choose either the man's name or the woman's as your family name. Have you heard of this?"* (Yes, heard of it = 83 percent)

"It would then also be possible for the man to take his wife's name. Do you consider this a good thing, a bad thing or doesn't it make any difference to you?"

"If such a bill were adopted, do you think many men would adopt their wife's last name, or don't you think so?"

	March 1975		
	Total	Men	Women
	%	%	%
Good thing	27	23	31
Bad	29	32	25
No difference	37	38	37
Undecided	7	7	7
	100	100	100

	March 1975		
	Total	Men	Women
	%	%	%
Men wouldn't adopt their wife's name	77	77	77
Yes, they would	6	7	5
Undecided	17	16	18
	100	100	100

EQUAL OPPORTUNITY

Question: *"In your opinion, in which areas should there be more equal opportunity for women here in West Germany than there has been up to now?"* (L)

	November 1979	
	Men	Women
	%	%
Salaries and wages	55	66
Opportunities for promotion at work	49	62
Political life, political appointments	38	44
Women appearing in public; the freedom of movement a woman has in public	27	41
Choosing a profession, the question of which professions are open to women	30	35
The rights one has in marriage and in the family	20	35
Sales and rental contracts, dealing with the authorities	17	26
The question of what children learn, what their training is to be	15	21
The education of children within the family	15	17
None of these	14	8

Question: *"If you hear of a family where the husband helps his wife regularly with the housework, would you say this appeals to you or does it not appeal to you?"*

A

	Appeals	Does not appeal	Undecided	
	%	%	%	
Total population - April 1970	74	13	13	= 100
- January 1976	80	12	8	= 100
- November 1979	77	11	12	= 100

PARENTAL MODELS

Question put to men/women: *"May I ask you a question about your father/mother? Would you say that you have followed your father's/mother's example in many ways, or not so much?"*

E

	April 1977									
	Father's example					Mother's example				
	Men	Age groups				Women	Age groups			
	total	14-29	30-44	45-59	60 and over	total	14-29	30-44	45-59	60 and over
	%	%	%	%	%	%	%	%	%	%
Followed his/her example:										
in many ways	22	13	18	27	35	32	21	22	35	47
in some ways	41	46	36	42	36	46	54	49	45	37
not at all	30	36	38	23	20	19	22	28	16	11
Other reply	7	5	8	8	9	3	3	1	4	5
	100	100	100	100	100	100	100	100	100	100

HAPPINESS IS CHILDREN?

Question: *"Do you believe a woman must have children in order to be happy?"*

E

	April 1977					
	Yes		No		Undecided	
	Women	Men	Women	Men	Women	Men
	%	%	%	%	%	%
Total population	38	38	41	35	21	27
AGE GROUPS						
14-29	19	18	58	51	23	31
30-44	33	37	48	38	19	25
45-59	43	47	36	25	21	28
60 and over	57	62	23	15	20	23

FATHER PRESENT AT DELIVERY

Question: *"There is a lot of talk right now about whether the father should be present at the birth of his child or not. What do you think? Are you in favor of or not in favor of allowing the father to be present during the delivery?"*

	In favor		Not in favor		Undecided, no reply	
	1975	1980	1975	1980	1975	1980
	%	%	%	%	%	%
Total population	54	58	30	26	16	16
FATHERS						
- who have already been present at delivery	85	80	10	8	5	12
- who have never been present at delivery	47	48	34	27	19	25
MOTHERS						
- whose husbands have already been present at delivery	85	95	9	4	6	1
- whose husbands have never been present at delivery	53	58	36	30	11	12

Question put to fathers: *"Were you yourself present at the birth of one of your children?"*

Question put to mothers: *"Was your husband present at the birth of one of your children?"*

A

		Fathers total	Mothers total	Age groups under 29	30-44	45-59	60 and over
Father was present -		%	%	%	%	%	%
Yes	1975	23	21	15	16	26	28
	1980	21	18	32	17	21	18

QUALITIES THAT COUNT

Question put to women/men: *"Which qualities do you value most in men (women)? Would you look at this list and name the five most important ones?"* (L)

Additional question: *"And sexual attractiveness—would you say it ranks among the five most important qualities?"*

Qualities in men	1964 Sept. %	1978 August %
Faithfulness	71	62
Warmth, cordiality	52	58
Sexual attractiveness	–	53
Honesty	55	49
Diligence	63	44
Naturalness	34	43
Intelligence	46	38
Humor	28	37
Efficiency at his job	–	36
Thrift	47	32
Cleanliness	34	27
Being practical-minded	–	20
Chivalry	28	17
Punctuality	20	17
Good looks	20	15
Tidiness	20	15
Discretion	8	10
	526	573

Qualities in women	1964 Sept. %	1978 August %
Naturalness	50	58
Faithfulness	62	54
Sexual attractiveness	–	53
Warmth, cordiality	50	51
Cleanliness	60	47
Thrift	65	46
Good looks	38	40
Honesty	45	38
Humor	25	33
Good cook	–	32
Diligence	45	30
Intelligence	29	30
Tidiness	35	23
Punctuality	15	12
Discretion	14	19
Efficiency at her job	–	7
Unselfishness	9	5
	542	578

– = not asked 1964

Question: *"How important is it, in your opinion, that a woman be able to cook well? I have a sheet here with black and white boxes. The uppermost white box means that it is extremely important that a woman be able to cook well; the lowest black box means that it is not at all important. You can choose any box."*

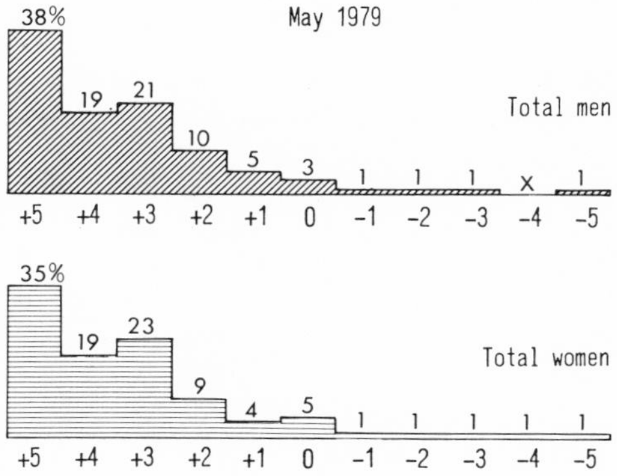

MEETING FOR THE FIRST TIME

Question to married, widowed and divorced persons: *"Could you tell me how you got to know your husband/wife - I mean, on what occasion you met for the first time?"*

	Men		Women	
	1963	1978	1963	1978
	%	%	%	%
At a party, the theater, the cinema, at sports activities, the market, dancing	45	53	50	40
Through friends, acquaintances, at a club or in the neighborhood	13	13	8	17
At work or through my profession	12	14	9	17
During holidays, on a trip	12	9	3	4
By chance, addressed me on the street, in a bar	12	3	3	8
Through the family	3	x	2	x
Knew each other as children	3	3	12	7
Through sports	x	x	5	3
Other or no answer	x	5	8	4
	100	100	100	100

TRUE LOVE . . . MORE OFTEN

Question: *"Do you believe in true love?" "Do you believe that you can only experience true love once, or can you experience it more often?"*

January 1980

	Men	Women	Age groups			
			16-29	30-44	45-59	60 and over
Believe -	%	%	%	%	%	%
Yes	52	63	57	59	58	58
No	32	25	27	29	28	28
Not sure	16	12	16	12	14	14
	100	100	100	100	100	100

	Men	Women
Experience -	%	%
Only once	37	47
More often	53	40
Not sure	10	13
	100	100

GETTING MORE TOLERANT

Question put to married persons: *"Do you think it's really necessary for husband and wife always to be of the same opinion in everything?"*

	Not necessary	Necessary	Undecided	
	%	%	%	
Married men - 1953	69	28	3	= 100
- 1979	84	11	5	= 100
Married women - 1953	62	33	5	= 100
- 1979	80	12	8	= 100

WHERE OPINIONS DIFFER

Question put to married persons: *"Could you tell me, with the aid of this list, where your wife/husband and you have* different *opinions?"*

	Married persons					
	Total		Men		Women	
	1953	1979	1953	1979	1953	1979
	%	%	%	%	%	%
Opinion about friends and acquaintances	30	39	32	42	27	36
Bringing up children	20	26	20	21	21	29
Money matters	28	25	29	22	27	26
Political matters	10	22	11	20	9	23
Religious matters	15	20	16	19	15	21
Furnishing our house	18	19	20	15	17	22
Professional matters	10	15	12	16	8	15
None of the above	5	1	6	x	4	1
We agree on everything	11	1	9	1	13	1
Other/no response	15	16	15	19	15	13
	162	184	170	175	156	187

WOULD MARRY THE SAME PERSON AGAIN

Question put to married persons: *"If you could choose again, would you marry the same man/woman?"*

G

	Married persons					
	Men			Women		
	1949	1963	1976	1949	1963	1976
	%	%	%	%	%	%
Yes, same person again	77	79	83	77	77	71
No	11	11	7	16	14	15
Undecided	12	10	10	7	9	14
	100	100	100	100	100	100

LIVING TOGETHER

Question: *"When a man and a woman live together without being legally married, do you feel that this is going too far, or would you not mind?"*

	June 1976								
	Total pop.	Men	Women	Age groups				Education	
				16-29	30-44	45-59	60 and over	Elementary	Secondary
	%	%	%	%	%	%	%	%	%
Wouldn't mind	66	69	64	86	76	51	44	62	80
Going too far	21	19	22	7	14	24	44	23	13
Undecided	13	12	14	7	10	25	12	15	7
	100	100	100	100	100	100	100	100	100

HESITANT IN OWN CASE

Follow-up question put to persons who don't mind or are undecided: *"Assuming you were faced wtih this question yourself, could you conceive of living with a man/woman without being legally married?"*

	June 1976				
	Conceivable	Would not consider it	Not so easy to say		
	%	%	%		
Total population	50	19	10	=	79
Men	54	15	12	=	81
Women	46	23	9	=	78
AGE GROUPS					
16-29	77	8	8	=	93
30-44	54	21	11	=	86
45-59	27	33	16	=	76
60 and over	34	16	6	=	56
MARITAL STATUS					
Single	78	7	7	=	92
Married	41	24	12	=	77

CHILDREN OUT OF WEDLOCK

Question: "When a man and a woman who have a child live together without being legally married, do you feel that this is going too far, or would you not mind?"

	June 1976				
	Wouldn't mind	Going too far	Undecided		
	%	%	%		
Total population	60	26	14	=	100
Men	66	22	12	=	100
Women	55	29	16	=	100
AGE GROUPS					
16-29	83	12	5	=	100
30-44	66	18	16	=	100
45-59	51	25	24	=	100
60 and over	34	52	14	=	100
MARITAL STATUS					
Single	81	11	8	=	100
Married	58	26	16	=	100

STRICTER RULES FOR IDOLS

Question: *"Would you find it disturbing if any of these people lived with someone without being legally married?"*

June 1976

	Pastor	Teacher	Neighbor	Politician	Doctor	Lawyer	None of these
	Would find it disturbing for a female -						
	%	%	%	%	%	%	%
Total population	48	25	19	18	17	14	47
Men	46	22	14	16	12	10	49
Women	50	27	24	19	21	16	46

	Pastor	Teacher	Neighbor	Politician	Doctor	Lawyer	None of these
	Would find it disturbing for a male -						
	%	%	%	%	%	%	%
Total population	45	21	18	17	16	11	51
Men	41	15	16	14	12	11	55
Women	48	26	19	19	19	12	48
AGE GROUPS							
16-29	29	6	10	9	4	5	67
30-44	43	15	11	9	10	4	53
45-59	52	31	23	22	24	16	44
60 and over	61	38	31	32	31	23	36
MARITAL STATUS							
Single	31	10	9	10	6	9	66
Married	49	23	20	17	17	11	47

EXTENDED FAMILIES

Question: *"Have you ever heard of the so-called extended families in which several men and women unite?"* (Yes, heard of them: 1972 = 91 percent; 1978 = 88 percent)

"Are you in favor of extended families in which various couples share the household and child-raising, or are you opposed to them? How would you answer according to this list?" (L)

	1972 Oct. Tot.	1978 Nov. Tot.	Men under 30	Men over 30	Women under 30	Women over 30
	%	%	%	%	%	%
Basically opposed to them	61	60	37	68	48	64
In favor, but only if there is no sexual partner swapping involved	19	24	36	16	38	23
In favor of them, even with sexual partner swapping	3	4	12	3	5	2
Undecided	17	12	15	13	9	11
	100	100	100	100	100	100

HAPPINESS WITHOUT SEX?

Question: *"In your opinion, is it possible to be happy in life without intimate (sexual) relations between a man and a woman?"*

Question: *"Is such an intimate relationship essential for you to be happy in life, or could you do without it?"*

	Persons between 20 and 30 years of age					
	Men			Women		
	1949	1963	1978	1949	1963	1978
	%	%	%	%	%	%
Happy without intimate relations -						
No	76	62	70	63	54	51
Yes	11	19	14	24	20	23
Undecided	13	19	16	13	26	26
	100	100	100	100	100	100
Intimate relations -						
Essential	81	67	84	56	46	65
Can do without	12	16	8	34	34	21
Undecided	7	17	8	10	20	14
	100	100	100	100	100	100

PROSTITUTION

Question: *"Do you consider prostitution to be a danger, a necessary evil, or a useful institution?"*

G

	Married men			Married women		
	1949	1963	1976	1949	1963	1976
	%	%	%	%	%	%
Necessary evil	44	58	56	45	50	51
Danger	29	12	6	33	27	12
Useful institution	25	29	38	14	19	37
No answer	2	1	x	8	4	x
	100	100	100	100	100	100

HOMOSEXUALITY

Question: *"How do you feel about homosexuality? Do you consider it to be a disease, a vice, a habit, or something very natural?"*

	Vice	Disease	Habit	Natural	No reply	
	%	%	%	%	%	
Married men - 1949	53	39	13	4	2	= 111
- 1963	47	38	14	5	1	= 105
- 1976	25	49	12	13	1	= 100
Married women - 1963	48	41	11	3	3	= 106
- 1976	20	46	14	20	1	= 101

THE FIRST TIME

Question: *"Can you remember your first sexual experience?"*

Question put to persons who remember their first sexual experience: *"Did you have this first experience with a girlfriend, a boyfriend, or with whom?" "How old were you then?"*

	Persons between 20 and 30 years of age					
	Men			Women		
	1949	1963	1978	1949	1963	1978
	%	%	%	%	%	%
Yes, can remember	80	80	93	85	68	93
The first experience was with						
- a partner of the opposite sex	74	75	91	80	68	91
- a partner of the same sex	6	5	2	5	x	2
No, can't remember, no reply	20	20	7	15	32	7
	100	100	100	100	100	100
Age of first experience -						
Under 13 years	–	1	1	–	1	x
13-15	–	8	22	–	3	12
16	–	13	17	–	6	18
17	–	15	22	–	12	29
18	–	17	13	–	9	14
19	–	7	6	–	10	9
20	–	7	5	–	11	8
21	–	2	2	–	4	1
22	–	1	2	–	2	2
23-25	–	3	1	–	3	x
26 and over	–	1	x	–	x	x
Don't know any more	–	5	2	–	7	x
Can't remember first experience	–	20	7	–	32	7
		100	100		100	100

SATISFACTION

Question put to single persons between 20 and 30 years of age: *"Do you find sexual satisfaction without being married?"*

	Men			Women		
	1949	1963	1978	1949	1963	1978
	%	%	%	%	%	%
Find sexual satisfaction through						
- normal intercourse	74	61	75	48	31	71
- masturbation	x	5	12	1	2	4
- prostitution	3	3	2	x	x	x
- homosexual/lesbian relationships	x	x	x	3	x	6
Find no sexual satisfaction	7	12	8	17	23	11
No reply	16	23	9	31	44	10
	100	104	106	100	100	102

EXTRAMARITAL RELATIONSHIPS

Question put to persons between 20 and 30 years of age: "*Do you condone or do you condemn it if married persons have extramarital relationships?*"

If "Condemn": "*Would you admit certain exceptions, e.g. if one of the marriage partners suffers from an incurable illness?*"

	1949		1963		1978	
	Men	Women	Men	Women	Men	Women
	%	%	%	%	%	%
Condemn it	51	68	76	79	45	48
- admitting no exceptions	17	30	34	36	23	21
- admitting certain exceptions	24	23	26	23	13	14
- undecided	10	15	16	20	9	13
	51	68	76	79	45	48
Condone it	7	3	2	4	25	14
That depends, undecided	42	29	22	17	30	38
	100	100	100	100	100	100

SEX AND MARRIAGE

Question put to married persons: "*Would you say that you in your marriage lead a regular and satisfying sex life?*"

Question put to married persons: "*Have you had sexual relationships outside of your marriage?*"

	Married persons between 20 and 30 years of age					
	Men			Women		
	1949	1963	1978	1949	1963	1978
	%	%	%	%	%	%
Yes, satisfying sex life	88	87	88	84	90	87
No	12	7	x	12	5	7
Undecided	x	6	12	4	5	6
	100	100	100	100	100	100
No outside relations	85	97	59	91	90	89
Yes	6	3	24	9	3	9
No reply	9	x	17	x	7	2
	100	100	100	100	100	100

IS SEX VITAL IN A MARRIAGE?

Question put to men: *"Do you believe that a marriage can fail just because husband and wife do not get along with one another sexually, or do you believe that this alone is not sufficient to break up a marriage?"*

H

	July 1977						
	Total men	Married	Not married	Age groups		Denomination	
				16-34	35-55	Protestant	Catholic
	%	%	%	%	%	%	%
Can break up a marriage	57	54	61	59	53	58	51
Not because of this alone	42	45	37	39	46	40	48
Depends on the person	1	1	2	2	1	2	1
	100	100	100	100	100	100	100

HAPPY SEX PARTNERS

Question put to men who have regular or occasional sexual intercourse (98 percent): *"How happy is the sexual relationship which you have with your partner?"*

H

	July 1977				
	Very happy	Fairly happy	Not particularly happy	No reply	
	%	%	%	%	
Total men	42	51	6	1	= 100
Married	42	51	7	x	= 100
Not married	44	51	4	1	= 100

CONTRACEPTION

Question: *"Are you in favor of or against contraception?"*

G

	Married men			Married women		
	1949	1963	1976	1949	1963	1976
	%	%	%	%	%	%
In favor of	68	66	88	62	62	86
Against	14	15	9	21	19	8
Undecided	18	19	3	17	19	6
	100	100	100	100	100	100

IMPROVEMENTS DESIRED

Question put to men: *"Do you think there are enough efficient methods of contraception, or do you think that investigation into improvements and new methods should continue?"*

H

	July 1977						
	Total men	Married	Not married	Age groups		Denomination	
				16-34	35-55	Protestant	Catholic
	%	%	%	%	%	%	%
There are enough efficient methods	60	62	57	55	65	72	52
Should look for improvements, new methods	33	30	37	37	28	20	41
Undecided	7	8	6	8	7	8	7
	100	100	100	100	100	100	100

RELUCTANT ABOUT THE PILL

Question put to men: *"Many people say that women today are extremely reluctant to take the pill. Do you share this belief or don't you?"*

H

	July 1977				
	Share this belief	Don't believe	Don't know	No reply	
	%	%	%	%	
Total men	41	35	21	3	= 100
Married	44	34	20	2	= 100
Not married	35	38	21	6	= 100

Question put to men: *"If the pill for men were as highly developed as the pill for women, would you yourself take this pill?"*

H

	July 1977				
	Yes - Certainly	Perhaps	No, probably not	Don't know	
	%	%	%	%	
Total men	15	43	32	10	= 100
Married	15	38	36	11	= 100
Not married	14	53	24	9	= 100

THE PILL FOR MEN

Question put to men: *"Scientists are currently involved in developing a new contraceptive—the pill for men. Have you already heard about it, or is this the first time?"* (Yes, heard = 86 percent) *"Various things which other people told us about the pill for men are listed here. Please read through the list. With which of the statements would you agree?"* (L)

H

	July 1977 Total men %
Pros	
If my partner couldn't take the pill it would be good if there were a pill for men	60
If I take the pill, then I can see to it myself that I don't become a father if I don't want to	55
I think that the pill for men is a good idea, because then women would not have to take the pill all the time	53
I should think the pill is less detrimental to men's health than to women's	27
A man who takes the pill would certainly stand a better chance with women	19
Men are certainly more careful than women and would definitely take the pill regularly	11
	225
Cons	
I would be concerned about the effect the pill for men might have on my health	34
I think it would be a nuisance to have to swallow the pill all the time	25
If I took the pill I would have to go to the doctor every six months or so for a check-up and a new prescription	21
Man's masculinity is somehow questioned when he has to take the pill	16
I fear that sex would no longer continue to be so enjoyable for the man if he took the pill	16
I think that the pill can cause impotence in men when taken for a long time	15
I am fundamentally opposed to contraception and hence I am also against the pill for men	7
I am against the pill for men because it is really the woman's job to take care of contraception	6
	140

THE OLDER GENERATION

AGE PYRAMID FOR RESIDENT POPULATION ON DECEMBER 31, 1977

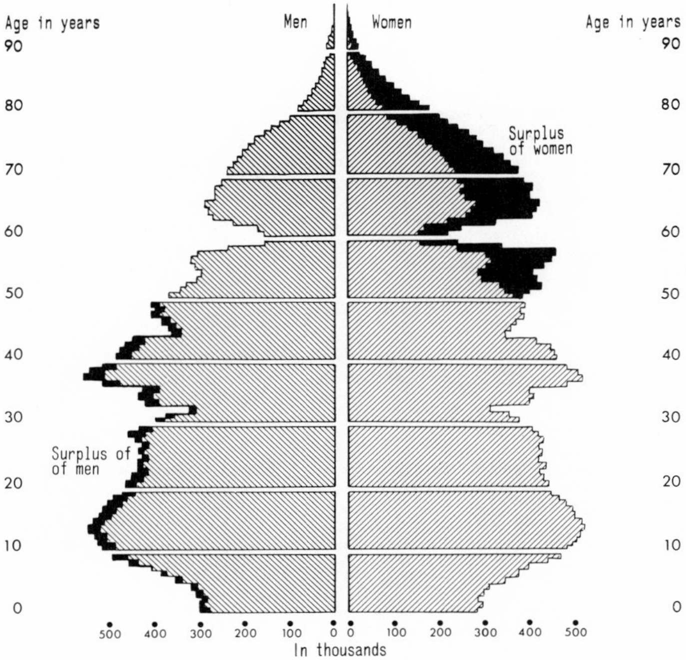

Question: *"How would you generally describe your state of health?"*

I

	Very good %	Pretty good %	All right %	Poor %		
Total population 55 years and over - November 1979	7	37	48	8	=	100
Men	7	40	45	8	=	100
Women	7	34	51	8	=	100

SHUNTED ASIDE?

Question: *''Someone said to us recently, 'When you get older, you soon get the feeling from everyone that you're not needed anymore; you feel as if you've been shunted aside.' Is this the way you see things, or are you of a completely different opinion?''*

I

	November 1979		
	Total	Household consists of -	
	55 years and over	single person	several persons
	%	%	%
Completely different opinion	59	50	62
See things this way too	21	27	18
Undecided	20	23	20
	100	100	100

Question: *''How satisfied are you with your living arrangements?''*

I

	November 1979		
	Total population	Household consists of -	
	55 years and over	single person	several persons
	%	%	%
Very satisfied	63	56	66
Rather satisfied	33	38	31
Unsatisfied	4	6	3
	100	100	100

FAST PACE

Question: *''Do you sometimes have the feeling that the pace is too fast these days, that you can barely keep up with it?''*

I

	Yes	No	Undecided	
	%	%	%	
Total population between 55 and 70 - June 1970	60	28	12	= 100
- November 1979	66	23	11	= 100

BOREDOM

Question: *''Are you familiar with the feeling of time dragging?''*

I

	November 1979		
	Familiar	Not familiar	
	%	%	
Total population 55 years and over	31	69	= 100
Men	32	68	= 100
Women	31	69	= 100

DISSATISFIED WITH FATE?

Question: "*Are you familiar with the feeling of sometimes being dissatisfied with your fate and thinking that other people have had better luck than you?*"

I

	Familiar with feeling - Yes	No	Undecided	
	%	%	%	
Total population between 55 and 70 - June 1970	44	42	14	= 100
- November 1979	41	45	14	= 100

TOGETHERNESS

Question: "*Some people prefer to be with others and only enjoy themselves when they are in a group. Other people are happy to be alone frequently. How do you personally feel?*"

I

	Prefer to be - with others	alone frequently	Other/no reply	
	%	%	%	
Total population between 55 and 70 - June 1970	41	48	11	= 100
- November 1979	47	39	14	= 100

Question: "*How often do you get together with other members of the family? Would you say -*"

I

	November 1979 Total population 55 years and over	
	%	
Daily, almost daily	39	84 (Daily through several times a month)
Several times a week	16	
Once a week	13	
Several times a month	16	
Several times a year	12	
Seldom, never	4	
	100	

YOUNG AND OLD TOGETHER

Question: "*In general, do you think it is good or not when the older and the younger generations of a family live together in one household?*"

I

	November 1979 Good	Not good	Depends	No opinion	
	%	%	%	%	
Total population 55 years and over	14	56	26	4	= 100
Men	12	57	27	4	= 100
Women	15	56	26	3	= 100

ACQUAINTANCES

Question: *"Do you have many acquaintances or only a few?"*

I

	November 1979		
	Total population 55 years and over	Household consists of - Single person	Several persons
	%	%	%
Many	43	34	47
Medium	39	45	37
Few	18	21	16
	100	100	100

Question: *"If you think of the people you enjoy being together with and whom you see often, are all of them approximately your age and older, or are many or some of them younger?"*

I

	November 1979			
	Same age or older	Many of them younger	Some of them younger	
	%	%	%	
Total population 55 years and over	32	22	46	= 100
Men	30	22	48	= 100
Women	34	21	45	= 100

Question: *"Whom do you get along with better - younger people, older people, people your own age, or does age not matter?"*

I

	November 1979				
	Younger	Older	Same age	Age doesn't matter	
	%	%	%	%	
Total population 55 years and over	8	5	26	61	= 100
Men	6	5	30	59	= 100
Women	9	5	24	62	= 100

AT CROSS PURPOSES?

Question: *"The other day, someone said to us 'there's no sense at all in spending a lot of time talking to younger people. They live in a different world, have other ideas and interests, and you just talk at cross purposes; no one is really interested in what the other is saying.' Do you think this is true, generally speaking, or are you of a different opinion?"*

I

	November 1979			
	Different opinion	Generally true	Undecided	
	%	%	%	
Total population 55 years and over	53	29	18	= 100
Elementary school	49	32	19	= 100
Secondary school	65	17	18	= 100

CHANGED PRINCIPLES

Question: *"There have been a great many changes in people's ideas and basic principles in the last few decades. Where would you not agree with present-day ideas, what is it that you are unable to accept?"* (L)

I

	November 1979 Total 55 years and over %
That duty doesn't count for so much any more nowadays	57
That many women take their occupation more seriously nowadays than they do their marriage and their family	57
How indifferent many people have become	57
How important money and material things are to people nowadays	49
That everything is criticized, authority is not recognized	46
The way children are raised nowadays	45
That people barely have ideals any more which they work for	40
That nothing is permanent, things are constantly changing	37
The way everyone trusts that the state will take care of them nowadays, instead of helping themselves	29
That the Germans aren't so patriotic anymore	28

ADVICE

Question: *"Are you often or seldom asked by young people for advice?"* ('Never asked' = 27 percent of total persons 55 years and over)

Follow-up question for 'yes'-responses: *"What are you asked for advice about? Could you tell me with the help of this list?"*

I

Excerpt of comparable items -	November 1979 Total persons 55 years and over %	October 1979 Total persons younger than 55 years %
Questions about training, in selecting a profession	35	25
Judging other people	33	38
How to carry on a household	27	26
Marriage problems	24	14
Political questions	19	17
What goals to set in life	18	23
The best way to invest	17	31
How to raise children	17	11
	190	185

ADVICE TO THE YOUNG

Question: *"On this list there are various pieces of advice which one could give to young people. Which of them would you also give as advice to young people?"*

I

	November 1979 Total population 55 years and over %
Learn as much as possible	81
Be aware of remaining independent, don't be dependent on other people	69
Cultivate a circle of good friends, otherwise life is empty	69
Develop interests and hobbies early in order to live a meaningful old age	54
Start working to acquire a home or an apartment early	50
Man needs religion, a strong belief	47
Travel as much as possible and get to know foreign countries	36
Try to enjoy life above all	32
Try to help shape and improve the world around you	30
Take your private life more seriously than your profession	28

GETTING ALONG

Question: *"Do you have the impression that generally speaking most pensioned people get along well enough, or do you believe that many have a difficult time getting by?"*

I

	November 1979			
	Get along %	Difficult time %	Don't know %	
Total population 55 years and over	42	43	15	= 100
Pensioners	38	47	15	= 100
Non-pensioners	49	36	15	= 100

FINANCIAL SITUATION

Question: *"Where would you place yourself on this list—which of these best applies to you?"* (L)*

I

	November 1979 Total population 55 years and over %
My financial situation is satisfactory. I have enough money to lead a good life	32
I have just enough. I manage well for the most part, but I can't do anything extravagant	56
Barely enough—just enough to live off, but I don't have enough left for anything else	11
I hardly have enough for the basic necessities. I often don't know how I will get by	1
	100

*see also page 304

PROVISIONS FOR OLD AGE

Question: *"Two people are talking here about financial provision for their old age. Which of the two does pretty much what you do?"* (ill. X)

I

	November 1979		
	Total 55 years and over	Men	Women
	%	%	%
"I'm trying to accumulate as much as possible for my old age, in addition to my pension. The pension alone isn't enough for me."	46	43	51
"I'm not going to go to any lengths to provide for old age. Whatever I get in the way of a pension will be enough for me."	41	45	35
Undecided	13	12	14
	100	100	100

Question: *"Of course, you don't really know how things will turn out—but do you expect to continue living as you always have when you're a pensioner, or do you expect you'll have to economize?"*

I

	November 1979				
	Total pop. 55 years and over	Men	Women	Household consists of - single person	several persons
	%	%	%	%	%
Live as always	58	57	59	48	60
Economize	32	31	32	39	30
Undecided	10	12	9	13	10
	100	100	100	100	100

CONTINUE WORKING

Question put to employed persons 55 years and over: *"Two people are talking here. Which of the two has about the same point of view you do?"* (ill.)

I

	November 1979				
	Total employed persons 55 years and over	Men	Women	Education Elementary	Secondary
	%	%	%	%	%
I would like to work as long as I can. I enjoy my occupation. I would hate to give it up	46	40	55	44	51
I'm not going to work one day longer than I have to. After that I'm finally going to be able to do all the things I enjoy	42	49	32	43	41
Undecided	12	11	13	13	8
	100	100	100	100	100

PLANS AND THEIR REALIZATION

Question: "*A number of things are listed here which you might plan on for your old age. Is anything included that you plan on, or rather, that you have definite plans for?*" (L)

Question: "*Is there anything on this list that you have done since you've begun receiving your pension?*" (L)

I

	November 1979 Persons over 55 years not yet retired	retired	
	%	%	
Spend more time on my hobbies	47	32	Have spent more time on my hobbies
Read more than before	36	34	Have read more than before
Be more sociable, get together with other people more	33	24	Have socialized more
Take extensive trips	32	24	Have taken extensive trips
Attend events more frequently	26	13	Have attended events more frequently
Work at my occupation as long as possible	24	3	Have worked longer in my occupation
Devote myself more to my children's household	22	24	Have devoted myself more to my children's household
Find a sideline job, make some additional money	13	10	Have got a sideline job, made some additional money
Work for a club, a party or in community politics	10	8	Have worked for a club, a party, in community politics
Fix up the apartment differently	8	19	Have redecorated my apartment
Move to a different apartment, a different house	8	15	Have moved to another apartment, another house
Move to an old-age home	6	3	Have moved to an old-age home
Build or buy my own house	5	5	Have built my own house
Move somewhere else	4	8	Have moved to different place
None of these, but have other plans ...	8	16	None of these
	282	238	

OLD-AGE HOMES

Question: "*What is your impression of our old-age homes - are they generally well run, so that the elderly feel comfortable there, or are conditions in most old-age homes rather unsatisfactory?*"

I

	November 1979 Well run	Unsatisfactory	Yes and no	Don't know	
	%	%	%	%	
Total population 55 years and over	20	21	39	20	= 100

LOOKING FORWARD TO RETIREMENT

Question: *"If you think of the time when you will no longer work professionally, do you actually look forward to that time, or not so much?"*

I

	November 1979				
	Look forward	Not so much	Sometimes	Undecided	
	%	%	%	%	
Total employed persons 55 years and over	40	18	30	12	= 100
Men	33	25	31	11	= 100
Women	50	9	28	13	= 100
EDUCATION					
Elementary	39	17	30	14	= 100
Secondary	42	21	29	8	= 100
HOUSEHOLD SIZE					
One person	38	24	33	5	= 100
Several persons	41	17	29	13	= 100

GOOD HEALTH AND A LONG LIFE

Question: *"If science made it possible for people to live until the age of 150 and still retain their vigor, would you like to live so long, or not?"*

I

	November 1979				
	Would like to	Depends	Rather not	Undecided	
	%	%	%	%	
Total population 55 years and over	39	24	32	5	= 100
Men	47	21	27	5	= 100
Women	33	27	35	5	= 100
Household consists of -					
single person	28	26	42	4	= 100
several persons	43	24	28	5	= 100

See also page 497

THE UNIVERSITIES AND RESEARCH

Question: "*Do academics, that is, people with a university education, have a special responsibility toward society because of their education?*"

"*Where would you say, e.g. in which fields, do academics have a special responsibility?*" (L)

	October 1972 Total population %
Yes, special responsibility	64
that is—	
generally	37
in their profession	32
in economics	22
in politics	21
No special responsibility	36
	100

INTEREST IN ACADEMIA?

Question: "*Are you interested in questions concerning the universities?*"

April 1979 - Total population

Very interested %	To a certain extent %	Not particularly %	Not at all %	No answer %	
8	25	35	27	5	= 100

Question: "*Has your opinion of the universities here in West Germany improved, got worse, or stayed the same during the past ten years?*"

	Improved %	Got worse %	Stayed the same %	Undecided %	
Total population - April 1979	16	26	34	24	= 100

THE PURPOSE OF STUDYING

Question: *"There are various reasons for studying at the university. What purpose do you see in university studies? Would you please name the* two *most important points on this list here?"* (L)

	October 1972 %
Realizing a professional dream	49
Higher income	35
Chances to get ahead	30
Thorough training in a field	23
Extending one's horizon, general education	17
Prestige, status	15
Personal development	13
Security in social terms	13
Independence	11
	206

TOO MANY STUDENTS

Question: *"Now I would like to read a few statements to you which one often hears in connection with our universities. Would you please tell me in each case whether you agree or don't agree?"*

	April 1979			
	Agree %	Don't agree %	Undecided %	
The vast numbers of people who are studying at present won't be able to find a job suited to their university training	78	7	15	= 100
There is too much talk about politics at our universities today	60	20	20	= 100
Too many students make a comfortable life for themselves at the taxpayers' expense	56	25	19	= 100
When parents let their children study they are bound to be afraid that their children will change completely, become strangers to them	40	36	24	= 100
Too much money is put into our universities, too much government support	32	39	29	= 100
The universities make an essential contribution to the wealth of West Germany	30	36	34	= 100
The government should give the universities more freedom	19	54	27	= 100

IMAGE OF THE UNIVERSITY GRADUATES

Question: *"If you think about the young people who have studied and completed their studies within the last few years—of course these descriptions won't apply to everyone, but which of the statements on these cards here apply to most of them?"* (C)

	April 1979 %
Have an extensive general knowledge	58
Can speak eloquently	57
Have good opportunities for advancement	52
Earn good money	49
Have no idea about professional life	48
Demand too much	47
Looked up to by society	44
Speech is too highbrow, use too many foreign words	44
Have varied interests	43
Politically are often radical	43
Have a well-founded specialized education	40
Think they know everything better	40
Look down on those who have not studied	36
Are suited for executive positions	35
Try to force their political views onto others	29
Don't want to make any efforts	24
Are efficient, industrious	21
Inexperienced in the ways of the world, have their heads in the clouds	21
Tolerant, unprejudiced	16
Honest, reliable	15
Stand up for public welfare	11
None of these	8
	781

SELF-ASSESSMENT

Question: *"There are various groups of people included on this list. Which of these groups would you say you belong to?"* (L)

	February 1978	December 1977	
	Total students*	Total pop.	Age group 16-29
	%	%	%
Independent thinkers	57	42	48
Liberals	44	23	22
Middle-class	43	50	42
Optimists	43	33	35
Progressives	38	17	29
Intellectuals	37	6	7
Active citizens	28	22	22
Plain folks	18	42	36
Religious people	15	22	9
Working-class	9	25	23
Conservatives	9	11	4
Employed persons	9	38	47
Successful, on the way up	8	5	5
Disadvantaged	7	9	9
	365	345	338

* The results published here and in the following tables are from a poll of 500 students at 33 universities and technical universities in West Germany and in West Berlin.

FINANCING STUDIES

Question: *"Where do you get the money you have at your disposal? Using this list, could you please tell me all the financial sources you have at your disposal?"* (L)

	Students	
	1966	1978
	%	%
From my parents, other family members, friends	74	88
From public funds that you don't have to pay back (scholarships, educational grants. Bafoeg*)	30	44
From working while attending the university or before going there	21	62
From loans	2	7
From a pension	8	3
Other funds	9	4
	144	208

*Bundesaubildungsfoerderungsgesetz = Federal funds for higher education.

CRITICISMS

Question: *"On these cards we have various opinions that students have expressed in our interviews. Would you read these views and distribute the cards on this list according to whether you agree or don't agree?"* (C, L)

	December 1978		
	Students		
	Agree - absolutely	Agree - partially	Don't agree
	%	%	%
Anybody who is working for a degree now must face the fact that they'll be out in the cold later and won't be able to realize his/her professional expectations	57	37	5
The introduction of the limitation on years of study is nothing but a way of disciplining the students	51	31	15
Overall, a large measure of freedom and legal security is a reality in our democracy	50	35	13
There is too little willingness on the part of the political parties to find a common solution to our burning problems, such as terrorism and unemployment	43	35	17
In our country, policy is determined by how strong pressure groups are and not by what is recognized as being right and necessary	43	43	11
You have to watch your words these days in West Germany because you can easily be labelled as a terrorist sympathizer	42	33	23
The university constitution is authoritarian	40	40	17
The university reforms have led to a regimented course of study. There is no room at the university any more for free intellectual development	36	41	20
The pressure to succeed at the university means that you're constantly under pressure and can't really develop as a person	34	46	17
Social contacts at the university are usually superficial; it's difficult to make friends and easy to become isolated	32	45	21
The schools and universities produce a conformist type, reward the opportunist and keep critical awareness from developing	32	41	25

continued

continued

	December 1978		
	Students		
	Agree - absolutely	partially	Don't agree
	%	%	%
Present-day youth is critical and independent. Anyone who says they don't dare to state their opinion doesn't know them	31	43	24
As a student, you often feel rejected and distrusted by the rest of the population	28	41	29
In our country, the Basic Law is being undermined increasingly; more and more, it is being falsified in a reactionary and authoritarian direction	27	34	36
Class conflicts are no longer argued out in West Germany; they are kept quiet	23	37	37
German politics should free itself of Western guardianship	21	39	37
The government and the parliament no longer represent the people's interests	21	44	32
Democracy does not rule in the parties	21	44	32
There is no more free and equal discussion in West Germany; no real opposition is tolerated	20	37	39
There is no more discussion in the parties because the people at the top won't have their policies questioned	17	49	32
The university is first and foremost the handmaiden of industry	17	40	41
Generally speaking, the best men and women in our country get to the top in the parties, labor unions and industry	13	34	49
There is no chance to get reliable information from the press anymore in West Germany	13	34	50

'No response' = the difference between 100 and the sum of the indicated responses.

CONTENT IN GERMANY

Question: *"If you look at all the aspects—material, cultural, political and private—are you content to be living in West Germany, or do you believe that life would be better in another country?"*

	Students 1966 %	Students 1978 %
Content to be living in West Germany	63	64
Life would be better in another country	22	15
Undecided	15	21
	100	100

MODEL COUNTRIES

Question: *"Is there any country you think could be a model for West Germany in terms of social policy?"* (L)

	December 1978 Students %
Sweden	37
The Netherlands	17
Switzerland	17
USA	7
France	7
England	6
China	6
Yugoslavia	5
Japan	2
GDR	2
Soviet Union	2
Albania, Brazil, South Africa	1
No, no country	32
Undecided	10
	151

OCCUPATIONAL FUTURE

Question: *"Do you already have a professional goal, that is to say, do you know what you want to become?"*

Question: *"Do you expect to be unemployed for a while after completing your studies, or don't you think so?"*

December 1978

Students

	Have professional goal - %		Unemployment upon completing studies - %
Yes, pretty exact notion	48	Yes, expect so	39
Yes, approximate notion	45	Don't expect to be unemployed	42
No, none at all	7	Impossible to say	19
	100		100

POLITICAL INTEREST

Question: *"Are you interested in politics?"**

	December 1978 Very	Pretty	Somewhat, but not especially	Not at all	
	%	%	%	%	
Total students	24	39	31	6	= 100

MEMBERSHIP

Question: *"Do you belong to one of these organizations?"* (L)

	Belong to - political party	political student organization	youth organization of a party	single-issue group	Don't belong to any political organization	
	%	%	%	%	%	
Students - 1966	4	6	3	—	88	= 101
- 1978	12	12	7	8	86	= 125

— = not asked

STUDENTS' ASSESSMENT OF PROFESSORS

Question: *"We would like to get an idea of how professors are judged these days. What we want is a specific image, not just a cliché of professors in general. Think of the professor whose lecture you will attend next. We're not interested in the name - we're just interested in having you tell us which of the things on these cards apply to him?"* (C)

	December 1978 Students
	%
Speaks well, can lecture well	51
Works hard at his lectures and courses	50
Has a sense of humor	44
Has breadth of knowledge	44
Very intelligent	43
Wants his students to do well, wants to support them	42
Obliging, likable	41
As far as I can tell, an excellent scholar	36
Mainly develops his theories, has his hobby horses	34
A persons who impresses me	31
Authoritarian	28
Stimulating, full of ideas	27
Hard to listen to him, lectures badly	20
Proud, condescending, arrogant	20
Doesn't like to inconvenience himself	20
Removed from reality	16
Eager beaver	15
Unwilling to find out about other things	12
Intellectually stagnant	10

THE PRESENT SITUATION

Question put to professors/young researchers:* *"There are various things listed on these cards which university teachers/other assistant professors and candidates for the doctorate have said about their own fields. Could you please pick out all the cards that apply to the situation in your field as well?"* (C)

	Winter 1976/77		
	Professors	Asst. professors/ research associates	Candidates for the doctorate
	%	%	%
Positive			
We have research results which look promising from the point of view of practical application	59	50	48
Our field has made great progress in the last ten years in Germany	51	47	45
Many productive research ideas come from assistants and candidates for the doctorate	48	62	61
In my field, research is conducted almost exclusively at the universities	48	49	45
We have excellent scholars at our institute who are among the leaders in our field	45	44	40
We haven't had any trouble up to now getting the funds for our work	28	29	28
The mass media often report on research results in our field	27	21	22
We have research results that can help improve life for many people	x	21	23
	306	323	312
Negative			
Not enough time for research	75	58	34
Poor job opportunities for those who finish the degree	55	60	61
Not enough non-teaching and non-research staff	49	45	32
There are barely enough funds for equipment for teaching; there's barely anything left for research	46	31	21
Too many students relative to the existing teaching personnel	44	47	44
It's hardly possible to replace outdated equipment from budgetary funds anymore	38	34	24
Our library is going to the dogs because the budget is insufficient	35	32	27
Not enough work space	33	34	38
We have trouble paying the current expenses for running and servicing our equipment	31	23	17
We don't have enough good people for the urgent work that needs doing	26	24	19
The institutes we work with are located too far apart	21	19	17
When research results are published, the contribution young scholars have made to the achievement isn't emphasized enough	6	23	31
We don't expect to establish fundamentally new findings in our field	5	10	10
Considering the extent of my research activities, I feel that I'm not paid well enough	x	17	30
	464	457	405

*see explanation p. 276.

HOW PROFESSORS VIEW THEIR FIELDS

Question: *''There are various thing listed on these cards that university professors have said about their own fields. Could you please pick out all those cards that apply to the situation in your field as well?''* (C)

Statements: *''We have had no problem to date with getting the funds for our work.'' ''Our field has made great progress in Germany in the last ten years.'' ''Too many students in relation to the existing teaching staff.''*

	Winter 1976/77		
	Statement referring to -		
	funds	progress	number of students
	%	%	%
Agree with this statement by -			
Total professors	28	51	44
Professors in the following fields or groups of fields -			
Electronics, Computer Science	44	64	49
Civil Engineering	39	57	39
Materials Technology and Process Engineering	38	67	9
Chemistry	38	52	20
Geological Sciences	35	51	41
Biological Sciences	35	58	47
Mechanical Engineering and Engineering Sciences	34	55	21
Physics	34	66	14
Mathematics	34	48	47
Near Eastern and Far Eastern Studies	33	49	8
Theoretical Medicine	31	57	55
Theology	29	32	9
Agricultural Sciences	28	56	23
Philosophy	27	27	47
Clinical Medicine	26	62	57
Economics	26	56	52
Language and Literature	24	30	31
Historical Sciences and History of Art	22	39	49
Psychology	22	55	73
History	19	36	29
German, English, Romance Languages	19	33	69
Sociology, Ethnology	18	49	58
Architecture, Area Planning, Surveying	17	62	62
Education	17	61	71
Law	15	20	63
Political Science, Journalism	15	60	51
Geography	14	43	68

A COMPARATIVE VIEW OF RESEARCH

Statement: "*Here in West Germany, research in my field has no chance of competing with developments abroad. We've gotten into a hopelessly marginal situation.*"

	Winter 1976/77 Agree %
Total professors	10
Professors in the following fields or groups of fields –	
Psychology	24
Sociology, Ethnology	20
Historical Sciences and History of Art	19
Clinical Medicine	18
Architecture, Area Planning, Surveying	15
Economics	15
History	13
Philosophy	12
Theoretical Medicine	12
Agricultural Sciences	11
Geological Sciences	10
Language and Literature	9
Geography	9
Biological Sciences	8
Mathematics	8
Near Eastern and Far Eastern Studies	8
German, English, Romance Languages	8
Education	7
Mechanical Engineering and Engineering Sciences	7
Theology	7
Chemistry	6
Law	6
Electronics, Computer Science	6
Physics	5
Political Science, Journalism	4
Materials Technology and Process Engineering	4
Civil Engineering	x

* These results are from a survey of 5,000 professors, assistant professors, research associates and candidates for the doctorate, conducted by the Institut fuer Demoskopie Allensbach during the fall semester of 1976-1977 in the Federal Republic of Germany and in West Berlin. The survey was suggested by the Deutsche Forschungsgemeinschaft and received financial support from the Stifterverband fuer die Deutsche Wissenschaft, the Volkswagenstiftung, the Fritz Thyssen Stiftung and the Robert Bosch Stiftung.

RESEARCH NECESSARY

Question: *"There are different opinions about whether every university teacher should do research. Some think every university teacher must do research. Others feel it isn't necessary for every university teacher to do research. Which of these two opinions do you tend to share?"*

	Winter 1976/77			
	Everybody must do research	Not absolutely necessary	Impossible to say	
	%	%	%	
Professors	79	18	3	= 100
Assistant professors and research associates	71	26	3	= 100
Candidates for the doctorate	66	31	3	= 100

INDICATORS OF GOOD RESEARCH

Question: *"What would you consider to be an indicator of especially good research? Could you select all those things from these cards that, in your opinion, are part of good research in your field?"* (C)

	Winter 1976/77		
	Professors	Assistant professors/research associates	Candidates for the doctorate
	%	%	%
Results that turn out to be productive for further research	89	86	84
Formulating the problem precisely, a clear hypothesis	82	84	75
Clear, comprehensible presentation of results	81	88	86
Choosing the methods which are best suited to our latest knowledge about the problem	67	70	67
Contributing to the development of methods	66	65	68
Publication, communication, passing things on	64	71	76
How consistent the argument is	64	67	70
Progress in theory, which simplifies existing, complicated explanations	60	62	59
Chances of duplicating the investigative process	60	66	71
Relevance to actual practice, applicability, usability	55	66	69
Something fundamentally new, unprecedented	46	32	29
Empirical demonstration	42	43	45
Results which prove to be a contribution to social progress	36	51	57
Recognition by other researchers	22	18	17
	834	869	873

EXCHANGING IDEAS

"A question about the exchange of scholarly ideas—given your present situation, what are your most important sources of scholarly ideas?" (L)

	Professors	Winter 1976/77 Assistant professors/research associates	Candidates for the doctorate
	%	%	%
Reading the literature in the field	87	89	89
Contacts with colleagues in my particular field of research	72	54	49
Listening to lectures and discussions at conventions and meetings	68	56	39
Lectures, colloquia with scholars from elsewhere	67	41	29
Regular talks with my co-workers (young scholars: with my professor, thesis supervisor)	66	51	73
Conversations that develop out of meetings and conventions	65	38	24
Discussions in connection with my own lectures at conventions	64	32	16
Trips abroad, stays abroad	59	24	18
Meeting foreign guests	55	23	14
Interdisciplinary seminars, colloquia	45	34	31
Exchange of manuscripts	42	25	17
Conversations with colleagues in my field, my particular division	39	60	64
Being in touch with those who do practical work in my field	39	27	32
Colloquia which are put on for the interested public	39	20	14
Seminars, courses and supervising students in the field	32	26	14
Conversations with colleagues at my university outside of my field or particular division	32	21	15
Conversations with colleagues over coffee, beer, food or when meeting by chance	25	33	37
Personal letters	22	13	8
Getting to know people at foundation meetings and symposia	18	6	7
Exchange of papers, bulletins, circulars, etc. from the institute	17	11	16
Private socializing, invitations from colleagues	10	9	15
	963	693	621

BOTTLENECKS

Question put to all university teachers as well as young researchers and candidates for the doctorate, insofar as they do research themselves: "*What do you lack most of all for your research, what are the most serious bottlenecks?*" (L)

	Professors	Winter 1976/77 Assistant professors/research associates	Candidates for the doctorate
	%	%	%
Being freed to do research	53	37	9
Assistants	41	12	5
Travel funds	41	27	18
Funds for materials	27	19	16
Typists, secretaries	26	21	10
Technical personnel	23	20	11
Purchase or use of large equipment belonging to the institute	17	13	12
Space for own use	16	15	14
Library, documentation, literature	15	14	14
Small equipment (up to 10,000 Marks each)	15	14	12
Student help	13	9	6
Candidates for the doctorate	7	2	1
Office equipment (Xerox, typewriter, calculator)	5	6	7
Allotted time in the university computer center	4	3	4
Use of large equipment from outside the institute	4	4	5
Candidates for the diploma	3	3	4
Services from sources outside the university	2	4	4
No response	8	17	32
	320	240	184

OPPORTUNITIES FOR TALENTS

Question: "*How do you view the situation in your field—is there no room for talented young researchers at the universities nowadays, or do really talented young researchers in your field still have the opportunity to take up careers as university teachers and researchers?*"

	Winter 1976/77 Professors			
	No room at the universities %	Still have the opportunity %	Depends on the field, no response %	
Total professors	50	46	4	= 100
Professors in the following fields, groups of fields -				
Language and Literature	76	22	2	= 100
German, English, Romance Languages	75	22	3	= 100
History	73	25	2	= 100
Philosophy	68	30	2	= 100
Political Science, Journalism	67	31	2	= 100
Chemistry	66	32	2	= 100
Geological Sciences	63	32	5	= 100
Near Eastern and Far Eastern Studies	63	31	6	= 100
Geography	59	41	x	= 100
Sociology and Ethnology	59	38	3	= 100
Archaeology and History of Art	58	40	2	= 100
Agricultural Sciences	56	42	2	= 100
Physics	56	42	2	= 100
Architecture, Area Planning, Surveying	53	41	6	= 100
Psychology	51	45	4	= 100
Biological Sciences	50	46	4	= 100
Materials Technology and Process Engineering	50	45	5	= 100
Economics	48	48	4	= 100
Mathematics	47	50	3	= 100
Theology	45	51	4	= 100
Law	42	52	6	= 100
Mechanical Engineering and Engineering Sciences	41	48	11	= 100
Theoretical Medicine	39	55	6	= 100
Education	35	58	7	= 100
Electronics and Computer Science	35	58	7	= 100
Civil Engineering	27	71	2	= 100
Clinical Medicine	21	72	7	= 100

A UNIVERSITY CAREER

Question put to young researchers: *"Do you intend to work full-time as a university teacher later on?"*

	Winter 1976/77 Yes %	Perhaps %	No %	
Assistant professors/research assistants	50	23	27	= 100
Candidates for the doctorate	18	28	54	= 100

URGENT PROBLEMS

Question put to young researchers: *"As a young scholar, what are the most urgent problems for you at the moment, what weighs heaviest on your mind at present?"* (L)

What weighs heaviest is -	Winter 1976/77 Assistant professors/ research associates %	Candidates for the doctorate %
The time limitation on positions for assistants and research projects	66	44
Limited opportunities for advancement within the universities	61	44
A great deal of competition when applying for a position	37	42
Time pressure, being forced to finish a piece of work quickly	34	41
Poor job opportunities outside of the university	35	37
The fact that many permanent positions are blocked by relatively young, immobile people	36	30
The pressure to have to publish quickly and in quantity	37	20
Having to be on good terms with important people	25	28
Constant insecurity about whether current projects will continue to be financed	21	26
Being very much overburdened	20	17
Too many teaching obligations	22	5
Problems with making a living	6	36
Problems with financing research projects	15	18
Fears about the future, existential fears	14	16
How removed from practical life my research and my university activities are	12	16
Too much work with self-government	18	4
The pressure to conform to prevailing opinions	9	13
The pressure to adjust to a certain political line	9	10
The pressure to choose the line of least resistance when selecting research topics, to avoid any risk	9	11
The pressure to repay graduate fellowships	2	15
Lack of motivation	4	8
Lack of freedom when selecting research topics	5	5
	497	486

FOREIGN WORKERS

Question: *"Are there actually many foreign workers here in the area, or have you not noticed?"*

	Many %	A few %	None %	Have not noticed %	
Total population - April 1964	61	25	3	11	= 100
- Fall 1971	69	25	2	4	= 100

PROBLEMS

Question: *"Do you think the foreign workers pose a difficult problem for us, or is everything quite all right with the foreign workers?"*

	Quite all right %	Difficult problem %	Undecided %	
Total population - Spring 1964	36	32	32	= 100
- Fall 1971	46	36	18	= 100

PROS AND CONS

Question: *"What do you think of foreign workers in general? Here are some cards containing various opinions about them. Which of them would you say apply?"* (C)

Pro statements	1964 Spring %	1971 Fall %
Thrifty	33	53
Industrious	22	43
Kind-hearted	17	30
Willing to help	15	27
Polite	16	25
Handy, skillful	16	19
Reliable	6	14
Honest	6	14
Resourceful, intelligent	8	9
	139	234
No opinion (refers to both pro and con)	31	10

Con statements	1964 Spring %	1971 Fall %
Loud	39	54
Not very clean, rather slovenly	30	41
Always after the girls	42	38
Quick-tempered, often violent	27	37
Obtrusive	19	22
Cannot be trusted	21	22
Work-shy, lazy	13	11
Impudent, arrogant	9	9
Quick to steal	6	7
Too pretentious	6	5
	212	246

MIXED FEELINGS

Question: *"Do you have a good opinion of the foreign workers here in West Germany or not such a good opinion?"*

	Good opinion %	Not good opinion %	Yes and no %	No opinion %	
Total population - May 1972	37	15	41	7	= 100
- July 1974	26	18	48	8	= 100
OCCUPATION					
Unskilled workers	16	24	54	6	= 100
Skilled workers	25	18	53	4	= 100
Non-managerial employees and public servants	32	12	50	6	= 100
Managerial employees and public servants	39	8	47	6	= 100
Self-employeds, professionals	30	19	49	2	= 100
Farmers	25	28	44	3	= 100

CONTACTS

Question: *"Do you sometimes meet foreign workers, I mean on the job or otherwise? Are you friends with foreign workers, or do you at least know them well, so that you sometimes get together privately?"*

		August 1974		
	Get together privately %	Meet them, yet have no private contacts %	Don't meet any %	
Total population	13	32	55	= 100
Men	16	39	45	= 100
Women	10	25	65	= 100
AGE GROUPS				
16-29	18	38	44	= 100
30-44	13	37	50	= 100
45-59	14	33	53	= 100
60 and over	7	16	77	= 100
OCCUPATION				
Unskilled workers	13	33	54	= 100
Skilled workers	19	35	46	= 100
Non-managerial employees and public servants	10	31	59	= 100
Managerial employees and public servants	11	27	62	= 100
Self-employed, professionals	12	38	50	= 100
Farmers	4	13	83	= 100

SCHOOL PROBLEMS OF FOREIGN CHILDREN

Question: *"It is often said that the children of foreign workers face difficulties at German schools. Do you think that this is an urgent problem, or is it not so important in your view?"*

	Urgent problem	Not so important	Undecided	
	%	%	%	
Total population - March 1978	61	23	16	= 100
- January 1980	65	21	14	= 100

PREJUDICED?

Question: *"There are different opinions about life with foreigners. Think of Blacks, Italians, Yugoslavs, Turks who are in about the same position as you. I'd like to read you a few questions now and have you tell me whether you would do this, or probably not."*

"Would you sit down in a bus next to an Italian, a Yugoslav, a Black or a Turk, or would you rather not?"

"Would you invite an Italian, a Yugoslav, a Black or a Turk whom you know personally to your home for dinner, or not?"

"Would you like having an Italian, a Yugoslav, a Black or a Turk as your neighbor, or not?"

"Would you like to see children of Italians, Yugoslavs, Blacks, Turks attend school with your own children, or not?"

"Would you dance with an Italian, a Yugoslav, a Black or a Turk, or would you rather not?"

"Would you marry an Italian, a Yugoslav, a Black or a Turk, or probably not?"

	February 1975			
	Italian	Yugoslav	Black	Turk
	%	%	%	%
Yes, sit next to them in the bus	81	84	77	73
Prefer not to	12	9	17	20
Undecided	7	7	6	7
	100	100	100	100
Yes, invite them home	53	59	61	47
Don't think so	34	26	31	42
Undecided	13	15	8	11
	100	100	100	100
Glad to have them attend same school	17	17	24	16
Prefer not to	16	12	12	16
Don't care	59	61	58	59
Undecided	8	10	6	9
	100	100	100	100

continued

continued

	February 1975			
	Italian	Yugoslav	Black	Turk
	%	%	%	%
Like them as neighbors	14	16	20	11
Prefer not	21	14	17	23
Don't care	57	60	58	60
Undecided	8	10	5	6
	100	100	100	100
Men				
Yes, dance with them	69	64	57	54
Rather not	19	15	28	30
Undecided	12	21	15	16
	100	100	100	100
Women				
Yes, dance with them	40	47	45	33
Rather not	40	30	44	54
Undecided	20	23	11	13
	100	100	100	100
Men				
Yes, marry one of them	22	30	14	16
Probably not	62	50	78	74
Undecided	16	20	8	10
	100	100	100	100
Women				
Yes, marry one of them	10	14	7	4
Probably not	78	74	82	90
Undecided	12	12	11	6
	100	100	100	100

GOOD WORKERS

Question: *"If you compare Germans and foreign workers, would you say foreign workers work just as well, almost as well or not nearly as well as Germans—if we assume the same training?"*

	February 1975				
	Just as well	Almost as well	Not nearly as well	Don't know	
	%	%	%	%	
Total population	54	22	9	15	= 100
AGE GROUPS					
16-29	66	17	6	11	= 100
30-44	58	23	7	12	= 100
45-59	51	24	11	14	= 100
60 and over	41	23	13	23	= 100
OCCUPATION					
Unskilled workers	44	27	11	18	= 100
Skilled workers	51	24	10	15	= 100
Non-managerial employees and public servants	62	18	7	13	= 100
Managerial employees and public servants	68	14	5	13	= 100
Self-employeds, professionals	55	18	10	17	= 100
Farmers	39	26	14	21	= 100

IMMIGRANTS OR GUESTS

Question: *"If foreign workers want to stay here permanently, should they be allowed to, or should they return to their home countries after a certain period of time?"*

	July 1974			
	Be allowed to stay	Should return	Undecided	
	%	%	%	
Total population	37	42	21	= 100
OCCUPATION				
Unskilled workers	28	49	23	= 100
Skilled workers	42	40	18	= 100
Non-managerial employees and public servants	43	34	23	= 100
Managerial employees and public servants	54	28	18	= 100
Self-employeds, professionals	40	44	16	= 100
Farmers	28	59	13	= 100

EQUAL RIGHTS ON THE JOB?

Question: *"There are several statements on this list about foreign workers in Germany and their position in their profession. Could you please read these and tell me where you would agree?"* (L)

	February 1975						
	Total pop.	Unskilled workers	Skilled workers	Non-managerial employees/public servants	Managerial employees/public servants	Self-employeds, professionals	Farmers
	%	%	%	%	%	%	%
Pro statements							
A foreign worker who has an important position as a skilled worker should be allowed to keep his job even if jobs are endangered	45	36	43	54	55	44	30
Foreign workers should be allowed to practice all professions in Germany	42	33	40	50	53	44	20
Foreign workers should have the opportunity to get white-collar jobs in Germany ...	32	22	32	40	40	30	14
It should in principle be possible for a foreign worker to be the boss of Germans ...	22	16	21	28	32	19	8
	141	107	136	172	180	137	72
Con statements							
In times of crisis, foreign workers should be fired first	57	66	59	51	45	55	69
Foreign workers should be allowed to work here for five years at most	41	49	44	35	32	39	42
Foreign workers should not be permitted to send for their whole families	34	39	34	31	29	33	34
Foreign workers should only be employed as blue-collar workers	21	28	18	18	14	21	30
	153	182	155	135	120	148	175

INTEGRATION

Question: *"There are various things printed on these cards which you sometimes hear people say. Could you read them through please and then distribute the cards onto these columns according to whether you agree entirely, only partially, or not at all? In case you cannot make up your mind, simply put the card aside."* (C, ill.)

	February 1975				
	Agree entirely %	Agree partially %	Not at all %	Undecided %	
Pro statements					
Foreign workers should be paid just as well as the Germans for doing the same work	72	19	4	5	= 100
Foreign workers should be able to get just as far as Germans under the same conditions	46	35	11	8	= 100
The inherent aptitudes and capabilities of foreign workers and Germans are equally good, basically speaking	44	34	12	10	= 100
Basically speaking, there is no objection to a German girl having a close friendship with a foreign worker	37	35	21	7	= 100
Competent foreign workers who have lived a long time in Germany should be able to participate in council or municipal elections	17	20	52	11	= 100
Con statements					
It is to be feared that the foreign workers will become a serious problem for us in the future	55	28	11	6	= 100
The majority of foreign workers are not at all interested in being able to participate in elections. They merely want to earn more and live better than at home	51	28	11	10	= 100
In itself it is not a good thing at all for Germans and foreign workers to become friends and to meet more frequently	13	25	53	9	= 100
German babies are more intelligent than those of foreign workers	8	14	69	9	= 100

IV. THE ECONOMY

INDUSTRY AND LABOR

INDUSTRIALIST

Question: "*On these cards are a number of things which one may hear said about* industrialists. *Of course no two are alike, but think for a moment in very general terms. Could you please pick out all the cards which, in your opinion, apply to industrialists in general?*" (C)

A

	1977 Sept. %	1965 May %
Hold a lot of responsibility, a lot depends on their decisions	71	47
Have too little time for their families, most often have no real family life	60	41
Played a big part in our post-war economic recovery, in improving our economic position	58	48
Have been instrumental in restoring our image abroad, in re-establishing our influence in the world	55	46
They are people who have to work a lot, have very little leisure time	49	32
Live in great luxury, spend heaps of money on themselves and their families	35	33
Have a different relationship today with the labor unions than before, consider the labor unions as genuine partners	30	29
Inconsiderate towards others, will stop at nothing	30	27
Do a lot for science and research	30	22
Are often on holiday, go on long hunting trips and world tours	29	30
Personally live very thriftily, do not throw their money away	28	23
Their fortunes have survived the monetary reform, they have become rich at the expense of others	27	32
Only acknowledge those who have money, nothing impresses them except money	27	27
Control politics, bribe politicians	27	21
Are affable towards the workers because they need them today, otherwise nobody would find jobs	23	46
Stubbornly impose their will, do not acknowledge any other opinion	22	19
Can only talk business, have no other interests	21	19
Do a lot for sports, spend a lot of money on sports facilities for their staff	18	16
Patronize the arts, lend support to artists	13	8
None of these	5	7
	658	573

HARD-WORKING

Question: "*When you hear about industrialists—do you think of hard-working people, or of people who only profit from the work of others?*"

A

	1952 Oct. %	1965 May %	1970 Sept. %	1976 June %	1980 Jan. %
Hard-working people	42	50	44	48	55
Profit from work of others only	22	23	27	22	18
Undecided	36	27	29	30	27
	100	100	100	100	100

SOCIAL-MINDED?

Question: "*Do you think the majority of industrialists think only of their personal gain today or are they also social-minded?*"

A

	1950 May %	1965 July %	1973 Aug. %	1980 Jan. %
Only of gain	60	40	34	39
Also social-minded	16	34	35	40
Undecided	24	26	31	21
	100	100	100	100

Question: "*Do you think that most manufacturers try of their own accord to meet the wishes of their workers and employees as much as possible, or must they be forced to do so by law?*"

A

	Must be forced %	Do so of own accord %	Undecided %	
Total population - June 1950	59	14	27	= 100
- March 1955	47	26	27	= 100
- December 1963	39	29	32	= 100
- January 1974	53	18	29	= 100
OCCUPATION				
Unskilled workers	57	14	29	= 100
Skilled workers	64	13	23	= 100
Non-managerial employees and public servants	55	14	31	= 100
Managerial employees and public servants	50	25	25	= 100
Self-employeds, professionals	33	41	26	= 100
Farmers	19	25	56	= 100

PROFITS

Question: *"Do you favor or object to the fact that industrialists make big profits?"*

	November 1975			
	Favor	Object	Undecided	
	%	%	%	
Total population	59	11	30	= 100
OCCUPATION				
Unskilled workers	45	14	41	= 100
Skilled workers	54	13	33	= 100
Non-managerial employees and public servants	59	10	31	= 100
Managerial employees and public servants	74	7	19	= 100
Self-employeds, professionals	85	3	12	= 100
Farmers	61	9	30	= 100

CRITICISMS

Question: *"A question about the large firms and companies in West Germany: Here are some criticisms of these large firms. Would you please read through this list and tell me which of these things personally bother you?"* (L)

	Nov. 1976
	%
They don't care about the environment, pollute the air and water	61
They make too much profit and thereby keep the prices high	55
Not enough employee representatives on the board of directors	32
They don't pay enough attention to the quality of their products	27
They bribe foreign government officials in order to get contracts	27
They don't pay enough attention to the safety of their products	26
They bribe German officials in order to get contracts	20
They don't employ enough unskilled workers (i.e. foreign workers, women)	15
None of these	17
	280

LABOR UNIONS

Question: *"Would you say the labor unions in Germany are too demanding, or too lax?"*

	1952 Oct. %	1963 Dec. %	1970 Nov. %	1978 April %
Too lax	24	19	20	14
Too demanding	18	21	25	29
Just right	21	30	31	39
Don't know	37	30	24	18
	100	100	100	100

	April 1978 Just right %	Too demanding %	Too lax %	Don't know %	
Total population	39	29	14	18	= 100
OCCUPATION					
Unskilled workers	37	18	19	26	= 100
Skilled workers	45	24	18	13	= 100
Non-managerial employees and public servants	43	26	14	17	= 100
Managerial employees and public servants	42	37	9	12	= 100
Self-employeds, professionals	22	54	5	19	= 100
EMPLOYED PERSONS total	48	21	17	14	= 100

Question: *"Do you believe that the unions* primarily *represent the interests of the worker and employee, or do the unions have other interests that are more important to them?"*

	1952 June %	1974 Aug. %	1978 April %
Interests of the worker and employee	45	59	65
Other interests	23	24	20
namely, Power politics	11	8	6
Material interests of the officials	10	4	4
Own interests as industrialists	–	4	3
Safeguard their own interests	–	5	4
Other and non-specific reply	2	3	3
	23	24	20
Don't know	32	17	15
	100	100	100

UNION MEMBERSHIP

Question: *"Would you say that a worker who is not a member of a union is at a disadvantage or not at a disadvantage?"*

	September 1976						
	Total gainfully employed	Employers	Employed persons	Blue-collar workers	White-collar workers	Unionized	Non-unionized
	%	%	%	%	%	%	%
At a disadvantage	42	45	41	41	40	35	44
Not at a disadvantage	35	20	38	37	38	52	30
Undecided	23	35	21	22	22	13	26
	100	100	100	100	100	100	100

D

	Fall 1980	
	Membership in labor unions	
	Men	Women
	%	%
Total employed persons	40	19
Total workers	52	23
Unskilled workers	14	18
Skilled workers	38	5
Total salaried employees	31	21
Non-managerial employees	26	20
Managerial employees	5	1
Total public servants	46	28
Non-managerial public servants	29	9
Managerial public servants	17	19

PARTY PREFERENCE OF LABOR UNION MEMBERS

	Fall 1978				
	SPD	CDU/CSU	FDP	Other parties	
	%	%	%	%	
Total population	39	50	7	4	= 100
Total unionized employees	59	31	6	4	= 100
Blue-collar workers	63	28	5	4	= 100
White-collar workers	57	32	7	4	= 100

Question: *"Do you approve of labor unions occasionally working together with Communist parties and groups, or should they under no circumstances do so?"*

C

	September 1980			
	Approve	Under no circumstances	Undecided	
	%	%	%	
Total population	12	68	20	= 100
Total labor union members	20	60	20	= 100

MIXED FEELINGS

Question: *"Are you satisfied with the way in which labor unions represent the interests of employees (1952 = 'workers') nowadays, or not?"*

	On the whole satisfied	On the whole dissatisfied	Don't know	
	%	%	%	
Total population - October 1952	26	26	48	= 100
- January 1979	40	40	20	= 100

POLITICAL INFLUENCE

Question: *"Do you think the political influence of the labor unions in West Germany during the past few years has increased or decreased?"*

A

	January 1979				
	Influence has -			Undecided	
	increased	decreased	remained the same		
	%	%	%	%	
Total population	63	3	17	17	= 100
OCCUPATION					
Unskilled workers	52	3	20	25	= 100
Skilled workers	59	5	21	15	= 100
Non-managerial employees and public servants	65	3	16	16	= 100
Managerial employees and public servants	69	1	20	10	= 100
Self-employeds, professionals	76	1	8	15	= 100
Farmers	71	x	10	19	= 100
UNIONIZED					
Labor union members	68	6	22	4	= 100
Non-members	62	3	16	19	= 100

Question: *"One sometimes hears the opinion that labor unions today are trying to gain more and more power and influence in politics. Do you also find this to be true, or not?"*

"And do you think it is good or not if the unions aspire to gain more political power?"

	August 1974	Spring 1979
	%	%
Aspire to gain more power and influence	64	59
and that is - not good	45	48
- good	11	6
Undecided	8	5
Do not attempt this	20	19
and that is - good	9	12
- not good	6	4
Undecided	5	3
No response	16	22
	100	100

CO-DETERMINATION

Question: *"Here are two people having a discussion. Which of the two matches your opinion?"* (ill., X)

	April 1974 Democracy in industry - Yes	No	Undecided	
	%	%	%	
Total population	53	27	20	= 100
OCCUPATION				
Unskilled workers	48	23	29	= 100
Skilled workers	62	22	16	= 100
Non-managerial employees and public servants	59	24	17	= 100
Managerial employees and public servants	53	34	13	= 100
Self-employeds, professionals	31	47	22	= 100
Farmers	29	44	27	= 100

LET THE WORKERS DECIDE

Question put to gainfully employed persons in private industry: *''Who should choose the representatives of the workers to the board of directors? Should those who work for the company decide this alone, or should the unions have a say in this?''*

	April 1974 Persons gainfully employed in private industry		
	Total	Union members	Non-union workers
	%	%	%
The workers alone	68	63	69
Unions have a say	16	29	12
Undecided	16	8	19
	100	100	100

HOPES AND FEARS

Question put to gainfully employed persons in private industry: *''Once co-determination is introduced in big companies, do you think this will tend to have advantages or disadvantages for the* economic development *of these companies, or won't it make any difference?''*

Question put to persons gainfully employed in private companies that employ 2,000 and more: *''If co-determination is introduced in* your *company, do you think this will have advantages for* you *personally, or will it have disadvantages, or won't it change anything as far as you're concerned?''*

	April 1974 Persons gainfully employed in private industry					
	personal involvement			company's involvement		
	Total	Union	Non-union	Total	Union	Non-Union
	%	%	%	%	%	%
Advantages	27	34	20	25	38	21
Disadvantages	3	1	5	22	12	25
No difference	50	48	53	28	34	25
Don't know	20	17	22	25	16	29
	100	100	100	100	100	100

Question: *''What do you think of the following statement: 'Without democracy in the* economy *there cannot be any real* political *democracy.' Do you generally agree with this or disagree?''*

	November 1978						
	Total pop.	Unskilled workers	Skilled workers	Non-managerial employees/public servants	Managerial	Self-employeds, professionals	Farmers
	%	%	%	%	%	%	%
Agree	54	47	50	57	60	55	44
Disagree	15	10	17	15	20	21	12
Undecided	31	43	33	28	20	24	44
	100	100	100	100	100	100	100

THE ECONOMIC SITUATION

Question: *"Which, in your opinion, is the most important question we in West Germany should primarily concern ourselves with at present?"* (O)

Excerpt*	1951 Oct. %	1955 Jan. %	1960 Jan. %	1965 Jan. %	1970 Jan. %	1975 Feb. %	1980 Jan. %
Economic problems	45	28	27	27	41	85	65
Selection from the specific replies-							
- oil crisis, energy crisis	–	–	–	–	–	–	33
- wages, prices, currency	–	–	–	21	24	25	9
- unemployment	–	–	–	–	3	53	12
- old-age pensions	–	–	–	–	–	1	3

*see also pages 127 and 140.

DEMANDS

Question: *"There are various demands relating to economic policy on this list. Which three points do you personally consider most important?"* (L)

	May 1969 %	June 1972 %	January 1978* %
Avoid a gradual devaluation of currency to keep prices from rising from one year to the next	70	81	70
Have enough secure jobs	60	61	82
More opportunities for workers to secure economic assets	40	38	29
The government should spend less	33	37	35
The government should reduce taxes	41	36	32
We should sell as many products as possible to other countries	13	11	16
We should help developing countries structure their economies	10	11	14
Rapid wage increases for all workers and employees	8	5	5
Our economy should grow as quickly as possible, even if this is connected with a rise in prices	3	4	5
	278	284	288

* = 2,000 respondents between 18 and 65 years of age

FREE ECONOMY

Question: *"In West Germany we have two possibilities. Which one do you prefer? A planned economy in which prices always remain stable because the government has fixed them, but often there are shortages of goods in which case they are rationed, or a free economy in which all goods may be had at all times but prices vary according to supply and demand?"* (L, X)

A

	1953 July %	1961 August %	1971 June %	1974 May %
Free economy	54	60	70	70
Planned economy	31	27	21	19
Undecided	15	13	9	11
	100	100	100	100

Question: *"Two people are talking here. With which of the two would you tend to agree?"* (ill., X)

The one:

"I think the government should decide which products are to be manufactured. If industry decides this, it does so with an eye to its profits, while the government tends to go by what people really need."

The other:

"I think it's best for the government not to have too much control of the economy. If industry is allowed to do its own planning and make decisions about which goods to produce, you have a better chance of being able to buy what you need."

	January 1980			
	Industry itself should decide %	Government should decide %	Undecided %	
TOTAL POPULATION	66	20	14	= 100
OCCUPATION				
Unskilled workers	55	28	17	= 100
Skilled workers	64	22	14	= 100
Non-managerial employees and public servants	67	18	15	= 100
Managerial employees and public servants	73	15	12	= 100
Self-employeds, professionals	76	12	12	= 100
Farmers	73	19	8	= 100

PRICE CONTROLS

Question: *"In your opinion, should government agencies set up price controls again?"*

A

	1948 Dec. %	1958 June %	1964 April %	1970 Nov. %
Yes	70	69	72	64
No	20	18	17	24
Undecided	10	13	11	12
	100	100	100	100

Question: *"Two men are talking about prices here. If you were asked, which would you decide in favor of?"* (ill., X)

A

	1969 %	1972 %
"I am in favor of stable prices as far as possible, so that wages and salaries only need to increase slightly"	89	87
"I am willing to accept price increases if wages and salaries increase even faster than prices"	6	7
Undecided	5	6
	100	100

THE PUBLIC AND PROFIT

Question: *"Someone said recently: 'In our economic system, the focus is too much on the greatest amount of profit; human needs are second in line.' Would you agree with this opinion completely, or only in part, or would you not agree?"*

A

	Agree completely %	Partly %	Don't agree %	Undecided %	
Total population - August 1972	33	46	11	10	= 100

REASONS FOR RISING PRICES

Question: *"In your opinion, what is the main reason that prices are so high? Here is a list - could you pick out the main reason?"* (L) (No more than two responses)

	February 1957 %	March 1962 %	December 1975 %
The raw materials of the world market	16	6	48
Taxes	30	24	38
The salary demands of the unions	39	40	36
The profit industrialists make	29	37	30
The profit trade makes	29	30	29
Duties, tariffs	9	6	4
The demands of agriculture	10	11	4
Undecided	6	7	4
	168	161	193

ECONOMIC EQUALITY IMPOSSIBLE

Question: *"Do you think it is possible to achieve an economic situation in Germany in which no one suffers any need?"*

A

	Possible	Perhaps	Impossible	Don't know	
	%	%	%	%	
Total population - December 1954	23	21	48	8	= 100
- December 1971	25	23	42	10	= 100

FAIR CONDITIONS

Question: *"Do you think economic conditions—that is, what people own and what they earn—are by and large fair in the Federal Republic or are they not fair?"*

	Fair	Not fair	Undecided	
	%	%	%	
Total population - August 1964	42	38	20	= 100
- February 1973	44	42	14	= 100
- January 1979	50	36	14	= 100

PERSONAL SITUATION

Question: *"If you think a moment about your* personal *situation, how would you describe it? Here is a ladder. The top rung of this ladder, 10, would mean that your financial situation is quite excellent, and zero would mean that you can hardly live off what you have. Which rung corresponds to your present financial situation."* (ill.)

	January 1977						
	Total pop.	Unskilled workers	Skilled workers	Non-managerial employees	Managerial and public servants	Self-employeds, professionals	Farmers
	%	%	%	%	%	%	%
Good to satisfactory*	29	18	23	34	54	41	20
Average	57	58	63	56	43	47	71
Not good	14	24	14	10	3	12	9
	100	100	100	100	100	100	100

*rungs 7-10; average: rungs 4-6; not good: rungs 0-3

EDUCATION AND INCOME

D

Summer 1976

	Gainfully employed men								
	Un-skilled workers	Skilled workers	Non-mana-gerial employees	Non-mana-gerial public servants	Mana-gerial employees	Mana-gerial public servants	Self-employeds	Profes-sionals	Farmers
	%	%	%	%	%	%	%	%	%
EDUCATION									
Elementary	95	91	54	59	25	10	48	10	84
Secondary	5	9	46	41	75	90	52	90	16
	100	100	100	100	100	100	100	100	100
NET MONTHLY INCOME									
Under 1,000 DM	11	4	3	1	1	x	2	x	21
1,000 - 1,499 DM	66	51	35	34	3	4	14	7	42
1,500 - 2,499 DM	23	43	56	61	46	58	46	19	29
2,500 DM and over	x	2	6	4	50	38	38	74	8
	100	100	100	100	100	100	100	100	100
	Gainfully employed women								
EDUCATION									
Elementary	94	83	49	27	33	4	56	38	87
Secondary	6	17	51	73	67	96	44	62	13
	100	100	100	100	100	100	100	100	100
NET MONTHLY INCOME									
Under 1,000 DM	25	15	9	4	x	x	5	x	19
1,000 - 1,499 DM	51	52	50	27	27	10	16	24	48
1,500 - 2,499 DM	23	29	34	55	53	73	47	30	25
2,500 DM and over	1	4	7	14	20	17	32	46	8
	100	100	100	100	100	100	100	100	100

GOOD WAGES

Question: *"Do you think that workers today earn good wages in West Germany, or not?"*

	1957 Aug.	1960 July	1963 July	1976 March	1980 Jan.
	%	%	%	%	%
Earn good wages	55	63	66	62	68
Just enough	30	25	25	26	23
Do not earn good wages	10	6	6	9	7
Don't know	5	6	3	3	2
	100	100	100	100	100

ASSESSMENT OF OWN FINANCIAL SITUATION

Question: *''Where would you place yourself on this list—which of these replies best applies to you?''* (L)*

1: My financial situation is satisfactory. I have enough money to lead a good life.
2: I have just enough. I manage well for the most part, but I can't do anything extravagant.
3: Barely enough—just enough to live off, but I don't have enough left for anything else.
4: I hardly have enough for the basic necessities. I often don't know how I will get by.

	July 1977					
	Answer:					
	1	2	3	4		
	%	%	%	%		
Total population	20	64	14	2	=	100
INCOME OF THE CHIEF WAGE EARNER						
Under 750 DM	x	49	40	11	=	100
750 - 999 DM	8	61	28	3	=	100
1,000 - 1,249 DM	9	66	23	2	=	100
1,250 - 1,499 DM	12	71	15	2	=	100
1,500 - 1,749 DM	18	66	14	2	=	100
1,750 - 1,999 DM	20	68	12	x	=	100
2,000 - 2,499 DM	31	62	5	2	=	100
2,500 - 2,999 DM	46	48	5	1	=	100
3,000 - 3,999 DM	50	46	2	2	=	100
4,000 DM and over	70	30	x	x	=	100

*see also page 262.

EXPECTATIONS

Question: *''How do you see our economic development: do you think that our economy will take an upswing or a downswing in the next six months?''*

	1966 Dec.	1968 April	1970 May	1973 March	1977 Feb.	1978 Nov.	1979 Oct.	1980 Jan.	1980 Oct.	198 Marc
	%	%	%	%	%	%	%	%	%	%
Downswing	40	17	26	30	27	19	18	40	45	55
Upswing	20	40	29	26	31	28	26	15	10	9
Stay the same	29	33	35	35	35	46	48	39	40	29
Undecided	11	10	10	9	7	7	8	6	5	7
	100	100	100	100	100	100	100	100	100	100

IMPORT OF CAPITAL

Question: "*There are various opinions about whether or not it is a good thing that the Arabs now have a share in German enterprises. There are three men discussing the matter here. With which one would you most tend to agree?*" (ill., X)

	February 1975 %
In principle I do *not* consider it a good thing if Arabs buy up shares of German firms and thus become co-owners of German enterprises	47
I have nothing against Arabs having a share in German firms as long as this is restricted to *special* cases	32
I think it is advantageous to our economy if the Arabs have a great share in German enterprises and we thus gain more capital	12
Undecided	9
	100

EXPORT OF TECHNOLOGY

Question: "*There are firms in the Federal Republic which export the most up-to-date machinery and entire factory facilities to the Soviet Union. There are various points of view concerning this. Some welcome it, saying that these exports are to our economic advantage and help to secure employment in the Federal Republic. Others are against it, saying we are reinforcing Communism with our modern technical facilities and that we are helping the Soviet Union do what it could not do on its own. What do you think? Are you for or against the delivery of up-to-date facilities to the Soviet Union?*"

A

	November 1977			
	For %	Against %	Undecided %	
Total population	52	20	28	= 100
OCCUPATION				
Unskilled workers	40	22	38	= 100
Skilled workers	57	16	27	= 100
Non-managerial employees and public servants	57	21	22	= 100
Managerial employees and public servants	55	21	24	= 100
Self-employeds, professionals	49	18	33	= 100
Farmers	35	34	31	= 100
PARTY PREFERENCE				
SPD	65	13	22	= 100
CDU/CSU	42	30	28	= 100
FDP	59	14	27	= 100

GOVERNMENT RESPONSIBILITIES

Question: *"There are various problems in our present economic situation, and the question is to what extent is the federal government responsible for these. Would you please read this and see if there is something listed that you would say is the fault of the federal government, that they have done too little in that area?"* (L)

	December 1976						
	Total pop.	Unskilled workers	Skilled workers	Non-managerial employees	Managerial and public servants	Self-employeds, professionals	Farmers
	%	%	%	%	%	%	%
That the government can't make ends meet, must go into debt ..	54	53	51	52	56	66	55
That so many people are unemployed ...	48	52	48	47	44	52	49
Rising prices	44	48	45	41	36	51	50
The collapse of companies, that many firms go bankrupt ..	28	25	26	25	30	44	30
That employers don't purchase enough new machines, new industrial plants, etc., that is to say, they invest too little	18	13	17	18	25	27	13
That the German economy is selling less to foreign countries, exports are decreasing	17	15	18	15	19	24	16
That consumers hesitate to buy, postpone purchases	17	16	18	15	20	26	10
None of these	18	18	19	21	22	10	12
	244	240	242	234	252	300	235

SQUANDERING MONEY

Question: *"Do you think that the government spends our tax money sensibly, or do you believe that the government squanders money away in doing its public duties, from road construction all the way to defense?"*

	1974	1975	1977	1978
	%	%	%	%
The government squanders money	52	59	57	60
- spends it sensibly	24	21	22	22
Undecided	24	20	21	18
	100	100	100	100

HIGH TAXES

Question: *"Do you feel that you pay high taxes or low taxes?"*

	June 1979					
	High taxes	Acceptable	Low taxes	Undecided	Don't pay taxes	
	%	%	%	%	%	
Total population	43	26	3	3	25	= 100
Men	49	28	4	3	16	= 100
Women	38	24	3	3	32	= 100
OCCUPATION						
Unskilled workers	43	22	5	2	28	= 100
Skilled workers	46	23	3	2	26	= 100
Non-managerial employees and public servants	40	31	3	3	23	= 100
Managerial employees and public servants	44	28	4	3	21	= 100
Self-employeds, professionals	52	19	2	2	25	= 100
Farmers	32	32	x	5	31	= 100

THE NATIONAL DEBT

Question: *"Two people are talking about the national debt. Which of the two says what you tend to think?"* (ill.)

The one:

"I think it is irresponsible for the government to continue going into debt, because someday our children are going to have to make sacrifices to straighten the whole business out."

The other:

"I don't think it's so bad for the government to go into debt. Every government has a certain amount of debts. We've gotten along all right with these debts so far and will continue to do so."

	January 1979			
	Debts irresponsible	Debts not so bad	Undecided	
	%	%	%	
Total population	49	37	14	= 100
OCCUPATION				
Unskilled workers	45	34	21	= 100
Skilled workers	51	39	10	= 100
Non-managerial employees and public servants	46	40	14	= 100
Managerial employees and public servants	47	39	14	= 100
Self-employeds, professionals	56	33	11	= 100
Farmers	65	17	18	= 100

WHERE TO SAVE

Question: *"The government is always being asked to save money, but there are different opinions about where the saving should occur. There are several things printed on these cards for which the government spends money. Would you sort these cards according to whether you think the government should save here or whether it should definitely not save here."* (C, L)

	March 1980			
	Here the government should definitely		Undecided	
	not save	save		
	%	%	%	
Fighting crime	83	6	11	= 100
Old-age pensions	78	9	13	= 100
Continued expansion of hospitals	77	11	12	= 100
Construction of old-age homes	74	8	18	= 100
Child support payments	74	12	14	= 100
Construction of incinerating plants and sewage plants	69	10	21	= 100
Financial support for families	69	13	18	= 100
Government housing	66	16	18	= 100
Support for research	64	15	21	= 100
Coal mining	64	11	25	= 100
Establishing new nursery schools	60	17	23	= 100
Financing noise prevention equipment	58	17	25	= 100
Construction of schools and universities	52	27	21	= 100
Developing public transportation for cities, suburbs	54	21	25	= 100
Improving the railroads	41	29	30	= 100
Unemployment benefits	41	39	20	= 100
Road construction	39	42	19	= 100
Power plants	34	46	20	= 100
Defense spending	32	52	16	= 100
Economic support for developing countries	28	54	18	= 100
Salaries, expenses for public servants	19	63	18	= 100

UNEMPLOYMENT

Question: *"Our government has two choices for how to deal with the present economic situation. Which would you prefer?"*

A

	1974 Aug. %	1976 April %
The government can combat rising prices as its first priority. The disadvantage is that we will have greater unemployment right now, but experts say that it will stabilize the whole economy in the future	52	50
The government can make full employment its top priority. Experts say that we will as a result have no problems with unemployment, but that in the future we will have to deal with ever more rapidly increasing prices	33	37
Undecided	15	13
	100	100

Question: *"Do you think the unempoyment figure will stay at about one million, or do you think the figures will once again decrease to the low level we enjoyed a few years ago?"*

	1976	1977	1978			Party preference		
	Total population			Men	Women	CDU/CSU	SPD	FDP
	%	%	%	%	%	%	%	%
Continued unemployment of about one million	33	61	53	59	48	58	48	56
Figures will decrease	47	19	23	23	23	17	31	35
Undecided	20	20	24	18	29	25	21	9
	100	100	100	100	100	100	100	100

Question: *"Do you believe that many of those who are presently unemployed do not want to work, or are these just isolated cases?"*

A

	1975 Oct. %	1976 April %	1977 Dec. %	1978 Dec. %	1979 Aug. %	1981 Jan. %
Many don't want to work	49	49	59	55	53	58
Only isolated cases	45	45	36	39	39	32
Undecided	6	6	5	6	8	10
	100	100	100	100	100	100

THOSE HIT HARDEST

Question put to gainfully employed white-collar and blue-collar workers: *"Have you personally ever been unemployed?"*

	Total blue-collar and white-collar workers		Unskilled workers		Skilled workers		Non-managerial employees		Managerial employees	
	1975*	1978	1975	1978	1975	1978	1975	1978	1975	1978
	%	%	%	%	%	%	%	%	%	%
Yes, have been unemployed	24	28	39	39	23	27	14	23	16	19
When was this?										
1978	–	3	–	5	–	1	–	2	–	4
1977	–	5	–	6	–	4	–	4	–	5
1976	–	4	–	6	–	4	–	4	–	x
1975	6	5	12	8	4	5	2	2	4	3
1973/74	9	4	17	8	8	3	4	2	6	4
1969 - 1972	4	4	9	8	3	3	1	3	1	1
1960 - 1968	6	5	12	6	5	6	2	4	3	1
1950 - 1959	6	5	7	8	6	4	5	5	3	x
Before 1950	3	3	4	4	2	4	1	3	3	1
	34	38	61	59	28	34	15	29	20	19
No, have never been unemployed	76	72	61	61	77	73	86	77	84	81
	100	100	100	100	100	100	100	100	100	100

*The comparison should take into account the fact that the surveys were not conducted at the same time of year.

FIRED

Question: *"When you were unemployed (the last time), what had happened? Were you fired by your employer or did you give notice?"*

	May 1978 Unemployed						
	Blue-collar workers	White-collar workers	Men	Women	Age groups under 25	25-44	45 and over
	%	%	%	%	%	%	%
Fired	68	50	68	50	61	57	71
Gave notice	22	40	20	43	21	35	24
Short-term contract had run out	5	8	9	2	7	6	5
Had not been employed previously	5	2	3	5	11	2	x
	100	100	100	100	100	100	100

MOBILITY

Question put to blue- and white-collar workers who have been unemployed within the last 12 months or who fear being unemployed with the next six months (21 percent of all workers): *''Suppose you suddenly became unemployed, would you only look for a job that was situated in this area, or would you be willing to move away from here if it meant you could find a job somewhere else?''*

	Only in this area	Move away	Undecided	
	%	%	%	
Blue- and white-collar workers - December 1975	55	31	14	= 100

Question: *''If a company offers an employee a very good position* somewhere else in West Germany, *and his family is against moving—in your opinion, should he accept the job and try to convince the family or should he reject the offer for the sake of his family?''*

A

	February 1979			
	Accept	Reject	Undecided	
	%	%	%	
Total population	47	30	23	= 100
OCCUPATION				
Unskilled workers	49	31	20	= 100
Skilled workers	44	32	24	= 100
Non-managerial employees and public servants	45	29	26	= 100
Managerial employees and public servants	56	27	17	= 100
Persons currently unemployed	50	39	11	= 100
Persons who have been unemployed from time to time in the last three years	54	30	16	= 100

AUTOMATION

Question: *''Two people are talking here about whether or not companies should continue automating production. Which of the two says pretty much what you think, too?''* (ill. X)

The one:

''I'm against replacing more and more workers by machines. The number of unemployed which results from this is too high a price to pay.''

The other:

''Companies have to keep automating production; otherwise our products will become too expensive and we won't be able to sell them, because other countries produce these products more cheaply. This also means people would have to be dismissed.''

	April 1978				
	Total pop.	Gainfully employed white-collar and blue-collar workers	Self-employeds	Unionized persons	Non-unionized persons
	%	%	%	%	%
Against continued automation	52	50	40	57	47
For automation	31	34	46	27	38
Undecided	17	16	14	16	15
	100	100	100	100	100

THE WAY PUBLIC MOOD ANTICIPATES THE GROWTH RATE*

A. Growth rates of the real gross national product

B. Percent that responded to the question posed in December, "Is it with hopes or with fears that you enter the coming year?" by answering "with hopes".

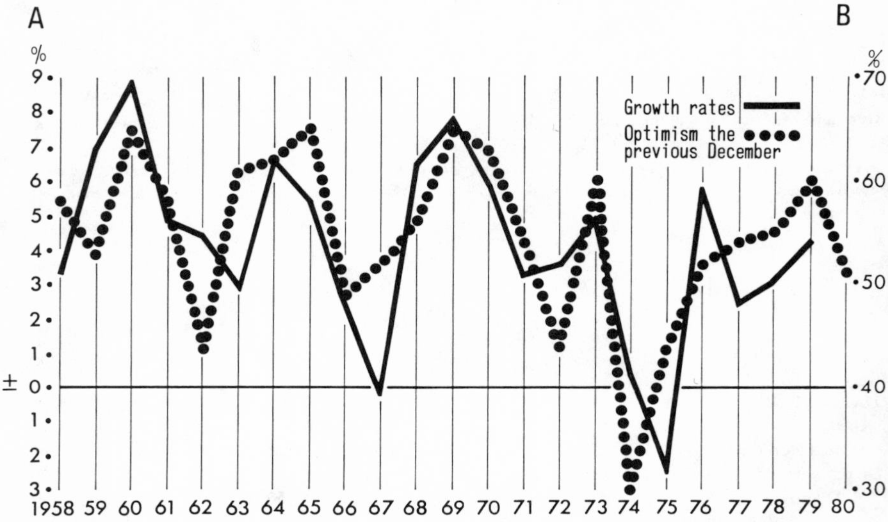

*Ascertained by Karl Steinbuch

See also page 499

ENERGY PROBLEMS

Question: *''There is a lot of discussion about whether nuclear power will usher in an era of good fortune or bring about the total destruction of mankind. Here are three points of view concerning this. Which of them comes closest to your opinion?''* (L)

A

	1957 Nov. %	1975 June %	1979 Jan. %
Nuclear energy in itself can greatly benefit mankind if we learn how to handle it intelligently	46	65	60
Nuclear energy will probably be harmful to us because it is doubtful that we will learn how to use it intelligently	20	12	20
Nuclear energy is bound to lead to destruction because one day things will end in nuclear war	20	5	7
Nuclear energy is certain to yield benefits and advantages for the whole of mankind	8	12	9
Undecided	6	6	4
	100	100	100

THREE MILE ISLAND

Question: *''A few days ago there was a serious accident in a nuclear energy plant in America. Did you follow the reports about it closely, or didn't it especially interest you?''*

B

	Followed it closely %	Of no special interest %	Didn't hear about it %	
Total population - April 1979	82	18	x	= 100

Question: *''Here are two opinions about nuclear power plants. Which of the two would you tend to agree with?''* (L)

	1978 December %	1979 July %
''The risks of nuclear power plants are too great, that's why under no circumstances should nuclear power plants be built''	40	52
''Only nuclear power plants are able to meet our energy needs; therefore it is necessary to put up with the possible risks that may arise''	39	30
Undecided	21	18
	100	100

OPTIMISM

Question: "*There are two opinions on the question of how mankind will live in the future: Some say we will strip the earth, squeezing out all the raw materials until we are left with nothing. Others say that mankind has always been able to help itself and we will do so once again by finding substitutes for the raw materials which are now scarce. What is your opinion?*"

	Will find substitutes	Will be left with nothing	Undecided	
	%	%	%	
Total population - March 1978	59	26	15	= 100
- December 1979	62	21	17	= 100

ENERGY CRISIS?

Question: "*Do you believe that there will be a major energy crisis in the near future, so that each household will only receive a rationed amount of gas, fuel oil and electricity, or don't you believe that it will come to that?*"

A

	Major energy crisis	Won't come to that	Undecided	
	%	%	%	
Total population - July 1979	33	48	19	= 100

Question: "*Do you think that it is presently necessary for West Germany to save energy, or don't you think it's necessary?*" (Yes, necessary = 84 percent)

Follow-up question put to people who consider it necessary to save energy: "*Who, in your opinion, could best save energy? Could you please answer with the help of this list?*" (L)

	Car owners	Industry	Government agencies	Private households	
	%	%	%	%	
Total population - July 1979	56	47	46	44	= 193

NOT BY LAW

Question: "*These days it is often suggested that West Germany's energy consumption be restricted by law, in order to safeguard the energy supply for the future. Do you agree with this suggestion, or are you against government regulation of energy consumption in private households?*"

	Against	For	Undecided	
	%	%	%	
Total population - December 1978	46	36	18	= 100
- July 1979	56	31	13	= 100

WAYS OF SAVING ENERGY

Question: "*Various proposals have been made about how energy can be saved, but the question is which is the most efficient. How do you think energy could best be saved?*" (L)

A

	July 1979 %
Request every individual to voluntarily use less electricity, fuel oil, coal, natural gas and gasoline	68
Restrict the heating of office rooms to a certain temperature	52
Put a speed limit of 100 km/hour into effect on the freeways	39
Not allow private driving on one day of every month (half group: week)	39
Raise the prices of all types of energy so that people become more economical on their own	22
Have the government ration energy: each household receives only a certain amount of electricity, fuel oil, gasoline, etc. per month	18
Require appliances using a lot of electricity to be used only at certain times	12
	250

DRIVING ECONOMICALLY

Question: "*There are various ways of saving gasoline. Which of them would you most be in favor of if you had to save?*" (L)

A

	May 1980 Drivers of private cars %
Do without all driving that's not absolutely necessary	57
Use public transportation more often	39
Buy a smaller car next time	37
Drive more slowly	30
Not drive at all on one day of the week	16
Sell the car	12
Drive as before	11

HEATING AND COOKING

Question: "*What kind of heating do you have?*"—"*What do you use for cooking?*"

	Coal %	Electricity %	Natural gas %	Fuel oil %	Other %	
Heating - 1963	61	13	3	22	3	= 102
- 1977	16	9	16	62	3	= 106
Cooking - 1963	35	54	37	x	x	= 126
- 1977	9	76	21	x	x	= 106

WHOSE FAULT?

Question: *"Who do you believe is most at fault that gasoline and fuel oil are becoming more and more expensive?"* (L)

	July 1979					
	International oil companies	Oil-producing countries	Federal government	Consumers	Don't know	
	%	%	%	%	%	
Total population	72	66	17	14	6	= 175

SUGGESTED WAYS OUT

Question: "What should the industrial nations who are dependent on oil do if the oil-producing countries stop the flow of oil or if the prices climb beyond reach? Here are three opinions on the subject—with which would you tend to agree?" (L)

	July 1979
	%
The industrial nations must ration energy strictly, for example with ration cards, and must thus put up with government control and a worsening of the economic situation	38
Like it or not, the industrial nations must pay the high prices and put up with inflation and unemployment	24
There's nothing left for the industrial nations to do except to occupy the oil fields and to force the delivery of oil, thereby risking military conflict	13
Undecided	25
	100

EASY LIFE NOT GUARANTEED

Question: *"Do you believe that technical progress is making our lives easier or more difficult?"*

	Easier	More difficult	Remains the same	Don't know	
	%	%	%	%	
Total population - May 1966	50	29	11	10	= 100
- January 1980	41	40	12	7	= 100
Men	45	37	12	6	= 100
Women	38	43	12	7	= 100
AGE GROUPS					
16-29	46	34	13	7	= 100
30-44	47	36	14	3	= 100
45-59	42	39	11	8	= 100
60 and over	31	51	11	7	= 100

WORKING CONDITIONS

Question: *"Do you think life would be most pleasant if we didn't have to work?"*

	Yes %	No %	Undecided %	
Total population - 1952	13	82	5	= 100
- 1960	13	80	7	= 100
- 1972	21	71	8	= 100
- 1976	16	76	8	= 100
- 1980	20	70	10	= 100
Men	23	67	10	= 100
Women	18	73	9	= 100
AGE GROUPS				
16-29	34	51	15	= 100
30-44	23	69	8	= 100
45-59	14	76	10	= 100
60 and over	9	84	7	= 100
OCCUPATION				
Unskilled workers	25	63	12	= 100
Skilled workers	23	66	11	= 100
Non-managerial employees and public servants	20	70	10	= 100
Managerial employees and public servants	17	76	7	= 100
Self-employeds, professionals	14	77	9	= 100
Farmers	5	91	4	= 100

ENJOY WORK AND LEISURE

Question: *"Which time do you like best - the time when you are at work or the time when you aren't working, or do you like both?"*

	1967 June %	1972 Aug. %	1975 Aug. %	1977 Oct. %	1979 Dec. %	1980 July %
Like both	46	61	58	53	48	47
When I'm not working	42	31	32	35	39	39
While I'm at work	7	3	5	4	4	7
Undecided	5	5	5	8	9	7
	100	100	100	100	100	100

MORE EFFORT NECESSARY

Question: *"Some people say you have to achieve a great deal to hold your own in your profession and to get ahead nowadays. What is your opinion on this? Do people have to work harder at their professions at present than they did ten or twenty years ago, or do they have an easier time of it today?"*

	Harder at present %	Easier %	No difference %	Don't know %	
Total population - August 1972	60	21	12	7	= 100
- August 1980	63	16	14	7	= 100

Question: *"Assuming a critic says the Germans don't work enough and do too much goldbricking, and to keep up with the competition in the international economic system, they are going to have to work harder again. Would you tend to agree with this criticism or would you tend to be against it?"*

	August 1980			
	Agree with this criticism %	Against this criticism %	Undecided %	
Total population	29	53	18	= 100

PRESSURE TO ACHIEVE?

Question: *"Do you often or sometimes fear that you are unable to keep up in your profession, that you are unable to achieve as well as others?"*

	Often %	Sometimes %	Never %	No reply %	
Total gainfully employed persons - April 1975	5	22	60	13	= 100
- December 1979	4	26	60	10	= 100
EDUCATION					
Elementary	5	27	58	10	= 100
Secondary	2	24	63	11	= 100

ANXIETIES

Question: *"Do you frequently or sometimes think about becoming unemployed or otherwise having less income, or don't you worry about this?"*

	Frequently %	Sometimes %	Don't worry %	No reply %	
Total population - April 1975	12	32	52	4	= 100
- December 1979	9	28	57	6	= 100
AGE GROUPS					
16-29	12	31	52	5	= 100
30-44	10	36	50	4	= 100
45-59	8	31	56	5	= 100
60 and over	5	12	70	13	= 100
OCCUPATION					
Unskilled workers	12	35	44	9	= 100
Skilled workers	12	32	51	5	= 100
Non-managerial employees and public servants	8	25	61	6	= 100
Managerial employees and public servants	3	19	71	7	= 100
Self-employeds, professionals	9	28	56	7	= 100
Farmers	1	14	80	5	= 100

EFFICIENCY

Question: *"If you would please read this conversation—which of the two says what you would also tend to think?"* (ill., X)

The one:
"By and large it is a fact that the person who works harder earns more. Good workmanship always pays off."

The other:
"Basically, it is a fact that good workmanship is hardly rewarded at all. Nowadays, the person who makes a greater effort hardly earns anything more for it."

	October 1977			
	Good workmanship - always pays off %	is hardly rewarded at all %	Undecided %	
Total gainfully employed persons	52	41	7	= 100
OCCUPATION				
Unskilled workers	40	50	10	= 100
Skilled workers	48	45	7	= 100
Non-managerial employees and public servants	51	39	10	= 100
Managerial employees and public servants	55	41	4	= 100
Self-employeds, professionals	71	29	x	= 100
Farmers	70	24	6	= 100

A GOOD EDUCATION ESSENTIAL

Question: *"Which, in your opinion, are the most important things for getting ahead professionally?"* (L)

	December 1973					
	Total pop.	Unskilled workers	Skilled workers	Non-managerial employees and public servants	Managerial	Self-employeds, professionals
	%	%	%	%	%	%
A good education/ good training	69	62	70	71	74	65
Industry and perseverance	65	68	67	59	61	73
Talent and ability	49	42	52	50	54	44
Interest and continued education	30	24	29	33	38	28
Sociability	30	26	24	32	43	37
Connections	23	26	24	25	18	19
Pushiness	20	20	20	20	16	24
Chance and luck	18	23	16	17	16	12
	304	291	302	307	320	302

GOALS

Question: *"After leaving school, everyone had some idea of what he/she wanted to be. Did you have a special goal when you left school? Did you also become what you wanted to be? Why didn't it work out?"*

C

	Men		Women	
	1953	1979	1953	1979
	%	%	%	%
Yes, had occupational goal	89	78	69	72
Became what I wanted to be	42	36	23	24
Became something else	47	42	46	48
due to -				
circumstances of the times	17	9	12	15
family reasons	15	6	19	11
shortage of money	12	6	14	8
no training positions open	4	9	3	2
insufficient schooling	–	3	–	1
reasons of health	2	2	2	1
other reasons/no reply	4	15	4	16
No, had no occupational goal	11	22	31	28
	100	100	100	100

MONEY AND STATUS

Question: *"Who in your opinion, is generally more respected, a white-collar worker who earns 300 Marks (1976: 1,500 Marks) a month, or the foundry worker who takes 450 Marks (1976: 2,000 Marks) a month home?"*

I

	1952 Oct. %	1955 March %	1960 May %	1976 March %
The white-collar worker	59	56	51	60
The foundry worker	24	21	20	14
Undecided	17	23	29	26
	100	100	100	100

Question: *"Here is a list of professions. Could you please select four or five of them that you hold most in esteem, that you respect most?"* (L)

	1966 %	1972 %	1978 %
Doctor	84	81	80
Clergyman	49	37	48
Professor	–	40	32
Lawyer	37	38	31
Ambassador, diplomat	29	33	31
Nuclear physicist	37	40	30
Pharmacist	34	29	26
Author	–	–	26
Elementary school teacher	37	25	25
Engineer	41	29	24
Politician	15	27	23
Director of a large firm	23	19	20
High school teacher	28	24	20
Independent businessman (1978: industrialist)	21	18	20
Army officer	12	13	13
Union leader	–	–	10
Newspaper editor	15	15	9
Book dealer	6	5	6
	468	473	474

– = not asked

USING POTENTIAL

Question: ''*Everyone's situation is different. Some people can put all their capabilities to full use, while others don't have this chance. How about your own situation—could you show me on this ladder? 10 means that so far in your life you have been able to make use of your capabilities; you could make the most of your potential. 1 means that up till now you haven't had the chance to show what you are capable of. Which step would you pick?*'' (ill.)

Men ▼ Women ●

Capabilities put to use, expressed in one-tenth intervals from the average value

October 1977

									−	Average point on the scale	+										
Total population										6,32											
Men											▼	▼									
Women								●	●												
16 - 29 years					▼	▼	▼	▼	▼												
						●	●	●	●												
30 - 44 years										▽											
											●	●	●								
45 - 59 years											▼										
										○											
60 and over											▼	▼	▼	▼	▼						
										○											
Unskilled workers	▼	▼	▼	▼	▼	▼	▼	▼	▼												
			●	●	●	●	●	●	●												
Skilled workers								▼	▼												
							●	●	●												
Non-managerial employees and public servants											▼	▼									
											●	●									
Managerial employees and public servants											▼	▼	▼	▼	▼						
											●	●	●	●							
Self-employeds, professionals											▼	▼	▼	▼	▼	▼	▼	▼	▼	▼	▼
											●	●	●	●	●	●	●	●	●	●	●
Farmers											▼	▼	▼	▼	▼	▼					
											●	●	●	●	●						

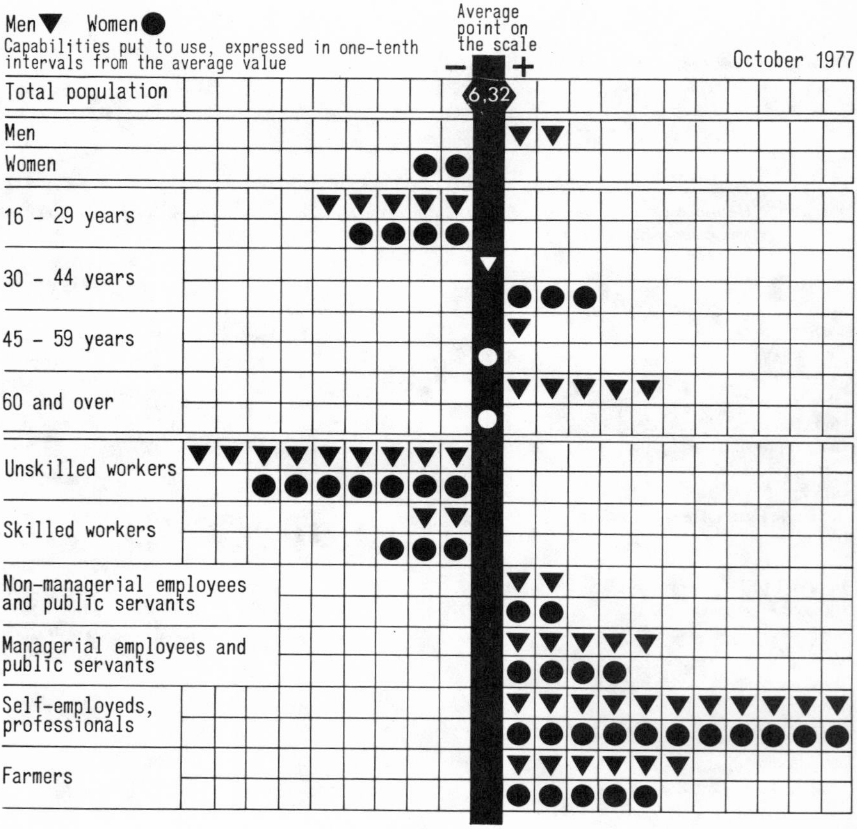

THE IDEAL OCCUPATION

Question: *"It's quite true that one cannot do everything at the same time in one's life. But which of these occupations listed here do you think would have given you the greatest pleasure, which ones would have most suited you? You may name more than one occupation."* (L)

	Women 1968 %	Women 1972 %
Nursery school teacher	19	25
Nurse	13	20
Teacher	9	17
Commercial artist	14	14
Dressmaker	10	14
Airline stewardess	8	13
Architect	14	13
Physician	11	12
Secretary	7	12
Saleswoman	12	11
Journalist	9	11
Hairdresser	14	11
Cook	14	10
Psychologist	6	9
Gardener	12	9
Photographer	5	9
Fashion model	15	8
Librarian	9	7
Actress	9	7
Public service official	4	8
Bookkeeper	11	6
Judge, lawyer	6	4
Ballet dancer	6	4
University professor	x	2
None of these	8	7
	245	263

	Men 1968 %	Men 1979 %
Forester	13	27
Engineer	13	24
Pilot, airline pilot	15	20
Architect	8	17
Teacher	25	14
Mechanic	12	14
Public servant	11	13
Professional soldier, officer	7	13
Physician	12	12
Journalist	11	12
Musician	12	12
Farmer	13	11
Chauffeur, professional driver	13	10
Judge, lawyer	5	10
Sailor	7	9
Psychologist	4	8
Cook or pastry cook	13	7
Locomotive driver	10	7
Chemical engineer	11	6
Politician	5	6
University professor	x	5
Priest, pastor	4	4
Sales representative	8	4
Hairdresser	8	7
None of these	6	7
	246	279

WORKMANSHIP

Question: *"What is your opinion of the skilled workmen of today?"*

	August 1977			
	Good opinion	Poor opinion	Undecided	
	%	%	%	
Total population	57	23	20	= 100

Question to persons who had had dealings with a skilled workman within the past two years: *"How well satisfied were you with this workman's work?"*

	August 1977			
	Satisfied	Not satisfied	No answer	
	%	%	%	
Total workmen	91	7	2	= 100
Carpenter	98	2	x	= 100
Electrician	97	3	x	= 100
Telephone workman	96	x	4	= 100
Metalsmith	96	4	x	= 100
Tailor	96	4	x	= 100
Painter, wallpaperer	96	2	2	= 100
Shoemaker	94	4	2	= 100
Window maker, glass worker	94	4	2	= 100
Tile worker	93	5	2	= 100
Heating technician	93	6	1	= 100
Mason	91	5	4	= 100
Clock/watch repair	90	5	5	= 100
Plumber	89	11	x	= 100
Radio repairman	89	9	2	= 100
Locksmith	88	10	2	= 100
Auto mechanic	87	11	2	= 100
Chimney sweep	87	4	9	= 100
Roofer	83	11	6	= 100

SETTING UP OWN BUSINESS

Question put to gainfully employed white-collar and blue-collar workers: *"Would you in principle be interested in setting up your own business?"*

	Yes, definitely %	Perhaps %	No %	
Gainfully employed white-collar and blue-collar workers				
Total - August 1962	17	20	63	= 100
- December 1976	7	21	72	= 100
- January 1980	13	25	62	= 100
Men	14	28	58	= 100
Women	11	21	68	= 100
AGE GROUPS				
16 - 29	17	35	48	= 100
30 - 44	14	25	61	= 100
45 - 59	5	17	78	= 100
EDUCATION				
Elementary	11	25	64	= 100
Secondary	16	26	58	= 100
OCCUPATION				
Unskilled workers	12	21	67	= 100
Skilled workers	13	31	56	= 100
Non-managerial employees	13	27	60	= 100
Managerial employees	15	27	58	= 100

TIME PRESSURE

Question put to employed persons: *"Are you able to finish your work comfortably within the normal work hours, or are you frequently under pressure and have to exert yourself in order to complete your work?"*

	February 1977			
	Comfort-ably %	Under pressure %	Sometimes yes, sometimes no %	
Total employed persons	36	34	30	= 100
OCCUPATION				
Unskilled workers	43	27	30	= 100
Skilled workers	39	31	30	= 100
Non-managerial employees and public servants	39	29	32	= 100
Managerial employees and public servants	32	48	20	= 100
Self-employeds, professionals	19	50	31	= 100

IMPORTANT CRITERIA

Question put to gainfully employed persons: *"Here are various things concerning your work. Please pick out the ones which you personally consider to be especially important for a job."* (C)

	Dec. 1973	April 1979
	%	%
Good working atmosphere	82	82
Secure position	76	70
Interesting work	69	69
Independent work	69	67
Recognition of achievements	68	67
A job which is perfectly suited to your disposition and capabilities	64	53
High income	63	53
Regular time off	63	60
Good opportunity for advancement	61	44
A job in which one can achieve something	54	45
A job which is recognized and respected	49	38
A lot of contact with other people	48	46
No stress (not asked 1973)	–	42
Tasks which require taking a lot of responsibility	41	39
A job in which it is important to have one's own ideas	41	36
A job in which one can do something to benefit the community	39	29
A job in which one can help others	35	24
The opportunity to be in charge of others	24	18
	946	882

CRUCIAL FOR THE GENERAL WELFARE

Question put to gainfully employed persons: ***"Some occupations are especially important for the general welfare, and others are less important. How would you view your occupation, what you do—does it belong to the activities that are especially important or to the less important ones?"***

	August 1979					
	Especially important		Less important		Undecided	
	Men	Women	Men	Women	Men	Women
	%	%	%	%	%	%
Total gainfully employed persons	43	34	43	53	14	13
Total salaried employees	40	33	48	56	12	11
Total public servants	67	70	25	25	8	5
Self-employeds, professionals	44	42	42	29	14	29
Farmers	88	77	12	18	x	5

WORKING CONDITIONS: FLEXIBILITY, COMMUTING, OVERTIME, SHIFT WORK

	1975/76 Gainfully employed	
	Men	Women
	%	%
Full-time	98	74
Part-time	2	17
Hourly	–	9
	100	100
Flexible working hours -		
not possible	55	47
not yet established	26	22
established	15	20
No reply	4	11
	100	100

	1975/76 Gainfully employed	
	Men	Women
	%	%
Non-commuters	54	69
Commuters	39	29
Work at no fixed place	7	2
	100	100
Is overtime paid?		
Yes	49	40
No	27	24
Don't do overtime	24	36
	100	100
Doing shift work	15	7

REDUCED WORKING TIME

Question: "*Supposing working time were to be reduced. Here is a list of various possibilities. Which of them do you think is the best, which one would you prefer?*" (L)

	July 1978	
	Total pop.	Age group 60 yrs. and over
	%	%
Lower the age of retirement	35	52
Increase the length of annual vacation	23	16
Work only a four day week	22	6
Reduce the daily working hours	11	9
Undecided	9	17
	100	100

JOB SATISFACTION

Question put to gainfully employed people: *"Would you say that your present occupation satisfies you completely, partially, or not at all?"*

	Completely %	Partially %	Not at all %	
Total gainfully employed people - March 1960	47	46	7	= 100
- July 1967	64	30	6	= 100
- February 1973	47	42	11	= 100
- September 1980	46	47	7	= 100
Men	47	47	6	= 100
Women	43	48	9	= 100
AGE GROUPS				
16-29	34	56	10	= 100
30-44	46	47	7	= 100
45-59	58	36	6	= 100
60 and over	62	37	1	= 100
OCCUPATION				
Unskilled workers	30	53	17	= 100
Skilled workers	47	46	7	= 100
Non-managerial employees and public servants	44	52	4	= 100
Managerial employees and public servants	54	41	5	= 100
Self-employeds, professionals	73	24	3	= 100
Farmers	53	40	7	= 100

Question: *"There are people who earn 5,000 Deutsche marks a month and more. What do you think - do these people differ from others, that is, are they especially capable and do they achieve* more, *or don't you think so?"*

	October 1977				
	Total	Age groups			
	pop. %	16-29 %	30-44 %	45-59 %	60 and over %
They achieve more	46	40	50	47	46
Don't think so	40	48	37	39	36
Undecided, no opinion	14	12	13	14	18
	100	100	100	100	100

Question put to gainfully employed persons: *"In all jobs there are hard-working people and people who don't work so hard. What is this like in your job? Do those who work harder earn more or not?"*

	October 1977				
Those who work harder -	Total	Age groups			
	pop. %	16-29 %	30-44 %	45-59 %	60 and over %
Earn more	45	35	49	49	59
Don't earn more	40	47	37	38	30
Undecided	15	18	14	13	11
	100	100	100	100	100

DECISION-MAKING

Question put to employed persons: *"Anyone who works can make his own decisions in some areas and is dependent in others. The question is how free the individual feels. What is your situation? Could you explain it with the aid of this ladder?*

It works like this: 0 would mean you had no freedom to make decisions in your profession, and 10 would mean you felt completely free and independent in your professional decisions. Where would you place yourself?" (ill.)

	(6-10) Comparatively free	(5) Neither, nor	(0-4) Comparatively unfree	
	%	%	%	
Total employed persons - January 1979	53	16	31	= 100
- August 1975	52	20	28	= 100
OCCUPATION				
Unskilled workers	33	19	48	= 100
Skilled workers	45	22	33	= 100
Non-managerial employees and public servants	48	23	29	= 100
Managerial employees and public servants	81	10	9	= 100
Self-employeds, professionals	91	5	4	= 100
Farmers	72	14	14	= 100

JOB ADVANCEMENT

Question put to people who have been employed for at least 10 years: *"Did you have the same occupation in 1967 as you have today, or do you now have a different occupation?" "Do you think your present position is an improvement in comparison to 10 years ago or would you not say so?"*

	October 1977				
	Blue-collar workers	White-collar workers	Public servants	Self-employeds, professionals	Farmers
	%	%	%	%	%
Same occupation	73	73	82	81	90
Different occupation	27	27	18	19	10
	100	100	100	100	100
Present position an improvement over that of 10 years ago	40	60	65	45	23
Would not say so	48	35	31	42	56
Undecided	12	5	4	13	21
	100	100	100	100	100

PROS AND CONS OF THE JOB

Question put to gainfully employed persons: *"On these cards are various things which one can say about one's job or occupation. Please take a look at the cards and lay out all those which apply to you."* (C)

	1979 March Gainfully employed persons Men	
	Men	Women
	%	%
Pros		
I feel comfortable with my colleagues, it can be fun working with them	65	57
My job is interesting, it never bores me	60	57
What I like about my job is that I have a lot of contact with people; people interest me	51	59
I get a lot of pleasure out of my work	43	49
I am aware that my work is highly esteemed	40	43
I have a pleasant superior, I like working with him/her	37	42
I have a great deal of responsibility in my occupation. Quite a lot depends upon my not making any wrong decisions	33	17
My work absorbs me completely, it gives my life a sense of purpose	32	25
	361	349
Cons		
If I compare myself to others and think about my job, I must say I earn too little	35	31
I would like to take on more responsibility	33	29
I actually work only because I have to earn money. If I didn't have to, I would certainly not work	26	26
My job leaves me too little time for my private life	26	17
I neither like nor dislike my job especially. After all, one has to do something	25	18
I have a very difficult superior	17	11
I am burdened with too much work. I have the feeling I am being taken advantage of	16	14
I sometimes think that not enough is demanded of me—I could do a lot more	16	12
At my work I seldom ever hear a cheerful or appreciative word. I miss that	15	16
The job I have suits neither my ability nor my education	11	13
Unfortunately colleagues make life difficult for me	9	7
	229	194

PRAISE

Question put to gainfully employed persons: *"Have you recently been praised for your work or were you paid a compliment that really made you feel good?"*

	March 1976					
	Unskilled workers	Skilled workers	Non-managerial employees and public servants	Managerial employees and public servants	Self-employeds, professionals	Farmers
Yes, have been praised—	%	%	%	%	%	%
Total women	22	37	41	48	36	8
Total men	17	32	38	44	43	12

THE BOSS

Question put to employed persons: *"If you were to describe your boss using these categories, which of them apply?"* (L)

	August 1962	June 1976
	%	%
Very good income	71	66
Owns his/her own home	58	65
Very hard-working professionally	66	57
Has a job with a lot of responsibility	59	54
You don't know much about his/her private life	43	43
Treats people fairly	54	41
Has a well-appointed place of work, an attractive office	48	40
Takes a big vacation trip every year	44	38
Works very hard, overtime and such	34	31
Is very popular with the other employees	39	30
Not in perfect health	29	26
Travels a lot, gets around a lot	29	24
Happy family life	33	21
Takes work home	14	15
Has a cozy life, doesn't have to work especially hard	18	15
Has lots of leisure time	11	9
	650	575

SOMEWHAT NOTICEABLE

Question put to gainfully employed persons: *"What would happen if your boss were to drop out for half a year, perhaps because he/she became sick or went on a long trip. Do you think it would be very noticeable if the boss disappeared for half a year or would everything continue the same as ever?"*

	Continue as usual	Somewhat noticeable	Very noticeable	
	%	%	%	
Total gainfully employed persons - 1962	49	26	25	= 100
- 1976	40	30	30	= 100
- 1980	44	31	25	= 100
Men	48	31	21	= 100
Women	38	30	32	= 100
OCCUPATION				
Unskilled workers	40	33	27	= 100
Skilled workers	41	30	29	= 100
Non-managerial employees/ public servants	45	30	25	= 100
Managerial employees/public servants	52	32	16	= 100

THE BOSS: NOT TOO BOSSY

Question put to blue-collar and white-collar workers: *''Are you sometimes annoyed about the way your boss talks to you?''* (Yes=44 percent)

	August 1972 Total employed persons	Men	Women
	%	%	%
Often	26	26	26
Not so often	41	41	40
Very rarely	33	33	34
	100	100	100

Question put to gainfully employed persons: *''Are you content with your boss or not so content?''*

	September 1980 Total employees	Age groups 16-29	30-44	45-59	60 and over	Unskilled workers	Skilled workers	Non-managerial employees and public servants	Managerial
	%	%	%	%	%	%	%	%	%
Content	62	57	65	64	61	62	64	60	62
Not so content	24	24	25	22	23	23	20	26	25
Undecided	14	19	10	14	16	15	16	14	13
	100	100	100	100	100	100	100	100	100

A WOMAN AS BOSS?

Question put to employed persons: *''Would you agree to having a woman as your superior?''*

	Women Yes	No	Undecided		Men Yes	No	Undecided	
	%	%	%		%	%	%	
Total employed persons - March 1978	81	9	10	= 100	57	23	20	= 100
- March 1974	85	11	4	= 100	57	29	14	= 100
AGE GROUPS								
16-29	88	9	3	= 100	59	25	16	= 100
30-44	81	14	5	= 100	58	29	13	= 100
45-59	87	11	2	= 100	55	32	13	= 100
60 and over	84	8	8	= 100	48	33	19	= 100
OCCUPATION								
Unskilled workers	82	12	6	= 100	47	37	16	= 100
Skilled workers	96	x	4	= 100	56	31	13	= 100
Non-managerial employees and public servants	87	11	2	= 100	64	21	15	= 100
Managerial employees and public servants	88	6	6	= 100	62	27	11	= 100

MERIT PAY

Question: *"There are two secretaries who are the same age and who do practically the same job. One day, however, the one finds out that the other one is earning 100 marks a month more. She goes straight away to complain to the boss. But the boss is forced to tell her that the other is more efficient and reliable and works faster than she does. Do you consider it fair that the one earns more, or do you not consider it fair?"*

In the parallel version the case reads, "... *two auto mechanics who are* ..."

	Secretaries			Auto mechanics		
	Fair	Not fair		Fair	Not fair	
	%	%		%	%	
Total population - May 1972	83	17	= 100	79	21	= 100
- November 1975	71	29	= 100	77	23	= 100

SICK LEAVE

Question put to employed persons (51% = 100): *"What is your opinion of colleagues who obtain a medical leave of absence and don't come to work owing to a bit of a headache or a cold?"* (L)

	January 1978
	%
It is unfair to those colleagues who go to work even when they don't feel up to the mark	59
I don't think it's right, for if everybody did it, the company would soon be jeopardized financially	27
They are within their full rights and I am in complete agreement. Often an additional day off is necessary to recuperate	18
Other or no reply	4
	108

PILFERING

Question: *"Many people who work in offices take writing paper, pencils etc. home with them for their private use.* (Half group: *Workers, too, often take small quantities of material that they can use at home.) Do you think they can go ahead and do so, should they only do so in exceptional cases, or should they not do so at all?"*

	The office employee —				The worker —			
	1959	1971	1975	1980	1959	1971	1975	1980
	May	March	Nov.	March	May	March	Nov.	March
	%	%	%	%	%	%	%	%
Can go ahead and do so	5	13	11	13	5	10	9	10
Only in exceptional cases	18	30	35	33	18	29	31	29
Should not do so at all	73	52	48	49	73	56	55	55
Undecided	4	5	6	5	4	5	5	6
	100	100	100	100	100	100	100	100

FRINGE BENEFITS

Question put to employed persons: *"In many companies there are various benefits and social services for the workers and employees. Which of the benefits on this list does the company where you are presently working have?"* (L)

	Employed persons 1961 %	1974 %	1979 %
Christmas money	85	92	54*
Gift on a professional anniversary (e.g. 25 years with the company)	49	55	58
Company parties, festivities (Christmas, May 1, etc.)	43	49	56
13th month salary	–	–	52*
Company cafeteria	43	45	42
Additional vacation pay	11	44	47
Company outings	38	39	38
Company pension plan	29	34	33
Gift on family occasions (e.g. weddings, baptisms)	25	31	31
Products manufactured by the firm can be bought at a discount	32	35	27
Medical treatment by a company doctor	18	14	23
Company sports, company sports club	14	22	21
Paid educational leave	–	–	19
Continuing education courses, company language courses	10	17	18
Some things can be bought at a reduction through the company or in the canteen	27	22	17
Interest-free loans	17	15	16
Company medical plan	18	16	16
Company housing at reduced rates or rent-free	–	–	16
Financial aid when there is serious illness	20	15	13
Company buses to take you to work	11	18	11
Company library, reading room	20	11	10
Company cars for private use	–	–	9
Merit bonus	–	–	8
Rest home, maternity home	14	10	5
Dormitory for single persons/apprentices	9	7	5
Company nursery school	3	5	4
14th month salary	–	–	4*
Movies, plays and concerts put on by the company	7	4	–
Financial aid if you have children attending college	3	2	1
None of the above	7	3	4
	553	605	658

*= in 1979, 'Christmas money' was subdivided into the categories Christmas money, 13th month salary and 14th month salary.

– = not asked

WOMEN ON THE JOB

Question put to women: *"Are you gainfully employed or do you have any other job aside from your housekeeping?"*

	March 1979					
	Employed— full time	Employed— part time	Employed— on an hourly basis	Only in the home	Neither, nor	
	%	%	%	%	%	
Total women	26	12	7	48	7	= 100
AGE GROUPS						
16-29	50	8	4	16	22	= 100
30-44	31	20	8	40	1	= 100
45-59	20	16	11	52	1	= 100
60 and over	3	4	4	81	8	= 100
EDUCATION						
Elementary	21	12	8	54	5	= 100
Secondary	35	12	4	36	13	= 100

LIKE WORKING

Question to employed women: *"Would you prefer to do your housekeeping only, or do you actually like going out to work as well?"*

	Employed women					
	Total		Full time		Part time employment	
	1973	1979	1973	1979	1973	1979
	%	%	%	%	%	%
Like to work as well	72	73	72	76	71	69
Prefer housekeeping only	14	15	14	13	13	17
Undecided	14	12	14	11	16	14
	100	100	100	100	100	100
	Employed, married mothers with children under 16 years					
Like to work as well	68	68	63	67	72	69
Prefer housekeeping only	19	19	24	30	16	14
Undecided	13	13	13	3	12	17
	100	100	100	100	100	100

PREFERENCES

Question to women exclusively occupied with housekeeping: *"Would you like to be gainfully employed or do you actually prefer working in the household only?"*

	Women exclusively occupied with housekeeping			Not gainfully employed, married mothers with children under 16 yrs.	
	1967	1973	1979	1973	1979
	%	%	%	%	%
Prefer housekeeping only	68	47	54	31	30
Would like to work as well	14	32	21	44	32
Prefer to be employed	10	12	14	19	23
Undecided	8	9	11	6	15
	100	100	100	100	100

MEN ADVANTAGED

Question: *"Is it your impression that women have equal professional opportunities as compared with men nowadays, provided that they achieve as much, or are men generally advantaged?"*

	1967	1972	1976	1979
	%	%	%	%
Men are advantaged	44	64	64	63
Women have equal opportunities	40	21	20	17
Undecided	16	15	16	20
	100	100	100	100

DOING MEN'S WORK

Question: *"More and more women are taking up what were traditionally men's occupations, such as assembly line work, painting, or masonry. Do you think this is good, or don't you especially like it?"*

A

	May 1979					
	Think it's good		Don't like it		Undecided	
	Women	Men	Women	Men	Women	Men
	%	%	%	%	%	%
Total	58	48	31	34	11	18
AGE GROUPS						
16-29	71	59	19	22	10	19
30-44	66	56	19	25	15	19
45-59	52	44	44	40	4	16
60 and over	46	29	42	55	12	16

WOMEN UNDERREPRESENTED

Question: *"It is a well-known fact that in business and politics women are much less represented in better-paid and important posts than men. Should that be changed, in your view, or do you find the state of things satisfactory as it is?"*

	Should be changed %	Satisfactory as is %	Undecided %	
Total population - April 1973	58	32	10	= 100
- March 1976	60	28	12	= 100
- May 1979	62	27	11	= 100
Men	52	34	14	= 100
Women	69	22	9	= 100
AGE GROUPS				
16-29	75	19	6	= 100
30-44	65	26	9	= 100
45-59	62	26	12	= 100
60 and over	46	38	16	= 100
OCCUPATION				
Unskilled workers	54	34	12	= 100
Skilled workers	56	32	12	= 100
Non-managerial employees and public servants	71	20	9	= 100
Managerial employees and public servants	68	21	11	= 100
Self-employeds, professionals	58	30	12	= 100
Farmers	36	50	14	= 100

BRINGING ABOUT A CHANGE

Question: *"There are two opinions about how women could change things. Which would you agree with?"* (L)

The one:

"Women will gradually gain more and more recognition in business and politics. The idea of justice and equality is gaining prominence in the modern world."

The other:

"If women energetically commit themselves and begin to fight for it, there will be greater equality. Without energetic protests it won't work."

	1973	1979	Total	Total	Women: Age groups			
	Total population		Men	Women	16-29	30-44	45-59	60 and over
	%	%	%	%	%	%	%	%
Equality will gradually gain ground	60	56	56	55	51	56	61	56
Women must fight for equality	25	29	27	30	39	33	21	18
Undecided	15	15	17	15	10	11	18	26
	100	100	100	100	100	100	100	100

THE CONSUMER

D

	Total households			
	1975	1976	1978	1980
	%	%	%	%
Investments				
Savings agreement for the purpose of home construction -				
- less than DM 40,000	} 39	} 40	26	21
- more than DM 40,000			12	12
Fixed interest bonds	12	12	9	10
Savings bonds	–	–	10	11
Stocks	8	8	6	7
Investment stocks	3	3	3	3
	62	63	66	64
Insurance				
Private life insurance				
- less than DM 20,000	38	35	25	25
- between DM 20,000 and DM 49,999	23	24	22	24
- more than DM 50,000	7	8	8	8
Private full health insurance	7	8	8	8
Private supplementary health insurance	24	24	15	17
Full coverage car insurance	10	13	13	17
	109	112	91	99

INVESTMENTS AND INSURANCE

D

	Spring 1980						
	Total households	Unskilled workers	Skilled workers	Non-managerial employees	Managerial and public servants	Self-employeds, professionals	Farmers
	%	%	%	%	%	%	%
Investments							
Savings agreement for the purpose of home construction -							
- less than DM 40,000	21	16	23	23	22	19	25
- DM 40,000 and over	12	7	10	13	19	17	13
Savings bonds	11	6	9	11	17	17	7
Fixed-interest bonds	10	4	7	11	19	20	8
Stocks	7	2	3	6	14	15	6
Investment stocks ...	3	1	1	3	6	6	1
Gold bars, gold coins	5	1	2	5	9	12	5
	69	37	55	72	106	106	65
Insurance							
Private life insurance	22	17	23	23	25	25	4
Private full health insurance	8	4	6	11	22	31	11
Private supplementary health insurance ...	17	8	12	18	28	24	16
Full-coverage car insurance	17	9	14	17	26	24	13
	64	38	55	69	101	104	44
Credit Cards							
Eurocheque	41	22	34	48	59	54	21
Other credit cards ...	2	2	2	2	2	3	1
	43	24	36	50	61	57	22

LOANS

Question: *"Nowadays many things are so expensive that one can hardly acquire anything without taking out a loan. Could you tell me whether you have taken out a loan for something during the last three years - either for yourself or for some other member of your household?"* (L)

D

	Total households borrowing	Purpose of loan - Car	House, apartment, property	Furniture	TV set, stereo	Setting up business	Vacation	Other
	%	%	%	%	%	%	%	%
1978	23	9	8	5	2	1	1	3
1979	22	7	9	5	1	1	1	7
1980	23	8	8	5	2	1	1	14

D

	Spring 1979						
	Total pop.	Unskilled workers	Skilled workers	Non-managerial employees and public servants	Managerial	Self-employeds, professionals	Farmers
	%	%	%	%	%	%	%
Have taken out a loan	22	18	24	23	23	23	18
No loan	78	82	76	77	77	77	82
	100	100	100	100	100	100	100
	Borrowers						
Purpose of loan							
Mortgage loan	38	28	29	39	52	48	45
Credit for goods:							
Car	33	33	38	35	26	19	22
Furniture, larger household appliances	23	33	25	26	13	11	11
Television, stereo equipment	6	11	4	4	4	4	5
Trips, vacation	6	6	4	4	4	7	5
Setting up business ..	5	x	x	x	4	26	x
Advanced professional training	3	5	x	4	4	4	11
Education, provision for children when older	2	x	4	x	x	4	x
Credit for other purposes	14	11	13	13	13	19	33
	130	127	117	125	120	142	132

CAR OWNERSHIP

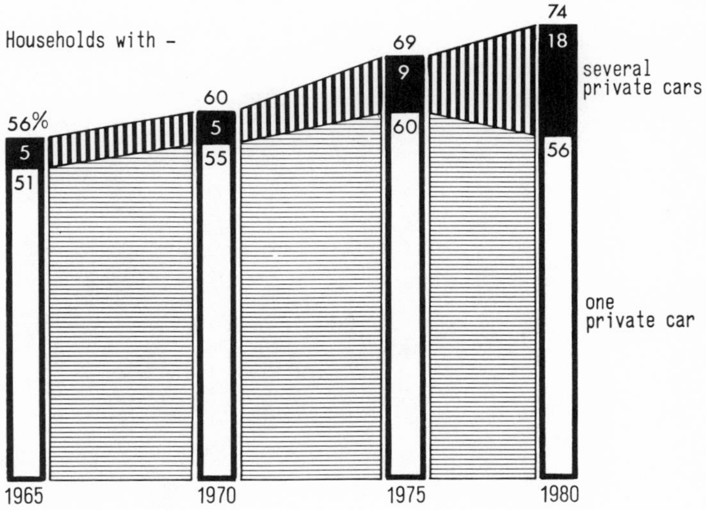

D

	Households with several private cars					
	1972	1976	1977	1978	1979	1980
	%	%	%	%	%	%
Total population	7	11	13	15	16	18
OCCUPATION						
Unskilled workers	3	4	6	8	9	10
Skilled workers	6	9	11	13	12	14
Non-managerial employees/public servants	6	11	13	14	16	16
Managerial employees and public servants	11	17	18	23	23	27
Self-employeds, professionals	19	24	23	30	31	32
Farmers	10	19	19	20	20	31

CAR DATA

D

	Spring 1979						
	Total owners of private cars	Unskilled workers	Skilled workers	Non-managerial employees and public servants	Managerial employees and public servants	Self-employeds, professionals	Farmers
	%	%	%	%	%	%	%
New or second hand -							
Bought new	54	43	49	53	64	67	51
Bought used	46	57	51	47	36	33	49
	100	100	100	100	100	100	100
Year of manufacture -							
1978/79	37	38	39	39	34	33	32
1976/77	40	38	39	39	43	43	36
1972-1975	20	21	20	20	20	22	28
Before 1972	3	3	2	2	3	2	4
	100	100	100	100	100	100	100
Make -							
VW	26	25	26	30	26	19	21
Opel	20	25	26	19	14	15	24
Ford	12	17	13	11	9	12	13
Mercedes	9	4	7	7	11	21	20
Audi/NSU	9	8	9	9	8	5	6
BMW	3	4	5	4	10	12	4
Fiat	4	4	4	4	3	2	2
Renault	5	5	4	6	5	3	2
Other French make ..	5	4	2	6	7	5	4
Japanese make	2	4	2	2	2	2	2
Other foreign make ..	5	x	2	2	5	4	2
	100	100	100	100	100	100	100
Horsepower -							
Under 55 hp	43	47	44	49	37	29	51
50-90 hp	41	44	43	39	40	39	40
Over 90 hp	16	9	13	12	23	32	9
	100	100	100	100	100	100	100

MILEAGE

D

Estimated kilometers driven per year -	Total drivers of private cars 1976 %	1977 %	1978 %	1979 %	1980 %
30,000 and over	6	5	6	6	5
20,000 to 29,999	14	13	14	12	11
15,000 to 19,999	22	24	23	24	24
10,000 to 14,999	34	34	34	35	34
less than 10,000	24	24	23	23	26
	100	100	100	100	100

WHO DRIVES?

Question: *"Is there a car in your household?" "Do you yourself mainly drive this car or does someone else drive it more frequently?"*

D

	Summer 1980					
	Total households	Men	Women	Selected age groups 18-24	60-69	70 and over
Car driven by -	%	%	%	%	%	%
respondent mainly	38	60	20	43	26	9
respondent very occasionally	10	4	14	13	5	2
respondent never	26	16	35	29	20	9
No car in the household	26	20	31	15	49	80
	100	100	100	100	100	100

EXTRAS

D

	Summer 1980						
	Total owners of private cars	Unskilled workers	Skilled workers	Non-managerial employees and public servants	Managerial employees and public servants	Self-employeds, professionals	Farmers
	%	%	%	%	%	%	%
Total automobile accessories	49	34	52	51	53	52	33
Of these							
- Fur seat covers	25	17	27	26	27	28	11
- Other seat covers	19	14	22	18	20	19	19
- Additional halogen headlights	17	11	19	17	18	21	12
- Wide track tires	9	5	10	9	11	11	6
- Aluminium rims	8	4	8	8	9	14	4
- Racing style steering wheel	6	5	8	6	7	6	4
- Spoiler	4	3	5	4	4	3	x
- Additional dashboard instruments	4	2	4	5	4	4	1
- Bucket seats	3	2	4	3	4	4	2
- Decoration set	2	1	3	1	2	1	2

Question put to car owners, who drive a car themselves: *"Which things do you generally fix yourself on your car?"* (L)

D

	Wash car	Wax, polish	Touch up damage to paint	Minor repairs	Major repairs	Have all done	
	%	%	%	%	%	%	
Total drivers - Spring 1980 ...	71	51	35	33	1	23	= 214
Men	95	82	66	65	1	22	= 331
Women	45	20	2	2	x	21	= 90

ENJOY DRIVING?

Question put to owners of private cars: *"Do you actually enjoy driving, or not?"*

	Enjoy driving	Drive because I have to	Yes and no	
	%	%	%	
Men - 1974	37	40	23	= 100
- 1980	43	35	22	= 100
Women - 1974	56	27	17	= 100
- 1980	52	26	22	= 100

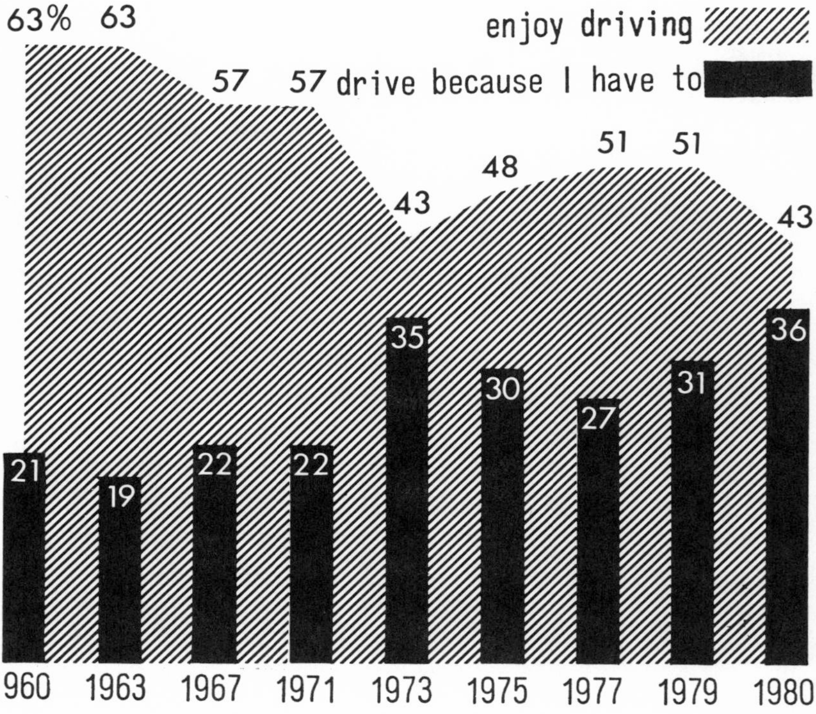

A GOOD DRIVER?

Question: *"If you were to say how well you drive, what would you say?"*

A

	August 1975					
	Characterize their own driving as -					
	Very good	Good	Mediocre	Not especially good	No opinion	
	%	%	%	%	%	
Total car owners	7	45	41	4	3	= 100

BUYING PLANS

Question: *"Do you intend to purchase a car in the next one or two years or don't you think so?"*

D

	Yes, intend to	No, not in the next 1-2 years	Don't know	
	%	%	%	
Total population - 1978	22	60	18	= 100
- 1979	20	63	17	= 100
- 1980	18	61	21	= 100

CAR RENTAL

Question: *"Have you rented a car or a small transport vehicle from a car-rental in the last 12 months?"*

D

	1980						
	Total pop.	Unskilled workers	Skilled workers	Non-managerial employees and public servants	Managerial	Self-employeds, professionals	Farmers
	%	%	%	%	%	%	%
Yes -	5	3	5	5	6	9	2
once	1	3	4	5	5	7	2
often	4	x	1	x	1	2	x
No	95	97	95	95	94	91	98
	100	100	100	100	100	100	100

WANTED: MORE INFORMATION ABOUT CARS AND CAR TESTING

D

	1980						
	Total pop.	Unskilled workers	Skilled workers	Non-managerial employees and public servants	Managerial	Self-employeds, professionals	Farmers
Especially interested in-	%	%	%	%	%	%	%
general information ..	19	14	25	18	18	16	14
economical driving ..	28	18	31	30	34	31	25

SELF-IMAGE

Question put to car drivers: *"Would you please read what it says on these cards and set aside those items that apply to you personally and that you agree with?"* (C)

E

	October 1971
	%
For my car, the oil is changed regularly after the required number of kilometers	76
When I drive, I often ask myself how some drivers ever got a license	59
I always take the car in for a check-up after the required number of kilometers	57
If the most recent tax raise on gas really goes toward road construction, I'm basically in agreement with it	55
I'd rather drive more slowly and be sure I get there	52
I've frequently been in situations where I barely escaped an accident	50
I always try to check and see how much gas my car uses, how long a certain quantity lasts	49
Taxi drivers often behave pretty inconsiderately in traffic	49
I've often avoided the autobahn and taken other roads because there were such traffic jams	48
When I drive, I often have the feeling that it's very dangerous and that I could be the next to whom something happens	47
If better use were made of the police, our traffic situation would be better	38
I really like to drive my car to full capacity	36
Truck drivers often behave pretty inconsiderately in traffic	36
You do find bad drivers among women somewhat more often than among men	36
When I drive, I like to smoke	35
I don't let anybody drive my car; I'm the only one who drives it	32
I try not to drive off in the car on weekends	26
You can often tell by the make what kind of driver you'll find behind the wheel	23
For license plates from certain towns or counties I know right away that it's going to be a bad driver	21
If someone on the road acts like an idiot, you should go ahead and tell him so (for example, by blinking, honking, making a sign, calling out)	21
It very seldom happens that someone passes me who's driving the same car I am	21
I wouldn't mind an autobahn fee if it meant that our highway net would be expanded more quickly	20
I regularly take colleagues along to work in my car	11
I regularly go to work in a colleague's car	2
	900

ANNOYING

Question put to drivers of private cars: *"Here is a list of snags which one encounters time and again in traffic. Could you tell me which of them you find particularly unpleasant?"* (L)

E

	1971 Fall %	1978/79 Winter %
When you get caught in rush-hour traffic	69	61
Traffic jams	64	56
When you have to look a long time for a parking place or wait until one is free	58	51
Road works and detours	48	41
Exhaust fumes when driving in close file	45	39
Speed limits on perfectly clear streets	44	34
When the traffic lights are badly timed	41	34
It is so difficult to find your way around strange towns	43	31
There are so many trucks on the roads	34	22
There are far too many traffic signs	30	21
When the red light is too long	19	17
When your car gets splashed just after being washed	28	13
The constant fear of accidents	18	12
You are always subjected to engine noise	9	5
You are never served immediately at gas stations	9	5
	559	442

CONSIDERATE DRIVERS?

Question: *"What is your impression of automobile traffic today? Are drivers by and large more considerate than they were about five years ago, or have they become worse in the last few years?"*

D

	August 1976				
	More considerate %	Have become worse %	Remained the same %	Undecided %	
Total population	37	29	27	7	= 100
Men	45	23	26	6	= 100
Women	30	35	27	8	= 100
Total drivers	45	25	26	4	= 100
Total non-drivers	26	36	27	11	= 100

TRAIN OR CAR?

Question: *"When you have to travel a distance of 500 kilometers alone, what is more convenient—to drive your car or to go by train?"*

E

	Drive my car	Go by train	Both equal	Don't know	
	%	%	%	%	
Total car owners/drivers - 1971	43	46	6	5	= 100
- 1978	58	31	4	7	= 100

AVERAGE SPEED: 128 km/h=80 mph

Question: *"How fast do you usually drive on the freeway?"*

km/h:	90	100	110	120	130	140	150	160	170	No answer	Never drive on freeway	
	%	%	%	%	%	%	%	%	%	%	%	
Total car drivers	1	7	8	23	24	12	8	3	3	2	9	= 100

Question put to drivers: *"Here are two people have a conversation. Which of the two would you tend to agree with - the one above or the one below?"* (ill.)

	July 1980
	%
"I have the feeling that the multinational oil companies use the rise in oil prices irresonsibly in order to make huge profits."	64
"You can say whatever you want about the oil companies, but you can hardly blame them for the rise in oil prices. The oil-producing countries impose these prices on them."	24
Undecided	12
	100

TRAFFIC VICTIMS UNDERESTIMATED

Question: *"How many people do you think died on German roads in 1975?" "How many people would you suspect were injured in traffic accidents in the Federal Republic in 1975?"*

D

August 1976

Estimated traffic deaths -	%
less than 1,000	6
1,000 - 5,000	14
5,000 - 10,000	11
10,000 - 15,000	15
15,000 (correct answer)	7
16,000 - 20,000	6
20,000 and over	24
Don't know	17
	100

Estimated traffic injureds -	%
less than 5,000	5
5,000 - 10,000	5
10,00 - 30,000	14
30,000 - 60,000	14
60,000 - 100,000	7
100,000 - 200,000	14
200,000 - 400,000	12
400,000 - 500,000 (correct answer)	4
More than 500,000	7
Don't know	18
	100

OIL PRICES

Question put to drivers: *''Here are two people having a conversation. Which of the two would you tend to agree with - the one above or the one below?''* (ill.)

	July 1980 %
''I have the feeling that the multinational oil companies use the rise in oil prices irresponsibly in order to make huge profits.''	64
''You can say whatever you want about the oil companies, but you can hardly blame them for the rise in oil prices. The oil-producing countries impose these prices on them.''	24
Undecided	12
	100

BICYCLE

Question: *''Do you ride a bicycle frequently or only occasionally?''*

D

	Frequently %	Sometimes %	Never %	
Total population - August 1976	24	26	50	= 100
- May 1980	26	32	42	= 100

	1980 Purchasers of bicycles and accessories in the past 12 months %
Total population	28
Unskilled workers	26
Skilled workers	28
Non-managerial employees and public servants	28
Managerial employees and public servants	30
Self-employeds, professionals	27
Farmers	25

VACATION TRIPS

Question: *"Did you go on a vacation trip last year?"*

D

	Year of vacation						
	1949	1957	1964	1972	1976	1978	1979
	%	%	%	%	%	%	%
Several vacation trips*	} 21	} 36	} 50	} 53	15 } 55	19 } 56	18 } 57
One vacation trip*					40	37	39
None	79	64	50	47	45	44	43
	100	100	100	100	100	100	100

* = for 6 days or more

MEANS OF TRANSPORTATION

Question put to vacationers: *"Did you travel* by train, in your own car, by bus, by plane, or by some other form of transportation?"*

D

	Vacation Year			
	1957	1960	1972	1979
	%	%	%	%
Train	54	48	22	22
Private car	26	35	56	58
Bus	12	14	10	13
Plane	x	x	18	22
Ship	x	x	2	5
Other	13	8	5	6
	105	105	113	126

*Vacation trips for 6 days and more

SUMMER PREFERRED

Question put to vacationers: *"During which season were you away on vacation?"*

D

	Vacation year 1978							
	Vacationers	Age groups						
	total	14-19	20-29	30-39	49-49	50-59	60-69	70 and over
	%	%	%	%	%	%	%	%
Spring	22	17	19	21	20	27	31	34
Summer	69	78	71	76	72	65	56	54
Fall	25	17	24	21	23	32	38	37
Winter	27	25	32	27	26	28	27	31
	143	137	146	145	141	152	152	156

LENGTH OF STAY

Question: *"How long was your last vacation trip, how long were you away from home?"*

D

	Vacation year 1976					
	Length of trip in weeks -					
	More than 3	About 3	About 2	Less than 2	No vacation trip	
	%	%	%	%	%	
Total population	6	15	20	14	45	= 100
AGE GROUPS						
14-19	4	14	30	9	43	= 100
20-29	4	15	28	11	42	= 100
30-39	5	16	25	13	41	= 100
40-49	6	17	21	12	44	= 100
50-59	6	16	19	10	49	= 100
60-69	9	15	14	13	49	= 100
70 and over	10	12	12	8	58	= 100
OCCUPATION						
Unskilled workers	4	10	13	11	62	= 100
Skilled workers	6	12	20	13	49	= 100
Non-managerial employees and public servants	7	19	23	14	37	= 100
Managerial employees and public servants	10	20	21	17	32	= 100
Self-employeds, professionals	7	18	19	15	41	= 100
Farmers	2	6	5	13	74	= 100

BOOKING IN ADVANCE

Question put to vacationers: *"Have you booked one or more of these vacation trips through a travel agency and had to pay for the vacation trip, flight, accommodation or board in advance?"*

D

	1978 Total pop.	1979 Total pop.	Occupation: Unskilled workers	Skilled workers	Non-managerial employees and public servants	Managerial employees and public servants	Self-employeds, professionals	Farmers
	%	%	%	%	%	%	%	%
Yes, booked in advance	41	45	44	44	45	47	51	43

ACCOMMODATION

Question put to vacationers: *"What sort of accommodation did you have during your vacation?"*

D

	Vacation year 1978: Total vacationers	Age group: 14-19	20-29	30-39	40-49	50-59	60-69	70 and over
	%	%	%	%	%	%	%	%
Hotel, boarding-house								
- with bath, shower	38	23	36	46	46	51	47	33
- without bath, shower	16	19	16	17	18	20	18	17
Vacation house or apartment	19	21	21	31	27	22	10	7
Private room	18	14	21	19	21	22	22	19
Tent, trailer	13	28	24	15	11	8	4	x
Stayed with relatives, friends ...	15	16	16	15	14	18	18	24
	119	121	134	143	137	141	119	100

CAMPING

Question: *"Have you gone camping within the past five years, i.e. with a tent or a trailer? (Weekend trips included)"*

A

	September 1976: Total pop.	Age groups: 16-29	30-44	45 and over
	%	%	%	%
Yes	19	35	23	9
No	81	65	77	91
	100	100	100	100

WHERE THEY WENT

Question put to vacationers: *"Which places have you been to on vacation in the last 12 months?"* (L)

D

	Vacation year				
	1957	1972	1978	Youth	
	Total	Total	Total	14-17	18-24
Vacation in -	%	%	%	%	%
Federal Republic of Germany	70	42	51	55	46
German Democratic Republic	5	3	5	3	5
Italy	10	12	16	16	15
Austria	7	21	25	24	25
Switzerland	3	5	8	5	8
France	2	4	11	12	21
Spain, Portugal	1	11	12	9	15
Belgium, Netherlands, Luxemburg	1	4	6	9	10
Scandinavia	1	3	5	5	7
Greece	x	1	4	2	5
England, Ireland	x	1	3	7	7
Yugoslavia	x	3	6	5	8
Eastern bloc	x	6	4	x	3
North America	x	x	2	2	2
North Africa	x	x	2	x	3
Central America, South America	x	x	1	x	x
Asia	x	x	1	x	2
	100	116	162	154	182

HONEYMOON

Question put to honeymooners (36 percent = 100): *"Did you spend your honeymoon in Germany or did you go abroad?"*

D

	August 1976									
	Germany	Italy	Austria	Spain, Portugal	Balkans	Switzer- land	Northern Europe	France	Else- where	
	%	%	%	%	%	%	%	%	%	
Spent honeymoon in	60	11	11	7	3	3	2	2	3	= 102

IF MONEY DIDN'T MATTER

Question: *"Which country do you personally like best, in which would you most like to travel often? - Assuming that money didn't matter."* (O)

A

	1955 Jan. %	1979 June %		1955 Jan. %	1979 June %
A Mediterranean country	39	27	Canada	4	3
Austria	5	15	England	1	2
A Scandinavian country	7	11	Holland	2	2
France	6	8	Israel	2	2
USA	8	8	Thailand	x	2
Switzerland	20	6	Africa	1	1
A Latin American country	2	6	Japan	1	1
An East bloc country	1	3	Australia	1	1

VACATION CHOICES

Question: *"There are many possible ways of spending one's vacation. Could you describe your vacation* more specifically - which of the things on this list apply to your vacation?"* (L)

D

	Vacationers 1979 %
Rest and relaxation	33
Vacation in the sun, swimming	17
Family vacation	15
Vacation with friends, relatives	12
Visiting relatives, friends	12
Skiing vacation, winter vacation	8
Adventure trip	6
Camping trip	6
Tour (from place to place with short stays)	6
Taking a trip to a big city	5
Educational trips, language-study vacation	4
Other active vacation, vacation involved with sports or hobbies	4
World tour, trip to far-away places	3
Cruise, sea voyage	3
Club vacation (i.e. Méditerranée, Robinson, etc.)	1
	135

*vacations of more than 6 days

WAYS OF SPENDING TIME AND MONEY

Question put to vacationers: *"Would you read this list and tell me what you did during your last vacation?"* (L)
D

	Vacation year 1975						
	Total pop.	Men	Women	Age group 14-29	30-44	45-59	60 and over
	%	%	%	%	%	%	%
Went swimming	62	65	60	75	69	59	33
Walked a lot	61	56	66	44	62	71	75
Hiked in the mountains	31	35	27	26	31	35	34
Went skiing	7	8	6	11	8	4	2
Went toboganning, ice-skating	3	3	3	3	5	1	1
Went yachting	4	5	3	5	6	4	1
Went water-skiing	2	3	2	3	3	2	x
Was at a nudist beach	6	6	6	7	8	5	2
	176	181	173	174	192	181	148
Made new friends	58	58	58	65	57	53	54
Ate well, got to know the cuisine of other regions	48	48	48	49	50	51	40
Went out alot in the evenings	39	41	38	59	38	32	19
Went dancing	19	20	18	36	18	9	4
	164	167	162	209	163	145	117
Took lots of photographs	38	44	32	43	45	35	20
Did some shopping	36	30	41	42	37	30	31
Drove around in my car to get to know the area	35	37	32	32	39	38	28
Took part in organized trips	16	16	15	15	10	16	25
Made some movies	11	12	10	10	16	10	4
	136	139	130	142	147	129	108
Went to see famous buildings, works of art	28	27	29	24	28	31	31
Read a lot	18	15	22	17	19	16	22
Brushed up knowledge of languages abroad	6	8	5	10	6	5	2
	52	50	56	51	53	52	55
Slept a lot, relaxed	54	50	58	54	55	55	52
Took a cure	6	7	5	x	2	9	13
	60	57	63	54	57	64	65

HAGGLING

Question: *''It often happens in shops today that people, before making a big purchase, will try to beat down the price. Some people are very good at haggling, others cannot do it at all. What about you? Can you haggle or do you not like doing it?''*

	Don't like doing it	Can haggle	Undecided	
	%	%	%	
Total population - September 1967	73	20	7	= 100
- April 1975	54	36	10	= 100

NICE THINGS NOT CHEAP

Question: *''When we go into a store to buy something, we often look over or are shown several things from which we can choose. Do you find that usually the nice things - the things you like the best - are also the most expensive, or are the nicest things not always the most expensive?''*

	February 1977						
	Total			Age groups			
	pop.	Men	Women	16-29	30-44	45-59	60 and over
The nicest things are -	%	%	%	%	%	%	%
the most expensive	54	45	62	55	55	58	51
not the most expensive	11	14	8	15	9	9	9
It depends	35	41	30	30	36	33	40
	100	100	100	100	100	100	100

SHOPPING HOURS

Question: *''In Germany all stores must close at the same time. In many other countries it is up to the stores themselves how long they stay open. Do you think it would be a good thing if store owners could decide whether they want to stay open longer in the evenings or on Saturday afternoons, or not? The working hours of staff would, of course, have to remain as they are at present.''*

	Good	Not good	Undecided	
	%	%	%	
Total population - December 1963	52	34	14	= 100
- May 1972	62	26	12	= 100
- February 1976	57	28	15	= 100

CONSUMER PROTECTION

Question: *"There is a lot being said today about consumer protection and consumer education. What would you say: Where is it most necessary to protect the consumers so that they receive flawless goods, are served properly and not overcharged - which companies have up to now shown too little interest in the consumer?"* (L)

	May 1979 %
Oil companies	54
Pharmaceutical manufacturers	44
Car dealers	37
Building contractors	32
The food industry	32
Private insurance companies	29
Tour operators	26
Car manufacturers	25
Electricity supply works	24
Newspaper publishers	23
Cosmetics industry	19
Manufacturers of electrical household appliances	19
Federal Postal Services	19
Manufacturers of detergents	17
Federal Railroad	16
Banks	16
Television and phono equipment manufacturers	15
Building and loan associations	8

ONLY THE BEST

Question: *"There are certain goods for which buying the best possible quality is important, and other goods for which this is not so important, either because quality is quite uniform or because one often buys something new. Please take a look at this list and tell me for which of these goods you personally adhere to the principle of buying the best possible quality and not a cheaper or more average quality."* (L, X)

	August 1974 %
Television set	52
Washing machine	51
Shoes	50
Refrigerator	43
Suits, coats	40
Upholstered furniture	38
Radio	37
Wrist watch	33
Carpet	32
Brandy, Cognac	25
Kitchen furniture	23
Dress shirts	21
Soap	18
Chocolate	13
Children's toys	12
Sports equipment	11
Socks	10
Ties	9
Tent, Camping equipment	8
Stationery	6

MAIL ORDERS

Question: *"Have you or someone in your household ordered articles from a mail-order firm within the last 12 months?" "Have you, within the last 12 months, bought anything directly from a store belonging to a mail-order firm, that is, from a branch of the mail-order firm?" "What did you buy from a mail-order firm?"*

	Total pop.	Unskilled workers	Skilled workers	Non-managerial employees and public servants	Managerial employees and public servants	Self-employeds, professionals	Farmers
	%	%	%	%	%	%	%
Yes, did so - 1978 ...	37	40	39	38	37	24	40
- 1979 ...	50	53	54	51	42	37	46
Women's wear	20	24	21	21	16	10	24
Men's wear	11	13	13	10	9	5	11
Children's wear	9	10	10	9	6	6	9
Underclothes	8	10	8	7	7	4	14
Shoes, leather goods .	7	10	8	7	5	3	6
Linens	7	9	7	7	7	4	8
Household goods	6	7	7	6	6	3	6
Sporting goods, camping supplies ..	4	4	4	4	4	2	1
Toys	3	4	3	3	3	2	3
Books	3	3	3	4	4	2	2
Watches, jewelry	3	3	3	3	3	1	3
Auto accessories	3	2	3	3	3	1	2
Tools	3	3	4	2	4	1	2
Furniture	2	2	3	2	3	2	2
Stationery	2	2	2	2	2	1	1
Television, radio	2	3	2	2	1	1	2
Toiletries	2	3	2	3	2	1	3
Bicycle, moped	1	1	1	1	1	1	x
Things for the baby ..	1	1	2	1	1	1	1
Food	1	2	1	2	1	1	2

JAPANESE PRODUCTS

Question: *"There are Japanese products on the market, for example textiles, binoculars, chinaware, cameras, transistors, etc. Have you personally bought any of these Japanese products yet?" (Yes, have bought = 47 percent)*

Question: *"Do you believe that Japanese products are just as good quality overall as German products, or are they better or worse?"*

A

	May 1970						
	Total pop.	Men	Women	Age groups 16-29	30-44	45-59	60 and over
	%	%	%	%	%	%	%
Just as good as German products	57	63	53	62	60	58	50
Better than German products	6	6	6	6	6	7	4
Worse than German products	19	20	17	22	19	17	17
Undecided	18	11	24	10	15	18	29
	100	100	100	100	100	100	100

ECONOMIZING

Question: *"Could you use this list to tell me where you have recently reduced expenditures or where you intend to reduce them?"* (L)

	1974 Dec. %	1975 Nov. %	1977 Nov. %	1978 Nov. %
Limitation of sizeable purchases	44	39	26	29
Spending less on alcoholic beverages	23	26	18	25
Smoking less	21	23	20	23
Doing things myself in the apartment, house or garden which one would normally have done by others	28	26	19	23
Spending less on clothes	26	22	17	18
Going to the theater or cinema less frequently	19	17	10	15
Saving money on vacations	20	15	10	13
Saving money on the car	20	17	12	13
Spending less on food	10	10	9	10
Don't cut down on any of the things listed	26	32	39	35
	237	227	180	204

THE HANDYMAN

Question: *"Which of the things in this list have you* yourself *done in your home within the last 12 months?"* (L)

D

	Spring 1979 Total %	Men %	Women %
Done the painting, varnishing	34	43	27
Done the wallpapering	33	40	27
Laid the carpets	18	23	14
Fitted and/or repaired electric appliances	14	24	5
Done some joinery	11	18	5
Done some masonry	8	13	3
Laid tiles	7	10	4
Done some plumbing work	6	10	3
Done some locksmith's work	5	10	1
Repaired the heating	5	8	2
Done none of these things	49	37	60
	190	236	151

NEW EXPERIENCES

Question: *"Have you done anything in the last three months that was completely new to you, possibly something that's included on this list?"* (L)

D

Excerpt from replies:	1980 Total pop. %	Men %	Women %
Been to a restaurant I hadn't been to before	33	37	30
Been to a town or a city I hadn't been to before	26	29	23
Gone to a store I hadn't been to before	25	23	26
Was invited over by someone whose house I'd never been to	21	21	22
Invited someone myself who'd never been to my house	14	14	14
Rearranged the furniture	14	13	15
Looked at a magazine I wasn't familiar with yet	11	11	11
Started a new hobby	6	6	5
Tried a new sports activity	5	5	4
	155	159	150

	Age groups 14-19 %	20-29 %	30-39 %	40-49 %	50-59 %	60 and over %
Been to a restaurant I hadn't been to before	52	47	37	32	26	17
Been to a town or a city I hadn't been to before	32	34	30	25	23	19
Gone to a store I hadn't been to before	32	32	29	25	20	16
Was invited over by someone whose house I'd never been to	38	32	24	19	17	11
Invited someone myself who'd never been to my house	20	21	19	14	10	7
Rearranged the furniture	14	17	17	14	12	11
Looked at a magazine I wasn't familiar with yet	21	13	11	10	9	7
Started a new hobby	11	8	5	4	5	3
Tried a new sports activity	11	8	5	3	2	1
	231	212	177	146	124	92

WHO DECIDES WHAT TO BUY?

D

	Spring 1975				
	Persons who decided what to buy*				
	Men	Women			Brand conscious buyers**
	%	%			%
Razor	88	12	=	100	25
Motorcycle	86	14	=	100	67
Electric drill	83	17	=	100	64
Electric razor	82	18	=	100	64
Car radio	77	23	=	100	54
Moped, Mofa	73	27	=	100	50
Tape recorder	71	29	=	100	68
Motor lawn mower	68	32	=	100	42
Movie camera	67	33	=	100	59
Travel radio, transistor	60	40	=	100	44
Cassette recorder	60	40	=	100	45
Camera	60	40	=	100	55
Car stereo	57	43	=	100	18
Ski equipment	55	45	=	100	37
Black and white television	55	45	=	100	75
Color television	54	46	=	100	75
Larger stereo set	52	48	=	100	25
Pocket camera	52	48	=	100	52
Clock radio	49	51	=	100	12
Camper	48	52	=	100	45
Built-in kitchen cabinets	44	56	=	100	39
Refrigerator	44	56	=	100	57
Freezer	43	57	=	100	58
Dishwasher	43	57	=	100	66
Photography equipment	42	58	=	100	14
Fully automatic washing machine	39	61	=	100	66
Grill	38	62	=	100	48
Coffee maker	35	65	=	100	47
Electric sweeper	34	66	=	100	63
Kitchen appliances, mixer	30	70	=	100	55
Juicer	28	72	=	100	38

*Persons who bought the objects during the last 3 years and decided on the purchases themselves. Example: out of 100 persons who were involved in the purchase of a vacuum cleaner 66 were women and 34 were men.

**Persons who decided what to buy and at the same time gave preference to brand name products. Example: out of 100 buyers of vacuum cleaners 63 preferred brand name vacuum cleaners.

DISTRIBUTION OF HOUSEHOLD EQUIPMENT

D

Households with -	1975 %	1976 %	1977 %	1978 %	1979 %	1980 %
Fully automatic washing machine	79	81	–	–	81	85
Electric coffee machine	56	63	71	75	76	81
Freezer	48	61	63	65	–	70
Dishwasher	15	16	17	21	23	25
Color TV-set (not portable)	34	41	45	55	60	69
Radio alarm clock	14	21	32	39	49	56
Hifi - record player	–	–	37	35	32	32
Stereo equipment for car	5	7	–	–	13	18
Electrical drill with supplements	44	46	44	47	49	55
Motor-driven lawn mower	24	27	28	30	30	32

– = not asked

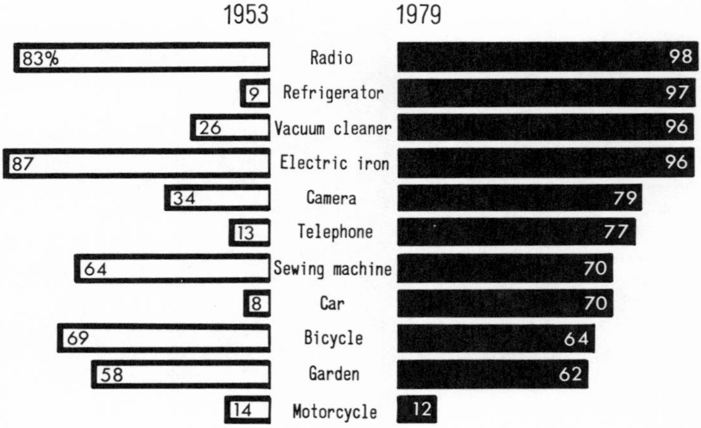

PHOTOGRAPHY

Took a photograph -	1977	1979	1980
	Total population		
	%	%	%
in the past 12 months	52	50	50
more than 12 months ago	17	18	18
No photographs taken	31	32	32
	100	100	100

Type of pictures taken -	1977	1979	1980
	Photographers*		
	%	%	%
Color prints	76	77	79
Slides	26	24	24
Black and white prints	10	9	6
	112	110	109

	Persons who took a photograph in the past 12 months		
	Total	Men	Women
	%	%	%
1980: total	50	59	42
Number of photographs -			
50 and over	18	26	11
25 - 49	13	15	11
15 - 24	12	12	12
less than 15	7	6	8

	Age groups						
	14-19	20-29	30-39	40-49	50-59	60-69	70 and over
	%	%	%	%	%	%	%
1980: total	62	67	64	58	45	30	13
Number of photographs -							
50 and over	15	28	25	20	17	8	4
25 - 49	18	17	16	15	13	8	2
15 - 24	17	14	14	14	10	8	5
less than 15	12	8	9	9	5	5	2

1980: Type of camera used within the past 12 months -

35mm camera	Pocket camera 110 film	Pocket camera 126 film	Instant developing camera	Other camera	
%	%	%	%	%	
44	22	18	6	12	= 102

WHO BUYS THE GROCERIES?

Question: ''*Who usually buys the groceries for your household and everything else that's needed every day?*''

	February 1976				
	Total pop.	Age groups 16-29	30-44	45-59	60 and over
	%	%	%	%	%
Men					
I do myself	12	15	8	7	19
Others and I	34	30	40	26	35
Others only	54	55	52	67	46
	100	100	100	100	100
Women					
I do myself	57	40	61	60	66
Others and I	36	46	36	37	27
Others only	7	14	3	3	7
	100	100	100	100	100

WHO IS THE COOK?

C

	Total households Men 1953	Men 1979	Women 1953	Women 1979
	%	%	%	%
I do the cooking myself	3	11	82	89
Other people do the cooking	93	87	17	10
Nobody, only eat out	4	2	1	1
	100	100	100	100

	Persons doing the cooking Men 1953	Men 1979	Women 1953	Women 1979
	%	%	%	%
Like it very much	31	51	69	51
Like it	33	44	29	44
Don't like to cook	36	7	2	5
	100	100	100	100

EATING OUT

Question: *"Do you sometimes go out for a meal in a restaurant? I don't mean a normal restaurant or lunchroom food during the working day." "About how often do you go out to eat?"*

	November 1978					
	At least once a week	Two to three times a month	About once a month	Less often than that	Never eat out	
	%	%	%	%	%	
Total population	8	20	21	23	28	= 100
Men	9	20	22	19	30	= 100
Women	7	19	21	26	27	= 100
AGE GROUPS						
16-29	11	27	25	23	14	= 100
30-44	7	25	25	21	22	= 100
45-59	5	15	20	29	31	= 100
60 and over	6	9	13	21	51	= 100
EDUCATION						
Elementary	5	15	22	24	34	= 100
Secondary	12	29	20	21	18	= 100

WOMEN'S ADVICE

Question put to women: *"When shopping with a man for men's clothing, when does he often ask you for advice—for which articles of clothing in particular?"* (C)

"With some articles of clothing one pays more attention to the fashion, and with others less so. Could you tell me in which things the male you buy for is especially fashion-conscious?" (C)

D

	September 1976						
	Suit	Coat	Pants	Shirt	Tie	Socks	Shoes
Women:	%	%	%	%	%	%	%
He often asks for my advice when purchasing	59	52	50	50	46	28	39
I see to it that he is fashionably dressed	64	36	53	59	53	10	32

REGULAR CONSUMPTION

Question: *"Which of these things have you yourself bought within the past two weeks?"* (C)

D

	Total population			
	1977	1978	1979	1980
	%	%	%	%
Dairy products				
Canned milk	51	51	48	47
Cheese in slices, ready packed	36	39	34	35
Foreign cheese specialities	21	24	21	22
Ice cream, family pack	27	29	27	27
	135	143	130	131
Candy, Snacks				
Milk chocolate	41	41	37	37
Chocolates	18	19	16	17
Filled chocolates	15	16	14	15
Semi-sweet chocolate	14	16	13	14
Cookies	35	35	32	31
Cheese crackers	9	11	9	9
Pretzel sticks, pretzels, nuts	33	32	30	29
Chewing gum	29	30	26	25
	194	200	177	177
Ready-to-serve meals, frozen foods				
Ready to serve meals, frozen	10	11	11	10
Pizza, frozen	8	10	10	12
Ready-to-serve packaged soups	18	19	17	17
Poultry, frozen	27	28	24	24
Meat/sausages, packed	–	27	24	–
Sausages, canned	–	22	22	–
	63	117	108	63
Coffee, Tea				
Coffee, whole beans	29	32	32	32
Coffee, ground	26	24	19	17
Instant coffee	17	17	15	14
Decaffeinated coffee (whole, ground, instant)	16	15	14	15
Tea, loose	16	18	16	16
Tea bags	20	20	18	18
	124	126	114	112

– = not asked.

PERSONAL HYGIENE

Question: *"How often should an adult take a bath?"*

	Every day	Every other day	Every third day	Once a week	Every two weeks		Average: number of days:
	%	%	%	%	%		
Total population - September 1964	10	8	24	57	1	= 100	3.3
- August 1975	15	21	30	33	1	= 100	2.5

Question: *"Which of these products have you used within the past week?"* (C)

D

Excerpt from replies:	Total households 1978 %	1980 %
Shampoo	84	84
Scented soap	78	72
Bath salts	62	63
Deodorant spray, deodorant stick	56	55
Mouthwash	44	40
Deodorant soap	41	39
Liquid shower soap	30	34
Special hand lotion	–	32
	Men	
After-shave lotion	64	65
Shaving soap, shaving cream	38	38
Hair lotion	24	23
Pre-shave lotion	25	21

Excerpt from replies:	Women 1978 %	1980 %
Multi-purpose skin cream	64	62
Day cream	58	54
Perfume	53	52
Hairspray	53	46
Lipstick	48	45
Special hand lotion	45	44
Hair conditioner	49	40
Nail polish	37	37
Night cream	36	34
Eye makeup	36	33
Facial makeup	33	30
Facial milk	35	30
Eau de cologne, lavender	32	29
Hair color	13	13
Facial mask	–	11

– = not asked.

SHAVING HABITS

Question put to men: *"Do you usually shave with an electric shaver or a razor?"*

D

	Men 1977	1978	1979	1980
	%	%	%	%
Electric shaver	57	60	58	59
Razor	36	34	35	33
Other reply	7	6	7	8
	100	100	100	100

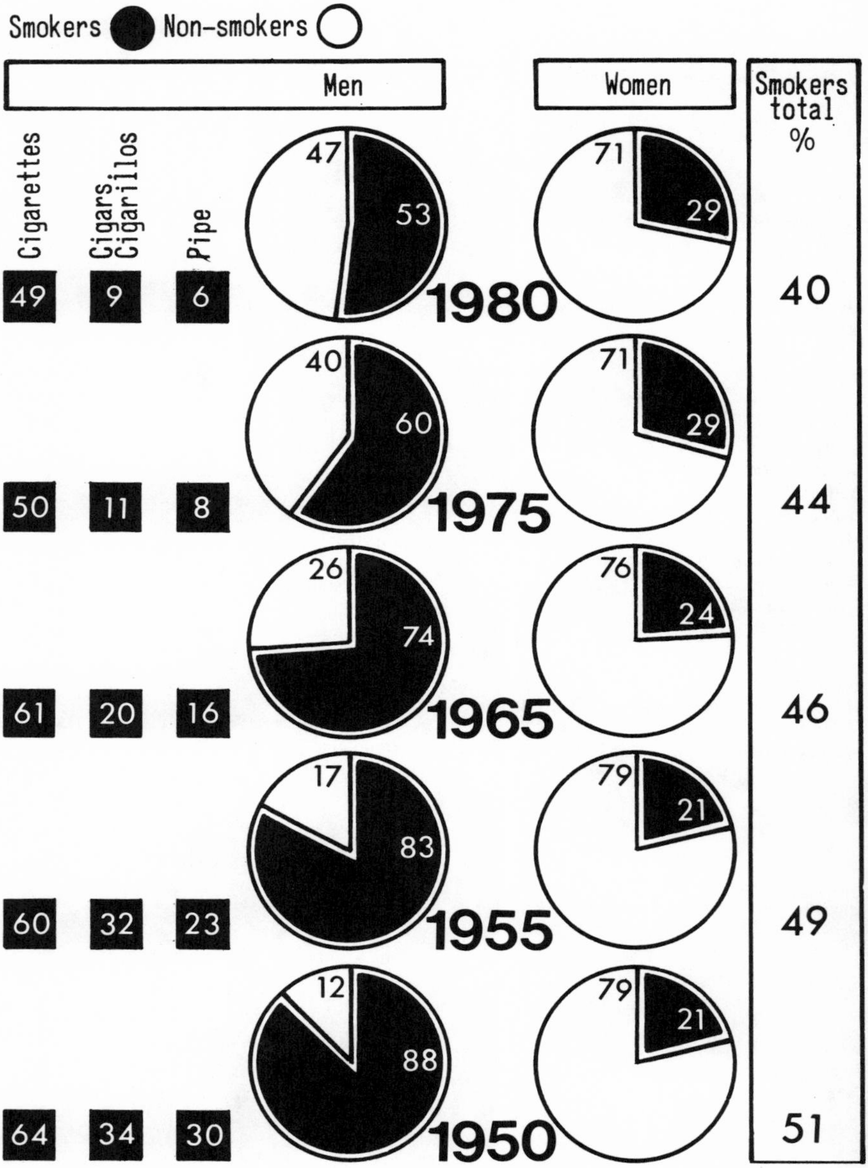
Smokers
Non-smokers
Men
Women
Smokers total %
Cigarettes
Cigars, Cigarillos
Pipe
1980
49
9
6
47
53
71
29
40
1975
50
11
8
40
60
71
29
44
1965
61
20
16
26
74
76
24
46
1955
60
32
23
17
83
79
21
49
1950
64
34
30
12
88
79
21
51

CIGARETTES ARE THE FAVORITE

D

Summer 1980

Smoking -	Total pop. %	Men %	Women %	Age groups 14-19 %	20-29 %	30-39 %	40-49 %	50-59 %	60 and over %
Filter cigarettes	33	37	28	39	47	40	34	28	21
Filterless cigarettes	6	11	2	10	12	6	6	5	3
Cigars, Cigarillos, cheroots	3	7	x	1	2	3	3	3	5
Pipe	3	5	x	2	3	3	3	2	3
Non-smoker	60	47	71	55	44	58	58	65	71
	105	107	101	107	108	100	104	103	103

Persons who smoke cigarettes

Daily -	Total %	Men %	Women %	Age groups 14-19 %	20-29 %	30-39 %	40-49 %	50-59 %	60 and over %
more than 20 cigarettes	25	31	14	9	24	29	28	31	24
10 - 20 cigarettes	46	48	45	39	51	46	46	47	46
less than 10 cigarettes	29	21	41	52	25	25	26	22	30
	100	100	100	100	100	100	100	100	100

NON-ALCOHOLIC DRINKS

Question: *"What have you personally bought in the past two weeks?"* (L)

D

	Summer 1980						
	Total pop.	Unskilled workers	Skilled workers	Non-managerial employees and public servants	Managerial	Self-employeds, professionals	Farmers
	%	%	%	%	%	%	%
Mineral water	49	44	45	53	54	47	44
Lemonade	40	40	41	42	38	37	33
Pure fruit juice	30	26	27	34	35	30	21
Cola	35	36	40	36	32	33	20
Tomato juice, vegetable juice	10	8	9	12	13	11	5
Concentrated juice	8	8	9	8	8	7	6
Tonic water, etc.	8	6	6	9	11	10	4
	180	168	177	194	191	175	133

ALCOHOLIC DRINKS

	Men %	Women %
WINE		
White wine, dry	21	21
Other white wine	26	31
Champagne	29	23
Sherry, port	5	9
	81	84
LIQUOR		
Clear schnaps	32	17
German brandy	24	14
Whisky	16	8
French cognac	11	7
Fruit schnaps	11	8
Rum	7	6
Vodka	7	3
Gin	3	3
	111	66

	Men %	Women %
BEER		
Pilsner	55	28
Export	36	24
Top-fermented dark beer	16	8
Near beer, malt beer	4	8
Low-calorie beer	2	2
	113	70
OTHER ALCOHOLIC DRINKS		
Liqueur	9	20
Bitter cordial	14	9
Half-bitter cordial	9	6
Ready mixed drinks with coffee and liquor	5	7
Apéritif	5	6
	42	48

ALCOHOLIC DRINKS

Question: "*What did you personally drink or buy in the past two weeks?*" (L)

D

	Summer 1980						
	Total pop.	Unskilled workers	Skilled workers	Non-managerial employees and public servants	Managerial	Self-employeds, professionals	Farmers
	%	%	%	%	%	%	%
BEER							
Pilsner	41	35	47	39	44	42	25
Export	29	31	32	27	29	29	31
Top-fermented dark beer	12	10	12	14	12	12	4
Near beer, malt beer	6	7	6	7	5	7	5
Low-calorie beer	2	2	1	2	2	2	2
	90	85	98	89	92	92	67
LIQUOR							
Clear schnaps	24	22	29	20	22	23	31
German brandy	18	16	21	18	21	19	17
Whisky	12	10	14	12	11	14	3
French cognac	9	5	8	8	15	12	3
Fruit schnaps	9	7	10	9	12	10	10
Rum	6	6	7	6	6	7	4
Vodka	5	3	5	5	4	6	3
Gin	3	2	3	3	5	4	1
	86	71	97	81	96	95	72
WINE							
White wine, dry	21	12	16	23	29	30	22
White wine, other	29	21	26	32	34	31	30
Red wine	27	19	22	29	38	33	20
Champagne	29	23	25	31	34	38	22
Sherry, port	7	3	4	9	14	11	5
	113	78	93	124	149	143	99
OTHER							
Liqueur	15	16	13	16	15	14	19
Bitter cordial	11	11	13	10	12	13	9
Half-bitter cordial	7	7	8	6	7	9	8
Ready mixed drinks with coffee and liquor	6	5	6	6	7	5	5
Apéritif	5	3	3	5	11	10	2
	44	42	43	43	52	51	43

THE MEDIA

Per week, spend time:	1967 hrs./min.	1973 hrs./min.	1977 hrs./min.	Index value (1967=100) 1973	Index value (1967=100) 1977	1977 Education Elementary hrs./min.	1977 Education Secondary hrs./min.
	Total population						
Watching television	9.40	12.22	11.31	128	119	12.23	9.32
Listening to the radio	5.17	7.38	7.26	144	141	7.35	7.07
Reading the newspaper	3.47	3.59	3.37	105	96	3.35	3.43
Reading magazines	2.19	2.23	2.22	103	102	2.25	2.17
Reading a book for enjoyment	2.08	1.56	2.05	91	98	1.44	2.55
Reading a book for further education	1.06	1.08	1.17	103	117	0.47	2.28
Listening to records	0.50	1.33	1.52	185	224	1.43	2.13
	25.07	30.59	30.10			30.12	30.15

TURNOVER BY MEDIA

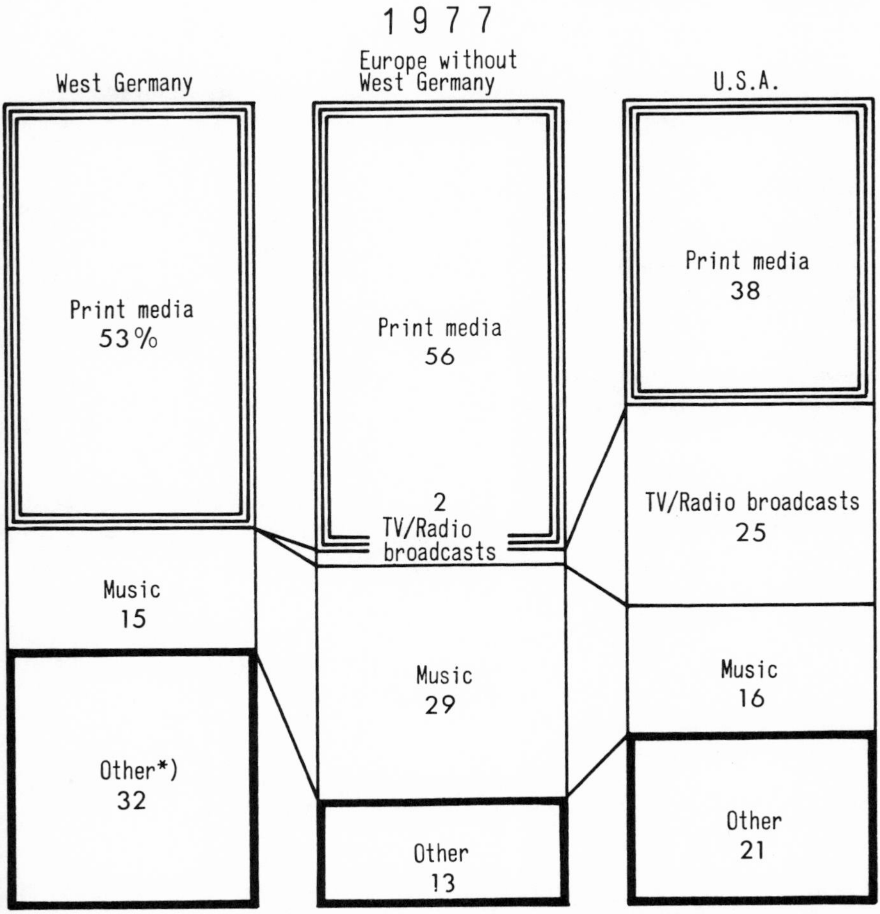

*Other business activities:	West Germany %	Europe without West Germany %	U.S.A. %
Commissioned distribution	17	5	x
Commissioned printing	13	4	5
TV program production	2	2	4
Films	x	2	12
	32	13	21

*In West Germany, commercial corporations are to date forbidden to broadcast TV or radio programs.

NEWS SOURCES

Question: *"How do you get the news and find out what's going on in the world?"* (L) (One response only)

	January 1980		
	Total	Education	
	pop.	Elementary	Secondary
	%	%	%
Although I find out a lot from television, I additionally get information from the paper	60	57	65
I get everything that's important from television; the newspaper isn't so important to me	23	27	13
I find out everything that's important from the paper; television isn't so important to me	11	9	16
Television and the newspaper aren't important to me; you get the news you need from the radio	5	5	6
I find out what I need to know from conversations. That way I don't need television, the newspapers, or the radio	1	2	x
	100	100	100

ANCHORMEN

Question: *"A question about the journalists and commentators who state their political opinions in the papers and weeklies and on radio and television. Whose statements and writings on political questions are you especially interested in?"* (O)

A

	1970	1971	1972	1974	1975	1976	1978	1979
	%	%	%	%	%	%	%	%
Friedrich Nowottny	1	2	4	12	13	22	10	14
Gerhard Loewenthal	12	22	16	17	17	13	9	12
Werner Hoefer	11	16	11	8	8	10	7	7
Peter Scholl-Latour	7	4	3	5	4	5	3	5
Ernst Dieter Lueg	x	1	1	3	4	9	5	5
Peter Merseburger	6	9	9	8	7	5	5	4
Claus-Hinrich Casdorff	3	3	3	4	4	3	3	4

Only those journalists who received at least 4 percent in 1979 are listed here.

TELEVISION SET DISTRIBUTION PER HOUSEHOLD

D

	Black and white %	Color %	None %		
1966	71	–	29	=	100
1968	78	1	21	=	100
1969	81	2	17	=	100
1970	82	5	13	=	100
1971	82	8	10	=	100
1972	79	11	10	=	100
1973	77	18	5	=	100
1974	71	25	4	=	100
1975	64	33	3	=	100
1976	57	40	3	=	100
1977	50	47	3	=	100
1978	40	57	3	=	100
1979	33	64	3	=	100
1980	23	75	2	=	100

	Summer 1980 Households with -			
	Several TV sets %	one TV set %		
Total population	28	73	=	100
OCCUPATION				
Unskilled workers	21	79	=	100
Skilled workers	27	73	=	100
Non-managerial employees and public servants	27	73	=	100
Managerial employees and public servants	35	65	=	100
Self-employeds, professionals	36	64	=	100
Farmers	20	80	=	100

PROGRAMMING

Question: *"There are various television programs listed on these cards. Which of these should television show more often than up to now, which should be shown less often and which do you think there is just the right amount of?"* (C, L)

	September 1979				
	Should be shown more often	Just right	Should be shown less often	No opinion	
	%	%	%	%	
Feature films	54	34	5	7	= 100
Comedies	44	37	10	9	= 100
Animal shows	43	43	6	8	= 100
Adventure movies	39	39	13	9	= 100
Family series	37	38	16	9	= 100
Folk drama in dialect	35	39	16	10	= 100
Movies with regional background	35	34	21	10	= 100
Folk music programs	34	34	21	11	= 100
Quiz shows	30	46	15	9	= 100
Detective stories	29	39	25	7	= 100
Television plays	29	48	11	12	= 100
Cabaret, satire	28	35	24	13	= 100
Circus	27	45	16	12	= 100
Musical hit shows, music shows	26	38	26	10	= 100
Operettas	25	38	24	13	= 100
Westerns	24	38	29	9	= 100
Slapstick	23	29	36	12	= 100
Talk shows	18	34	34	14	= 100
Musicals	18	41	26	15	= 100
Variety shows	16	42	26	16	= 100
Puppet and marionette shows	15	37	28	20	= 100
Jazz programs	12	26	46	16	= 100

RELAXING AND FUNNY

Question put to persons who watch entertainment programs (85 percent = 100): *"What do you expect an entertainment program to do for you if you're going to like it?"* (L)

It should	September 1979 %
- make me relax	79
- make me laugh	68
- distract me from my everyday preoccupations	68
- stimulate my imagination	27
- make me think	25
- make being alone easier	21
- help educate and inform me	20
- appeal to my feelings	18
- call my attention to social problems	12
- help me solve my problems	7
- provide me with models	5

PRIVATE STATIONS: BETTER OR WORSE?

Question: *"Imagine what it would be like if we had commercial television stations, in addition to the existing broadcasting corporations. What would this mean? What would be likely to change?"* (L)

A

	November 1979 %
If there's more competition, the individual station tries harder and the program improves	44
If there are more programs, you can more easily find something you like	39
There will be too many commercials	37
If there are more programs, there's going to be even more squabbling in the family over what to watch	30
More programs mean you won't know what to watch at all anymore	26
More programs mean that varying political opinions will have a greater voice	21
There will be too many entertainment programs and too few informative programs	12
None of the above	10
	219

GIVE THEM WHAT THEY WANT

Question: *"There are various arguments for or against privately run television stations. Two people are talking about this. Which of the two says what you think, too?"* (ill.)

A

	November 1979
	%
"Private television stations would mainly show light programs because that way they could expect to have the largest audience. Private stations would not take upon themselves television's role of informing the public."	28
"I think it's good for private television stations to adjust to what people really want to see, instead of forever trying to educate and to inform them."	46
Undecided	26
	100

TOO UPSETTING?

Question: *"When watching a movie or television, do you sometimes look away if there is something that upsets you too much?"*

	November 1978		
	Total pop.	Men	Women
	%	%	%
Look away	36	13	56
Don't look away	48	73	27
It depends	16	14	17
	100	100	100

HOLOCAUST

Question: *"The other day, a movie about the persecution of the Jews in the Third Reich was shown on the third channel over a period of four days. Did you see the programs in this Holocaust series?"*

Question put to persons who have seen programs in the series (63 percent = 100): *"If you think back on the effect Holocaust had on you, could you compare this with the impression other films or programs on television have made on you?"*

	March 1979			
In watching Holocaust, did you have the same kind of feelings you have when watching -	Completely different	Similar	Undecided	
	%	%	%	
exciting westerns?	90	4	6	= 100
reports about terrorist attacks?	69	21	10	= 100
reports about refugee boats from Vietnam?	57	33	10	= 100

The following are the results of a representative survey among television households with children between the ages of 3 and 9 in the Federal Republic of Germany and West Berlin. 414 interviews with children and a parent or guardian were conducted.

CHILDREN AND TELEVISION

Question: "*Would you please look through these cards and lay out the ones where you would say that you agree?*" (C)

	Winter 1974/75		
	Total parents or guardians	Education of head of household	
		Elementary	Secondary
	%	%	%
Children learn a lot of useful things for school from television	63	66	50
We often talk to our child about the things that he/she saw on television	67	64	73
As a parent, one often doesn't know which programs are appropriate for children. Television should give more information and advice	60	63	54
Our child often imitates what he/she sees on television	53	56	43
Children learn a lot for later life from television	50	54	40
We have the rule that when eating, we do not watch television	47	51	59
Our child is allowed to watch television so that when his/her friends talk about it, he/she isn't shut out of the conversation	45	49	34
We often watch certain programs only because our child wants to see them	45	47	40
You sometimes have to do without television for the child's sake	42	39	43
Children should be able to decide for themselves which programs they want to watch	40	44	21

continued

CHILDREAN AND TELEVISION

continued

	Winter 1974/75		
	Total parents or guardians	Education of head of household	
		Elementary	Secondary
	%	%	%
If our child is naughty, he/she is not allowed to watch television	36	34	37
As a reward we sometimes let our children watch programs that he/she otherwise is not allowed to see	34	34	34
Our child doesn't sleep well at night if he/she has seen something upsetting on television	34	36	31
Our child enjoys television so much - that's why I let him/her watch TV as often as possible	32	36	23
Children must first and foremost comply with the wishes of adults when watching television	29	34	21
If our child gets bad grades at school, we see to it that he/she watches less television	29	30	22
Through television children learn too early about the evil and cruelty in this world	24	29	13
For children too, television provides a means of relaxation from the strain of daily life	28	28	24
I approve of children watching television, because then they're not running around in the streets	22	28	10
If it weren't for television, one would have a lot more time for the children	21	21	18
Television doesn't leave enough time for children to play	12	14	7
Because of television children don't take enough time for their schoolwork	11	11	11
I often let my child watch television so that I have some time for myself	7	8	4
I don't like to let my child watch television because he/she learns so many bad things from it	5	6	3
Television is the reason why children and young people don't listen when called; ignore their parents	5	7	x

FAVORITE PROGRAMS

Question put to parents/guardians: *"There are various kinds of television programs listed here. Which of them does your child especially like to watch?"* (L)

Question put to children: *"What do you like to watch on TV? You can name more than one program."* (O)

	Winter 1974/75	
	According to	
	the parent/ guardian	the child
Especially likes to watch:	%	%
Animal programs (Lassie, Flipper, Daktari, Animals of this World)	81	30
Cartoons (The Pink Panther, The Flintstones)	76	43
Preschool educational programs (Sesame Street, The Red Playmobile, the Program with the Mouse, the Rattling Box)	66	59
Punch and Judy show, puppet shows	60	3
Childhood experiences (Pippi Longstocking, Huck Finn)	56	6
Westerns, Indian films, adventure films (Bonanza, Tarzan)	53	31
Music programs (The Hit Parade, Disco)	46	9
The Sandmen	45	15
Fairy tale films	42	2
Advertising	40	6
Police/Detective programs	16	3
Family programs	13	6
Movies, television plays	12	7
Sports programs	7	2
Educational programs about nature and technology, adventures of our times, experiments	5	3
Comedy (Laurel and Hardy, Fathers of Slapstick)	x	22
	618	247

PERMISSION NEEDED?

Question: *"Does your child have to ask first to watch television?"*

	Winter 1974/75					
					Education of head of household	
	Total parents or guardians	Child's age 3-4 yrs.	5-7 yrs.	8-9 yrs.	Elementary	Secondary
	%	%	%	%	%	%
Always has to ask	50	64	50	39	43	68
Sometimes, it depends	18	14	18	23	22	14
Doesn't have to ask	32	22	32	38	35	18
	100	100	100	100	100	100

VIEWING TIME

	Spring 1976					
	Monday - Friday			Monday - Sunday		
	Broadcast begin to sign-off	Broadcast begin to 8:00 p.m.	6:00 p.m. to 8:00 p.m.	Broadcast begin to sign-off	Broadcast begin to 8:00 p.m.	6:00 p.m. to 8:00 p.m.
Percent viewing by time slot	%	%	%	%	%	%
Total children*	13	15	21	13	15	20
AGE GROUPS						
3- 7	9	14	20	9	13	17
8-13	14	15	22	15	16	22
For comparison:						
Total adults**	22	14	21	22	15	22
Length of time	Min.	Min.	Min.	Min.	Min.	Min.
Total children	62	40	25	74	48	24
AGE GROUPS						
3- 7	46	38	24	50	41	21
alone	10	9	5	9	8	4
with other children	9	8	5	9	8	4
with adults	27	21	14	32	25	13
8-13	69	41	26	85	51	26
alone	13	11	6	15	13	6
with other children	10	8	5	12	9	4
with adults	46	22	15	58	29	16
For comparison:						
Total adults	107	36	25	121	47	26

* = 560 children aged 3-13
** = 2640 adults aged 14 and over

BACKGROUND TV

Question: *"Does your child sometimes play while watching television—or do something else like reading, doing schoolwork or eating dinner?"*

	Winter 1974/75				
	Plays	Does nothing	Eats dinner	Does schoolwork	
	%	%	%	%	
Parents or guardians	48	37	10	5	= 100

ACTIVE GAMES

Question: *"Games which involve a lot of running around, like hide and seek, tag, ball games, etc.—does your child play such games frequently, occasionally, seldom or never?"*

	Winter 1974/75						
	Total parents/ guardians	Children aged:			Amount of television watched by child		
		3-4	5-7	8-9	little	average	much
	%	%	%	%	%	%	%
Frequently	66	61	67	67	67	65	69
Occasionally	23	29	22	21	25	24	17
Seldom, never	11	10	11	12	8	11	14
	100	100	100	100	100	100	100

CHILDREN VIEWING POLICE AND DETECTIVE SERIES

	Spring 1976				
	Total house-holds with children	Households with children who view police and detective series			
		often	occasionally	seldom	never
	%	%	%	%	%
SIZE OF HOUSEHOLD					
2 -3 persons	31	17	11	22	47
4 or more persons	69	83	89	78	53
	100	100	100	100	100
AGE OF HEAD OF HOUSEHOLD					
Under 30	8	0	2	4	15
30 -49	82	74	82	88	80
50 and over	10	26	16	8	5
	100	100	100	100	100
EDUCATION OF HEAD OF HOUSEHOLD					
Elementary	70	80	69	74	68
Secondary	30	20	41	26	32
	100	100	100	100	100

TWO-THIRDS OF POPULATION EXPOSED TO TV ADVERTISING

Coverage of television advertising in four weeks -	1977 %	1978 %	1979 %	1980 %
First channel	68.0	62.6	64.3	64.6
Second channel	69.1	65.1	65.6	65.7

TYPE OF EXPOSURE

Question: "*Do you usually watch the whole sequence of television advertising or only in part, or do you not at all and only listen to what is being said, or do you not really pay attention to all this?*"

	1980				
	Watch whole sequence %	Only in part %	Listen, do not watch %	Don't pay attention %	
Total viewers per average advertising sequence	17	59	7	17	= 100
Men	14	58	8	20	= 100
Women	18	60	7	15	= 100
AGE					
14-29	11	58	6	25	= 100
30-44	11	59	8	22	= 100
45-59	14	62	10	14	= 100
60 and over	24	57	7	12	= 100
OCCUPATION					
Self-employeds, professionals	11	59	3	27	= 100
Managerial employees and public servants	11	57	10	22	= 100
Non-managerial employees and public servants	13	61	10	16	= 100
Skilled workers	20	57	5	18	= 100
Unskilled workers	23	60	5	12	= 100
Farmers	12	56	16	16	= 100

LISTENING TO THE RADIO

Question: "*Do you listen to the radio?*" (Yes: 1953=84 percent, 1979=91 percent) "*Could you estimate the average number of hours you listen to the radio on weekdays?*"

C

	Average time on weekdays					
	Less than 1 hour %	1-2 hours %	Up to 4 hours %	More than 4 hours %	It varies %	
Total radio listeners - 1953	23	37	19	9	12	= 100
- 1979	27	38	17	13	5	= 100

EASY LISTENING

Question: *"Do you like to listen to music?"* (Yes = 97 percent) *"What kind of music do you especially like to listen to?"*

	Hits	German folk music	Operettas	Beat, pop, rock	Classical music	Foreign folk music	Jazz, soul
	%	%	%	%	%	%	%
1978 - May	56	52	39	33	31	22	18

DON'T DISTURB

Question put to radio listeners: *"Here is a list of various programs. Could you take a look at it and tell me which of these programs would interest you to the extent that you don't want to be disturbed while listening to them?"* (L)

"For which of these programs would you turn off the radio or change stations, if you were the only one listening to the radio?" (L)

C

	Don't want to be disturbed				Turn off radio			
	Men		Women		Men		Women	
	1953	1979	1953	1979	1953	1979	1953	1979
	%	%	%	%	%	%	%	%
News	58	64	35	51	2	2	4	2
Sports	42	54	10	13	15	10	35	29
Local news	32	42	22	38	7	8	10	4
Political commentaries	27	42	7	23	22	11	46	22
Economic programs	14	21	6	7	22	15	31	22
Programs by political parties	11	19	3	10	34	18	49	26
Radio plays	45	18	57	25	9	13	8	10
Programs by the unions	9	7	2	3	33	23	45	48
Church service broadcasts	17	6	29	15	19	40	9	21
Agricultural programs	18	6	15	8	24	32	23	23
Church news	10	4	14	11	22	38	14	20
Programs for housewives	3	2	42	30	33	41	6	7
None of these	9	10	17	19	22	18	18	22
	295	295	259	253	264	269	298	256

THE LEADING PUBLISHING COMPANIES

Represented by summed monthly circulation figures per magazine category

1978/79

	Publisher									
	Bauer	Springer	Burda	Gruner + Jahr	Jahres-zeiten	Aug-stein	Motor-verlag	Das Beste	Other	
Magazine category:	%	%	%	%	%	%	%	%	%	
TV magazines	38	47	8	–	–	–	–	–	7	= 100
Yellow press	43	–	2	–	–	–	–	–	55	= 100
Current illustrated magazines	41	–	25	30	–	–	–	–	4	= 100
Teenage magazines	62	2	19	–	–	–	–	–	17	= 100
Women's magazines ...	–	–	22	41	31	–	–	–	6	= 100
Home construction	–	–	39	–	–	–	–	–	61	= 100
Fashion magazines	16	–	44	–	14	–	–	–	26	= 100
Newsmagazines	–	–	–	–	–	100	–	–	–	= 100
Car, motorcycle	11	–	–	–	–	–	52	–	37	= 100
Cultural entertainment ..	–	–	–	20	–	–	–	56	24	= 100
Sports	–	–	–	–	–	–	–	–	100	= 100
Parents' magazines	–	–	–	47	–	–	–	–	53	= 100
Health, nutrition	–	–	–	–	40	–	–	–	60	= 100
Cuisine	–	–	75	25	–	–	–	–	–	= 100
The home	–	–	27	37	36	–	–	–	–	= 100
Hobbies and photography	14	–	–	–	23	–	–	–	63	= 100
Business	–	–	–	25	–	–	–	–	75	= 100
Men's magazines	40	–	–	–	–	–	–	–	60	= 100
Consumer magazines ...	–	–	–	–	–	–	–	–	100	= 100
Total magazines with a circulation of 100,000 and over	37	15	12	9	2	2	1	1	21	= 100

SIGNIFICANT PUBLISHING CENTERS

in percent of summed monthly circulation figures

1978/79

Magazine category:	Hamburg %	Offenburg %	Munich %	Location Cologne/ Duesseldorf %	Stuttgart %	Frank-furt %	Other %		
TV magazines	85	8	–	–	–	–	7	=	100
Yellow press	56	2	–	13	–	–	29	=	100
Current illustrated magazines	71	25	–	–	–	–	4	=	100
Teenage magazines	8	19	70	1	–	–	2	=	100
Women's magazines	78	–	22	–	–	–	–	=	100
Home construction	–	39	–	–	–	–	61	=	100
Fashion magazines	31	46	2	2	–	–	19	=	100
Newsmagazines	100	–	–	–	–	–	–	=	100
Car, motorcycle	–	–	4	10	68	–	18	=	100
Cultural entertainment	28	–	–	56	8	–	8	=	100
Sports	5	–	–	24	–	–	71	=	100
Parents' magazines	47	–	–	–	–	–	53	=	100
Health, nutrition	23	–	–	15	–	–	62	=	100
Cuisine	25	–	75	–	–	–	–	=	100
The home	73	27	–	–	–	–	–	=	100
Hobbies and photography	27	–	37	–	18	–	18	=	100
Business	–	–	–	60	–	20	20	=	100
Men's magazines	–	–	60	10	–	–	30	=	100
Consumer magazines	–	–	–	11	–	–	89	=	100
Total magazines with a circulation of 100,000 and over	60	10	6	6	1	x	17	=	100

THE MAGAZINE WITH LARGEST CIRCULATION BY CATEGORY

D

	Location of publisher	1978/79 Circulation in thousands	Readers per issue	Readers in publication interval millions
TV and Radio Magazines				
Hör Zu	Hamburg	4,064	3.4	13.64
Yellow Press				
Neue Post	Hamburg	1,683	2.2	3.84
Current Illustrated Magazines				
STERN	Hamburg	1,745	7.4	12.99
Teenage Magazines				
BRAVO	Munich	1,234	2.8	3.41
Women's Magazines				
Brigitte	Hamburg	1,413	5.0	7.06
Home Construction				
Das Haus	Offenburg	2,738	2.1	5.72
Fashion Magazines				
Burda Moden	Offenburg	1,524	3.5	5.40
Newsmagazines				
DER SPIEGEL	Hamburg	1,000	6.5	6.53
Car, Motorcycle				
Auto, Motor und Sport	Stuttgart	485	5.5	2.65
ADAC-Motorwelt (Membership magazine)	Munich	5,873	1.7	9.92
Cultural Entertainment				
Das Beste	Duesseldorf	1,439	3.7	5.29
GEO	Hamburg	415	–	–

continued

continued

	Location of publisher	1978/79 Circulation in thousands	Readers per issue	Readers in publication interval millions
Sports Magazines				
Kicker Sportmagazin (Monday issue)	Nuremburg	247	11.2	2.76
Parents' Magazines				
Eltern	Hamburg	663	5.5	3.65
Leben und Erziehen	Aachen	659	2.6	1.70
Health, Nutrition				
VITAL	Hamburg	320	5.4	1.72
Cuisine				
Meine Familie & ich	Munich	864	2.4	2.09
Essen & Trinken	Hamburg	243	6.6	1.61
Housekeeping				
Schoener Wohnen	Hamburg	423	9.3	3.93
Hobbies and Photography				
Selbst ist der Mann	Cologne	148	13.5	2.00
Photo	Munich	123	8.1	1.00
Business				
Capital	Hamburg/ Cologne	212	7.7	1.64
Men's Magazines				
Playboy - Germany	Munich	437	6.3	2.77
Lui - Germany	Munich	241	3.8	0.92
Consumer Magazines				
Test	Berlin	780	6.4	5.02
Satire				
Pardon	Frankfurt	133	13.8	1.84

*estimated

NUMBER OF MAGAZINES WITH CIRCULATION FIGURES OF 100,000 OR MORE BY CATEGORY

D

	1978/79				
	Number of magazines according to frequency of publication			Summed monthly circulation figures	
	Weekly	Bi-Weekly	Monthly	Sale in millions	Percent of all magazines
Magazine category:	No.	No.	No.	Mil.	%
TV magazines	6	–	–	54.5	31.9
Yellow press	14	–	–	45.5	26.6
Current illustrated magazines	4	1	–	23.0	13.5
Teenage magazines	3	3	3	9.3	5.4
Women's magazines	–	4	–	7.0	4.1
Home construction	1	1	–	6.9	4.0
Fashion magazines	–	–	8	4.3	2.5
Newsmagazines	1	–	–	4.0	2.3
Cars, motorcycles*	–	4	4	2.7	1.6
Cultural entertainment	–	–	8	2.5	1.5
Sports	2	1	3	2.2	1.3
Parents' magazines	–	–	3	1.5	0.9
Health, nutrition	–	–	6	1.4	0.8
Cuisine	–	–	2	1.2	0.7
The home	–	–	3	1.1	0.6
Hobbies and photography	–	1	5	1.1	0.6
Business	1	–	3	1.0	0.6
Men's magazines	–	–	5	1.0	0.6
Consumer magazines	–	–	2	0.9	0.5
	32	15	55	171.1	100

Example: The 6 weekly television magazines have a circulation of 54.5. mil. figured on a monthly basis; this represents 31.9 percent of all the magazine issues published in the course of a month (of the big magazines with a circulation over 100,000).

*Not including the membership magazine of the automobile club ADAC, with a monthly circulation of 5.9 mil.

MAGAZINE CATEGORIES AND DEMOGRAPHIC CHARACTERISTICS OF READERS

D

	1978/79		
	Selected groups of readers		
	Women	Age group 14-29	Gymnasium graduates* with Abitur degree
Magazine category:	%	%	%
TV magazines	54	31	8
Yellow press	73	26	3
Current illustrated magazines	52	29	9
Teenage magazines	57	62	x
Women's magazines	89	37	7
Home construction	53	28	11
Fashion magazines	87	36	7
Newsmagazines	38	31	25
Car, motorcycle**	19	48	7
Cultural entertainment	48	30	23
Sports	22	39	9
Parents' magazines	69	34	13
Health, nutrition	67	24	7
Cuisine	69	32	14
The home	58	29	11
Hobbies and photography	24	41	13
Business	28	27	36
Men's magazines	30	50	12
Consumer magazines	36	29	16
Satire	37	54	27
For comparison:			
Population 14 years and over	54	29	9

Example: Among 100 readers of current illustrated magazines, 52 are women, 29 are between 14 and 29 years of age and 9 have completed the Abitur degree.

*) 38% are in schools beyond the nine-year grade school

**) Excluding the automobile club membership magazine "ADAC-Motorwelt"

NEWSPAPER CATEGORIES

D

	1978/79 Scheduled appearance	Purchase mainly by/at	Number of titles
Daily regional newspapers	daily ex. Sun.	subscription	420
Daily national newspapers	daily ex. Sun.	subscription	3
Weekly newspapers	weekly	subscription	5
Business newspapers	daily ex. Sat. Sun.	subscription	1
Business newspapers	weekly	subscription	4
Sunday newspapers	Sundays	newsstand	2
Regional yellow press	daily	newsstand	7
National yellow press	daily ex. Sun.	newsstand	1

	Circulation per edition	summed weekly	percent of total weekly circulation	Coverage per issue
	Mil.	Mil.	%	%
Daily regional newspapers	23.3	139.8	74	70
Daily national newspapers	0.8	4.0	2	7
Weekly newspapers	0.9	0.9	x	–
Business newspapers, daily	0.08	0.4	x	–
Business newspapers, weekly	0.5	0.5	x	–
Sunday newspapers	3.1	3.1	2	30
Regional yellow press, daily	1.6	11.2	6	8
National yellow press, daily ex. Sun.	4.9	29.4	16	28

NEWSPAPERS

D

	First quarter of 1979		
	Number of titles	Circulation sold per issue Mil.	Coverage per issue %
All daily newspapers	406	23.41	
Regional daily newspapers (subscriptions)		16.07	70.4
National daily newspapers	3	0.84	6.7
-Frankfurter Allgemeine Zeitung		0.30	
-Sueddeutsche Zeitung		0.32	
-Die Welt		0.22	
Weekly newspapers	5	1.83	2.6
-Deutsche Zeitung		0.13	0.8
-Sonntagsblatt		0.13	0.8
-Die Zeit		0.37	3.9
-Rheinischer Merkur		0.06	
-Bayern-Kurier		0.17	1.2
Business newspapers	5		
daily: Handelsblatt		0.08	
weekly:			
-Deutsche Handwerkszeitung		0.35	0.9
-Nordwestdeutsches Handwerk			
-Boersenzeitung			
-Deutsches Wirtschaftsblatt			
Sunday newspapers	2	2.78	
-Bild am Sonntag		2.45	27.4
- Welt am Sonntag		0.33	3.6
Regional yellow press	7	1.63	7.8
- Der Abend		0.05	
- Abendpost/Nachtausgabe		0.13	
- Abendzeitung/8 Uhr Blatt		0.28	
- B.Z. (Berlin)		0.33	
- Express		0.45	
- Hamburger Morgenpost		0.23	
- tz - Muenchen		0.16	
National yellow press (Bild)	1	4.87	27.5

TOPICS OF INTEREST

Question: *''Everyone has certain interests, i.e. things we would like to find out more about, just as there are other things we are less interested in. Could you please take a look at these cards and then distribute them on this sheet according to whether you would be interested in finding out more on the subject, or if it wouldn't interest you so much or wouldn't interest you at all.''* (C, ill.)

D

	Spring 1976						
	Total	Age groups					
	pop.	14-19	20-29	30-39	40-49	50-59	60 and over
Excerpt from reply ''very interested'':	%	%	%	%	%	%	%
Vacation and travel	44	47	51	50	46	42	31
Good nutrition	44	24	36	44	47	49	54
Good food and drink	40	31	48	45	44	40	32
Home decorating	39	24	47	50	46	39	25
Social security, provisions for old age	37	12	27	38	47	50	38
Plants, flowers, gardening	35	9	17	34	43	46	49
Cooking, recipes	35	20	33	37	38	40	34
Skin care, body care	35	40	38	38	35	34	28
Leisure time activities	35	52	45	40	34	27	19
Sports, sports events	34	47	39	40	33	30	25
Music (popular)	33	62	42	33	29	26	20
Money, investments	30	20	34	37	36	31	20
Housekeeping	30	10	26	34	37	38	30
Medical questions	30	13	23	28	32	36	41
Fashion	29	37	36	32	28	29	20
Continuing education, professional advancement	28	52	42	36	27	16	7
Hair care, hair styles	27	35	32	29	26	25	18
Children, child raising	27	16	35	44	33	19	10
Cars	25	34	34	30	24	21	11
Sewing, tailoring, needlework	22	14	17	22	24	28	25
Handicrafts, do-it-yourself work	20	22	22	26	25	17	13
Classical music	17	15	13	18	17	21	18
Photography, filming	16	20	23	20	16	12	8
Beauty care and make-up	14	23	21	17	13	12	5
Dieting	14	7	10	11	15	19	20
Antiques	11	7	10	13	12	13	10
Alcoholic beverages	9	9	13	10	8	6	6
	760	702	814	856	815	766	617

THE DAILY PAPER

Question: *"There's so much in the daily newspapers these days that you simply can't read everything. Could you tell me, with the aid of this list, what it is you generally always read?"* (L)

	1977 Dec. Total population	1976 Aug.	Men	Women	Age groups 16-29	30-44	45-59	60 and over
	%	%	%	%	%	%	%	%
Local reports from this area	76	80	79	81	77	80	83	81
Political news and reports on Germany, domestic policy	59	61	76	47	51	69	58	65
Advertising/personals	48	54	46	61	51	53	55	58
Political news and reports from abroad	45	46	61	32	40	49	45	48
The sports section	40	41	66	18	52	45	35	30
News reports on daily life	38	40	34	46	37	37	40	47
Letters to the editor	36	37	32	42	25	41	40	44
Editorials	35	34	41	27	31	37	35	33
The women's section	30	33	5	58	32	32	32	35
Reports on court cases and current trial proceedings	29	30	32	29	27	28	35	33
The arts section	25	27	20	34	29	28	23	27
The business section, business news	24	26	39	15	13	31	34	27
The section on science and technology	20	25	41	11	24	30	26	20
Serialized novels	14	13	4	21	8	11	15	21
	519	547	576	522	497	571	556	569

JOURNALISM AS A CAREER

Question: *"If you had a son - would you like it or not if he became a journalist?"*

	November 1972			
	Like it	Dislike it	Undecided	
	%	%	%	
Total population	42	18	40	= 100

JOURNALISM AND DEMOCRACY

Question put to journalists*: *"It is often said that if we didn't have any journalists, our democracy would be in bad shape—because the journalists are the people who, through their criticism, see to it that democracy functions. Would you agree with this view, or do you find it to be exaggerated?"*

	Subeditors		Editors		Editors-in-chief	
	1969	1973	1969	1973	1969	1973
	%	%	%	%	%	%
Completely agree	39	47	49	62	45	73
Only partly agree	30	34	29	27	25	20
Find it exaggerated	31	19	22	11	30	7
	100	100	100	100	100	100

SATISFACTION WITH JOB

Question put to journalists*: *"Are you for the most part satisfied working here for this newspaper or not?"*

	Subeditors		Editors		Editors-in-chief	
	1969	1973	1969	1973	1969	1973
	%	%	%	%	%	%
Satisfied	70	69	87	82	94	91
Not so satisfied	27	26	10	16	6	9
Undecided	3	5	3	2	x	x
	100	100	100	100	100	100

*see explanation p. 397.

WHO DETERMINES CHARACTER OF PAPER?

Question put to journalists*: *''Who mainly determines the character of your paper, that is, the style, line, tone, the whole image—is it mainly the publisher, or more the editor-in-chief, or the editorial staff as a whole, or is it someone else?''*

	December 1969		
	Sub-editors	Editors	Editors in-chief
The character of the newspaper is determined by:	%	%	%
The editorial staff as a whole	71	53	64
The editor-in-chief	16	17	24
Mainly the publisher	9	5	x
The senior editor of the department	x	31	16
Other responses	7	10	4
	103	116	108

FREEDOM OF EDITING PROTECTED

Question put to journalists*: *''If you hear it said that the publisher doesn't threaten the freedom of editing, he protects it—would you agree with this or would you not agree?''*

	Editors		Editors		Editors-in-chief	
	1969	1973	1969	1973	1969	1973
	%	%	%	%	%	%
Agree	29	51	61	56	68	76
Don't agree	48	29	15	25	17	7
Yes and no, that depends	12	11	8	9	8	15
Undecided, no response	11	9	16	10	7	2
	100	100	100	100	100	100

*210 journalists from 75 newspaper offices in the Federal Republic and West Berlin

PUBLISHER'S INFLUENCE

Question: *"Can you tell me with the aid of this list how the publisher influences editorial work?"* (L)

	December 1969		
	Sub-editors total	Editors	Editors-in-chief
	%	%	%
He has a considerable hand in shaping the newspaper's basic line *or* He alone determines the paper's editorial policy	51	49	51
Always reads the paper with attention and says what he didn't like, what should have been done differently	48	51	51
Suggests which topics should be treated for economic reasons or reasons of publishing policy	35	27	22
Influences editorial work through his voice in selecting new editors	35	17	29
Determines the paper's position on specific questions and for specific events	35	12	11
Gives exact instructions as to what is not to be treated in the paper	25	3	13
Says which topics should be treated in greater or in lesser detail	22	20	11
Has reserved the right to okay business trips	12	19	24
Distributes rules of writing which all editors must stick to	9	7	7
Largely determines how the editorial budget is used	8	3	9
Looks at the layout and then sometimes determines whether something should be deleted from the paper	8	2	2
Participates substantially in the editorial work by providing suggestions and ideas	6	12	11
None of the above	4	10	11
	298	232	252

ADVERTISING

Question: *"What is your opinion of the advertisements we see everywhere on posters, in newspapers, periodicals and on television? Do you think it is good to have advertising and in this way let people see all the various goods available, or do you find it annoying?"* (1960: television not mentioned)

A

	1960	1965	1975	Age groups			
	Total population			16-29	30-44	45-59	60 and over
	%	%	%	%	%	%	%
Good	52	45	48	53	42	51	44
Annoying	34	38	32	27	35	29	37
Don't know	14	17	20	20	23	20	19
	100	100	100	100	100	100	100

DIRECT-MAIL ADVERTISING

Question: *"Many firms send out advertising direct to the home by mail, by that I mean printed advertisements, such as form letters, pamphlets, brochures, catalogs, etc. How often are you sent such advertising?"*

	1970 Spring %	1976 Spring %
Daily, almost daily	12	15
Several times a week	30	30
Several times a month	36	34
Even less	16	15
Never	6	6
	100	100

Question: *"When you receive such advertising, what do you usually do with it?"* (L)

	1970 Spring %	1976 Spring %
I usually read it rather carefully	8	8
I read only those things that interest me	34	34
I usually just look it over very quickly	34	32
I usually don't read any of it	18	20
Never get such advertising	6	6
	100	100

PRIZE COMPETITIONS

Question: *"Have you taken part in any prize competition in the last three months? By that I mean solving a puzzle, guessing a word, etc. and then sending in the answer."*

"Do you remember where the competition you took part in appeared—in your daily paper, a magazine or elsewhere?"

	Total population %	Men %	Women %
Yes, took part in a prize competition - 1975	28	24	31
- 1980	31	27	35

	The prize competition appeared in a - daily paper		magazine		Elsewhere	
	1975 %	1980 %	1975 %	1980 %	1975 %	1980 %
Total persons who took part	5	5	19	22	8	9
Men	5	5	15	18	7	8
Women	4	4	21	26	8	9

BOOKS

Question: "*Approximately how many books would you say you read per year?*"

	November 1979				
	1 book	2 - 3 books	More than 3 books	Impossible to say	
	%	%	%	%	
Total population	7	27	61	5	= 100
Men	6	30	58	6	= 100
Women	8	24	63	5	= 100
AGE GROUPS					
16-29	6	23	67	4	= 100
30-44	6	24	63	7	= 100
45-59	7	30	57	6	= 100
60 and over	10	32	53	5	= 100
EDUCATION					
Elementary	9	34	51	6	= 100
Secondary	4	16	75	5	= 100

TOTAL NUMBER OF BOOKS PUBLISHED INCLUDING PAPERBACKS

	1961	1965	1970	1975	1979
			in thousands		
Total number of books	23.1	27.2	47.1	43.6	62.0
of these: paperbacks	1.0	1.3	3.9	4.9	7.4

(By kind permission of the Boersenverein für den deutsche Buchhandel e.V., Frankfurt/Main)

BOOK CLUBS

Question: "*Have you ordered a book from a book club or a book society in the last twelve months, or have you bought one from a book club store?*" (Yes = 26 percent)

Question put to buyers (26 = 100 percent): "*There are various things on these cards that are said about buying from book clubs or book societies. Where would you agree—could you please take out those cards?*" (C)

A

Positive arguments	Feb. 1978 %
There is something for everyone in a book club catalog	61
You get books considerably more cheaply through the book club	54
It's fun to sit down and pick out a book from the book club magazine after work	52
Even if I don't want to buy anything, I think it's interesting to leaf through the book club magazine	51
My whole family can help pick out the books	48
I can order everything I'd like to read from a book club, without any inhibitions	44
There's no salesperson to pressure you when you pick something from the book club magazine	43
The book club magazines give me lots of ideas for how to put together my library	24
What I like about the book club is that you're really always forced to buy a new book	23
	400

Negative arguments	
The thing that's a bother about the book club is that you have to accept books regularly	41
There are inexpensive books in the bookstore too; you don't have to be a member of a book club	20
The way the book club treats you is so impersonal; I miss being advised on an individual basis	11
The book club doesn't offer me enough books	11
What bothers me about the book club editions is that they all look so much alike	7
	90

HOME LIBRARY

Question: "*Could you tell me about how many bound books and paperbacks you have in your household?*"

	1967 %	1973 %	1978 %
400 books and over	3	5	4
200 to 400 books	8	10	12
100 to 200 book	15	16	18
50 to 100 books	19	19	21
30 to 50 books	14	16	16
20 to 30 books	14	12	12
10 to 20 books	12	11	10
Less than 10 books	6	5	2
No books in household	9	6	5
	100	100	100
Average number of books per household	82	91	78

BUYING BOOKS

Question: "*Have you personally bought a book, received one from a book club, or ordered one from somewhere else within the past 12 months?*"

	Total population		Persons who read a book during their leisure time at least once a week - for entertainment		for further education	
	1967 Oct. %	1978 Jan. %	1967 Oct. %	1978 Jan. %	1967 Oct. %	1978 Jan. %
Yes,	47	50	73	72	80	76
No	53	50	27	28	20	24
	100	100	100	100	100	100

	October 1977		
	Total	Education	
Number of books purchased during last 12 months—	pop. %	Elementary %	Secondary %
10 books and more	16	9	29
5 - 9 books	13	10	22
3 - 4 books	14	13	16
1 - 2 books	11	11	11
Have bought no books	46	57	22
	100	100	100

DEMOGRAPHIC DATA OF BOOK BUYERS

I

	January 1978 Books %		January 1976 Paperbacks %
Total buyers in the past year	50	Total buyers	60
Men	23	Men	60
Women	27	Women	60
AGE GROUPS		AGE GROUPS	
16-29	15	16-29	71
30-44	17	30-44	66
45-59	11	45-59	54
60 and over	8	60 and over	45
EDUCATION		EDUCATION	
Elementary	28	Elementary	48
Secondary	23	Secondary	88

PAPERBACKS

Question: *"Have you ever bought a paperback - either for yourself or as a present for someone else?"*

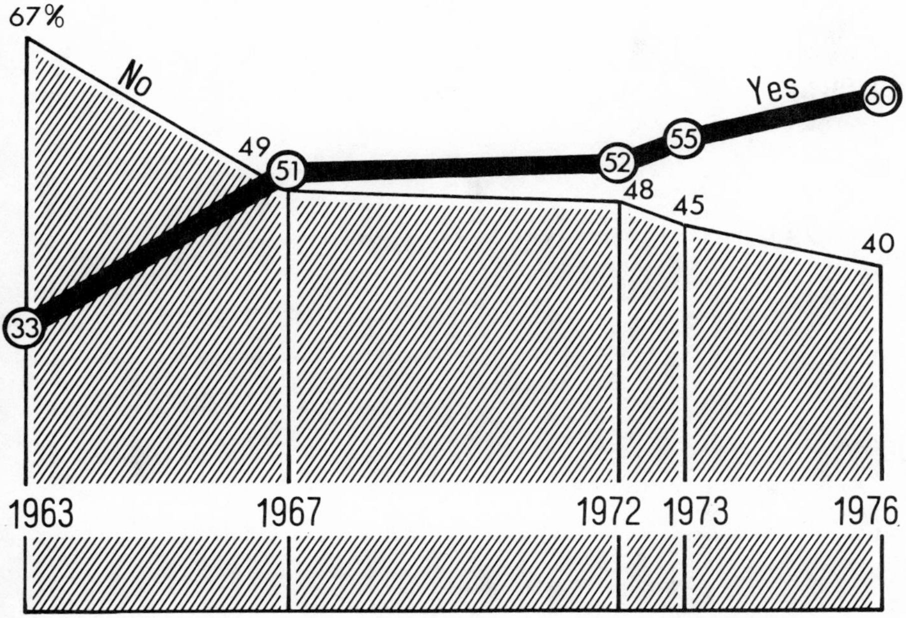

MOVIE ATTENDANCE DECLINING

Question: *"How often do you go to the movies?"*

	1965 %	1970 %	1975 %	1980 %
One or more times a week	5	3	1	1
One to three times a month	21	18	15	15
Less than once a month	28	28	28	26
Haven't been in years	46	51	56	58
	100	100	100	100

MOVIE-GOERS PER WEEK

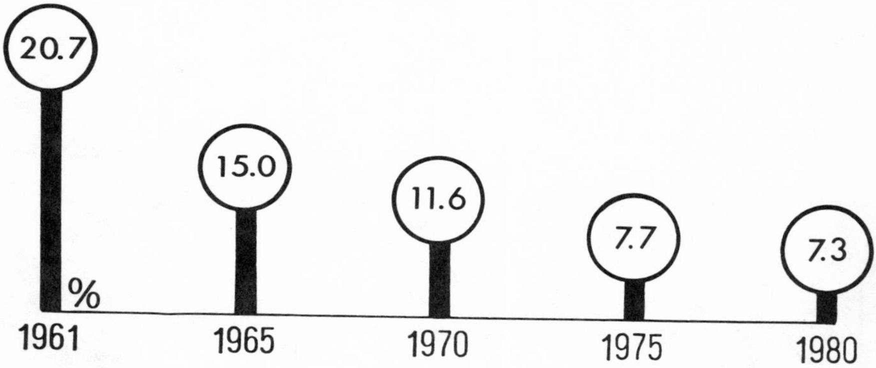

COVERAGE OF MOVIE THEATER ADVERTISING

D

	Movie attendance—					
		Weekly			Monthly	
	Total %	Men %	Women %	Total %	Men %	Women %
1974	6	8	4	18	22	15
1975	8	9	7	21	23	18
1976	6	8	5	17	21	15
1977	6	7	4	16	20	13
1978	6	7	5	18	21	15
1979	6	7	5	18	21	15
1980	7	9	6	18	22	16

THEATER AND OPERA ATTENDANCE

Question: *"Have you been to the theater or to the opera within the past one or two years, or did you not get around to going?"*

E

	April 1975				
	Several times %	Once %	Not in the past two years %	Never %	
Total population	25	11	48	16	= 100
AGE GROUPS					
16-29	30	14	34	22	= 100
30-44	26	11	49	14	= 100
45-59	26	10	48	16	= 100
60 and over	17	7	61	15	= 100
EDUCATION					
Elementary	16	11	52	21	= 100
Secondary	51	10	36	3	= 100
TOWN AND COUNTRY					
Villages	19	11	53	17	= 100
Small towns	22	10	49	19	= 100
Medium cities	24	11	46	19	= 100
Large cities	31	12	45	12	= 100

SUBSIDIES

Question: *"Many opera houses and theaters can no longer exist on their income alone. Therefore they are publicly subsidized. What is your view—are you for or against public subsidies for theaters?"*

E

	April 1975				
	Total pop. %	Elementary School %	Secondary School %	Have attended the theater/ opera in the last two years %	%
For	57	50	78	80	45
Against	17	20	8	8	22
Undecided	26	30	14	12	33
	100	100	100	100	100

V. GERMANY AND THE WORLD

FOREIGN POLICY

Question: *"Which country in the world do you consider to be Germany's best friend?"* (O)

	1965 May %	1977 Sept. %	1980 Jan. %	1980 Sept. %
USA	49	54	53	51
France	9	10	14	17
Austria	5	6	5	6
Switzerland	3	3	2	2
Great Britain	6	2	1	2
The Netherlands	2	2	1	2
Italy	1	1	1	x
Other country	7	5	5	5
Has no friend	x	9	9	4
Don't know	20	14	13	14
	102	106	104	103

	September 1980						
	Total	Age groups				Interested in politics -	
Excerpt from replies:	pop. %	16-29 %	30-44 %	45-59 %	60 and over %	yes %	no %
USA	51	48	53	52	52	52	51
France	17	18	16	19	15	19	14
Has no friend	4	5	4	4	5	5	4

Note: as of 1977, "Germany" replaced by "the Federal Republic" in the question.

NEXUS

Question: *"With which of these countries should we seek the closest possible cooperation?"* (L)

	1954 Aug. %	1959 Sept. %	1963 Aug. %	1968 Nov. %	1972 Aug. %	1975 Sept. %	1980 Aug. %
USA	78	81	90	81	76	79	80
France	46	48	70	68	63	63	69
Britain	58	49	65	59	55	47	46
Japan	35	32	31	35	44	35	40
China	–	–	–	–	–	–	39
Italy	34	31	30	32	33	24	26
Russia	22	31	27	35	49	38	20
Poland	11	25	27	25	32	21	20
Spain	42	27	20	21	21	16	19
Israel	13	19	17	24	25	19	18
Egypt	–	–	–	–	–	–	16
Portugal	–	–	–	–	–	12	13

– = not asked.

SUCCESSFUL?

Question: *"Do you consider that West German foreign policy of recent years has been successful, or would you say that, if anything, the German position has deteriorated?"*

	1961 Oct. %	1964 Dec. %	1970 Nov. %	1972 Dec. %	1974 Sept. %	1979 Nov. %
Successful	14	15	53	54	30	35
Deteriorated	36	31	13	15	35	12
Unchanged	24	29	20	15	29	33
No opinion	26	25	14	16	6	20
	100	100	100	100	100	100

OF NO ACCOUNT

Question: *"Please read the conversation between these two people here. Which of them would you tend to agree with?"* (ill.)

	March 1976 %
"I feel that West Germany has caught up a lot in foreign policy. We are respected abroad and have a say in all the important committees—in the EC, in the UN, etc."	25
"I am of a different opinion. Admittedly we are members of the EC and the UN and we pay out money all over the place. But West Germany doesn't have a say at all."	60
Undecided	15
	100

INTEREST IN FOREIGN POLICY

Question: *"Are you interested in foreign policy?"*

	Yes %	Not much %	Not at all %	
Total population - September 1979	40	41	19	= 100
- October 1980	47	37	16	= 100
AGE GROUPS				
16-29	46	39	15	= 100
30-44	50	38	12	= 100
45-59	51	34	15	= 100
60 and over	43	38	19	= 100
EDUCATION				
Elementary	38	43	19	= 100
Secondary	65	28	7	= 100
PARTY PREFERENCE				
SPD	47	36	17	= 100
CDU/CSU	50	38	12	= 100
FDP	56	34	10	= 100

OF VITAL IMPORTANCE

Question: *"A few statements about foreign affairs have been listed here. Which of them would you yourself make?"* (L)

	September 1979 %
Foreign policy is of vital importance for a country like West Germany	59
In foreign affairs one never really finds out what is actually happening, all the important things take place behind closed doors	34
It is impossible to be well informed about foreign policy because simply too much happens	31
Foreign policy is so complicated that one can hardly understand what is going on	31
The most able politicians are to be found in the field of foreign policy	17
Foreign affairs are exciting	16
Foreign policy is not so interesting for the individual citizen; it hardly affects him/her	15
In West Germany there are very few differences of opinion about foreign policy between the political parties	12
Foreign policy is repulsive, many of the governments with whom we negotiate are unjust and cruel	9
None of these	9
	233

AID TO DEVELOPING COUNTRIES

Question: *"Are you for or against our providing financial assistance to the developing countries in Asia and Africa?"*

	1959	1963	1968	1974	1980	Party preference		
	Oct.	Nov.	Nov.	Jan.	Febr.	SPD	CDU/CSU	FDP
	%	%	%	%	%	%	%	%
For	62	47	48	49	50	53	48	62
Against	17	27	26	24	23	23	24	19
Undecided	21	26	26	27	27	24	28	19
	100	100	100	100	100	100	100	100

PRIORITIES

Question: *"Political issues which people all over the world are concerned with have been included on these cards here. Could you please pick out the issues wich you personally consider to be the most important?"* (No more than 5) (C)

	September 1979 %
See to it that there is a secure energy supply	66
Environmental protection	57
See that people in all countries receive adequate nutrition	54
Détente, mutual understanding between East and West	54
Protect human rights in all countries	51
See to a stable world economy	43
See that peace is maintained through a military balance between East and West	38
Disarmament	35
Control of population growth in developing countries	38
See that the citizens in all countries have a sufficient say in political decision making	20
Support the independent development of an efficient economy in the developing countries	18
Give the UN more influence worldwide on the political affairs of individual nations	9

MORE AID OR LESS?

Question: *"If it were up to you, would you say we should support the developing nations more or less than we have in the past?"*

C

	Total pop.	Age groups 18-29	30-59	60 and over	Party preference SPD	CDU/CSU	FDP
	%	%	%	%	%	%	%
More aid	15	25	14	8	18	12	20
Less	38	34	38	41	36	40	36
As before	36	32	39	36	40	34	37
Undecided	11	9	9	15	6	14	7
	100	100	100	100	100	100	100

ARGUMENTS

Question: *"Could you explain your view of development aid in more detail? - This list contains several things we have already been told. With which of them would you agree?"* (L)

C

	Total pop.	July 1977 Party preference SPD	CDU/CSU	FDP
	%	%	%	%
Pros				
Our own industry will benefit if we support economic progress in these countries	48	55	44	49
We get our oil and other raw materials from the Third World countries and therefore we have to cooperate with them	48	51	47	51
Financial aid to Third World countries is obligatory for humanitarian reasons, we may not shirk giving it	44	51	39	51
Aid to Third World countries will help us win friends whom we can well use in the arena of international politics	35	37	33	39
We must help the countries of the Third World, as otherwise war between the poor and rich nations will one day break out	25	29	22	30
	200	223	185	220
Cons				
The countries of the Third World are a drain on our resources, the money often falls into the hands of the wrong people	48	47	49	44
We need the money for our own country, there is enough to to be done at home	41	40	43	36
Why are we always the ones who have to help, the oil-rich countries could also do a lot more	37	37	38	33
Self-help is the most important thing for Third World countries; continual foreign assistance prevents them from learning how to tackle their problems themselves	36	32	40	44
Most of the developing countries are communist. It we support them, then we are supporting world communism	21	16	28	14
	183	172	198	171

SELECTIVE AID

Question: *"The demand has been made that West Germany give development aid only to those countries where independent, democratic conditions prevail and which are friendly toward the West. What do you think—do you agree with this request or not?"*

A

	December 1977			
	Total pop.	Party preference SPD	CDU/CSU	FDP
	%	%	%	%
Agree	60	60	69	58
Don't agree	17	21	13	28
Undecided	16	15	13	8
Against development aid on principle	7	4	5	6
	100	100	100	100

POLITICAL MODELS

Question: *"Which type of political system do you think will eventually prevail in the developing countries, e.g. in Asia, Africa and Latin America—the Western democratic system or the communist system, or do you think they will work something out for themselves?"*

	December 1977							
	Total pop.	Age groups 16-29	30-44	45-59	60 and over	Party preference SPD	CDU/CSU	FDP
	%	%	%	%	%	%	%	%
Will differ from country to country	32	35	34	33	26	30	32	32
Work something out for themselves	22	22	24	23	21	26	20	25
Communist system	19	21	19	18	17	20	20	18
Western democratic system	8	6	9	8	8	8	10	9
Impossible to say	19	16	14	18	28	16	18	16
	100	100	100	100	100	100	100	100

POSSIBILITIES OF ALIGNMENT

Question: *"West Germany has several possibilities as to how to align its foreign policy. Various possibilities are described on this list. Which of them do you consider the best; which of these should West Germany especially emphasize?"* (L)

	September 1980							
	Total	Age groups						
	pop.	16-29	30-44	45-59	60 and over	CDU/CSU	SPD	FDP
	%	%	%	%	%	%	%	%
Continue to stand by the U.S.	57	49	60	60	58	71	49	58
Pursue an independent policy with the countries of the European Community	40	39	45	41	36	40	41	59
Pursue a policy of neutrality between the great powers in the East and in the West	31	36	32	29	26	22	28	36
Take a neutral position of friendly cooperation with the Soviet Union	15	19	16	15	11	11	21	10
Work closely together with the Soviet Union	4	4	4	5	2	2	5	4
Undecided	9	9	7	7	12	7	7	4

CLOSER COOPERATION WITH U.S.?

Question: *"In the future, should we cooperate equally with the U.S. and the Soviet Union, or more closely with the Soviet Union, or more closely with the U.S.? What is your opinion?"*

	1973	1977	1978	1980	1981
	May	Nov.	Oct.	Jan.	May
	%	%	%	%	%
Equal cooperation	54	38	36	41	32
More closely with the U.S.	36	49	51	49	56
More closely with Soviet Union	3	2	1	2	1
Undecided	7	11	12	8	11
	100	100	100	100	100

COEXISTENCE

Question: *"Do you believe that the West and the East can coexist peacefully, or don't you believe so?"*

	Can coexist peacefully %	Don't think so %	Undecided %	
Total population - December 1954	20	66	14	= 100
- July 1956	46	40	14	= 100
- April 1959	46	38	16	= 100
- June 1962	36	51	13	= 100
- June 1976	49	33	18	= 100
- September 1979	56	27	17	= 100
- February 1980	51	38	11	= 100
AGE GROUPS				
16-29	48	38	14	= 100
30-44	53	38	9	= 100
45-59	55	37	8	= 100
60 and over	48	41	11	= 100
PARTY PREFERENCE				
SPD	60	30	10	= 100
CDU/CSU	40	50	10	= 100
FDP	58	31	11	= 100

EUROPEAN SECURITY CONFERENCE

Question: *"Here is a question about the Conference for Security and Cooperation in Europe, CSCE, which has just been concluded in Helsinki. Two people are talking about this conference. Which of them says what you also tend to think?"* (ill., X)

A

	August 1975			
	Total pop. %	Party preference SPD %	CDU/CSU %	FDP %
"I don't think the declarations signed in Helsinki make Europe safer for peace; for, in the end, the East will interpret the decisive points differently from the West."	46	38	61	46
"In my view, East and West have taken a decisive step toward securing peace. Even if some points should later be interpreted differently, the whole thing is a great success for the peaceful coexistence of the peoples of Europe."	29	40	17	39
Undecided, no reply	25	22	22	15
	100	100	100	100

APPREHENSIONS

Question: *"Do you worry about our being threatened by the East, or not?"*

	Worry %	Don't worry %	Undecided %	
Total population - February 1976	51	37	12	= 100
- January 1978	44	43	13	= 100
- November 1979	41	41	18	= 100
- January 1980	64	26	10	= 100
- May 1981	50	35	15	= 100
AGE GROUPS				
16-29	40	45	15	= 100
30-44	49	34	17	= 100
45-59	58	31	11	= 100
60 and over	56	30	14	= 100
PARTY PREFERENCE				
SPD	57	32	11	= 100
CDU/CSU	75	17	8	= 100
FDP	68	24	8	= 100

AMERICA OR RUSSIA?

Question: *"If we had to decide between these two possibilities, which is more important for the future of the German people: a good relationship with America or a good relationship with Russia?"*

	America %	Russia %	Undecided %	
Total population - June 1954	62	10	28	= 100
- December 1957	61	6	33	= 100
- October 1975	52	12	36	= 100
- November 1979	63	12	25	= 100
AGE GROUPS				
16-29	52	19	29	= 100
30-44	64	10	26	= 100
45-59	66	8	26	= 100
60 and over	68	11	21	= 100
PARTY PREFERENCE				
SPD	57	15	28	= 100
CDU/CSU	75	6	19	= 100
FDP	47	16	37	= 100

A DIFFICULT CHOICE

Question: *"What, in your view, would be the best foreign policy - should we continue the military alliance with the Americans, or should we close ranks with the other European states to form a political bloc in Europe?"*

A

	May 1981 Total pop. %	March 1979 Total pop. %	Party Preference SPD %	CDU/CSU %	FDP %
Political bloc in Europe	32	38	44	32	36
Alliance with Americans	44	36	30	48	38
Undecided	24	26	26	20	26
	100	100	100	100	100

NEUTRAL

Question: *"Which do you think would be the better foreign policy—should we remain militarily allied with the U.S. or should we attempt to be neutral?"*

	Military alliance with the U.S. %	Neutral %	Undecided %	
Total population - September 1961	40	42	18	= 100
- September 1965	46	37	17	= 100
- May 1969	44	38	18	= 100
- June 1973	41	42	17	= 100
- February 1975	49	36	15	= 100
- October 1978	57	27	16	= 100
- July 1980	54	27	19	= 100
AGE GROUPS				
16-29	48	33	19	= 100
30-44	57	25	18	= 100
45-59	57	27	16	= 100
60 and over	53	23	24	= 100
PARTY PREFERENCE				
SPD	49	34	17	= 100
CDU/CSU	69	16	15	= 100
FDP	47	37	16	= 100

THE UNITED STATES

Question: *"How confident are you that the United States is capable of taking a wise leadership role today?"*

A

	Very confident %	Fairly confident %	Not so confident %	Not at all %	Undecided %	
Total population - August 1979	8	26	42	12	12	= 100
- May 1980	7	27	46	10	10	= 100
- September 1980	6	28	43	10	13	= 100
AGE GROUPS						
16-29	5	27	40	13	15	= 100
30-44	5	28	47	10	10	= 100
45-59	6	28	46	10	10	= 100
60 and over	7	28	38	6	21	= 100
EDUCATION						
Elementary	6	29	39	7	19	= 100
Secondary	4	26	51	14	5	= 100
PARTY PREFERENCE						
SPD	5	27	42	10	16	= 100
CDU/CSU	7	32	44	5	12	= 100
FDP	5	26	48	14	7	= 100
PERSONS WHO SAY -						
they like the Americans	9	39	38	3	11	= 100
they don't like the Americans	1	12	51	25	11	= 100

continued

continued

Question: *"How confident are you that the United States is capable of taking a wise leadership role today?"*

A

	May 1981					
	Very confident	Fairly confident	Not so confident	Not at all	Undecided	
	%	%	%	%	%	
Total population	8	34	39	8	11	= 100
AGE GROUPS						
16-29	5	30	41	10	14	= 100
30-44	9	33	46	7	5	= 100
45-59	11	35	43	6	5	= 100
60 and over	8	40	26	7	19	= 100

LIKEABLE

Question: *"Generally speaking, do you like the Americans, or don't you like them particularly?"*

	1957 Dec.	1961 April	1965 May	1967 Jan.	1973 May	1975 March	1979 Aug.	1980 Sept.
	%	%	%	%	%	%	%	%
Like them	39	51	58	47	48	42	50	51
Not particularly	24	16	19	24	24	21	23	22
Undecided	37	33	23	29	28	37	27	27
	100	100	100	100	100	100	100	100

	September 1980				
	Like them	Not particularly	Undecided	No opinion	
	%	%	%	%	
Total population	51	22	17	10	= 100
Men	52	25	15	8	= 100
Women	50	19	18	13	= 100
AGE GROUPS					
16-29	52	21	17	10	= 100
30-44	52	23	15	10	= 100
45-59	50	23	15	12	= 100
60 and over	48	22	19	11	= 100
EDUCATION					
Elementary	52	21	16	11	= 100
Secondary	49	25	17	9	= 100

continued

continued

REGIONAL DISTRIBUTION					
Northern Germany with West Berlin	53	20	15	12	= 100
North-Rhine Westphalia	52	21	16	11	= 100
Rhine-Main/Southwest	48	25	17	10	= 100
Bavaria	51	20	19	10	= 100
Former American occupation zone	50	24	17	9	= 100

OPINION UNCHANGED

Question: "*Would you say that your opinion of the Americans has gotten better of late—or has it tended to get worse?*"

	1968 Nov. %	1972 April %	1977 Feb. %	1980 Jan. %	1980 Sept. %
Got better	5	10	20	19	6
Got worse	36	34	18	26	18
Stayed the same	48	42	51	46	66
Undecided	11	14	11	9	10
	100	100	100	100	100

	September 1980				
	Got better %	Got worse %	Stayed the same %	Undecided %	
Total population	6	18	66	10	= 100
AGE GROUPS					
16-29	8	18	64	10	= 100
30-44	6	22	63	9	= 100
45-59	6	19	66	9	= 100
60 and over	5	14	70	11	= 100
EDUCATION					
Elementary	6	15	68	11	= 100
Secondary	7	24	62	7	= 100

Question: "*Here are two people tallking about the relationship between the U.S. and the Federal Republic. Which of the two comes closer to what you think - the one above or the one below?*"

"The Federal Republic needs the Americans for protection purposes today just as much as 30 yeas ago when the alliance was established. Nothing has changed in this regard. This is why we must stand by the U.S. and accept their leadership."	48
"A lot has changed in the last 30 years. The Federal Republic has gained importance among the great powers. With the Germans' new role in world politics, it is no longer tolerable for us to always subordinate ourselves to American leadership."	35
Undecided	17
	100

TYPICALLY AMERICAN

Question: *"There are various opinions about the Americans. A few of them are listed here. Which of these would you say are typical of the Americans, which of these really apply to them?"* (C)

	1958 %	1962 %	1980 %
Efficient, capable in business	67	56	62
Progressive, stay in step with the times	–	61	58
Mechanically-minded, inventive	44	46	55
Put personal freedom first	46	50	53
Very patriotic, proud of their country	–	39	53
Extravagant, place too much emphasis on luxury	47	36	49
Energetic, full of initiative	47	47	48
Enjoy life, they get something out of life	–	49	41
Comradely, eager to help	44	39	37
Natural, unaffected, sincere	26	35	35
Cheerful	–	31	33
Brag, boast too much	32	22	32
Honest, straightforward, open	22	30	29
Probably live more happily than we do	–	41	29
Religious, believing	16	22	28
Have a good sense of humor	–	21	27
Soft, spoiled	26	25	25
Hard-working, industrious	24	24	22
Everyone has to have what the others have, must keep up with their neighbors	–	15	22
Don't know how to behave, have bad manners	–	–	21
Reliable, dependable	–	–	19
Poor soldiers	19	16	18
Polite, obliging	–	23	18
Cultivated, well-educated	–	20	17
Inconsiderate toward others	–	13	16
Unpredictable	12	13	15
Arrogant, conceited	17	11	12
Raise their children well, know how to raise children	–	13	12
Are not superficial, take life seriously	–	10	11
False, deceitful, insincere	4	3	4
Don't know, no response	9	15	10
	502	826	911

– = not asked

NIXON

Question: *"How do you think our relationship with America will develop under Nixon—will it be better than under Johnson, or worse, or will nothing change?"*

"What is your opinion of President Nixon—do you have a good opinion or not such a good opinion of him?"

Relationship under Nixon -	1969 Jan. %
will be better	16
will be worse	8
nothing will change	53
Undecided	23
	100

Opinion of Nixon -	1969 Jan. %	1973 Nov. %
good	41	19
not so good	8	51
neither	42	30
Know nothing about Nixon	9	x
	100	100

Question: *"Are you pleased that Nixon has resigned or do you regret this?"*

	Pleased %	Regret it %	No opinion %	
Total population - August 1974	64	13	23	= 100

JIMMY CARTER

Question: *"In America, Jimmy Carter has been elected president. What do you personally think of Jimmy Carter? Is he a likeable person, or don't you like him very much?"*

"What do you think, is it a good thing for Germany that Jimmy Carter has been elected President, or not?"

A likeable person -	1976 %
Yes	40
No	22
Undecided	38
	100

Good for Germany -	1976 %
Yes	24
No	15
Undecided	61
	100

A BETTER CHANCE

Question: *"Do you believe that Carter will be able to assert himself better with the Russians than his predecessor, not as well, or the same?"*

	May 1977				
	Better	Not as well	The same	Don't know	
	%	%	%	%	
Total population	35	9	26	30	= 100
PARTY PREFERENCE					
SPD	33	11	29	27	= 100
CDU/CSU	38	9	24	29	= 100
FDP	38	12	31	19	= 100

SALT II

Question: *"The American President Carter and the Soviet party leader Brezhnev recently signed a treaty in Vienna limiting nuclear armament, the so-called SALT II Treaty. Did you know this or is this the first time you've heard about it?"* (Yes, knew = 77 percent) *"What is your impression of this treaty? Do you think that peace between the East and West is more certain now, or don't you think that this is necessarily the case?" "For whom does this treaty have more advantages—for the West or for the East?"*

	Sept. 1979
	%
Peace -	
More certain	20
Don't think so	40
Impossible to say	17
Know nothing about SALT II	23
	100

	Sept. 1979
	%
Advantage for the East	21
Advantage for the West	3
Equal for both	31
Impossible to say	22
Know nothing about SALT II	23
	100

Question: *"With which of these two opinions do you tend to agree."*

	September 1979
	%
"It's a considerable step forward if the superpowers sit down at one table and negotiate about the limitation of nuclear weapons. At least it's a first step toward disarmament."	46
"Negotitations like that don't realy mean a thing. The superpowers talk about disarmament but the arms race still goes on at the same time."	24
Impossible to say	7
Don't know anything about SALT II	23
	100

SECRETARIES OF STATE

Question: *"Do you happen to know the name of the American Secretary of State?"* (O)

"Have you ever heard of Henry Kissinger—do you know that name?" (Yes, know it = 92 percent) *"Could you tell me who Henry Kissinger is, what he does?"*

	February 1980			
	Correct answer	Incorrect answer	Don't know	
	%	%	%	
Cyrus Vance	58	3	39	= 100
Henry Kissinger	55	37	8	= 100

RELATIONSHIP THE SAME

Question: *"Has the relationship between West Germany and the United States improved of late, or worsened, or would you say it has remained the same?"*

	Remained the same	Worsened	Improved	Don't know	
	%	%	%	%	
Total population - August 1973	50	27	10	13	= 100
- August 1975	59	12	17	12	= 100
- September 1980	53	28	7	12	= 100
AGE GROUPS					
16-29	51	28	8	13	= 100
30-44	53	30	7	10	= 100
45-59	53	30	7	10	= 100
60 and over	53	24	7	10	= 100
PARTY PREFERENCE					
SPD	60	17	10	13	= 100
CDU/CSU	46	39	5	10	= 100
FDP	55	32	4	9	= 100
Persons who say -*					
they like the Americans	56	27	9	8	= 100
they don't like the Americans	48	38	4	10	= 100

*see page 13.

THE ELECTION CAMPAIGN

Question: *"Are you interested in the election campaign in the U.S. and in who the next president will be?"*

	September 1980			
	Yes	Not especially	Not at all	
	%	%	%	
Total population	40	42	18	= 100
POLITICAL INTEREST				
Interested in politics	60	32	8	= 100
Not interested in politics	17	54	29	= 100

PRESIDENTIAL CANDIDATES

Question: *"Here are the names of several American politicians. Would you please tell me which of them you have heard of?"* (L)

Follow-up question put to persons who named at least one politician: *"And do you consider this politician qualified for the U.S. presidency or not?"*

	September 1980							
	Jimmy Carter		Edward Kennedy		Ronald Reagan		John Anderson	
	Have heard of	Quali-fied	Have heard of	Quali-fied	Have heard of	Quali-fied	Have heard of	Quali-fied
	%	%	%	%	%	%	%	%
Total population	98	43	93	23	78	10	32	3
POLITICAL INTEREST								
Interested in politics	99	40	97	23	91	10	44	4
Not interested in politics	96	45	88	23	63	8	18	1

RONALD REAGAN

Question: *"In the U.S., Ronald Reagan has been elected President. What do you personally think of Ronald Reagan? Is he a likeable person, or don't you like him very much?"*

"What do you think, is it a good thing for Germany that Ronald Reagan has been elected President, or not?"

A

November 1980

A likeable person -	Total pop. %	SPD %	CDU/CSU %	FDP %
Yes	36	31	44	42
No	22	29	13	28
Undecided	42	40	43	30
	100	100	100	100

Good for Germany -	Total pop. %	SPD %	CDU/CSU %	FDP %
Yes	27	26	34	29
No	17	21	10	19
Undecided	56	53	56	52
	100	100	100	100

AMERICAN WITHDRAWAL

Question: *"If you read in tomorrow's paper that the Americans are to withdraw their troops from Europe, would you welcome or regret this step?"*

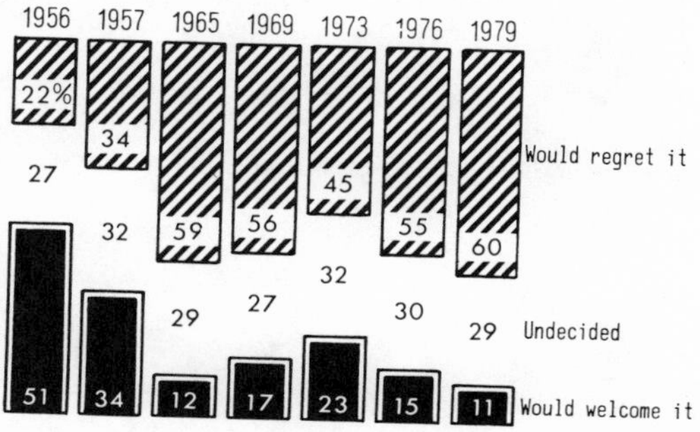

TROOP DEPLOYMENT

Question: *"Of course it's difficult to say, but under which conditions do you think the Americans would be prepared to deploy their troops? Here on these cards are a number of events. Please set aside those for which you feel the Americans would react with military measures and send out their troops."* (C)

	Spetember 1980		
	Total pop.	People who say they*- like the Americans	don't like the Americans
In case of -	%	%	%
West Germany being attacked	77	84	67
Canada being attacked	65	69	59
the Russians marching into West Berlin	63	69	53
the American hostages being killed in Iran	51	54	46
the Arabs stopping delivery of oil to the West	45	44	50
France being attacked	44	48	37
the Russians marching into Austria	34	36	31
the Russians marching into Yugoslavia	27	29	26
Israel being threatened by defeat to the Arabs in a war	25	27	24
North Korea beginning a war against South Korea	20	23	19
the People's Republic of China invading Taiwan (Nationalist China)	8	9	7
None of the above	7	4	11
	466	496	430

*see page 13.

THE SOVIET UNION

Question: "*Do you feel that the Russian government is basically willing to seek a reconciliation with the West at present, or don't you think so?*"

	Believe this %	Don't believe this %	No opinion %	
Total population - April 1959	17	57	26	= 100
- April 1965	23	56	21	= 100
- April 1970	33	46	21	= 100
- July 1974	29	55	16	= 100
- February 1977	27	60	13	= 100
- January 1980	17	69	14	= 100
AGE GROUPS				
16-29	18	63	19	= 100
30-44	18	70	12	= 100
45-59	17	72	11	= 100
60 and over	14	72	14	= 100
PARTY PREFERENCE				
SPD	25	62	13	= 100
CDU/CSU	9	81	10	= 100
FDP	25	60	15	= 100

DISTRUST

Question: *"Here two people are discussing Russia. With which position would you tend to agree?"* (ill., X)

	1965 April %	1970 April %	1974 July %	1976 June %
"We have no reason to distrust Russia less today than years ago. Russia itself hasn't changed, but has only altered its methods. Russia is essentially just as dangerous for us today as it was before."	55	52	58	59
"We should stop distrusting Russia and acting as though the people were still the 'bad Russians', as in Stalin's time. A lot has changed in Russia since then."	27	34	29	26
Undecided	18	14	13	15
	100	100	100	100

RUSSIAN EXPLOITATION OF DETENTE

Question: *"Here are two men discussing Russia. With which of the two would you tend to agree?"* (ill., X)

A

	November 1977			
	Total pop. %	Party preference SPD %	CDU/CSU %	FDP %
"I think that the Russians take advantage of our good will in the matter of reconciliation with the East. They use our readiness to negotiate in order to extend their power further in the world."	61	53	78	54
"I think the Russians are serious about their policy of détente. They do not abuse our confidence in order to extend their power in the world."	19	30	10	25
Undecided	20	17	12	21
	100	100	100	100

CHANGE OF OPINION

Question: *"Would you say that your opinion of Russia has gotten better in the last 2 or 3 years, or has it tended to get worse?"*

	1977 Feb.	1980 Jan.	Age groups				Party preference		
	Total population		16-29	30-44	45-59	60 and over	SPD	CDU/CSU	FDP
	%	%	%	%	%	%	%	%	%
Stayed the same	46	25	23	25	27	25	28	21	23
Got worse	25	61	62	63	62	58	58	69	62
Got better	18	5	5	5	6	5	7	3	6
Undecided	11	9	10	7	5	12	7	7	9
	100	100	100	100	100	100	100	100	100

A MENACE

Question: *"Do you feel we are menaced by Russia, or not?"*

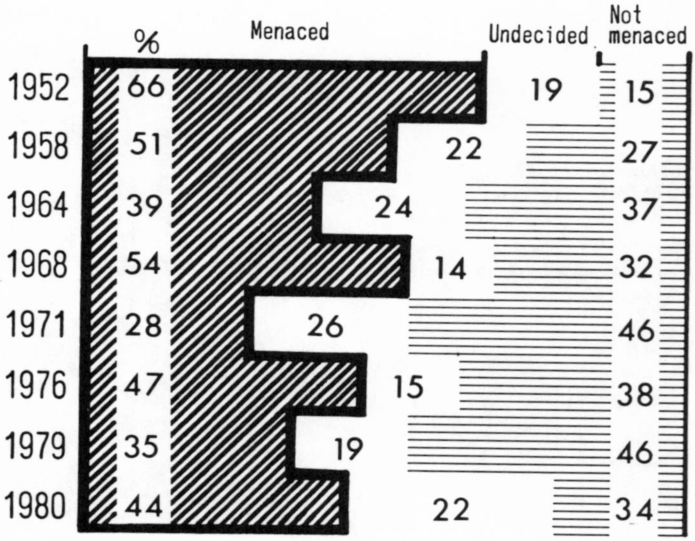

THE BALANCE OF POWER

Question: *"Who do you think is more powerful in the world today - America or Russia?"*

A

	February 1977				
	Russia %	America %	Both the same %	Undecided %	
Total population	29	29	30	12	= 100
AGE GROUPS					
16-29	30	30	27	13	= 100
30-44	27	31	30	12	= 100
45-59	32	27	32	9	= 100
60 and over	29	29	29	13	= 100
PARTY PREFERENCE					
SPD	29	26	34	11	= 100
CDU/CSU	33	33	25	9	= 100
FDP	22	33	31	14	= 100

LEONID BREZHNEV

Question: *"Brezhnev will be visiting Germany shortly. What do you think of this visit? Do you think it is a good thing and useful to us for him to come, or will this visit not accomplish anything, or perhaps even be detrimental?"*

"From all that you've seen or heard of Leonid Brezhnev—How likeable do you find him as a person?"

	1973 May %	1977 Nov. %
Brezhnev's visit -		
Good and useful	51	37
Won't accomplish anything	28	45
Perhaps detrimental	3	4
No opinion	10	11
Brezhnev unknown	8	3
	100	100

	1973 May %	1977 Nov. %
Very likeable person	3	2
Quite likeable	29	22
Not so likeable	20	34
Unpleasant	6	14
No opinion	34	25
Brezhnev unknown	8	3
	100	100

Question: *"Do you believe that the Soviet head of state Brezhnev aims for peaceful cooperation with the West, or is his main goal the Soviet domination of Western Europe?"*

A

	November 1977							
	Total	Age groups				Party preference		
	pop. %	16-29 %	30-44 %	45-59 %	60 and over %	SPD %	CDU/CSU %	FDP %
Soviet domination	53	42	53	55	61	45	66	36
Peaceful cooperation	23	30	23	23	17	36	12	43
Undecided	24	28	24	22	22	19	22	21
	100	100	100	100	100	100	100	100

IMPROVED RELATIONS MEAN MORE BUSINESS

Question: *"Several opinions are listed here. Would you please read this? Where would you agree - what would be your opinion as well?"* (L)

	1977 Nov. %
Advantages for the Federal Republic	
If we improve our relations with the Soviet Union, we will do more business with the East	55
An improvement in relations with the Soviet Union gives us more security vis-a-vis the East	38
Improved relations with the Soviet Union get us closer to German reunification	17
	110
Advantages for the Soviet Union	
Improved relations mainly produce advantages for the Soviet Union because it thereby has the chance to acquire goods and credits cheaply	48
If we improve our relations with the Soviet Union, it will gain in influence and reputation in the West	21
An improvement in our relations with the Soviet Union mainly means that the Soviet hegemony in Eastern Europe is strengthened	15
	84

YOUTH FOR UNDERSTANDING

Question: *"It has been suggested that certain German youth groups regularly spend their vacation in Russia, and in this way get to know the Soviet Union. Do you think that this is a good idea or not such a good idea?"*

A

	May 1973			
	Good idea	Not a good idea	Undecided	
	%	%	%	
Total population	80	10	10	= 100
AGE GROUPS				
16-29	91	5	4	= 100
30-44	86	6	8	= 100
45-59	77	13	10	= 100
60 and over	68	15	17	= 100
PARTY PREFERENCE				
SPD	94	3	3	= 100
CDU/CSU	69	16	15	= 100
FDP	82	8	10	= 100

WAR MUST BE AVOIDED

Question: *"No one knows what will happen, but what do you think—If we are confronted with the choice of either letting Europe become Soviet or resisting the move with every means at our disposal, which is more important - to defend democratic freedom, even if it leads to a nuclear war, or to avoid war above all, even though it means having to live under a communist government?"*

	1955 May	1960 July	1976 April	1979 Sept.	1980 March
	%	%	%	%	%
Avoid war above all	36	38	52	44	41
Defend democracy	33	30	28	30	31
Impossible to say	31	32	20	26	28
	100	100	100	100	100

NATO

Question: *"It is 30* years ago that NATO, the Western defense alliance, was founded, of which West Germany also is a member. A few views about NATO you can hear today are listed here. Could you read them through and tell me which of them you would agree with?"* (L)

	1971 Sept. %	1976 April %	1979 Sept. %
NATO has brought the Western countries closer together	51	52	46
The Western world owes its freedom to NATO	39	46	40
Had it not been for NATO we would have been attacked by the Communists a long time ago and would have been integrated into the Eastern Bloc	32	35	33
NATO is not powerful enough to defend Europe against a serious attack from the East	28	31	29
The NATO member countries agree too seldom with one another, each is too concerned about its own interests	24	31	26
NATO is a defense alliance which the Russians fear	29	28	25
NATO is of greatest use to the Americans	18	17	15
France's policy since de Gaulle has weakened NATO	–	–	14
NATO does not have strong leadership, not enough influence over its members	15	21	14
As long as NATO exists, there will be no real détente between East and West	13	–	8
None of these	4	7	5
Don't know what NATO means	15	11	13
	268	279	268

*) In previous years, the equivalent question was posed.

SUPREMACY

Question: *"Which NATO country, in your opinion, has the most say—the U.S., England, France, or Germany?"*

	U.S. %	Germany %	France %	Britain %	Undecided %	Don't know NATO %	
Total population - September 1971	74	1	1	x	9	15	= 100
- September 1979	67	3	2	1	14	13	= 100

ADVANTAGES

Question: *"All in all, does NATO have more advantages or disadvantages for us West Germans?"*

	1956 Sept. %	1959 April %	1971 Sept. %	1979 Sept. %
More advantages	29	43	47	48
More disadvantages	11	6	9	7
Undecided	28	26	29	32
Don't know what NATO is	32	25	15	13
	100	100	100	100

NATO COMMAND

Question: *"The German army is under the general command of NATO. Do you think that is all right, or would you prefer its being under a West German supreme command, if this were possible?"*

	1971 Sept. %	1976 April %	1979 Sept. %
NATO command all right	51	49	51
West German supreme command	18	16	16
Undecided	16	24	20
Don't know what NATO is	15	11	13
	100	100	100

DEFENSE

Question: *"Supposing the Russians were to start a war, do you think that we, together with NATO, would have enough troops and be sufficiently well armed to stave off an attack from Russia and prevent them from entering our country, or don't you think that we could defend ourselves against a serious Russian attack?"*

	1971 Sept. %	1976 April %	1979 Sept. %	1980 Feb. %
Couldn't defend ourselves	37	29	31	35
Sufficiently armed	27	26	27	33
Impossible to say	21	34	29	25
Don't know what NATO means	15	11	13	7
	100	100	100	100

REINFORCEMENT

Question: *"Would you be for or against NATO reinforcing their troops?"*

A

	1971 Sept. %	1976 April %	1979 Sept. %	1980 Feb. %
For reinforcement	25	41	38	50
Against	36	20	24	25
Undecided	24	28	25	18
Don't know what NATO is	15	11	13	7
	100	100	100	100

NEUTRON WEAPONS

Question: *"Have you ever heard about the neutron bomb or neutron weapons?"*

"Do you believe that the West needs neutron weapons in order not to fall behind the East militarily, or don't you consider neutron weapons necessary?"

A

	Necessary %	Not necessary %	Undecided %	Never heard of them %	
Total population - April 1978	39	30	23	8	= 100

DEPLOY MISSILES IN WEST GERMANY?

Question: *"NATO plans to deploy American medium-range missiles in the European member countries of NATO, for example in West Germany, to counterbalance Russian medium-range missiles. Are you in favor of this or not?"*

	In favor	Not in favor	Undecided	
	%	%	%	
Total population - November 1979	38	34	28	= 100

EAST MORE POWERFUL

Question: *"A question about armament in the East and West—From all that you've heard, how would you assess the present power relationship? Is the East more powerful, the West more powerful, or are they equally powerful?"*

	1976	1977	1978	1979	1980	1981
	Feb.	Nov.	Jan.	Sept.	May	May
	%	%	%	%	%	%
East more powerful	57	48	46	48	49	46
West more powerful	5	6	7	5	7	6
Equally powerful	24	33	34	31	27	31
Don't know	14	13	13	16	17	17
	100	100	100	100	100	100

EXTEND NATO

Question: *"Some people are now afraid that the Soviet Union will invade other countries in order to get closer to the Indian Ocean and to be able to cut off the West's oil supply. That is why some politicians demand that NATO Policies also cover these countries, for their own protection, and thus also to protest our oil supply, as well as for the protection of Western Europe. What is you opinion—should NATO also see to the protction of these countries in the Middle East or had they best keep out of this?"*

	Include these countries	Keep out	Undecided	
	%	%	%	
Total population - January 1980	50	38	12	= 100

THE EUROPEAN COMMUNITY

Question: *''Various things come to mind when you hear of the EC, the ''European Community''. Let me read a few to you and please tell me each time whether you might think of this when of the ''European Community''. Would you for example think of . . .''*

A

	March 1979				
	Yes	No	No reply		
	%	%	%		
Future	84	8	8	=	100
Peace	79	11	10	=	100
Progress	77	11	12	=	100
Friendship	74	17	9	=	100
Security	73	15	12	=	100
Bureaucracy	68	17	15	=	100
Butter surplus	66	21	13	=	100
Freedom	66	19	15	=	100
Power	56	31	13	=	100
Unemployment	52	33	15	=	100
Wealth	49	33	18	=	100
Socialism	32	46	22	=	100

HAVE MOVED CLOSER

Question: *''Do you think that the countries of the European Community have come closer to each other in recent years or not?''*

	1974	1975	1977
	March	Oct.	Aug.
The countries of the EC have -	%	%	%
come closer	43	53	43
not come closer	37	29	33
Undecided	20	18	24
	100	100	100

FOR GOOD REASON

Question: *"Is your interest in the question of a United Europe essentially based on reason or is it based on sentiment?"*

	August 1977				
	Total	Age groups			
	pop.	16-29	30-44	45-59	60 and over
	%	%	%	%	%
Reason	47	44	51	50	43
Sentiment	30	33	31	28	28
Undecided	23	23	18	22	29
	100	100	100	100	100

WOULD REGRET IT

Question: *"Supposing you were to suddenly hear that the EC, the European Community, was being dissolved— how would you react to this news? Would it, in your eyes, be -"*

A

	1970 March	1977 Aug.	1978 April	1979 March
	%	%	%	%
Very regrettable	38	29	33	29
Rather regrettable	30	36	31	41
Unimportant	16	18	16	17
Something rather positive	6	6	7	6
No opinion	10	11	13	7
	100	100	100	100

WEST AND EAST UNITED?

Question: *"Should only the countries of Western Europe belong to a United Europe, or should a United Europe also include Russia and the Eastern European countries? What is your opinion?"*

	West European countries only	East European countries also	Undecided	
	%	%	%	
Total population - March 1979	56	25	19	= 100

EC AS POLITICAL COMMUNITY

Question: *"Are you for or against the EC, i.e. the European Community, expanding to become a political community—a United Europe?"*

	1970 March %	1972 February %	1974 March %	1975 November %	1979 March %
For	69	73	72	71	68
Against	10	9	9	9	11
Undecided	21	18	19	20	21
	100	100	100	100	100

. . . OF WHAT KIND?

Question: *"What should this United Europe be like—how would you visualize it? Could you please answer with the help of this list?"* (L)

	1970 %	1979 %
A superordinate European government to fulfill certain tasks. But each country still has a government of its own to fulfill that country's special tasks of government	52	54
No European government. The governments of the individual countries meet regularly to make decisions on their common policies	16	22
Only one European government, the national governments having been abolished. All tasks hitherto fulfilled by the national governments are taken over by the European government	15	7
None of these	4	6
Undecided	13	11
	100	100

FUNCTION OF EUROPEAN PARLIAMENT

Question: *"How much influence should the directly elected European Parliament have? Should it only be able to advise the governments of the member countries, or should it be able to determine the policies of the member countries in certain matters or in all matters?"*

		March 1979		
	Total	Party preference		
	pop.	SPD	CDU/CSU	FDP
	%	%	%	%
Determine in certain matters	42	44	40	56
Only advise	35	34	37	34
Determine all matters	8	9	9	6
Undecided	15	13	14	4
	100	100	100	100

GERMAN INFLUENCE

Question: *"In our neighboring European countries, the way things are done leaves a lot to be desired. You often hear the view that we Germans should increase our influence and assume more of the leadership, and then relations within the European Community would soon improve. Would you agree with this or not agree?"*

A

	Do not agree	Agree	Undecided		
	%	%	%		
Total population - April 1975	40	31	29	=	100
- March 1979	47	30	23	=	100
OCCUPATION					
Unskilled workers	33	36	31	=	100
Skilled workers	46	31	23	=	100
Non-managerial employees and public servants	52	23	25	=	100
Managerial employees and public servants	55	29	16	=	100
Self-employeds, professionals	50	36	14	=	100
Farmers	30	38	32	=	100

EUROPEAN GOVERNMENT?

Question: *''In June of this year the European Parliament will be elected. This means that, just as in federal elections, the political parties put forward candidates for whom the population votes and the same process takes place in all of the countries of the European Community. Have you already heard something about these European elections or not?''* (Yes, heard about it = 88 percent in March 1979)

Question: *''Would you be willing to accept, over and above the federal government, a European government responsible for a common policy in foreign affairs, defense and the economy?''*

	1970	1971	1974	1979
	Jan.	Oct.	March	March
For foreign affairs, defense, economy -	%	%	%	%
Willing to accept a European government	56	58	55	45
Not willing	20	22	21	31
Undecided	24	20	24	24
	100	100	100	100

EUROCURRENCY

Question: *''If there were no longer a deutschmark, but only a single common European currency - would you favor or oppose that?''*

	1970	1974	1977	1979
	Jan.	March	Aug.	March
Common European currency -	%	%	%	%
Favor	52	57	35	39
Oppose	26	22	49	40
Indifferent	14	13	11	15
Undecided	8	8	5	6
	100	100	100	100

SECURITY AT STAKE?

Question: *"Here are two people discussing whether the military defense of the Federal Republic will be more secure or less secure in a United Europe. Which of the two says what you tend to think?"* (ill., X)

A

"I believe that the security of the Federal Republic -	March 1979 %
will be strengthened in a United Europe. It doesn't matter what role the Communists play; a United Europe is simply a power block which cannot be attacked so easily."	64
against the military power of the East would worsen in a United Europe. For in a United Europe the Communists will have a voice and thus our security system will be undermined."	17
Undecided	19
	100

GERMAN REUNIFICATION POSTPONED

Question: *"Here are two people discussing the reunification of Germany. Please read this and tell me which of the two says what you tend to believe."* (ill., X)

A

	March 1979 %
"The reunification of Germany cannot be attained at the moment, but the unification of Europe is possible. Therefore all energies should now first of all be channelled into creating a United Europe."	69
"I have reservations about the unification of Europe as it is now planned, including only the countries of Western Europe. I am afraid that we are thereby destroying our chances for German reunification."	12
Undecided	19
	100

FOREIGN WORKERS

Question: "*Another question about the foreign workers from the countries of the European Community, that is the countries listed on this sheet. Foreign workers from these countries have the right to live and work here whenever they wish. Did you know that, or is this the first time you've heard of it?*" (L) (Yes, knew = 71 percent)

"*What do you think of this freedom of choice of residence and employment within the whole European Community; do you consider this ruling good or not good?*"

A

	March 1979			
	Good	Not good	Undecided	
	%	%	%	
Total population	59	24	17	= 100
OCCUPATION				
Unskilled workers	48	31	21	= 100
Skilled workers	59	26	15	= 100
Non-managerial employees and public servants	62	21	17	= 100
Managerial employees and public servants	71	18	11	= 100
Self-employeds, professionals	60	20	20	= 100
Farmers	54	30	16	= 100

A EUROPEAN FLAG

Question: "*Would you approve or disapprove if the German flag was no longer raised at major official ceremonies, and a European flag was raised instead?*"

	Approve	Disapprove	Indifference	Undecided	
	%	%	%	%	
Total population - January 1970	35	41	18	6	= 100
- March 1979	27	43	25	5	= 100

DESIRABLE PACE

Question: "*How rapid should the development toward a United Europe be? Faster, or slower, or the same as in the past?*"

	1973	1975	1976	1978
	%	%	%	%
Faster	49	47	41	38
Slower	4	6	9	7
As in the past	34	36	37	34
Undecided	13	11	13	21
	100	100	100	100

WON'T LIVE TO SEE THE UNITED STATES OF EUROPE

Question: "*Do you think that you will live to see the day when the Western European countries join together to form the United States of Europe?*"

	1953 Feb. %	1961 Oct. %	1969 May %	1974 March %	1979 March %
Yes, I do	41	36	38	30	31
No, I don't	29	30	42	51	47
Undecided	30	34	20	19	22
	100	100	100	100	100

WEST GERMANY - EUROPEAN COMMUNITY - USA

Statistical data for comparison[1]

Country	Area in 1000 km^2	Population[2] in thousands	Mid-Year	Population density (Pop. per km^2)
West Germany	248.6	61,310	1978	247
Belgium	30.5	9,840	1978	323
Denmark	43.1[3]	5,110	1978	119
France	547.0	53,302	1978	97
Gr. Britain and N. Ireland	244.0	55,822	1978	229
Ireland	70.3	3,192	1977	45
Italy	301.2	56,697	1978	188
Luxembourg	2.6	356	1977	137
The Netherlands	40.8[4]	13,937	1978	342
EC	1,528.1	259,566	1977/78	170
USA	9,363.1[5]	219,800[6]	1978	23

[1]Source: Statistisches Jahrbuch 1979 für die Bundesrepublic Deutschland, Appendix 2.

[2]predominantly resident population, i.e. not including foreign armed forces within the country and not including those members of the country's own armed forces that are presently residing outside the country.

[3]not including Faeroes and Greenland.

[4]includes inland waters.

[5]total area; land area = 9,191.8.

[6]includes U.S. Armed Forces stationed abroad.

POPULATION BY AGE

Country	Age groups under 15 %	15-30 %	30-45 %	45-65 %	65 and over[1] %		Year
West Germany	20	22	21	22	15	= 100	1977
Belgium	22	23	18	23	14	= 100	1976
Denmark[2]	22	22	20	22	14	= 100	1977
France	23	24	19	21	14	= 101	1978
Great Britain	22	22	19	23	14	= 100	1978
Ireland	31	24	15	19	11	= 100	1976
Italy	23	22	20	22	13	= 100	1977
Luxembourg	20	23	21	23	13	= 100	1976
The Netherlands	25	25	19	20	11	= 100	1976
EC	22	23	20	22	13	= 100	–
USA	24	27	18	20	11	= 100	1977

[1]includes "age unknown"
[2]not including Faeroes and Greenland

MARRIAGES, BIRTHS, DEATHS

Country	Marriages per 1,000 inhabitants	Birth Rate (Live births per 1,000 inhabitants)	Death Rate (Deaths, not including stillbirths, per 1,000 inhabitants)	Year
West Germany	5.4	9.4	11.8	1978
Belgium	7.0	12.4	11.4	1977
Denmark[1]	6.2	12.2	9.9	1977
France	6.7	13.8	10.3	1978
Great Britain	7.2	11.8	11.7	1977
Ireland	6.1	21.4	10.5	1977
Italy	6.1	13.2	9.6	1977
Luxembourg	6.2	11.4	11.5	1977
The Netherlands	6.7	12.5	7.9	1977
EC	6.4	11.7	10.7	–
USA	10.1	15.3	8.8	1977

[1]not including Faeroes and Greenland

EMPLOYMENT

Country	Percent of total population employed Total %	Men %	Women %	Unemployed %	Year
West Germany	44	58	32	4.5	1978
Belgium	41	54	29	9.9	1977
Denmark	51[1]	59[1]	42[1]	7.7	1977
France	43	?	?	6.3	1977
Great Britain	47	60	35	6.2	1977
Ireland	36	?	?	11.8	1976
Italy	38	?	?	7.2	1978
Luxembourg	41	?	?	0.6	1977
The Netherlands	38	54	21	5.3	1977
EC	43	?	?	6.1	—
USA	46	57	36	7.0	1977

[1] 15-75 year olds

Note: The comparability of the figures is limited by the fact that in the individual countries there are in some cases greatly differing definitions of "employed person".

EMPLOYMENT BY SECTOR OF THE ECONOMY

Country	Agriculture, forestry and fisheries	Manufacturing[1]	Trade[2]	Other
	in % of employed persons			
West Germany	6.0	43.0	19.6	31.4
Belgium	3.0	33.8	24.0	39.2
Denmark	8.5	30.4	20.8	40.3
France	10.8	37.2	22.5	29.5
Great Britain	2.5	36.2	21.7	25.0
Ireland	23.8	28.4	22.9	25.0
Italy	14.6	35.5[3]	21.9	28.0
Luxembourg	6.0	46.3[3]	47.7	
The Netherlands	6.5	32.7	24.7	36.0
EC	8.0	37.5	21.6	32.9
USA	3.6	29.2	25.1	42.1

[1] includes construction
[2] includes restaurant business
[3] includes power production and water supply

COST OF LIVING

Price index: 1970 = 100

Country	1977
West Germany	146.3
Belgium	174.8
Denmark	188.7
France	183.2
Great Britain	249.0
Ireland	249.9
Italy	236.6
Luxembourg	166.0
The Netherlands	176.4
EC	—
USA	156.1

EXPORT

Country	1977 Export in millions of DM
West Germany	273.614
Belgium	86.973[1]
Denmark	23.350[2]
France	147.353
Great Britain	133.440[2]
Ireland	10.191[2]
Italy	104.476
Luxembourg	—[3]
The Netherlands	101.332
EC	880.728
USA	278.779[2]

[1] includes Luxembourg
[2] general trade
[3] included under Belgium

PRIVATE CARS IN USE

Country	Private cars in thousands	Private cars per 1,000 inhabitants	End of year
West Germany	20,377	326	1977
Belgium	2,871	292	1977
Denmark	1,375	270	1977
France	16,990	320	1977
Great Britain	14,300	291	1977
Ireland	573	179	1977
Italy	16,650	295	1977
Luxembourg	117	324	1975
The Netherlands	3,768	274	1976
EC	—	—	—
USA	110,351	513	1976

HOW THE BRITISH AND THE GERMANS VIEW EACH OTHER

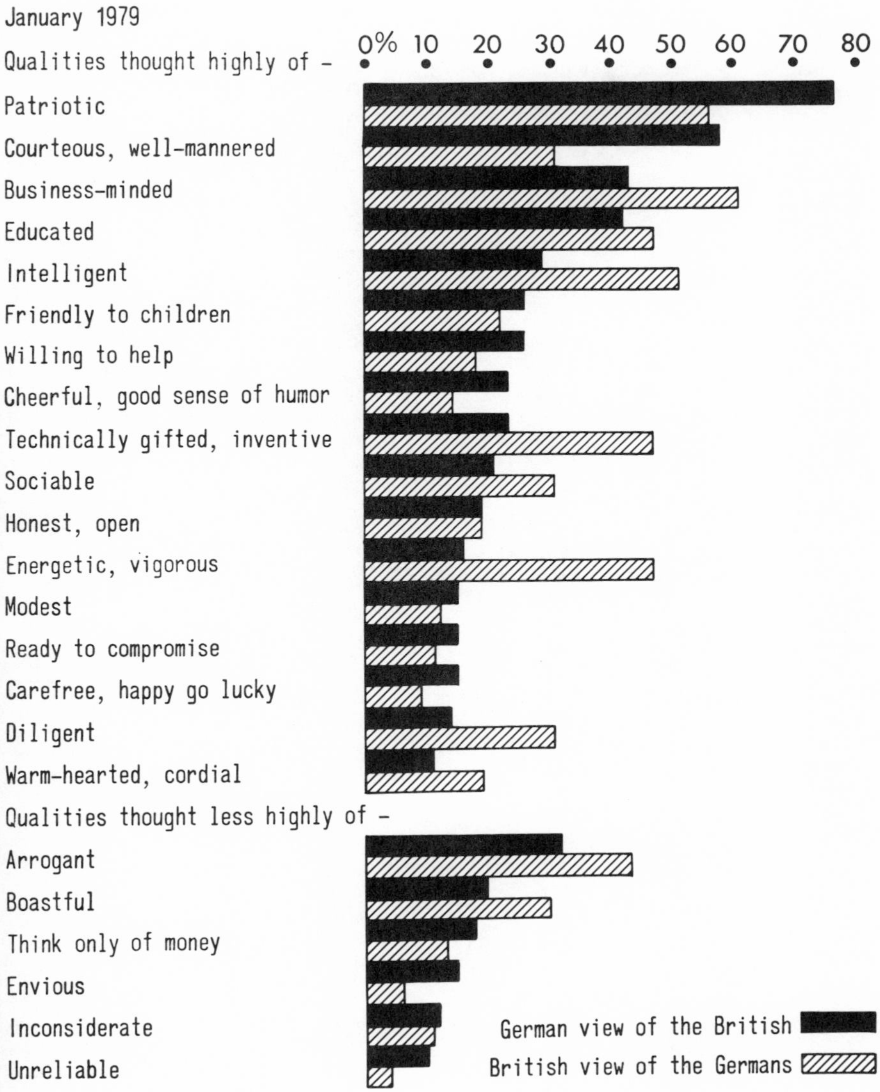
January 1979
Qualities thought highly of –
0% 10 20 30 40 50 60 70 80
Patriotic
Courteous, well-mannered
Business-minded
Educated
Intelligent
Friendly to children
Willing to help
Cheerful, good sense of humor
Technically gifted, inventive
Sociable
Honest, open
Energetic, vigorous
Modest
Ready to compromise
Carefree, happy go lucky
Diligent
Warm-hearted, cordial
Qualities thought less highly of –
Arrogant
Boastful
Think only of money
Envious
Inconsiderate
Unreliable
German view of the British
British view of the Germans

IMAGES

Question put to Germans (British): *"Here are some phrases to describe the British (German) people. I'd like you to tell me which of the phrases, in you opinion, best describe the British (German) people."* (C)

see also illustration on page 449

	January 1979							
	German view of the British				British view of the Germans			
	Age groups				Age groups			
	16-29	30-44	45-59	60 and over	16-29	30-44	45-59	60 and over
Qualities thought highly of -	%	%	%	%	%	%	%	%
Patriotic	73	80	79	76	50	62	57	52
Courteous, well-mannered	57	60	54	59	24	33	35	32
Business-minded	41	41	41	48	55	65	62	60
Educated	41	41	40	46	44	47	50	47
Intelligent	25	29	29	32	45	50	58	55
Friendly to children	29	26	25	25	17	22	27	25
Willing to help	30	25	21	29	17	18	21	18
Cheerful, good sense of humor	27	24	18	23	13	14	15	15
Technically gifted, inventive	21	24	25	22	38	48	51	52
Sociable	27	21	18	19	32	29	31	31
Honest, open	19	20	20	17	17	18	19	21
Energetic, vigorous	14	14	15	22	40	50	52	48
Modest	16	14	15	14	7	7	5	8
Ready to compromise	18	16	12	13	12	9	12	13
Carefree, happy-go-lucky	16	16	12	14	8	9	10	11
Diligent	15	12	14	17	24	24	34	33
Warm-hearted, cordial	14	11	7	12	15	19	21	20
Qualities thought less highly of -								
Arrogant	26	34	34	32	38	46	46	43
Boastful	18	20	20	20	31	27	32	29
Think only of money	13	15	20	25	12	12	15	11
Envious	13	14	15	18	6	5	9	5
Inconsiderate	8	11	12	15	9	12	15	8
Unreliable	8	11	11	10	3	4	5	6

A MUTUAL LIKING

Question put to Germans (British): *"Do you like the British (German) people or not?"*

	Germans referring to British			British referring to Germans		
	1962	1965	1979	1976	1977	1979
	%	%	%	%	%	%
Like them	32	46	36	46	53	54
Do not like them	32	25	24	10	7	12
Undecided	36	29	40	44	40	34
	100	100	100	100	100	100

	January 1979							
	Germans Age groups				British Age groups			
	16-29	30-44	45-59	60 and over	16-29	30-44	45-59	60 and over
	%	%	%	%	%	%	%	%
Like them	41	39	30	35	52	53	56	53
Do not like them	20	22	28	27	10	12	13	12
Undecided	39	39	42	38	38	35	31	35
	100	100	100	100	100	100	100	100

PERSONAL EXPERIENCE

Question put to Germans (British): *"Do you know any British (Germans) personally?"*

	January 1979				
	Know one	Know several	Know many	Know none	
	%	%	%	%	
Germans referring to British	9	26	5	60	= 100
British referring to Germans	13	26	6	55	= 100

Question to Germans (British): *"Have you ever been to Britain (Germany)?"*

	January 1979			
	Once	Several times	Never	
	%	%	%	
Germans been to Britain	13	10	77	= 100
British been to Germany	16	11	73	= 100

CHANGE OF OPINION

Question put to Germans (British): *"Would you say that over the last five years views about the British people (German people) have changed for the better or for the worse or have they not changed at all?"*

	January 1979				
	For the better	For the worse	Not changed	Don't know	
	%	%	%	%	
Germans referring to British	13	10	65	12	= 100
British referring to Germans	52	6	32	10	= 100

POPULAR

Question put to Germans (British): *"In general, do you believe that the Germans (British) are popular or unpopular abroad?"*

	January 1979									
	German view of the British					British view of the Germans				
	Total	Age groups				Total	Age groups			
	pop.	16-29	30-44	45-59	60 and over	pop.	16-29	30-44	45-59	60 and over
	%	%	%	%	%	%	%	%	%	%
Popular	48	52	46	50	46	58	68	52	54	57
Unpopular ...	30	26	33	28	31	34	25	39	36	35
Other answer .	8	5	9	8	8	3	2	4	3	3
Don't know ..	14	17	12	14	15	5	5	5	7	5
	100	100	100	100	100	100	100	100	100	100

HOME IS BEST

Question put to British (Germans): *"Where do you believe personal freedom is greater overall, in Britain or in West Germany - or is there no difference?"*

A

	In West Germany	In Britain	No difference	Don't know	
	%	%	%	%	
Germans say - 1976	40	10	32	18	= 100
- 1979	26	13	48	13	= 100
British say - 1976	8	50	15	27	= 100
- 1979	2	64	25	9	= 100

FAVORITE NATIONALITY

Question put to Germans (British): *"Could you indicate on this list which nationality you would prefer to have if you were not German (British)?"*

	January 1979									
	Germans					*British*				
	Total pop.	Age groups 16-29	30-44	45-59	60 and over	Total pop.	Age groups 16-29	30-44	45-59	60 and over
	%	%	%	%	%	%	%	%	%	%
North American	21	22	19	21	19	28	28	26	30	28
Swedish	18	19	20	15	17	14	15	17	13	9
French	17	24	17	15	13	13	19	14	9	10
Dutch	12	9	12	12	16	12	10	12	14	11
British/German	6	6	7	5	6	8	8	9	9	7
Spanish	4	3	4	6	3	3	4	4	2	3
Finnish	3	3	4	3	2	1	1	1	x	1
Russian	1	1	2	1	x	1	1	x	1	1
Other	11	9	12	13	12	9	8	9	9	11
No answer ...	7	4	3	9	12	11	6	8	13	19
	100	100	100	100	100	100	100	100	100	100

WHICH GERMANY?

Question put to British: *"When you hear the word 'Germany', what do you think of right off—of the Federal Republic, of the German Democratic Republic or of both at the same time?"*

	January 1979				
	Total pop.	Age groups 16-29	30-44	45-59	60 and over
	%	%	%	%	%
The Federal Republic	43	43	44	45	41
The German Democratic Republic	4	5	4	3	4
Both at the same time	50	51	50	50	49
That depends	3	1	2	2	6
	100	100	100	100	100

VIEW OF EACH OTHER'S GOVERNMENT

Question put to Germans (British): *"All in all, do you have a good or not such a good opinion of the British (German) government?"*

	January 1979									
	Germans					*British*				
	Total pop.	Age groups 16-29	30-44	45-59	60 and over	Total pop.	Age groups 16-29	30-44	45-59	60 and over
	%	%	%	%	%	%	%	%	%	%
Good opinion	23	22	25	23	22	51	44	55	52	54
Not so good opinion	29	25	32	30	28	7	9	6	5	7
Undecided ...	48	53	43	47	50	42	47	39	43	39
	100	100	100	100	100	100	100	100	100	100

POLITICIANS

Question put to Germans: *"Here on this list are the names of five British politicians. Which of them have you heard of?"* (L)

Question put to the British: *"Here on this list are the names of five German politicians. Which of them have you heard of?"* (L)

Follow-up question for each politician known: *"Do you personally like . . . or not?"*

	Like		Dislike		Neither, nor		Politician unknown		
British with reference to -	1976	1979	1976	1979	1976	1979	1976	1979	
	%	%	%	%	%	%	%	%	
Willy Brandt	41	52	3	5	24	23	32	20	
Helmut Schmidt	14	37	3	7	28	28	55	28	
Franz Josef Strauss ...	4	7	2	4	15	13	79	76	
Helmut Kohl	1	3	x	2	5	9	94	86	
Hans-Dietrich Genscher	1	3	x	1	3	4	96	92	
Germans with reference to -									
Harold Wilson	–	38	–	11	–	30	–	21	= 100
Edward Heath	–	32	–	9	–	26	–	33	= 100
James Callaghan	–	26	–	8	–	35	–	31	= 100
Margaret Thatcher	–	24	–	14	–	16	–	46	= 100
David Owen	–	10	–	4	–	21	–	65	= 100

– = not asked.

THE FRENCH

Question: *"Do you like the French?"*

	1965 %	1977 %
Yes, like the French	39	50
Don't especially like them	35	20
Undecided	26	30
	100	100

Question: *"Have you ever been to France?"*

	1964 %	1977 %
Have been to France -		
Yes	35	54
No	65	46
	100	100

ASSOCIATIONS

Question: *"When one hears about a country, there are various things that come to mind. If you think of France, what enters your mind - what things do you usually think of when you hear France mentioned? Could you answer with the help of this list?"* (L)

	February 1973 %
Good cuisine	73
Paris	67
Fashion	62
Pleasure, night life	53
History, Napoleon, the revolution	52
Cosmetics, perfume	51
Alcoholic drinks	46
Adenauer - de Gaulle, German-French friendship	46
Famous buildings	43
Sidewalk cafés	37
Charming women	36
National pride	34
Beautiful countryside	29

	February 1973 %
Enjoying life	29
A difficult foreign language	25
Modern art	24
Automobile companies	22
Vacation, travel	22
Expensive, high prices	21
Alsace-Lorraine	20
Beggars, bums	20
Residential districts, bars, dives	17
Disorder, neglect	16
Communists	14
World power	7
Sports	4

DE GAULLE

Question: *"How strong is your faith in de Gaulle as a wise leader in dealing with world problems—very strong, pretty strong or not so strong, or do you have no faith at all in him?"*

"Do you have the impression that de Gaulle is a friend of Germany or not?"

	1968 Sept. %
"Very strong faith"	5
"Pretty strong"	17
"Not so strong"	40
"No faith at all"	24
No opinion	14
	100

	1968 Sept. %
A friend of Germany -	
yes	17
no	29
yes and no	41
No opinion	13
	100

PATRIOTISM

Question: *"The French are said to be patriotic. Would you say that patriotism is a good thing, or do you not consider it to be a good thing?"*

	A good thing %	Not a good thing %	No opinion %	
Total population - August 1974	68	16	16	= 100

FRENCH OR AMERICAN PRIORITY?

Question: *"What is your opinion?"*

	1965 Jan. %	1966 Nov. %	1980 Jan. %
"America is the only one that can guarantee our security; therefore our first priority is not to annoy the Americans."	48	29	45
"We should work closely with France to make Europe strong, and America is going to have to make allowances for this."	19	29	22
Undecided	33	42	33
	100	100	100

THE ITALIANS

Question: *"Do you like the Italians or do you not especially like them—aside from the foreign workers, that is?"*

Question: *"Have you ever been to Italy?"*

A

	1964 July %	1977 Oct. %
Like the Italians	19	33
Don't especially like them	45	37
Undecided	36	30
	100	100

	1964 July %	1977 Oct. %
Have been to Italy -		
Yes	34	54
No, never	66	46
	100	100

SECURITY AT STAKE?

Question: *"Assuming that after the next election in Italy the Christian Democrats and the Communists would form a coalition government, would this pose a threat to our security, or not?"*

	May 1976			
	Would pose threat %	No threat %	Undecided %	
Total population	33	37	30	= 100
PARTY PREFERENCE				
SPD	27	48	25	= 100
CDU/CSU	44	28	28	= 100
FDP	34	47	19	= 100

OSTPOLITIK

Question: *"You sometimes hear that the government is too much concerned with Ostpolitik and doesn't think enough about our relationship with the West* (halfgroup: Europe and European unification). *Do you think this is true or is it not correct to say this?"*

	October 1975							
	Ostpolitik is at the expense of -							
	relationship with the West				European unification			
	Total	Party preference			Total	Party preference		
	pop.	SPD	CDU/CSU	FDP	pop.	SPD	CDU/CSU	FDP
	%	%	%	%	%	%	%	%
True	33	20	57	20	30	17	53	19
Not correct to say this	50	69	28	69	52	70	30	77
Undecided	17	11	15	11	18	13	17	4
	100	100	100	100	100	100	100	100

SATISFIED?

Question: *"Are you generally satisfied with the federal government's policy for the East or not?"*

	1974	1975	1980	Party preference		
	Total population			SPD	CDU/CSU	FDP
	%	%	%	%	%	%
Dissatisfied	40	41	38	19	61	28
Satisfied	32	31	35	56	16	51
No opinion	28	28	27	25	23	21
	100	100	100	100	100	100

DETENTE

Question: *"Here on these cards are various opinions. Could you please tell me with which you would completely agree, with which you would partly agree and with which you would not at all agree?"* (C)

	July 1970				
	Agree completely %	Agree partly %	Don't agree %	No response %	
25 years after the end of the war, we have to make a clean break with the past. If we want to get anywhere in politics, we have to deal with the situation as it is now	51	24	13	12	= 100
For 20 years, nothing was done about détente with the East. It's about time that something happened	45	25	17	13	= 100
Nothing that took place after the war in the East is final yet. How things should be in the future must first be decided in a peace treaty	41	29	14	16	= 100
We would be traitors to the German people's right of self-determination if we recognize the East German government as long as the people are held there under pressure and free elections are prohibited	37	23	22	18	= 100
We can offer the East what we will; recognition and nonagression: they will give us nothing in return, instead will remain mistrusting and hostile	36	29	19	16	= 100
We have to stop seeing East Germany as our poor brother who needs help. The people in East Germany don't want us to meddle in their affairs	35	34	17	14	= 100
Even if West Germany and East Germany were in agreement on all points, there would still be no reunification, because the Great Powers in the background don't want this	32	31	22	15	= 100
The division of Germany and the loss of the Eastern parts are the results of lost war- results which we can no longer change. It doesn't make any sense to pretend that it's not final	32	31	22	15	= 100
There is no reason for us to have a treaty with East Germany at any price. We can wait until East Germany is ready to concede	29	30	25	16	= 100

continued

DETENTE

continued

	July 1979				
	Agree completely %	Agree partly %	Don't agree %	No response %	
In 1952, the Adenauer government missed our big chance at reunification	27	25	25	23	= 100
We have to conclude an agreement with East Germany as quickly as possible. The longer we wait, the higher East Germany's demands	23	25	36	16	= 100
Recognizing East Germany and the present boundaries would overcome the mistrust of the East bloc nations and would make cooperation possible	22	33	28	17	= 100
There's no sense in continually demanding the right of self-determination for the people in East Germany. That way we won't achieve anything, instead we will only anger the East German government	21	30	31	18	= 100

THE ODER-NEISSE LINE

Question: *"Do you think that we should resign ourselves to the present German-Polish border—the Oder-Neisse Line—or shouldn't we accept this?"*

	1951 March %	1964 Sept. %	1972 May %	Party preference SPD %	CDU/CSU %	FDP %
Should resign ourselves	8	22	62	80	42	85
Shouldn't accept this	80	59	18	7	34	10
Undecided	12	19	20	13	24	5
	100	100	100	100	100	100

THE WARSAW TREATY

A question about the Warsaw Treaty, that is the treaty between Poland and the Federal Republic of Germany: *"Do you think that through this treaty we will be able to achieve a lasting good relationship with Poland or don't you think so?"*

A

	August 1972			
	Yes, think so	Don't think so	Undecided	
	%	%	%	
Total population	43	24	33	= 100
AGE GROUPS				
16-29	50	18	32	= 100
30-44	48	21	31	= 100
45-59	40	26	34	= 100
60 and over	32	31	37	= 100
PARTY PREFERENCE				
SPD	61	11	28	= 100
CDU/CSU	30	39	31	= 100
FDP	64	12	24	= 100

OUR POLISH NEIGHBOR

Question: *"One hears such widely differing views about the Polish people. What do you like and dislike about the Poles? What is your general opinion of them?"* (O)

Summary:	1959 Sept. %	1963 Oct. %	1972 Aug. %
Basically positive opinion	24	24	18
Ambivalent or neutral opinion	12	23	30
Basically negative opinion	36	18	19
No opinion	28	35	33
	100	100	100

QUID PRO QUO

Question: *"Western Germany has committed itself to pay 1.2 billion DM as reparation and besides this has granted a loan of one billion. In return, Poland will allow 125,000 people who want to settle in West Germany to leave the country. All in all, would you agree that this treaty should be concluded?"*

	February 1976			
	Agree	Don't agree	Undecided	
	%	%	%	
Total population	35	47	18	= 100
PARTY PREFERENCE				
SPD	56	25	19	= 100
CDU/CSU	17	64	19	= 100
FDP	39	38	24	= 100

THE POLISH CRISIS

Question: *"In Poland there have recently been strikes and demonstrations in several cities. Have you heard of or read about this, or is this the first you've heard of it?"* (Yes, heard, read = 98 percent)

"Do you think that the Russians will enter Poland if the Polish government fulfills the strikers' demands for freedom of the press, free labor unions and freedom of the church, or do you think the Russians won't risk this?"

A

	August 1980			
	Total pop.	Party preference		
		SPD	CDU/CSU	FDP
	%	%	%	%
Russians will enter Poland	27	21	35	25
Won't risk this	47	56	43	55
Undecided	26	23	22	20
	100	100	100	100

THREAT OF WAR?

Question: *"Do you think that the events in Poland have created a real threat of war, or don't you think so?"*

	August 1980				
	Total pop.	Age groups			
		16-29	30-44	45-59	60 and over
	%	%	%	%	%
Created a threat of war	20	16	18	23	23
Don't think so	63	65	71	60	56
Undecided	17	19	11	17	21
	100	100	100	100	100

KEEP OUT!

Question: "*Opinions differ as to which stand the German government should take to the present crisis in Poland. Here are two people talking about this. Which of the two best matches your opinion?*" (ill.)

A

	Total pop. %	August 1980 Party preference SPD %	CDU/CSU %	FDP %
"I think our government should demonstrate some understanding for the strikers in Poland. The demands for prosperity and freedom deserve our open sympathy."	30	26	35	35
"I have a different point of view. Even though we may have sympathy for the strikers in Poland and for their demands, the federal government should keep out of things, so that the situation, which is tense as it is, doesn't heat up even more."	54	59	50	57
Undecided	16	15	15	8
	100	100	100	100

ELIMINATING TROUBLE WITH ECONOMIC AID

Question: "*A few German banks and the federal government want to grant the Polish government a loan of 1.2 billion DM. Two people are talking here about what it means for us to provide the Poles with a large loan in the present situation. Which of the two says pretty much what you think, too?*" (ill., X)

B

	Total pop. %	August 1980 Party preference SPD %	CDU/CSU %	FDP %
"I think it is right to give Poland a loan, even if we are not in agreement with the regime there. Economic aid can be an important contribution to eliminating a source of trouble."	42	50	33	63
"I think Poland should not be given a loan. The present unrest shows that the money is used to keep an undemocratic regime in power."	35	25	48	29
Undecided	23	25	19	8
	100	100	100	100

CZECHOSLOVAKIA

Question: "*As of a few months, there are now new people in the government in Prague. Have you heard of this?*" (Yes, heard = 77 percent) "*Do you believe that this marks the beginning of a general tendency towards a freer development of the Eastern bloc or not?*"

	June 1968				
	Marks freer development %	Doesn't mark freer development %	Impossible to say %	Never heard of this before %	
Total population	50	14	13	23	= 100

REACTIONS

Question: "*Do you remember hearing the first news about Czechoslovakia? Here is a list of a few statements. For which of them would you say 'That's what I thought—those were also my feelings'?*" (L)

B

	September 1968 %
I was shocked	52
I pitied the people there	51
I was worried	50
I thought that really shows how dangerous the Russians are	46
I had the feeling that the détente policy of the last few years has been all for nothing	28
At one blow, I lost my faith in a more humanitarian development under the Communists	27
I though this means the Cold War all over again	24
The West can't do anything	24
I was furious	17
I didn't get upset	14
It's the Communists' business—it's none of our business	9

CONTINUE OSTPOLITIK

Question: "*In your opinion, what is the right policy to follow after the events in Czechoslovakia: Should we continue having ministers from Bonn meet with Ministers from East Berlin, or shouldn't we conduct such alks?*"

	Continue talks %	No talks %	Undecided %	
Total population - September 1968	58	22	20	= 100

AFTERTHOUGHTS

Question: *"Here are a few views on what has happened in Czechoslovakia. Which of them do you agree with?"* (L)

	September 1968 %
It's a good thing that the Czechs didn't immediately put up military resistance but instead offered only non-violent resistance	68
Czechoslovakia belongs to the Eastern sphere of influence; there the West can't intervene militarily, instead they have to limit themselves to protests	38
The Western powers should have immediately and decisively countered Russia and put economic and diplomatic pressure on Russia	26
Just like Czechoslovakia, the Russians could take over West Berlin anytime, and the Western Powers couldn't do a thing about it	24
West Berlin is under the special protection of the Western Powers and therefore the Russians wouldn't dare to occupy West Berlin	24
The West shouldn't get involved in the affairs of the Eastern Bloc nations. They have to work out how to get along with each other by themselves	23
The Czechoslovakian army should have offered the Russians military resistance from the beginning	9
The Western Powers should have immediately threatened Russia with military measures and, if necessary, they should have intervened	6
No answer	7
	225

A NEW TREND?

Question: *"The events in Czechoslovakia have clearly shown that there are two groups in the East: the conservative Communists who want to govern as in the past—with rigid leadership and censorship of the press—and the progressive or Reform-Communists who want to govern democratically with freedom of opinion and less pressure. In your opinion, which of these trends will be successful in the next 10 or 20 years in the Eastern European countries—the conservative or the progressive?"*

B

	Conservative %	Progressive %	It depends %	No opinion %	
Total population - September 1968	22	45	23	10	= 100

DISAPPOINTED

Question: *"In the last few years there have been treaties concluded between our government and the governments of the Soviet Union, Poland, Czechoslovakia and East Germany. What is your impression—are you satisfied with the developments that have taken place or are you disappointed?"*

	Satisfied %	Disappointed %	Undecided %	
Total population - September 1974	22	57	21	= 100
- September 1975	22	39	39	= 100

BUT NONETHELESS

Question: *"Do you think negotiations with the eastern European socialist countries are worth the effort, or not?"*

	Worth the effort %	Not worth the effort %	Undecided %	
Total population - 1973	49	29	22	= 100
- 1980	51	28	21	= 100

. . .CONTINUE DETENTE

Question: *"Should the Federal Republic continue the policy of détente in the future, or don't you think it makes sense to continue?"*

	January 1980							
	Total	Age groups				Party preference		
	pop. %	16-29 %	30-44 %	45-59 %	60 and over %	SPD %	CDU/CSU %	FDP %
Continue détente	74	74	77	75	72	89	59	85
No sense in continuing	17	17	19	15	17	7	28	8
Undecided	9	9	4	10	11	4	13	7
	100	100	100	100	100	100	100	100

Question: *"Who do you believe has profited most overall from improved German-Soviet relations—the Soviet Union or West Germany?"*

	1973 May %	1977 Nov. %	1980 Jan. %
The Soviet Union	45	44	55
West Germany	9	6	6
Both equally	31	33	25
Impossible to say	15	17	14
	100	100	100

THE MIDDLE EAST

Question: *"There has been a war between Israel and the Arab countries. The Israelis have, as a result, occupied various territories* (halfgroup: the part of Jerusalem that belongs to Jordan). *What is your opinion—should Israel give back all occupied territories* (halfgroup: the occupied section of Jerusalem) *or should Israel retain it all?"* (X)

A

	July 1967
	%
Israel -	
should retain all of Jerusalem	59
should give back occupied section	21
Other answer/don't know	20
	100

	July 1967
	%
Should keep all territories	19
Should keep parts	36
Should give back all	16
Other answer/don't know	29
	100

WHAT ISRAEL SHOULD DO

Question: *"Here are two people talking about what Israel should do. Which of the two would you tend to agree with?"* (ill., X)

	April 1971
	%
"It would be too dangerous for Israel to give up the occupied territories before the Arabs recognize the existence and independence of Israel."	45
"If Israel pulls out of the occupied territories, then the Arabs will be willing to enter into negotiations and then there is the prospect of coming to an agreement that would take into consideration the interests of both sides."	23
No opinion	32
	100

TAKING SIDES

A question about the conflict between Israel and the Arab nations: *"On whose side are you, on the side of the Israelis or more on the side of the Arabs?"*

	1970 %	1971 %	1974 %	1978 %
On the side of the Israelis	46	43	50	44
On the side of the Arabs	7	8	7	7
Neither	32	29	29	33
No reply	15	20	14	16
	100	100	100	100

Question: *"Do you believe that Israel will, in the long run, be able to maintain itself against the Arabs, or will the Arabs eventually prevail?"*

	1970 %	1974 %	1978 %
Israel will maintain itself	29	26	40
The Arabs will prevail	27	34	20
Undecided	44	40	40
	100	100	100

ANWAR SADAT

Question: *"President Sadat of Egypt and Prime Minister Begin of Israel recently negotiated with President Carter in America. Have you heard of this?"* (Yes = 96 percent)

"Do you think that Sadat will be able to gain the support of other Arab states for his Israel policy, or don't you think so?"

A

	Sadat will gain support %	Don't think so %	Undecided %	Not heard of negotiations %	
Total population - December 1977	35	30	35	x	= 100
- October 1978	25	38	33	4	= 100

IRAN

Question: *"There has been a revolution in Iran. The Shah and his government have been deposed. Why do you suppose this happened—mainly for religious reasons or because of dissatisfaction with social and political conditions under the Shah's regime?"*

	February 1979 %
Dissatisfaction with the Shah's regime	43
Religious reasons	21
Due equally to both reasons	30
No opinion	6
	100

CONCERNS

Question: *"Does the Shah's overthrow entail considerable disadvantages for us in West Germany and for our economy, or are there no noticeable disadvantages? What do you think?"*

A

	Considerable disadvantages %	No noticeable disadvantages %	Undecided %	
Total population - February 1979	60	24	16	= 100

AMERICAN HOSTAGES

Question: *"The American Embassy has been occupied in Iran. In return for freeing the hostages, the United States is required to extradite the Shah to Iran. Do you think America should extradite the Shah, or should he not be extradited?"* (Not be extradited = 71 percent)

Question: *"The Americans attempted to free the hostages in Iran by means of a military mission. Do you think that President Carter did the right thing in attempting to free the hostages, or shouldn't this have been attempted?"*

A

	Carter did the right thing %	Shouldn't have attempted it %	Undecided %	
Total population - May 1980	60	26	14	= 100

THE FAR EAST

Question: *"There are various things on this list that might be said about people in different countries. If you were to describe the Japanese, which of these things would you say apply?"* (L)

A

	May 1970		
	Total pop.	Education	
		Elementary	Secondary
	%	%	%
Positive qualities:			
Hardworking, industrious	80	80	79
Polite	61	61	64
Active	57	54	64
Intelligent	57	57	56
Disciplined, in control	45	43	51
Conscientious, dutiful	43	42	43
Exact, precise	27	26	30
Energetic	25	23	30
Reliable, trustworthy	25	25	26
Peace-loving	19	22	11
Reformers	17	15	23
Cheerful, happy	16	17	14
Idealists	16	16	17
Democratic	15	15	13
Emotional	12	13	8
Conservative	7	7	6
	522	516	535
Negative qualities:			
Authority-conscious	19	19	19
Have only their own advantage in mind	8	9	6
Stiff	4	4	4
Rebellious	4	4	6
Hot-headed, quick-tempered	3	4	2
Aggressive, quarrelsome	3	3	2
Superficial, capricious	1	1	1
Lazy, comfort-loving	x	1	x
Haughty, arrogant	x	1	x
Stupid, simple-minded	x	x	x
Don't know, none of these	3	3	4
	45	49	44

LEARNING ABOUT JAPAN

Question: *"People acquire their knowledge about other countries from diverse sources. If you try to remember, where did you receive your information concerning Japan? This list contains several possibilities. Which of them apply to you?"* (L)

A

	May 1970			
	Total	Education		
	population	Elementary	Intermediate	Secondary
I learned what I know about Japan mainly from -	%	%	%	%
Television	67	65	72	71
The daily newspaper	60	56	70	71
School	31	27	41	46
Films	31	27	41	46
Radio broadcasts	29	28	35	23
Books	28	22	43	46
Travel descriptions, lectures	13	9	24	23
Stories and reports from relatives or friends	8	8	10	14
Contact and meetings with Japanese	4	3	6	16
A stay in Japan	2	1	2	7
None of these, don't know about Japan	8	10	2	2
	281	256	346	365

ALLIED WITH THE WEST?

Question: *"How do you see Japan's position in the world—is Japan on the side of the West and the Americans, or on the side of the Russians, or of the Chinese, or is the country neutral?"*

	May 1970		
	Total	Education	
	pop.	Elementary	Secondary
	%	%	%
On the side of the West and the Americans	48	45	57
Neutral	2	2	2
On the side of the Russians	2	2	2
On the side of the Chinese	2	2	1
Don't know	46	49	38
	100	100	100

THE PEOPLE'S REPUBLIC OF CHINA

Question: *"Have you heard that the Chinese party leader Mao Tse-tung died, or is this the first time you've heard this?"* (Yes, have heard = 99 percent)

"If someone said that Mao was one of the greatest statesmen of the century, would you agree, or do you think this is somewhat exaggerated?"

	September 1976			
	Agree	Exaggerated	Undecided	
	%	%	%	
Total population	53	32	15	= 100
AGE GROUPS				
16-29	62	27	11	= 100
30-44	56	31	13	= 100
45-59	46	38	16	= 100
60 and over	46	34	20	= 100
PARTY PREFERENCE				
SPD	55	30	15	= 100
CDU/CSU	51	34	15	= 100
FDP	67	26	7	= 100

LOOKING AHEAD

Question: *"Russia and Red China are fighting for control over the Communist world. What is your impression as to who has the greater influence on Communism today—Russia or China?"*

"And which country do you think will have established itself as the leader of the Communist world in ten years' time?"

	Today		In 10 years	
	1966	1976	1966	1976
	April	December	April	December
	%	%	%	%
Russia	47	59	18	26
China	18	16	33	32
Both equally	14	11	9	11
Impossible to say	21	14	40	31
	100	100	100	100

WAR NOT LIKELY

Question: *"Do you think that in the next one or two years war will break out between Russia and China, or don't you think so?"*

	March 1974					
	Total pop.	Education		Party preference		
		Elementary	Secondary	SPD	CDU/CSU	FDP
	%	%	%	%	%	%
War will break out	8	7	9	7	9	9
Don't think so	61	60	64	69	59	65
Undecided	31	33	27	24	32	26
	100	100	100	100	100	100

CHINA NO. 1 IN THE YEAR 2000

Question: *"In your opinion, which country will be the most powerful in the year 2000?"* (O)

	USA	Russia	China	Other country	No answer	
	%	%	%	%	%	
Total population - April 1967	38	19	17	5	25	= 104
- December 1979	20	20	29	7	27	= 103

CHINESE-WESTERN ALLIANCE

Question: *"Do you think China and the West might ally themselves against the Soviet Union, or don't you believe in this possibility?" "If there were such an alliance, would you be in favor of it or not?"*

	January 1980			
	Yes	No	Undecided	
	%	%	%	
Chinese-Western alliance - possible	61	22	17	= 100
- favored	48	19	33	= 100

VIETNAM

Question: *"Do you follow the news about the war in Vietnam, or are you not really interested in this?"*

	1966 July %	1967 Feb. %	1968 Feb. %	1971 Aug. %
Follow it	65	72	77	57
Not really interested	35	28	23	43
	100	100	100	100

Question: *"What do you suppose—do the majority of Americans agree with the American Vietnam policy, or do they not agree?"*

	Majority don't agree %	Agree %	Half for, half against %	Don't know %	
Total population - July 1966	30	27	16	27	= 100

NEGOTIATIONS

Question: *"There are very different opinions about how America should act in Vietnam. The choices are listed here. What are you in favor of?"* (L)

The Americans should -	Aug. 1965 %	Feb. 1967 %
stay in South Vietnam but stop bombing North Vietnam and try to establish negotiations with the Communists	29	36
withdraw from Vietnam, withdraw American troops	21	33
continue bombing to the same degree as up to now and at the same time continue offering negotiations	15	11
continue to increase the attacks on North Vietnam; commit more troops and weapons until the Communists there give in	10	7
wage a declared war against North Vietnam, make a total military commitment there and, if necessary, extend the war to include China	5	3
No opinion	20	10
	100	100

NO RIGHT

Question: *"Some pople say the Americans should pull out of Vietnam. It's not their country and they have no right to be at war in that country.*

Others say that the Americans are defending Vietnam's freedom against Communism. They have to do this or else Communism will continue to spread and become an ever growing danger. What is your opinion?"

	1966 March %	1967 Sept. %	1968 Feb. %	1971 Aug. %
Have no right	25	37	31	46
Must defend freedom there	44	33	38	29
Undecided	31	30	31	25
	100	100	100	100

STOP FIGHTING

Question: *"Are you for or against the Americans continuing to fight in Vietnam?"*

	Against %	For %	Undecided %	
Total population - January 1966	44	25	31	= 100
- February 1968	56	19	25	= 100
- June 1971	80	7	13	= 100

NO POSSIBILITY OF WINNING

Question: *"Do you have the impression that the Americans could win the war in Vietnam, or do you think that the situation is hopeless?"*

	Could win %	Hopeless %	No opinion %	
Total population - March 1966	41	23	36	= 100
- February 1968	33	36	31	= 100
- June 1971	12	55	33	= 100

WILL THERE BE PEACE?

Question: *"A short time ago an armistice agreement was signed for Vietnam. What is your opinion: Will there now once and for all be peace, or is the fighting likely to continue in spite of this?"*

	Continue fighting %	Peace %	Undecided %	
Total population - February 1973	75	10	15	= 100

WHICH WAY?

Question: *"The Americans are withdrawing all troops from Vietnam. Do you believe that South Vietnam will also become Communist now or not?"*

	Become Communist	Don't think so	Undecided	
	%	%	%	
Total population - February 1973	36	27	37	= 100

LEAVE IT ALONE

Question: *"The entire resistance to the Communists in South Vietnam has now collapsed. There are two viewpoints on this matter. Which of these would you agree with?"* (L)

	April 1975			
	Total pop.	Party preference SPD	CDU/CSU	FDP
	%	%	%	%
"It was right for the Americans to leave Vietnam on its own and not to reinforce their aid. They had no right to interfere there and wage war."	45	51	38	65
"When the peace agreement was broken, the Americans should have again intervened in Vietnam. They should never have left Vietnam to the Communists."	32	28	38	22
Undecided	23	21	24	13
	100	100	100	100

VIETNAM: AN AMERICAN WAR

Question: *"If someone says that the Americans lost their war in South Vietnam, would you say they were right, or wasn't it really an American war any more?"*

A

	Americans lost their war	Not an American war	Undecided	
	%	%	%	
Total population - April 1975	50	26	24	= 100

OTHER COUNTRIES

Question: *"Soviet troops have marched into Afghanistan. Have you followed the events in Afghanistan in detail, or only as part of the news in general, or weren't you so interested in all of this?"*

	Followed in detail	As part of the news	Not interested	Not heard of it	
	%	%	%	%	
Total population - January 1980	51	42	6	1	= 100

AFGHANISTAN

Question: *"There are different opinions about how the events in Afghanistan affect world politics. I'd like to read you some opinions on this, if I may, and please tell me after each if you agree or if you don't agree."*

	February 1980			
	Agree	Don't agree	Undecided	
	%	%	%	
The European countries, especially West Germany, should in any case continue the policy of détente	78	9	13	= 100
The West must use all the means at its disposal to prevent a return to the Cold War	78	9	13	= 100
The invasion of Afghanistan has shown us the Soviet Union's true goals and intentions in terms of power politics	75	9	16	= 100
The Soviet Union's relations with the Third World will be upset for a long time to come because of the Russian intervention in Afghanistan	66	13	21	= 100
The policy of détente in Europe has been shattered by the events in Afghanistan	39	39	22	= 100
Under the pressure of world opinion, the Soviet Union will eventually withdraw from Afghanistan	14	64	22	= 100

DANGER OF WAR

Question: *"Do you believe that the events in Afghanistan have created a real danger of war, or don't you believe so?"*

	Yes, danger of war	No danger	Undecided	
	%	%	%	
Total population - January 1980	52	35	13	= 100
- February 1980	56	31	13	= 100

SANCTIONS

Question: *"Because of Afghanistan, America has severely limited trade with the Soviet Union. Some people think that we should also restrict our trade with the Soviet Union as a protest over the invasion of Afghanistan. Others are against this because they fear that with such measures we will only hurt ourselves. What do you think—should we limit our trade with the Soviet Union or not?"*

B

	Limit trade	Don't limit trade	Undecided	
	%	%	%	
Total population - January 1980	46	40	14	= 100

SUPPORT AMERICAN POLICY?

Question: *"There are different opinions about how the federal government should respond to American policy. Two opinions have been included here; which of these would you tend to agree with?"* (L)

A

	May 1980			
	Total pop.	Party preference SPD	CDU/CSU	FDP
	%	%	%	%
"I think that if we expect the Americans to come to our aid in Europe, we must show them by our actions that we support their policies in other parts of the world, even if we are not in agreement with all their measures and this requires sacrifices."	39	33	51	38
"I am of a different opinion. We should certainly create a solid front with the Americans as far as possible, but if they establish policies that are unreasonable, they can't expect us to go along with measures that run counter to our own interests."	49	55	39	55
Undecided	12	12	10	7
	100	100	100	100

SOUTH AFRICA

Question: *''When you hear of a country, you are likely to have various associations. If you think of the Republic of South Africa—the country way down in southern Africa* (ill.)*—what, above all, comes to your mind when you hear about South Africa? Could you answer with the aid of this list?''* (L)

Political associations -	1975 Feb. %
Racial segregation of Blacks and Whites	68
White supremacy	54
Black struggle for equality	54
Supression, exploitation of Blacks	45
Many countries reject this country's policies	36
Riots, political unrest	36
Colonies	25
Authoritarian state	24
Nationalism	15

General associations -	1975 Feb. %
Dr. Barnard, heart transplant	64
Very hot climate	64
Gold, diamonds	58
Wild animals, wildlife preserve	57
Cape of Good Hope	53
Developing country	35
Beautiful sea, beautiful beaches	32
Thriving economy, rich country	21
Other/no answer	2

WHITE SUPREMACY?

Question: *''In southern Africa, disputes between the black and the white population occur more and more often. Have you heard anything about this lately?''* (Yes, heard about it = 81 percent)

''Do you think the whites should retain their position of dominance, or should they hand the power over to the blacks?''

''Should Europe and the U.S. support the white government, or the black majority government?''

A

Whites should -	May 1976 %
give up dominant position	41
keep dominant position	17
Impossible to say	42
	100

U.S. and Europe should support -	May 1976 %
black majority government	41
white government	10
Undecided	49
	100

THE COUP IN CHILE

Question: *"There was a coup in Chile last year; the socialist head of state Allende was toppled by the military. According to what you know or have heard, do you believe that the people of Chile would have liked to keep Allende, or were the majority of the Chileans glad that he was overthrown?"*

E

	Wanted to keep Allende	Glad that he was overthrown	Undecided	Never heard about it	
	%	%	%	%	
Total population - May 1974	28	18	44	10	= 100

WHO TOPPLED ALLENDE?

Question: *"Do you believe that it was mainly the Americans who were behind the coup in Chile or not?"*

	Americans behind the coup - yes	no	Undecided	Never heard of coup	
	%	%	%	%	
Total population - October 1973	29	33	32	6	= 100

MIXED FEELINGS

Question: *"What do you think the situation is in Chile today? Two people are talking about it here—which one would you tend to agree with?"* (ill., X)

	May 1974
	%
"The present military dictatorship in Chile suppresses the people and rules by brute force. The democratic freedoms and rights have been abolished, and the ruling class has no intention of reinstating them."	30
"In my opinion, the military dictatorship in Chile is trying to re-establish order and to prepare the way for a democratic constitutional state. Considering all that preceded them, one can't expect that this will be achieved overnight."	30
Undecided	40
	100

THE UNITED NATIONS

Question: "*Have you ever heard anything about the 'United Nations' or the 'UN', as it is also called?*"

"*All in all, would you say that the UN has done a good job of solving the problems it has been faced with, or not such a good job?*"

	Good	Average	Bad	Undecided	Never heard of the UN	
	%	%	%	%	%	
Total population - June 1976	12	34	33	16	5	= 100

ADMITTING CHINA

Question: "*This year, the UN will take a vote on whether the People's Republic of China, i.e. Red China, should be admitted to the UN or not. As it is, only Nationalist China, i.e., Formosa, is a member of the United Nations. Here are three views on this matter. Which would you be for?*" (L)

	November 1971
	%
I am for the admission of the People's Republic of China (Red China) into the UN and for Nationalist China likewise remaining in the UN	49
I am for the admission of the People's Republic of China (Red China) into the UN as the sole representative of China, in place of Nationalist China	13
I am for Nationalist China remaining the only representative of China in the UN and for the People's Republic of China not being admitted	9
Undecided	29
	100

ADMITTING GERMANY

Question: *"Admitting West Germany and East Germany to the UN, the United Nations, has been a topic of discussion lately. Do you think that this should take place soon or should this be postponed for the time being?"*

A

	Should be soon	Should be postponed	Undecided	
	%	%	%	
Total population - September 1971	34	42	24	= 100

BENEFICIAL OR DETRIMENTAL?

Question: *"Here is a list of things that others have said about West Germany's admission to the UN. Which of them would you agree with?"* (L, X)

	October 1973
	%
West Germany's reputation in the world would be promoted by joining the UN	46
Membership in the UN costs a lot of money - we have to make great financial sacrifices for this	36
Through the UN West Germany has more influence on world politics	35
In case of a catastrophe the help of the UN would be valuable	33
Membership in the UN commits us to helping developing nations more than we have up to now	28
West Germany's international economic relations will be improved by joining the UN	26
If we are ever threatened or attacked, we receive help and support from the UN	22
The influence of the UN has continually decreased from the time of its founding; for this reason our membership does not mean a lot today	20
Joining the UN doesn't do a lot for West Germany, except for creating new government posts	18
If the UN intervenes militarily in some trouble spot, then we have to send our soldiers there too	16
None of these	11
	291

CHANCES FOR REUNIFICATION

Question: *"West Germany is now a member of the UN, the United Nations. Do you approve of West Germany's joining or not?"* (Approve = 63 percent; disapprove = 10 percent; undecided = 27 percent)

"At the same time as West Germany was admitted to the UN, so was East Germany. Two people are talking about this here. Which of the two would you tend to agree with?" (L, ill.)

	October 1973 %
"Now that both German states are members of the UN, the rest of the world will say that there is no longer any political necessity for the reunification of Germany. No country will advocate this anymore."	36
"The membership of both German states in the UN keeps the German question out in the open in front of the whole world, and now we will be able to work at our goal of reunification much better in international politics."	33
Undecided	31
	100

BIAFRA

Question: *"Have you heard of Biafra and could you tell me where it is located?"* (Yes = 76 percent)

"Biafra seceded from Nigeria. As a result, bitter civil war is raging. The majority of the population is threatened with destruction, either from enemies or from hunger. Some people say that something has to be done—intervention is necessary, for example by the United Nations. Others say that they have to work this out for themselves, and no foreigners should be allowed to get involved. How do you fell about this?"

	For intervention %	Against it %	Undecided %	
Total population - August 1968	59	25	16	= 100

THE OLYMPIC GAMES

Question: *"Have you ever seen this symbol?"* (ill.) (Yes, have seen it = 96 percent in May 1980)
"Could you tell me what this symbol stands for?" (Correct answer = 93 percent in May 1980)

PRESTIGE

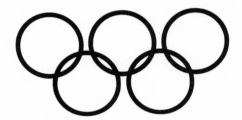

Question: *"If a country wins a lot of gold medals at the Olympics, do you believe that this increases its prestige in the world, or doesn't this have any influence?"*

	Increases prestige			No influence			Undecided		
	1968	1972	1980	1968	1972	1980	1968	1972	1980
	%	%	%	%	%	%	%	%	%
Total population	53	48	44	31	39	46	16	13	10
Men	56	51	46	33	41	47	11	8	7
Women	50	45	42	29	38	45	21	17	13
AGE GROUPS									
16-29	57	47	44	33	44	48	10	9	8
30-44	53	48	41	32	41	54	15	11	5
45-59	53	49	44	31	40	44	16	11	12
60 and over	46	49	47	26	28	38	28	23	15

PROMOTE SPORTS

Question: *"Do you think we should promote and support our athletes as much as possible in order to win a lot of gold medals, or shouldn't we push it?"*

B

	Promote	Don't push	Undecided	
	%	%	%	
Total population - January 1968	66	22	12	= 100

MEXICO 1968

Question: *"Are you content overall with how the athletes from West Germany did at the Olympic Games or are you not content?"* (Content = 51 percent)

"Do you think it was essentially for financial reasons that our team wasn't further ahead in Mexico or was this due to other reasons?"

	Financial reasons %	Other reasons %	No opinion %	
Total population - December 1968	24	50	26	= 100

MUNICH 1972

Question: *"Here are two people discussing the Olympic Games. Which of the two would you tend to agree with?"* (ill.)

	1970 April %	1972 February %
"It is a great honor for a country to be allowed to organize the Olympic Games. This is no time for financial considerations. For such a one-time event, one has to be ready to make some sacrifices."	53	50
"I basically have nothing against the Olympic Games, but I feel that in our country during the coming years there are much more important tasks for which we should spend our money first. That is why I don't really like the fact that the next Olympic Games are going to be held here."	38	39
Undecided	9	11
	100	100

MOSCOW 1980

Question: *"The next Olympic Games will take place in Moscow in 1980. Some have demanded that West Germany boycott the Olympics as long as Russia continues to violate the human rights of its citizens. Others say politics should be kept out of sports and that West Germany should in any case take part in the Olympics. What is your opinion?"*

	Take part %	Don't send any teams %	Undecided %	
Total population - September 1978	76	11	13	= 100

A POLITICAL ISSUE

Question: *"After the military intervention by the Soviet Union in Afghanistan, some politicians demanded that, as a means of protest, there be no participation in the Olympic Games. Are you for or against our athletes participating in the Olympic Games in Moscow?"*

	January 1980							
	Total	Age groups				Party preference		
	pop.	16-29	30-44	45-59	60 and over	SPD	CDU/CSU	FDP
	%	%	%	%	%	%	%	%
Should participate	48	54	51	47	38	53	42	43
Should not participate	29	26	30	28	32	27	35	31
Undecided	23	20	19	25	30	20	23	26
	100	100	100	100	100	100	100	100

Question: *"The federal government and the Parliament have recommended that no German athletes be sent to the Olympic Games in Moscow. Do you think that this was the right decision or not?"*

A	May 1980							
	Total	Age groups				Party preference		
	pop.	16-29	30-44	45-59	60 and over	SPD	CDU/CSU	FDP
	%	%	%	%	%	%	%	%
Right decision	58	47	58	61	65	54	70	58
Not right	40	51	40	35	34	44	29	42
No reply	2	2	2	4	1	2	1	x
	100	100	100	100	100	100	100	100

KEEP ON PLAYING

Question: *"Let's assume the Olympic Games are to be done away with and there will be no more Olympic Games in the future. Would you be pleased by this, would you regret it, or wouldn't you care?"*

	1976	1980				
	Aug.*	Aug.	Age groups			
	Total population		14-29	30-44	45-59	60 and over
	%	%	%	%	%	%
Would regret it	55	63	67	66	62	55
Wouldn't care	34	28	25	25	28	34
Would be pleased	8	5	5	5	5	4
Undecided	3	4	3	4	5	7
	100	100	100	100	100	100

*2,000 respondents aged 16 or over

VI. THE FUTURE

OUTLOOK

Question: *"When you think of the future, do you think life will become easier or increasingly difficult for people?"*

	January 1980								
	Total pop.	Men	Women	Education Elementary	Education Secondary	Age groups 16-29	Age groups 30-44	Age groups 45-59	Age groups 60 and over
	%	%	%	%	%	%	%	%	%
Increasingly difficult	63	60	66	66	58	60	63	61	68
Easier	14	16	12	12	18	16	12	14	13
Will remain the same	19	20	17	17	22	18	22	18	15
Don't know	4	4	5	5	2	6	3	7	4
	100	100	100	100	100	100	100	100	100

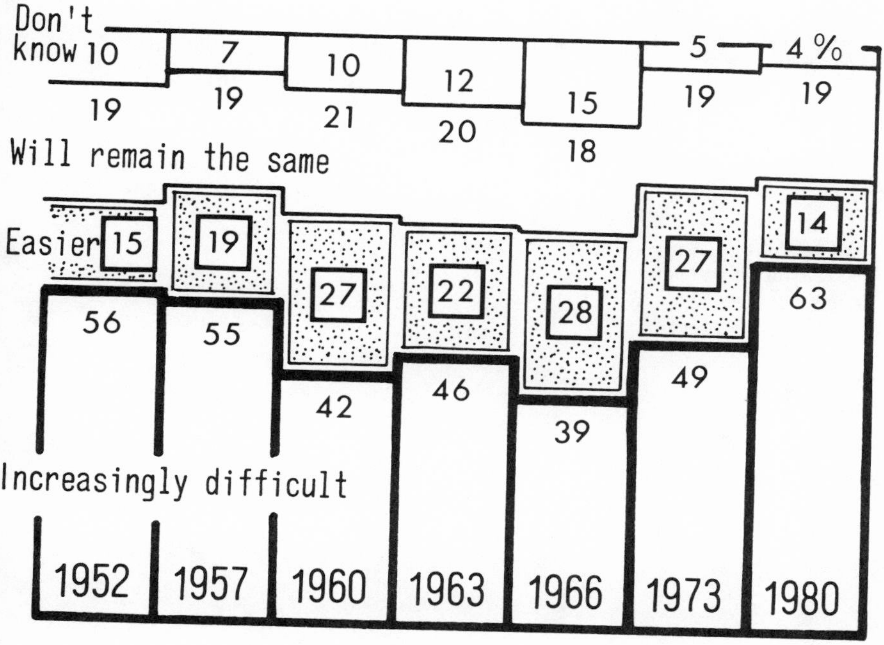

OPTIMISM

Question: *"Do you think that people who marry and set up a family these days can face the future with equanimity or must they constantly be afraid of another war?"*

A

	1963 Jan. %	1965 Febr. %	1968 Nov. %	1971 April %	1973 Febr. %	1976 Febr. %	1979 Jan. %
Afraid of another war	45	38	43	27	14	33	25
Can face the future with equanimity	21	27	29	42	62	43	44
Undecided	34	35	28	31	24	24	31
	100	100	100	100	100	100	100

ANOTHER WORLD WAR?

Question: *"Do you feel we must reckon with another world war, or do you think no one will ever risk a large-scale war again?"*

	1961 Sept. %	1967 June %	1975 Dec. %	1979 Nov. %	1980 May %	1981 Jan. %
Must reckon with world war	46	38	29	32	37	34
No one will risk world war	45	54	63	59	54	59
Impossible to say	9	8	8	9	9	7
	100	100	100	100	100	100

	May 1980							
	Total	Age groups				Party preference		
	pop. %	16-29 %	30-44 %	45-59 %	60 and over %	SPD %	CDU/CSU %	FDP %
Must reckon with world war	37	34	32	38	43	33	42	27
No one will risk world war	54	57	60	51	47	61	47	70
Impossible to say	9	9	8	11	10	6	11	3
	100	100	100	100	100	100	100	100

SURVIVAL

Question: *"Do you think the time will come when the human race will no longer be allowed to multiply, so that everybody can have enough to eat, or do you think people will always find a way for everybody to have enough to survive, even with a growing population?"*

	August 1974				
	Total pop.	Men	Women	Education	
				Elementary	Secondary
	%	%	%	%	%
Limit growth	34	37	32	31	44
Will find a way	45	45	45	45	44
Difficult to say	21	18	23	24	12
	100	100	100	100	100

BE FRUITFUL AND MULTIPLY

Question: *"The birthrate has been declining in West Germany in the last few years. A few scholars think that it may be good for such a densely populated country to have a reduction in population in the future. Overall, do you think it would tend to be a good thing or not such a good thing for West Germany if the population shrinks?"*

A

	October 1979			
	Not good	Good	Undecided	
	%	%	%	
Total population	74	12	14	= 100
Men	72	16	12	= 100
Women	75	10	15	= 100
AGE GROUPS				
16-29	66	17	17	= 100
30-44	79	6	15	= 100
45-59	79	13	8	= 100
60 and over	69	16	15	= 100
EDUCATION				
Elementary	75	12	13	= 100
Secondary	70	13	17	= 100

A DAMPER ON EXPECTATIONS

Question: *"If you take a look at these cards, what do you believe will come true in 10 years? What will things be like in 1990? I don't mean what you hope will come true, but what things will actually be like."* (C)

"And could you tell me what you hope for? Which of these things should occur in 10 years, i.e., around 1990 if it were up to you?" (C)

	December 1979	
	Ideal	Probable
	%	%
Diseases which were incurable will have cures for the most part, even cancer will be curable	89	56
Due to technical progress it will be possible to keep the air and the water clean	79	34
Any kind of atomic bomb experiment will be prohibited, people will no longer need to be afraid of the atomic bomb	76	18
The new sections of a city will be built so as to eliminate noise almost completely	68	28
Free medical care for all citizens	66	18
Hard manual labor will for the most part be done by machines; people will no longer have to struggle with this	65	63
The welfare state will be fully developed; no one will have to suffer extreme poverty anymore	63	18
Every talented young person will have the chance to study at a university	62	43
The streets will be wider and improved, so that there will be by far fewer accidents than today	61	28
Because people will have much more leisure time than they used to, most people will have many interests: learning handicrafts, do-it-yourself-building, photography, painting, playing musical instruments, etc.	60	50
Retirement at the age of 50, after this you receive a good pension	58	21
Many sports which only the rich can afford today will be open to all, i.e. tennis, horseback riding, sailing, etc.	56	47
Everyone will go for an obligatory physical examination once a year	54	34
Many more people will live in houses of their own than at present	50	44
Older people will live in especially quiet neighborhoods, in housing developments built especially for older people	40	22
Married women will no longer go to work; instead they will only take care of the household	40	11
Because people will have more time, they will get more involved in political activities	29	19
Great scientists and artists will be very well paid and highly regarded. Their contribution to society will be recognized more than it is today	24	21
	1040	575

WORLD DEVELOPMENTS

Question: *"No one can say for sure what is going to happen in the world in five or ten years, but what do you think things will be like in 1985—which of the events on this list will have occurred by then?"* (L)

	1976 Dec. %	1979 Dec. %
The whites will have been stripped of power in all of Africa	53	45
The communists will have seized power in several Western European countries	52	38
The Soviet Union will have gained more influence in the world	38	35
America will have lost influence in the world	31	50
The industrial nations will no longer be able to withstand the pressure from the developing countries	27	30
China will be the most powerful nation in the world, outranking Russia and the U.S.	26	24
Peace will have been established between Israel and its Arab neighbors	26	25
The United States of Europe will have come into being	24	29
West Germany will be the leading power in Europe	22	23
Disarmament will have made great progress in the world	13	22
America will have gained influence in the world	12	10
The Soviet Union will have lost influence in the world	12	17
NATO will have broken down	9	9
A new world war will have broken out	5	9
Germany will have been reunited	4	7
None of these	7	9

CONSULTING THE CRYSTAL BALL

Question: *"Normally we don't know what the future will bring. But if it were possible, would you like to know what your future will be like, or would you rather not know?"*

A

	1979 Dec.	1976 Sept.	Age groups			
	Total population		16-29	30-44	45-59	60 and over
	%	%	%	%	%	%
Would not like to know in advance	61	59	56	53	57	69
Would like to know	27	33	35	37	34	23
Undecided	12	8	9	10	9	8
	100	100	100	100	100	100

BURNING ISSUES

Question: *"There are some problems that are of special concern to us now and will continue to be in the next year or two and others that may not be such burning problems now but that may give us serious trouble in five or ten years. Would you read what is printed on these cards? Which of these items will be of special concern to us in the Federal Republic in the next year or two and which of them, while they will presumably not become acute soon, will be burning problems in five or ten years? Could you distribute the cards on this sheet accordingly?"* (C)

	November 1980	
	Will be of special concern to us -	
	in the next year or two	in five or ten years
	%	%
West Germany		
Unemployment being on the increase in West Germany	76	13
Being able to afford less because of price increases for raw materials	58	25
Inflation, the constant devaluation of money	57	26
Increasing tensions between foreign workers and Germans in West Germany	50	31
For West Germany to become less productive and lose influence globally if its economic situation deteriorates	28	35
For foreign countries not to be able to afford our products anymore	23	35
A new crisis developing over Berlin	18	30
For West Germany to be drawn into armed conflicts outside of Europe	10	29
	320	224
Europe		
For the policies of the GDR to cause the policy of détente to fail in Europe	39	22
European unity not getting anywhere	35	28
European interests taking a back seat to the East in matters of policy	25	22
Great Britain withdrawing from the European Community	23	29
The advance of communism in Europe	23	40
The U.S. having to withdraw troops from Europe because of crises in other parts of the world	21	32
The European Community not being able to cope with the admission of Portugal, Spain and Greece	14	30
The U.S. not being willing to defend Europe	9	33
	189	236

continued

Question: *"There are some problems that are of special concern to us now and will continue to be in the next year or two and others that may not be such burning problems now but that may give us serious trouble in five or ten years. Would you read what is printed on these cards? Which of these items will be of special concern to us in the Federal Republic in the next year or two and which of them, while they will presumably not become acute soon, will be burning problems in five or ten years? Could you distribute the cards on this sheet accordingly?"* (C)

	November 1980	
	Will be of special concern to us -	
	in the next year or two	in five or ten years
	%	%
East - West		
The East adopting a tougher course toward the West	55	21
For the East to take military action again in an Eastern European country	44	22
The failure of the East-West talks about arms limitations and arms control	41	22
Not keeping up with the East's armaments pace	40	25
The West not being unified enough in its approach to the East	37	22
Not enough being done about disarmament	36	22
The East not being able to handle its own problems	30	37
The Western defensive alliance, NATO, not holding up well anymore	14	33
	297	204
The World		
Energy and raw materials getting scarcer and more expensive	67	23
Terrorism and the use of force being on the increase all over the world	59	25
The flood of refugees from the Third World becoming a great problem	53	29
For an ever tougher competitive struggle to develop between the industrial nations over raw materials	47	32
Our supply of raw materials being interrupted by crises in the Third World	44	35
The influence of the East on developing countries becoming greater and greater	32	36
The bad economic situation in the poor countries becoming dangerous for us as well	29	45
The possibility that Third World conflicts might lead to a world war	14	44
	345	269

AMERICA AND RUSSIA IN 50 YEARS

Question: *"Of course no one can see into the future, but what do you think the world will be like in fifty years? Who will be more powerful—America or Russia?"*

A

	January 1980						
	Total	Age groups				Education	
	pop.	16-29	30-44	45-59	60 and over	Elementary	Secondary
	%	%	%	%	%	%	%
Russia	27	24	25	31	29	29	25
America	20	20	21	20	17	20	21
Both equally	22	23	22	25	20	22	21
Impossible to say	31	33	32	24	34	29	33
	100	100	100	100	100	100	100

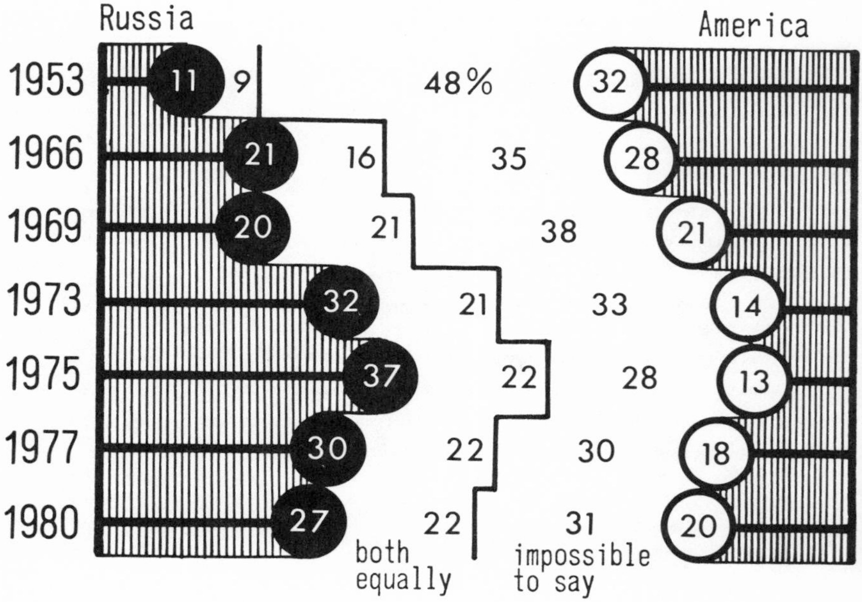

LIVE TO BE 150?

Question: *"If scientists made it possible for people to live until the age of 150 and still retain vigor, would you like to live that long, or not?"*

	1956 May %	1964 March %	1967 June %	1973 July %	1978 January %
Like to	32	55	47	49	46
Depends	17	16	19	21	23
Rather not	44	24	30	27	27
Undecided	7	5	4	3	4
	100	100	100	100	100

LOOKING AHEAD

Question: *"Is it with hopes or with fears that you enter the coming year?"*

	December 1980				
	Hopes %	Fears %	Skepticism %	Undecided %	
Total population	36	26	28	10	= 100
Men	33	24	33	10	= 100
Women	38	27	24	11	= 100
AGE GROUPS					
16-29	48	16	25	11	= 100
30-44	35	24	32	9	= 100
45-59	32	31	27	10	= 100
60 and over	27	34	29	10	= 100
EDUCATION					
Elementary	34	29	27	10	= 100
Secondary	39	21	30	10	= 100
OCCUPATION					
Unskilled workers	34	27	25	14	= 100
Skilled workers	34	27	30	9	= 100
Non-managerial employees and public servants	37	23	29	11	= 100
Managerial employees and public servants	41	26	24	9	= 100
Self-employeds, professionals	35	31	29	5	= 100
Farmers	27	34	29	10	= 100
PARTY PREFERENCE					
SPD	44	21	26	9	= 100
CDU/CSU	28	34	29	9	= 100
FDP	40	20	30	10	= 100

Question: *"Is it with hopes or with fears that you enter the coming year?"*

(1949-1969)

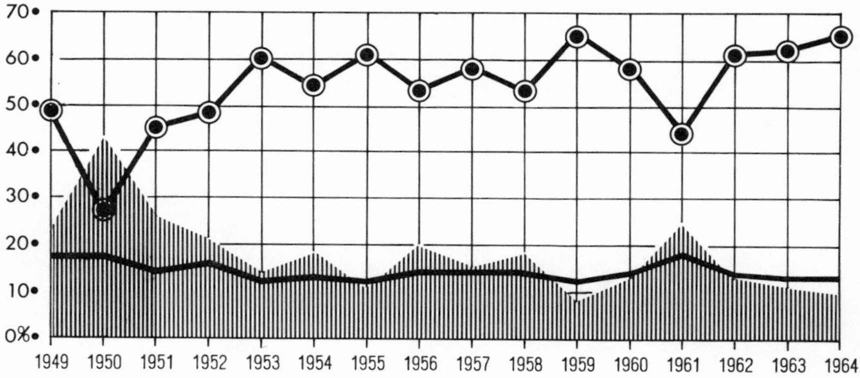

Question: *"Is it with hopes or with fears that you enter the coming year?"*

(1965-1980)

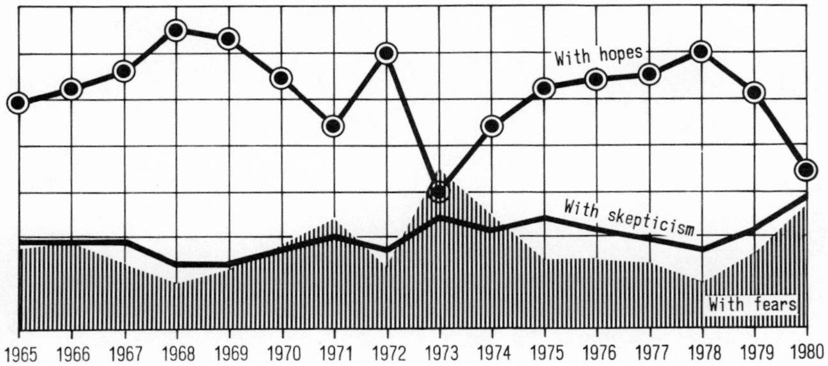

INDEX

A

B

C

D

E

O

P

Q

R

S

T